FOR COUNTRY,
CAUSE & LEADER

CHARLES B. HAYDON

For Country, Cause & Leader

THE CIVIL WAR JOURNAL OF CHARLES B. HAYDON

Edited by
STEPHEN W. SEARS

TICKNOR & FIELDS *New York* *1993*

For information about permission to reproduce selections
from this book, write to Permissions, Ticknor & Fields,
215 Park Avenue South, New York, New York 10003.

Library of Congress Cataloging-in-Publication Data
Haydon, Charles B., 1834–1864.
  For country, cause & leader : the Civil War journal of Charles
B. Haydon / edited by Stephen W. Sears.
    p.   cm.
  Includes index.
  ISBN 0-395-66360-1
  1. Haydon, Charles B., 1834–1864 — Diaries. 2. United
States. Army. Michigan Infantry Regiment, 2nd (1861–1865) —
Biography. 3. Michigan — History — Civil War, 1861–1865 —
Personal narratives. 4. Michigan — History — Civil War, 1861–
1865 — Regimental histories. 5. United States — History —
Civil War, 1861–1865 — Personal narratives. 6. United States
— History — Civil War, 1861–1865 — Regimental histories.
7. Soldiers — Michigan — Diaries.   I. Sears, Stephen W.
II. Title.   III. Title: For country, cause, and leader.
E514.5 2nd.H38   1993
973.8'98 — dc20
[B]   92-46272   CIP

Printed in the United States of America

MP 10 9 8 7 6 5 4 3 2 1

Frontispiece photograph of Charles B. Haydon, courtesy of
Michigan Historical Collections, Bentley Historical Library

Contents

Introduction

THE GOOD SOLDIER HAYDON: that was how he wanted to be remembered. He was loyal, trustworthy, obedient, brave, and certainly he was motivated. On July 4, 1862, in one of the darker hours of the war following the Federal retreat from Richmond, he could write without self-consciousness that he "cheered most heartily for country, cause & leader." To Charles B. Haydon the Union meant as much as life itself, and by way of documenting his belief he kept one of the most striking of Civil War journals.

Charles Haydon was not the typical Civil War soldier. When he enlisted in the first rush to the colors in April 1861 he was twenty-seven, half a dozen years older than most of his fellow volunteers. He was also considerably better educated than most of them, with four years of college and a beginning law practice when he signed up. His favorite campfire reading was the *Atlantic Monthly*, the most intellectually challenging American magazine of the day. When in the field he went to some lengths to obtain a copy of Dickens's newly published *Great Expectations*. (In comparison to the author's earlier work, he thought, "his best days are past.") He filled the long hours of boredom by recalling passages of poetry he had committed to memory, and he enlivened his journal-writing by quoting from the likes of Byron, Addison, Whittier, and William Cullen Bryant, hardly the usual fare of Civil War diarists.

While at first, like most of his fellows, Haydon expected little more than a three-month war, he sensed that this military experience promised to be a unique chapter in his life. He determined to make a full, careful, and analytical record of it; like a traveler embarking on the Grand Tour, he wanted by means of his journal to be able to relive the experience in later years. His effort at "journalizing," as he called it, never faltered through nearly three years of soldiering. He did his journalizing in pocket-sized notebooks, and as each was filled he sent it home for safekeeping. In all he would fill twenty of these notebooks; a twenty-first has been lost, leaving the only gap in his record of service. Because of the care he took in this regard, it may be supposed he intended someday to write a memoir of his experiences in this great American Civil War.

It may also be supposed that had that memoir been written, it would have depicted history with the bark on, for Charles Haydon's is one of the most candid, unblinking Civil War journals on record. He had not been in the army a week when he remarked that if the men would only pursue the enemy "as vigorously as they do the whores they will make very efficient soldiers." The men pursue liquor in these pages with the same single-mindedness, and they plunder everything not nailed down, and often enough even that did not stop them. The war as Haydon describes it is not a picture-book war.

Born in 1834 in Vermont, Charles B. Haydon was raised in the new (1837) state of Michigan, in the old Northwest Territory. His home was Decatur, a village in the southwestern corner of the state twenty-five miles from Kalamazoo. In 1857 he completed four years' study at the University of Michigan. Electing to enter the legal profession, he read law in a firm in Kalamazoo, where by his account he was earning five dollars a week as a law clerk when war broke out. "God only knows how much I loved the Law & how hard it was to give it up," he wrote. He had one sibling, his younger brother Arthur. His mother was dead. His father, Philotas Haydon, had recently taken a second wife, a young woman of Charles's generation, and started a second family. Although Charles was unmarried, he was interested enough in a woman he calls only "Mary R." at least to give thought to a wartime marriage.

On April 22, 1861, one week after President Lincoln called on the Northern states for militia to suppress "combinations too powerful to be suppressed by the ordinary course of judicial proceedings," Charles Haydon enlisted in a local militia company, the Kalamazoo Light Guard. While later he expressed regret that he had not joined the Light Guard at an earlier day so as to be better trained for wartime service, his maturity and standing in the community were enough to see him appointed 3rd sergeant of the company.

Haydon did not agonize over his decision to enlist. To him it was simply his patriotic duty. The Secessionists, as he termed the enemy, must not be allowed to destroy the Union. When the Kalamazoo Light Guard was subsequently told it would be required to serve not three months in state service but three years in federal service, Haydon did pause. Three years, he was sure, would mean for him the loss of his chosen career in the law. The hesitation was brief, soon overcome by the pull of duty. On May 25 he gave his oath of service to the United States. He was bound to the army for three years.

By then the Kalamazoo Light Guard was officially Company I, 2nd Michigan Infantry, and training in Detroit. Haydon quickly became inflexibly conscientious about his sergeant's duties. On the fourth day of keeping his journal he recorded that the 2nd Michigan's colonel, Israel B. Richardson, had "sharply berated" him for not knowing his job. After Richardson's censure he swore, "I shall not be caught again on that point," and he never was. Acquiring a copy of Hardee's *Tactics,* he studied the drills until he knew them forward and backward. Charles Haydon's military education was to be largely the result of his own efforts but it was no less thorough and complete for that.

The Civil War statistician William F. Fox included the 2nd Michigan Infantry in his list of 300 Union "fighting regiments," and with good reason. Of the more than 2,000 regiments in the Northern armies, just 20 suffered more battle dead than the 2nd Michigan. Of the men who enlisted originally in the 2nd, plus those who joined later as replacements, 21.5 percent died in battle or of disease; the regiment's total wartime loss — wounded, missing, dead from all causes — came to 55 percent. At times, as Haydon notes, this attrition reduced the regiment to a shadow. In its fight at Jackson, Mississippi, in 1863, for example, in which Haydon was severely wounded, he records that his company, with an on-paper strength of 101 men, brought but 20 to the battle line.

In 1861 Michigan was the first western state to send troops to
the eastern theater in any numbers, and the 2nd Michigan arrived
in Washington less than two months after Mr. Lincoln's call. It
participated in skirmishing engagements at First Bull Run and then
went into eight months' training with General McClellan's Army
of the Potomac. During 1862 it was in McClellan's Peninsula campaign against Richmond from first to last, then with Pope at Second
Bull Run and, after missing the Antietam campaign, with Burnside
at Fredericksburg. Assigned now to the peripatetic Ninth Corps,
the 2nd Michigan went west in February 1863 for service in Kentucky and in Grant's campaign against Vicksburg. Haydon was
wounded in Mississippi on July 11, shortly after Vicksburg's surrender, and while he recuperated his regiment defended against
the Confederate besiegers of Knoxville.

Charles Haydon's final service with the 2nd Michigan was in
Tennessee early in 1864. Having survived numberless perils in
camp and battle, he was on his way home to Michigan for a thirty-
day furlough awarded the regiment for re-enlisting when he fell
ill with pneumonia. On March 14, in Cincinnati, age thirty, he
died. The last entry in his journal is dated February 21, 1864. His
regiment, returning east and rejoining the Army of the Potomac,
would serve out the war in Grant's final campaign against Richmond.

During the thirty-four months that he kept his journal Haydon
was very much interested in the phenomenon of military leadership, particularly as he moved up the ladder of command himself — during his service he rose from 3rd sergeant to lieutenant
colonel — and the 2nd Michigan furnished him with an excep-
tional example for study. The skills needed for field command,
and the attendant risks, are starkly apparent here.

Israel Richardson, the regiment's first colonel, was a West
Pointer with a reputation for hard fighting and a special knack for
training volunteers to face the trials of the battlefield. He would
in time rise to the command of a division and the rank of major
general, and he would die of wounds received at Antietam. When
Richardson gained his first star he was replaced as head of the 2nd
Michigan by Orlando M. Poe, also a West Pointer and also an
exceptionally able officer; Haydon considered Poe the very model
of a regimental commander. In 1863 the Senate failed to confirm
Poe as a brigadier (apparently because of his earlier association

with the now discredited McClellan) and he reverted to his regular-army rank of captain; nevertheless he would make a distinguished record as chief engineer in Sherman's campaigns.

On the Peninsula the 2nd Michigan was assigned to the brigade of another hard fighter Haydon admired, Hiram G. Berry; Berry would be killed at Chancellorsville. But the fighting general Haydon admired above all others was his division commander, one-armed Phil Kearny. "The bravest man in the Army of the Potomac has fallen," he wrote in shock when Kearny was killed at Chantilly. It was precisely this fighting spirit that was missing in the high command, he thought. "We are fooled, beaten, bamboozled, out-flanked, hoodwinked & disgraced by half our numbers," he wrote angrily after the army's defeat at Second Bull Run. "When did the Rebels ever have occasion to boast over an encounter with the Divs. of Hooker, Richardson, Kearney?"

Haydon gives us revealing portraits of these various command-ers, but he is equally adept at smaller vignettes. He writes of Mr. Lincoln (whom he admired) having to review the troops on horse-back at a run, "his hair & coat tails horizontal"; of Brigadier General Sam Heintzelman cursing like a muleskinner in the heat of battle at Williamsburg; of a German-born corporal who had the experience to be the best drillmaster in the company but for his accent, which set the men to laughing so hard they could not carry out his orders. Haydon had a keen eye for the ridiculous.

While the journal is a virtual history of the 2nd Michigan during Haydon's service with it, one member of the regiment who would gain a particular notoriety is unmentioned here. One of Haydon's fellow enlistees of 1861, Private Franklin Thompson of Company F, contracted malaria when the regiment moved to Kentucky in 1863. Thompson failed to report to the hospital for treatment, however, and was subsequently carried on the Company F roll as a deserter. Private Franklin Thompson was in reality Private Sarah Emma Seelye, who had concluded that her two-year masquerade would be exposed in the hospital. She served out the war as Miss Seelye, army nurse, and the company roll was duly corrected.

The heroes of Haydon's story are the men of the 2nd Michigan, and especially the men of Company I. He observed them closely, and displayed a Dickensian talent for characterization. He relished describing, among others, the resourceful Benson, the insouciant Sid Prentice, the hapless Seward. Young Seward, he explained, "would starve to death if the boys did not take care of him. He never has anything in his haversack, no cup, no canteen, no shelter tent nor anything he needs." For his own part, Haydon admitted that he was surprised at his genuine liking for army life. "I think I must have been intended for a soldier," he wrote at one point, and as he rose in rank he began to give thought to the military as a career.

When in camp between battles Haydon used his journal-writing as a way to pass the time. He might discourse on such subjects as the pluses and minuses of the Northern war effort, the qualifications for company-level command, the need for disciplined leadership, or his own "elastic nature" that allowed him to continue to have hope for victory even in the darkest times. On one occasion he wrote a long and thoughtfully analytical study of his impressions on being subject to an artillery attack. When on campaign he produced more tightly focused, reportorial entries. His running account of operations on the Peninsula in 1862, for example, stands above any other of the scores of such diary accounts; indeed, it is the best single eyewitness account of that campaign to have survived.

Charles Haydon was greatly interested in the countryside through which the armies passed, and especially in how the war was affecting the civilian population there. While he followed Victorian decorum in rendering profanity as (for example) "give them h--l G-d d--n them . . . ," that was about the only Victorian convention he honored. He wrote his journal for himself, he said, and he intended that only his father and brother read the notebooks as he sent them home, and thus he was frank and outspoken about such things as the manners and morals of the Southern women he encountered. It seemed to him that there was a high rate of illegitimacy in the South, reflecting a low state of morals there. Then he learned that no fewer than three young ladies of his acquaintance back in Kalamazoo had recently found (as he put it) "babies for their cradles before they had husbands for their beds." He decided that the war must be affecting morality in both sections equally.

His comments on the manners and morals of his fellow soldiers are marked by a similar candor. Haydon had unwavering pride in his regiment and regarded the men of the 2nd as the best fighting men in the army. Yet, he said, they would patronize prostitutes every chance they could, and the regimental sick list reflected the consequences. They displayed a remarkable talent for finding liquor in spite of the government ban on selling liquor to soldiers. Haydon was not a teetotaler and he records one occasion when overindulgence left him with a headache of several days' duration. Still, he knew from experience what tried the soul of a company commander. "There is seldom any difficulty so long as you can keep them away from liquor & women," he wrote, "but there always is if you do not."

In the pages of Haydon's journal the army in the field and on the march invariably leaves a trail of devastation, beginning, as he notes, on the march to the First Bull Run battlefield. The range was wide, from casual raids on cornfields and orchards and the taking of farmers' fences for firewood to outright vandalism and wholesale destruction. At the Battle of Fredericksburg in December 1862 he describes in detail the wanton looting of the town by the men of the 2nd Michigan — this, be it remembered, one of the best-officered regiments in the Union army. He believed it was the attitude of most Federal soldiers (himself included) that Southern secessionists had started this war and therefore Southern property was not deserving of protection. "War is awful in the extreme," he commented, "but if *we* can risk *life & limb* do not hesitate over a few paltry *chattels* of the *enemy.*"

It seemed to Charles Haydon that there had to be something good to come in return for all this suffering and hardship, and for all this killing, and he found it in the cause of Union. God grant the sufferers, he wrote, "some kind reward at last, not only for them but for those who have given their all to a sacred cause." On April 4, 1862, at the start of the Peninsula campaign, he completed one of his notebooks and sent it back to Michigan along with a brief note to his brother, Arthur. If he should fall on the soil of Secessia in the coming battle, he said, he prayed that his body might be recovered and interred in Michigan "or *any loyal state*. . . ." His death would not come in battle, but his wish was granted.

* * *

Charles B. Haydon kept his journal in pencil in a series of what he called pocket memorandum notebooks, 5⅜ by 3⅜ inches, a size easy to carry securely while in the field. By way of further security he sent each notebook as completed to his father's home in Decatur, Michigan. After about a year of this practice, Haydon began to make copies of notebooks as he filled them on four-page stationery sheets, the pages of which measured 7 by 10 inches. He then sent these home periodically. He seems to have discarded five notebooks after making copies of them; the copies, and fifteen notebooks, survive. One notebook, for a seven-week period in the fall of 1862 and for which there is no copy, is missing. Most probably it was lost at some time after the war, or at least after Haydon's death, for it is of an early enough period that he would have noted its loss and left some record or summary of the period covered.

During World War II, starting in 1943, the *Decatur Republican,* the small weekly newspaper in his hometown, printed excerpts from Haydon's journal, continuing them into 1946. Subsequently a Haydon descendant, Ione Haydon, presented the original journal to the Michigan Historical Collections, held at the Bentley Historical Library of the University of Michigan at Ann Arbor.

Haydon's journal is published here by the kind permission of the director of the Bentley Historical Library, Francis X. Blouin, Jr. Others at the library who have provided assistance are Nancy R. Bartlett, Ann Flowers, Karen L. Jania, and Anne Frantilla. Norma Strickler of Decatur furnished useful information. An earlier transcription, prepared by Ida C. Brown of the Bentley Library, has been a helpful guide in making the present transcription.

In common with most diarists, to save time and space Haydon frequently resorted to abbreviations and used initials to indicate people and places. These are retained so long as meaning and identification are clear; where the abbreviations and initials are unclear they are silently expanded. Where Haydon left out essential punctuation, as he often did, it too has been supplied without notice. Such editing reflects Haydon's own intentions, for in the copies he made there is an editorial polish that is lacking in the original notebooks. After he began this practice of making copies, Haydon in his notebooks became more and more laconic, relying increasingly on abbreviations and initials and notations that he intended later to expand. His final journal notebook, which of course he had no opportunity to copy, is heavily laced with initials, not all of which can now be identified.

In the interest of clarity the entry dates have been standardized and paragraphing made consistent. Identifications or clarifications are supplied within brackets in the journal text or in footnotes. The editor has divided the journal into chapters and supplied stage-setting headnotes for each. It was Haydon's habit to use the last pages of his notebooks for bookkeeping purposes, recording loans and debts, listing promotions and resignations, and the like. These have been deleted, as have his brief notes to his father or brother written when he sent the notebooks home; as he told them, everything he had to say was in the journal.

With these exceptions, Charles Haydon's journal is transcribed here just as he left it.

FOR COUNTRY,
CAUSE & LEADER

One

THE KALAMAZOO
LIGHT GUARD
JOINS UP

The opening section of Charles B. Haydon's journal records his first five weeks of soldiering. In response to the president's call for 75,000 militia to put down the rebellion, on April 22, 1861, Haydon signed on with the Kalamazoo Light Guard, destined to be Company I, 2nd Michigan Infantry. He was made 3rd sergeant. Company I, along with several other three-month militia units (including Company K, also of Kalamazoo), entrained for Detroit to join in the formation of the 2nd Michigan at Cantonment Blair.

In addition to its introduction to the ways of the army, the Kalamazoo Light Guard encountered the hard reality of having to serve not the expected three months, but three years. The Fort Wayne Haydon mentions was a military post on the Detroit River on the outskirts of Detroit. Company I's captain was Dwight May. The 2nd Michigan's colonel was Israel B. Richardson, West Pointer, veteran of the Seminole and Mexican wars, a rough-hewn regular who had well earned his nickname "Fighting Dick." The Kalamazoo Light Guard was in the army now.

*   *   *

§ APRIL 30, 1861   Left Kalamazoo in Kalamazoo Light Guard for Detroit to join the 2nd Regt. Mich. Vols. At Mirengo we threw off James McEvoy for drunkeness & insubordination. We left K. at 11 A.M. & got nothing to eat on the road because the boys (principally the Battle Creek Co.) stole everything movable at some of the first stations, which was telegraphed in advance & all the groceries &c were closed agt us on the rest of the road. They cleared out several groceries almost entirely & their officers seemed to make no effort to restrain them.

We arrived at Det. about sundown & at the quarters abt an hour after in the midst of a heavy wind & rain. Most of us were wet through. We were marched into what was once Floral Hall or more properly shed. The mud was about two inches deep in the shed which was open at both ends. Some loose boards were all there was to keep us out of the mud. At 9 oclock we got a very fair supper of bread, butter, beef & tea. About 11 P.M. we got the men's quarters changed to neighboring barns where they were much more comfortable.

Lieut. Dake, Sergt. Ford & self by the kindness of a citizen were taken to good quarters in his own house. I never appreciated a good bed more than I did after the prospect of sleeping in the mud & wind of the shed. While we were lodged in the shed one of the boys declared that he would never complain again when his mother did not make his bed right. We need a little hardship sometimes to make us appreciate our blessings.

§ MAY 1, 1861 came in with a smart snow squall which continued from time to time during the day. We did very little except to fit up our quarters with berths & straw beds. We are thickly stowed in one above another but the quarters are warm & reasonably comfortable.

§ MAY 2 Weather very fine, the men still working on their quarters when off duty. The regular camp orders are given. We have to rise at 5 & drill 1 hour, then wash, breakfast &c. All lights out at 9 P.M. The men are writing letters, playing cards & lounging in the sun. There was much complaint this morning abt hard times & poor board. Several wanted to leave but I believe none went. We got part of our arms to day & I bought a knife large enough to chop wood with.

We had battalion drill in the afternoon.* I was pleased to see Capt. Charles May of Co. K & Prosecuting Atty. of our county. He knew nothing abt the drill & was compelled to trot up & down through the mud for 2 hours in great heat, vexation & confusion,

---

* In the Civil War, battalion drill meant drilling by regiment.

his boots at first nicely polished, soon after loaded with as much as 15 pounds clay & mud each. I have seldom seen a man more blowed & he swore most prodigiously, which I never heard him do before. There was a German Capt. in the other Co. of his Div. with a most ferocious moustache who roared out to him from time to time in a manner which fairly lifted him off his feet.

§ MAY 3 Sergt. Ford & self quartered with the men last night. We had a straw bed & each a blanket & a shawl so that we were warm enough & slept well, but Ford complains considerably. Nearly all the men have bad colds & 3 are sick. The duties of the day commenced at 5 by washing at the pump &c. The day like the latter part of yesterday is cold & disagreeable with fair prospect of another storm which would make the parade ground impass-able. I acted as second Sergt. this P.M. & was sharply berated by the Col. [Israel B. Richardson] for not knowing my business. I very soon learned it however & shall not be caught again on that point. We are becoming more accustomed to camp life &c. Still there is some grumbling amg the men. Those who are living better now than they ever lived before grumble most in many cases. Such are always first to complain when they are away from home.

§ MAY 4 We had to day the first fine day of camp life. The weather was really comfortable. We could lounge in the sun. I could laugh as heartily to day to hear the Col. blow up others as they did yesterday at my berating. I had the satisfaction of seeing Lieut. Dake on the full run several times (a rare sight). The Capt. [Dwight May] did not fare much better.

§ MAY 5 Sunday. Corpl. Ball & self went up to Ft. Wayne after breakfast to see how the other Regt.* was faring. We had a fine ride up & back on a steam boat & saw the fort & men &c. We returned to a late dinner. At 3 P.M. we mustered 18 men in our Co. to march to religious services. We march before breakfast for one hour & after church we drilled 2 hrs. They were busy drilling at the Ft.

We are now quite comfortable & used to camp life. I am sur-prised to see how quick I came into it. Capt. C. S. May says we shall never know anything again except facing, flanking, filing, marching &c &c. I think he is to some extent correct. I can easily

---

* The 1st Michigan, a three-month regiment.

see that if we remain here 6 or 8 weeks it will be dull beyond all description. If we are to remain here for three months I shall be very sorry that I enlisted. I came because I thought we were needed & if we are I shall be well content.

We got news yesterday that one man who enlisted in our Co. at Kalamazoo was dead. His name was Henry Carrier — a good stout boy — he was taken sick the day before we started & died soon after. This is the first death in our Co. & I believe the first in the Regt. There are several on the sick list.

§ MAY 6 Some rain last night, weather fair this morning. If the men pursue the enemy as vigorously as they do the whores they will make very efficient soldiers.

A smart rain P.M. We were to day examined & took the oath of alligiance to the State. The examination was not rigid, & none were rejected on acct of physical incapacity. Abt a doz. spare men had to be thrown out & will very reluctantly (most of them) go. Some will return home & others will enter other companies of this Regt. to supply the place of those who have been thrown out or have deserted. Many enlisted hastily & from some Co's., especially the Adrian Guards, desertions have been frequent. Till to day the stay of all was merely voluntary, henceforth it will be compulsory. An opportunity was given before taking the oath by our Co. for any who desired to withdraw. Only one went & he (Dennis Stockwell) among abundant groans & hisses from the Co. He returned before the oath & would have come in again if he had been permitted.

Camp life is not much different from what I expected. Card playing, profanity & the stealing of provisions are among the most noted characteristics outside of the duties. There are 4 Co's. of us quartered together, 2 from Kalamazoo, the East Saginaw Guards, & Constantine Union Guards. I noticed at one time this P.M. 15 4-hand games of euchre going on at the same time. No gambling is allowed in camp & strong measures are taken to prevent stealing.

I have not as yet regretted that I enlisted. I went from a sense of duty & I expect that to sustain me in the hardships which I may be called to endure. Only one thing troubles me seriously. That is to get up at 5 A.M. & drill at double quick time before breakfast.

§ MAY 7 Rain A.M. light. I have been on the go pretty briskly for two days, acting as second & sometimes as first Sergt. owing to the sickness or absence of the other. The battalion drill makes busy work for a new guide & for one who is the only file closer for a large part of the time. The rascals steal everything they can put hands on — stole Ford's shawl (an important part of our bed clothes) to day.

It is reported that we cannot go into service unless we enlist for three years or during the war. I should very much dislike 3 years & I also very much dislike to return without doing anything. If it was not for business I would not hesitate for a moment. After all we can do little while the war continues & we should do all we can to aid the vigorous measures which the Administration is taking.

§ MAY 8 I am to day Sergt. of the Guard & I find it dull business. It will probably be duller yet before 10 A.M. to morrow. We are out in all abt 26 hours — 2 hours on & 4 off. This is the first time I have been on. There is something exceeding solitary in the looks of a sentinel placing slowly up & down in stillness of the night. The weather is fine & we shall have a good night.

The morals of camp life are bad & manners likewise. It is doubtful whether the effect which war has upon the morals of a people is not more to be regretted than its more ostensible evils. I believe I have kept on abt as usual. This open air life will be good for me I think. It seems like old times to be out doors all day.

§ MAY 9 Morning watch 6 A.M. We passed the night, which was a fine one, in comparative quiet. The Corporals Guard was called for but twice during my watches. The first time my Corpl., a very worthy German, ran without the countersign & was himself arrested & sent to the guard house. I laughed heartily at the joke on the Corpl. I slept well abt 3 hours. My head aches a little & I feel dull & tired this morning. This standing guard is the most tiresome service I have. I believe I would rather march all the time. We were finally relieved abt 11 A.M. after abt 27 hours duty. I have not felt quite as well as usual to day. I have a sour stomach & a tendency toward looseness of the bowels. I do nothing for it save to stop eating.

§ MAY 10 It rains hard this morning & I am not sorry I can assure on any account save the condition of the grounds. I feel better this m'g but am not yet entirely well. Nearly all the men have diarhea & several are in the hospital quite sick. This is caused by the indiscretion of the men & by the quality of the food. Our victuals are cooked & served out by a contractor at one of the Fair buildings. The quantity is ample & the quality before cooking is good enough. There is a good deal of dirt mixed with it when we get it & some of it comes in very bad shape. The butter is bad & I eat very little of it. We have soup for dinner, made I presume from the fragments of breakfast. I think this soup is one of the principal causes of sickness. The potatoes are of poor quality. The bread thank God is good. We have in addition fresh & salt beef & pork. The provisions would be ample if well served. We have also tea, coffee, sugar & sometimes milk.

It is certain that this Regt. will not be recd for 3 months. We must enlist for 3 yrs during the war unless sooner discharged. I have not yet positively decided to do that. The Co. will stand abt half & half. If I had poorer prospects at home or a better place here I would not hesitate.

Our grounds will be all afloat by night. I wish the state could find dry land enough for us to camp. I would rather sleep in the open air than be quartered in the mud. I fear we shall all be sick when warm weather comes. The boys behaved rather bad in some cases yesterday. The guard house was pretty well filled & one came near being flogged.

§ MAY 11 It rained nearly all day yesterday & we had no drill except a private one for a few who saw fit to take part in it. I went to town once & spent the balance of the day in studying Hardee [William J. Hardee's *Tactics*] &c. This m'g is fine but the grounds are very bad. We have drilled but little to day owing to the state of the ground.

There is a good deal of reluctance to enlist for the war or three years. There are all manner of doubts & excuses raised. I can not wonder very much at it. A step which involves the possibility of 3 yrs in the army is a pretty serious one for most men. I have pretty much decided to go. It seems to me that I cannot honorably do otherwise. I should very much dislike to return to Kalamazoo in this juncture of affairs.

There is a general laxity of discipline in the camp partly because of 2 days idleness & partly because many of the men expect soon to be discharged & having no prospect of fighting before them care very little whether they do anything or not. There was some disturbance last night at the other building. Several were sent to the Guard House & pistols were freely drawn but none fired. A new made acquaintance of mine, 3d Sergt. of the Hudson Guards, is on trial by a Court Martial to day in consequence. We have no uniform as yet & shall soon be a very ragged Regt. if we do not get it.

§ MAY 12 Sunday. A fine day, no drilling. Dissatisfaction among some Co's. because the uniform has not been furnished. Meetings were held last night & strong indignation expressed & resolutions passed not to drill after Monday noon if they were not supplied. The consequence is that the men who were foremost in them have gone to the Guard House. Capt. C. S. May has trouble with his Co. He will not be well liked.

Our Capt. [Dwight May] was found fault with yesterday for the first time. There is a general outcry agt officers. It is without just cause. Many of the men seem to think they should never be spoken to unless the remarks are prefaced by some words of deferential politeness. Will the gentlemen who comprise the first platoon have the kindness to march forward, or will they please to halt, &c is abt what some of them seem to expect. An officer would need 3 yrs under a French dancing master before he could satisfy them.

I wanted to go to town to day to bathe & be shaved but they refuse to let us out. It surprises me to see how quickly I have fallen into this mode of life. I feel little more uneasiness or inconvenience than if I had been bred to it from youth. I have hardly a thought abt law. I eat, drink, sleep, drill & study Hardee's Tactics as much of course as if I knew no other business. I think I must have been intended for a soldier. If I were but Lieut. instead of 3d Sergt. I should be better satisfied than at present. My pay is very small. I have however money enough for the present.

The boys will upset the table before many days I think. The contractor gets over $3.25 per week for our board & might give better. I bought a pie & some cakes of a peddler this m'g & filled up for once.

We succeeded in getting out about 25 men to church to day. Many of them absolutely refused to go. We must have more discipline or we shall have nothing.

§ MAY 13 The 1st [Michigan] Regt. starts for Washington to morrow. It rained hard this m'g & we have done nothing to day. It is irksome to lie here in this way. I hope we shall be sent to the Fort. It is farther from town & discipline would be stricter. Several of the men came back from town last night very drunk but there was no serious disturbance. Co. K of Kalamazoo called for volunteers from its ranks for 3 yrs or the war. They made raise of 5 officers & 7 privates. I went to town P.M. & took a bath which refreshed me very much. This P.M. is very warm & fine but the grounds are too wet for drilling.

§ MAY 14　We recd order at 11 A.M. to take up our march for Ft. Wayne at 1 P.M. Previously we were called upon to sign for 3 yrs & we obtained 63 of 78, the largest Co. on the ground except the Scott Guards. We had a march of abt 5 miles to the Ft. where we arrived abt 4 P.M. & were at once marched to our quarters on the Steam Boat Mississippi moored opposite the Ft. The change from the mud of Cantonment Blair to the convenient Ladies Cabin of a first class lake steamer was so great as to fill us all with lively satisfaction. The stained glass windows, the arched ceiling & gilded paneling & clean tables contrasted strongly with the dirt & rough boards of Camp. Nor was the conduct of the men less marked. At supper there was not a word above the ordinary tone of conversation whereas at the Cantonment the air was loaded with shouts & curses the whole time in spite of all endeavors in our present state of discipline & the then surroundings to prevent it. The present quarters are better than a majority of the men ever saw before.

§ MAY 15　The m'g was very fine, cloudless. We had Co. drill in the forenoon. Rain at noon. Matters all quiet during the day. Our situation is a beautiful one — it commands a full view of the city & of both shores as far down as Wyandotte. The Detroit is a beautiful river, clear, cold, good banks & a lively current. From one to two hundred vessels of different kinds pass daily. The river is alive with business. It seems a pity to see so fine a boat as the one we are quartered on rotting down in idleness. It was one of the Michigan Central R.R. line & was laid up after the Great Western R.R. was built. There is now no other route on which they can profitably be employed. This with 2 others, 3 of the finest boats in the U.S., have since lain at the dock in idleness.

§ MAY 16　Was a still beautiful cold day. We had Co. drill in the m'g & officers drill afterwards. Battalion drill P.M. during which I got my shoes full of mud. The living is no better here than at the Cantonment except that it is cleaner. We hear no complaint abt it now. We have a very beautiful location & it will be left with regret. To be removed from a hog pen to a boat which cost near $300,000 is a desirable change. Still, I have been a little down in spirits & I can give no reason for it unless it be that our good quarters here are destined to decay unenjoyed. It looks too much like the decline of former greatness & good fortune.

Perhaps also the thought of 3 years soldier life with its varied chances & dangers & the possible breaking up of long cherished plans for life had something to do with it. Come what may my destiny is to follow the fortunes of the Stars & Stripes during the war.

§ MAY 17 gave us a beautiful but very sharp m'g. All uncertainty was removed to day by the administration of the oath for three yrs or during the war. Henceforth war is the business & nothing else. Several men stepped out & refused to take the oath, assigning as a reason that they were afraid they would not be allowed to go home before they went.

Lieut. Dake was dropped from service to day on the ground of alleged incompetency. A man outside the Regt. & a stranger to all is said to take his place. This creates much dissatisfaction. I think Dake could have been cast out by a vote of the Co. 3 days ago, but now he has abundance of sympathisers. We had a very fatiguing battalion drill in the afternoon.

§ MAY 18 Cold east wind. Many of the men gone home on leave. I had a good patriotic letter from Father last night. It did me good.

§ MAY 19 Sunday. I walked down to town this m'g & suitably refreshed myself by eating & drinking & after which I returned & attended church service on board. Co. I mustered 12 men for that duty. Many of the men have gone home on a visit. It is bad business. They all come back discontented.

§ MAY 20 A drizzling rain in the m'g. The Orderly* & 2d Sergt. were both suddenly ill so I had to go out with the guards & stand in the rain a couple of hours. I should have cared little for that had I have had anything on but my jacket. But I did not & therefore was wet to the skin. One of the Corpls. had business which made it absolutely necessary for him to go. Still just before he started he declared to me that he could not think of going home unless he could wear a military great coat. I lent him mine. The men seem perfectly crazy to go home & show their uniforms. Blue cloth & brass buttons enlist more soldiers than patriotism if we are to

---

* Another name for the company orderly was sergeant major.

judge from their actions. I am sorry so many have gone home. They are not worth a rush for a week after they get back.

§ MAY 21 I go on guard to day. I do not like the business very well. We took in 12 fine recruits last night & shall to day have a full company.

I was called off guard duty abt 10 A.M. to act as Marshal of the Court Martial to try a soldier for drunkenness & disorderly conduct. He was convicted & sentenced to wheel dirt for two days & be confined during the nights in the guard house. They use one of the sally ports for a guard house & it is not a pleasant place to stay. It is all stone & brick except the doors which are oak plank 8 inches thick. There is no light in it when the doors are closed. Standing guard is a very necessary duty but by no means a pleasant one.

§ MAY 22 10 A.M. I am sitting on the stone wall of the entrance of the east sally port of Ft. Wayne waiting for the morning guards to bring in my relief so that I can march them to quarters. I slept very little last night. The weather was sharp & frosty so that I preferred to be up most of the time.

We had a passably quiet time & took only four men whom we retained. Two men sentinels were found asleep on their posts & nailed. Two boys engaged in the unprofitable enterprise of stealing soldiers' shirts which were hung out to dry. They were taken. One waiter at the boat thought to enjoy the evening air without the countersign & brought up at the guard house. One tall poetic looking gentleman recently arrived went out in a like condition to enjoy a morning walk before the drum beat the reveille & brought up at the same place greatly to his astonishment. Some dozen men were arrested for pissing on forbidden ground. This made up the haul of the night.

§ MAY 23 We have a fine day. We are very busy drilling the recruits of whom we have over 40. We had battalion drill yesterday afternoon. Lt. Handy who usually conducts it was absent. The Capt. [Dwight May] took charge alone & it was soon evident that he had not yet learned the whole of his duty. I never saw a man who was more at a loss than he during part of the P.M. I hope we shall not have to go into battle till he has more experience. We should be ingloriously & unnecessarily cut to pieces.

A deserter from our Co. W. A. McKnight was arrested this morning. They shaved his head & drummed him out of camp. He had a splendid looking foretop, his hair cut & haggled in some places tight to his head & in others left abt 1 inch long. The tonsorial operation was performed in presence of the whole Co.

The small pox is in camp & we were all vaccinated to day. There are now over 1000 men in the Regt. & we shall soon march. I was called off a part of the forenoon to act as clerk of the Court Martial. One man from the Adrian Guards passed himself off to a raw sentinel as an officer & went out & passed several others out with him. He was sentenced to 3 days wheeling stone & 2 days cleaning privies, rather poor work for *an officer*. When not at work he is to be imprisoned in the guard house.

The wind which had been east for 3 days changed at noon yesterday to W. & a fleet of abt 30 vessels came up the river within 20 minutes of each other. It was the finest fleet I have ever seen. The sail covered nearly the whole width of the river. We could not see the city for some time when they passed. The breeze was fair & nearly all were under full sail.

Battalion drill P.M. as usual. The captains of Co's. I & K marched them into the field before the rest of the Regt. went & in consequence were sent for & ordered to march back to the Fort at double quick time giving us abt 2 miles extra travel. The drill afterwards was fatiguing. Some of the men said they could scarcely drag themselves along & it was impossible to keep them up to their places in line. I acted as left guide as usual & am somewhat tired myself. The guide's post in battalion drill is no sinecure. Two of the men fainted when they were vaccinated. That shows rather weak nerves for a soldier. Still they may be brave.

§ MAY 24 Co. I was reexamined yesterday with a view to the 3 years service. Several were thrown out & more ought to have been. Col. Richardson tried to displace 3 Lts. on ground as he alleged of incompetency. This caused an immediate disturbance. The flag was at half mast abt 1 P.M. & after which it was understood to mean that there is mutiny in the camp. The soldiers know nothing abt it yet. There is a petition in circulation to have Col. R. resign. The Governor has been telegraphed. It is said that several of the Capts. will refuse to serve under Col. R. There was a great celebration of Queen Victoria's birthday yesterday in Canada.

§ MAY 25 This m'g the Coldwater Light Artillery upset their table 100 ft. long & danced on the victuals & dishes, cause poor living.

We took the oath of allegiance to & promised faithfully to serve the U.S.A. agt all its enemies for the term of 3 yrs unless sooner discharged. Matters in camp are satisfactorily arranged. We are it is said to march to Ft. Gratiot with the 3d & 4th [Michigan] Regts. for Brigade drill. It is a good place as far as health is concerned & a fine journey to commence camp life on.

Some very pretty ladies visit us at camp nowadays. They are all looking for brothers or cousins who they heard had enlisted. They are pretty sure to find them but the boys are so hard up for money that in most cases unless love is more powerful than avarice the meetings terminate unsatisfactory.

§ MAY 26 Sunday. Co's. I & K were presented this m'g with a Testament for each man by the Kalamazoo County Bible Society. I immediately read the 1st Chap. of Rev., it being the first I have read since I came to camp. As usually happens on rainy mornings I had to march out the guard. I am invited to attend a soldier's wedding to night. One of our boys is going to be married. The manners & morals of camp have improved since we left Cantonment Blair.

§ MAY 27 According to appointment Lt. Handy, Corpls. Ball & Mason & self went immediately after dress parade down town to attend the wedding of our friend Johnston. He was married as appointed to a very pretty young lady whose eyes promise the sweetest disposition imaginable. She came alone 300 miles to be married before he went to wars. She will be a faithful friend to him as long as she lives or he needs one. We had a very pleasant time.

I fell in with an old school mate whom I had not seen before for several years. I also made the acquaintance of several very pretty & intelligent ladies whom I saw for the first & probably for the last time. Johnston has leave of absence for to day for which will be the last he will spend with his lady for some time. I leave this flower here to remember Johnston's wedding by. Its mates I promised to carry to the wars.

The m'g is cold & rainy. It is said we are to go South at once. The murder of the gallant Col. Ellsworth excites the liveliest indignation & should we ever go to battle will not be forgotten.*

§ MAY 28 I spent most of yesterday at the Adjutant General's office in the city copying Muster Rolls. I would rather be drilling. I always dislike to be shut up.

§ MAY 29 I worked all day yesterday on Muster Rolls at the Adjt. Genls. office in the city. I am excused from further duty there. I do not feel quite as well to day as I have heretofore. I have a touch of the prevailing bowel complaint. Several of the boys are sick & some are home sick. I am invited to a party in the city to night. I should like to go but parties are a great drain back on rising at 5 & drilling before breakfast.

§ MAY 30 I did not go to the party last night. I was not ready when the others went & when Corpl. Ball & self got ready there was no boat or omnibus to be found & we thought a 3 miles walk rather too much.

Notwithstanding the many excellent men who have recommended early rising, I cannot bring myself into any great love for drilling before breakfast. The drum beats at 5 A.M. so that no one can sleep & in as much as everyone has to go on guard who does not answer to roll call immediately after I contrive to be on hand.

Col. Richardson was married yesterday morning. The effect was excellent. He was never so pleasant before as at battalion drill yesterday. He said no less than three times that we did well, a thing he never did before. He begins to be pretty well pleased with his Regt. & was no doubt modified in his manner by the resolution of the Capts. not to serve under him unless he behaved better.

This is a beautiful morning. The river is almost as still as an inland lake. There is no wind to raise a ripple on the surface but there is always more or less dead swell which however does not break the surface of the water.

§ MAY 31 On guard. It is not my turn to day & I dont like it. Co. I has furnished 4 Sergts. for the guard already within 10 days. The day is fine but I do not feel very well & have not for the last 3 days. Perhaps guard duty will cure me.

---

* Col. Elmer Ellsworth, of the New York Fire Zouaves, attempting to tear down a Confederate flag at a hotel in Alexandria, Virginia, was shot and killed by the hotel proprietor. The incident was widely reported and Ellsworth was regarded by Northerners as a martyr.

In so much as after writing the above I recd an invitation to a party I concluded to give Sergt. Stevenson ½ a dollar to take my place.

We had a sharp drill this afternoon & fired our first blank cartridges. The noise seemed to confuse the men a little. We need more of it. Some of them fired almost their first guns. It all went off very well except that one man shot away his ramrod at the second fire. We are now called upon to wear our blankets, canteens &c at drill. The straps cause some soreness abt the shoulders. When we get on our blankets, overcoats, haversacks, cartridge boxes, cap boxes & our extra clothing we shall feel the weight.

§ JUNE 1, 1861 I went to the party last night and enjoyed myself pretty well although I was tired & partly sick. We got back to camp abt 1 A.M. I gave ½ dollar to get off guard yesterday & would have given double the amt to have laid abed this m'g.

I bought the Atlantic last night & read two articles. I will keep up with that if possible. It keeps me pretty busy to tend to duties & write what letters are necessary & study tactics some time each day.

We are greatly in need of well drilled officers. Had I joined the Kalamazoo Light Guard when I thought of it I should [have] done better.* I believe I begin to know my business but I had too much to learn & was sometimes taken off my guard. It is amusing & at the same time painful to me to see our Capt. at battalion drill. He seems to think we ought to come to our place without orders for the most part. "Boys why in h--l don't you come out, you know where to go just as well as I. Dont wait to be told every time." This is the way he often speaks & we come out & are strictly speaking liable to be sent to the guard house or served still worse every time we do it. Col. Richardson, Lt. Col Chipman, Capts. Dillman & Bretschneider (both Germans) of Co's. A & E & our 1st Lt. (Handy) are abt the only well drilled officers in the Regt. Lt. Handy is one of the best. If he were in the Capt.'s place it would be no great loss to the Co.

Capt. Chas. May was officer of the day to day & as usual made very vigorous efforts to clear the camp of lewd women & with abt the usual success. That is they did exceedingly abound thereabouts.

We had this P.M. a very lively drill & did the best work we have

---

* The Kalamazoo Light Guard had been a peacetime militia organization.

ever done. I acted as left guide as usual & was on the run the greater part of the time for 3 hours. The weather was very warm and the sweat fairly poured off me. We did no firing for want of cartridges. We were constantly on the move, mainly on the march in columns by Co. & by division, deploying columns by Div., changing direction by flank & front, forward & rear, with some forming of squares & charging. Col. Richardson seemed well pleased. He did very little scolding & I saw him smiling several times.

§ JUNE 2 Sunday. I have to stay here to day with the men & let the other boys go to town. I must try & march the men to church I suppose. It is dull business. I last Sunday, when aided by the 1st Lt. succeeded in marching out 2 men — new recruits — who had not yet learned the ways of camp.

There is an alarming amt of sickness in camp if the men are to be believed at roll call. It is strange how few get to the hospital. We can muster near 100 men at dinner but 60 is a large yield for drill. No man ever saw the beat of the bandaged heads & arms, the limping legs, bent backs, wry faces & contortions & dislocations which present themselves at morning roll call. This dodge is getting so threadbare that good soldiers sometimes suffer much pain & inconvenience rather than incur the suspicion of shirking duty.

§ JUNE 3 A very quiet day. Battalion drill dull. I wish our 1st Lt. had the Capt.'s post. There is some prospect that we shall leave soon.

§ JUNE 4 Since breakfast has been a very rainy day. Benson 2nd Sergt. had an altercation with Capt. Bretschneider this A.M. & is under arrest in consequence. Our Sergt. was undoubtedly wrong in a military view. The old German officer however needs to learn that there is a wide difference between German & American soldiers. He is a good officer in many respects, one of the best in the Regt., but holds to military rules stricter than we are as yet accustomed to do.

The Co. was to day divided into squads of 10 privates each & 1 squad assigned to each corporal (or corpuler as some of the boys get it) for messing & camp duties. Each Sergt. except the 1st has the general supervision of 2 corporals & their squads. G. H. Ball & M. H. Card, 2 of the best corporals in the Co., fall to me. We three have to look after the provisions, clothing, washing, equipments & in short all the wants of the men.

§ JUNE 5 Just after supper last night orders came to have all our things packed & in readiness for moving within 3 hours. Soon after we were informed that we were to march for Washington to day. We shall not probably be able to do so. It will take 1 day longer to get ready.

This is what we have been wishing for & all are glad the order has come, yet the hour of departure brings with it some sober reflections. I will not stop to record them. Any one can guess what they are — home, friends, dangers & hardships to be met, ties & associations broken, and that peculiar feeling which always attends going away.

It is well described by Byron & I shall not try to better his description.* He says on leaving the most unpleasant places one looks back occasionally at the steeple. I found it so even when I left Cantonment Blair. I am sure I have not less affection for the good old steamboat Mississippi, the gravelly yard & dry hot ditches of Ft. Wayne, or the good people of the pleasant city of Detroit, by most of whom we have been well used & by some with the utmost kindness & hospitality.

This has been a busy day. We have been distributing equipments all day. We leave to morrow at 3 P.M. going by way of Cleveland, Pittsburgh & Baltimore to Washington.

---

* In *Childe Harold's Pilgrimage*.

Two

TO THE SEAT
OF WAR

June 6, 1861, saw the Kalamazoo Light Guard setting off by train for the seat of war in Virginia. Sergeant Haydon was singularly impressed by the enthusiastic welcome Ohioans accorded the volunteers. "Our journey through Ohio was a glorious one," he wrote. The passage through Baltimore, by contrast, was nerve-racking, marked by recollection of the four soldiers and the dozen or so civilians killed in rioting three weeks earlier when the 6th Massachusetts made a similar passage.

The 2nd Michigan was assigned to the Department of Washington, Brigadier General Joseph K. F. Mansfield commanding, and was posted at Camp Winfield Scott on Georgetown Heights, on the outskirts of the capital. In careful detail Haydon records the volunteers' introduction to camp life in the field. After five weeks of it, on July 15, the 2nd Michigan was ordered to prepare to go to war.

* * *

§ JUNE 6, 1861 Up in the A.M. early, all my personal effects packed & rolled up in a blanket & slung over my shoulders. These cursed bundles are the greatest draw back on soldiering. They are a worse burden than Christian's was.* We had dress parade at 9

---

* In John Bunyan's *Pilgrim's Progress.*

A.M. & at this, 12 noon, they are loading the company baggage on board the propeller Missouri. We are to carry rations for three days, cooked.

We had an early dinner and abt half past one all embarked on board the prop. Missouri — more than 1000 in number — which was crowded with 500 — and proceeded to the Michigan Central R.R. dock. There we landed, formed & stood out in the hottest sun I ever saw without shelter for an hour & a half. It was enough to scorch one's ears off in as much as we had nothing on our heads but little Sardinian caps not larger than a ladies bonnet.

We then marched up to Fort Street, then up Fort St. to Woodward Av., then up Wd. Av. a ways, then back to the Russell House. Then we closed in mass, then changed direction by the left flank, then deployed columns, then wheeled by platoons into column, then marched to Jefferson Av., up Jefferson Av. 2 miles, then back to Woodward a part of the way on double quick, then back to the dock, another halt of an hour. During all this time we had heavy bundles on our backs which we were carrying for the first time. I was ready to throw mine down, it hurt & pulled so on my shoulders in addition to its weight. Many of the men could scarce keep their places in the ranks. It was perhaps a good show for others but it was rather tough on us. Abt 7 P.M. we were stowed (5 Co's.) on board the Missouri.

There was a great desire on the part of the boys to shake hands with everybody & bid them good bye, & the desire on the part of others was equally great. We shook hands with hundreds of persons whom we never saw before. The waiters on the boat [*Mississippi*] cried lustily when we went. We left it in charge of its four watchmen & of them only. The grass will again have a good opportunity to grow in the yard of Ft. Wayne, the most solitary place about Detroit. The ladies of Detroit & everywhere else have done well by us from the day we started till the present. The men have done well but they have done still better. I have known cases in our own Co. where the lowest of the sex walked 2 miles a day & back to bring refreshments to their new found favorites & I know that it was not done for money, for the boys were destitute of it.

We obtained or at least I & several others did, enough good provisions for supper without resorting to rations. We left abt 7 P.M. & were soon after followed by the other 5 Co's. on the steamer Ocean. We passed the old Mississippi. 2 men were standing on the bow who cheered us on our way. The night was pleasant with a brisk breeze.

§ JUNE 7 Morning. I passed rather a poor night. We slept on the bare deck & were very much crowded. I slept 4 or 5 hours but feel rather sleepy to day. The wind was fresh enough this m'g to make the boat pitch considerable & a good many men sick. I was not sick but I am sure I was not far from it. I was up at daylight & saw the sunrise for the first time in my recollection when out of sight of land. A dense fog came on soon after sunrise & in consequence we were delayed 2 hours & arrived at Cleveland abt 10. We took rations for the day this morning, 6 hard biscuits & a chunk of cold salt boiled beef for each man. Each had a good cup of warm coffee at Cleveland which refreshed us very much and nearly all of us obtained more or less provisions. I am not going to eat salt beef & hard bread when I can buy or otherwise obtain better eatables.

I saw very little of Cleveland. It was busy and dirty so far as I saw. It is said to be a handsome place. We here take cars (28 in number) on the Cleveland & Pittsburgh R.R. There are 2 trains where the road is crooked & one train with 2 engines where it is straight. There is a sentinel at each door & no one is allowed to leave the cars. The men would lose themselves & everything they have if they could get out. One has already lost his rammer, another his gun, 4 or 5 their caps.

Our journey through Ohio was a glorious one. Every hat & handkerchief & apron & bonnet along the road was thrown into the air. All manner of shouts & cheers of encouragement. Hurrah for Michigan, hurrah for the union, God bless you, farewell, give 'em h--l &c, greeted us at every step. All the little toils of war were forgotten at once.

I observed one thing in particular, to wit, that there are an immense number of pretty women in Ohio. Some of the handsomest I ever saw. Two places in particular are to be remembered. Hudson on the Western Reserve 40 or 50 miles I think from Cleveland — perhaps not so far. We were there recd by the firing of cannon, music &c. They furthermore brought provisions of all kinds, bread, biscuits & butter, rich cakes, cheese, dried meat, apples &c by the basket & apron full & pails of water cold as ice & milk in abundance, all gratis with smiles & blushes in abundance besides. The place is small, not as large as Kalamazoo I think. It is the site of the Western Reserve College & seemed so far as could be seen to be a place of great beauty.

The other place is Wellsville, a small village on the Ohio River at the foot of the Allegany Mountains. There is just room enough between the river & mountains for the R.R. & one handsome street which constitutes the whole village. It is a place of great beauty & unsurpassed in hospitality. May the prosperity & happiness of both places be ever equal to the patriotism & generosity of the inhabitants. I shall long remember them.

Our whole reception was such as only the soldiers of liberty & civilization receive. The whole country where we pass is in a blaze of patriotism. We passed along the borders of Va. but as the stars and stripes were flying & the people cheered us lustily we perceived little change. It was eleven P.M. when we arrived at Pittsburgh. We changed cars here & stood in the streets 2 hours waiting for coffee & change of cars. The first 7 Co's. got the coffee. They were piggish & the 300 gallons of coffee provided all disappeared before our turn came.

§ JUNE 8 We left at 1 A.M. & I slept till four. At 4 A.M. we arrived at Altoona where the last Co's. drank all the coffee we desired & the others waited. We bought some provisions & I made a good breakfast of ginger bread & coffee. At abt 1 P.M. we arrived at Harrisburgh & marched to Camp Curtin just out of the city. 4500 Penna. troops were quartered there. They were without uniforms & very ragged and dirty & many of them barefooted. They looked far worse than we ever did at Cantonment Blair. Indeed we are called a fancy Regt., said to be the best looking & best equipped of any that have passed this way. We are no better equipped however than our 1st Regt. Both receive the highest praise for appearance. Mich. is doing nobly. I hope our acts will tell as well as our appearance.

We pitched our tents on the fairground & were glad to throw ourselves on the ground & get a little rest. We got coffee, hard biscuit & salt beef & took dinner & supper both at once. I bought a cup of milk which with a hard biscuit served me. We had so much to do that it was after 10 when we rolled into blankets.

§ JUNE 9 We were up at 4 A.M. to make preparation for a Sunday journey to Washington via Baltimore. The day is beautiful but very warm. We are loaded with all sorts of arms & munitions. We begin to realize that we are approaching the enemies country. 10 rounds of ball cartridge were issued to each man. I distributed & took the precaution to put 20 rounds into my box. Orders are given how & where to form in case of an attack, which is expected at Baltimore. We shall enter the city with loaded guns & fixed bayonets. I do not believe there is any danger but am fully prepared. We have orders to abstain from eating or drinking anything except what we bring with us after we cross the Maryland line. This is to guard agt poison.

We had coffee, bread & fresh beef for breakfast. Marched to the railroad soon after 8.15. This journal is written on the cars a few miles out, just on the bank of the Susquehanna. We are taking on water from a fine spring for the balance of the journey. If this journal should come to a sudden termination on this fine Sunday afternoon in the streets of Baltimore the finder will please notify Philotas Haydon of Decatur, Michigan as soon as convenient & greatly oblige Charles B. Haydon.

One man of Co. K when we were passing through Ohio climbed on top of the cars contrary to express orders of his officers & bumped his head agt a bridge. If we had been going faster he would have been killed — perhaps he will die as it is.

We have not yet got to Maryland. The cars run so slow a part of the time that the men walk by the side. I am getting duced hungry & with little prospect of anything to eat.

After crossing the Md. line we saw very little to indicate the change, save picket guards of U.S. troops at all bridges & embankments & curves. We see abundance of places where bridges have been burned & the track torn up, but all is now in temporary running order. Union flags are even more abundant than in the free states & every one greets us with cheers of apparent welcome.

Fifteen miles from the city we halt, get out of the cars & load our guns. I ram down the first ball that I ever intended for a human mark. Cheers for the union continue unabated. The scenery is beautiful. Many of the residences are the finest I ever saw. Picket guards in large numbers. We arrive at the city & by the time we are formed it is quite dusk. We have strict orders not to cheer or speak to anyone unless it be to answer civil questions in as few words as possible.

We have two miles to march.* The streets are densely crowded on both sides. The children & ladies cheer in great numbers for the union & several wave flags. The men are much more careful what they do. Cheers for Jeff Davis are heard occasionally from groups of 3 or 4. With very few exceptions we march in perfect silence & in excellent order. There is now & then an insulting remark or threat but considering the crowd their number was very few. A very pretty girl offered me a bouquet but I declined to step beyond the line to receive it, so she threw it to me & I thanked her & went on. I presumed at first that it was a ruse to decoy me beyond the line & in reach of the men who were standing around but I guess it was not. One or two attempts were made to trip up our men marching on the flanks but without success. In other cases they took pains to remove obstructions from our way. We pass over the way pursued by the Mass. 6th & saw the place where those who were killed fell.

We arrive at the cars & halt without molestation. Many persons crowd around us to ask questions & many to congratulate. Appearances deceive or the union feeling is strongly predominant.

Just as we are getting on the cars a man threw a heavy stone striking the 1st Sergt. of the Niles Co. on the leg, hurting him considerably. He instantly fired & the man fell.

We get into the cars between 9 & 10 P.M., unfix bayonets & unsling our knapsacks & prepare to rest a little. Just as we are settled into our seats an order is sent through the train to put on our knapsacks, fix bayonets as quietly & quickly as possible which is done at once. We then proceed quietly & very slowly, the picket guard exploring the way at dangerous points. Abt 12 there were a few shots fired close by us & men came running past. We are instantly on the alert. It proved to be a collision between the pickets & the enemy. Reports are various, some say that two or three were killed. I think no one fell. We are very tired & hungry & it is almost impossible to keep awake.

I think we could have given the Secessionists a good one if we could have got at them & I am sure they might have troubled us badly if they had managed properly. Latest reports say that the

---

* That is, from one depot to another; there was no direct rail connection through Baltimore.

pickets killed 6 men last night who were advancing to attack us. I would have disliked to fire in the streets on account of the women & children. Col. Richardson was laughing in his sleeve all the time after they began to talk about fighting.

§ JUNE 10 The man who was shot at Baltimore last night has since died. There is skirmishing going on all the time. The city [Washington] is alive with troops. 85,000 are counted in the vicinity & several thousand are arriving daily.* The heat is intense. Several men have fallen down with sun strokes. I care very little abt marching in hot weather if it were not for my knapsack. I however begin to get along with that better than at first.

I visited the Capitol this m'g & went all through. I went to Post Office Building & this afternoon Patent Office. The Regt. marched out at 4 P.M. and paid its respects to the President & Genl. [Winfield] Scott. I have seen an abundance of interesting things to day but they are too numerous to describe. We were to have moved out of town to day but the weather was so hot that it was deferred.

I have eaten very little since we left Ohio. I have not got hungry enough yet to eat bacon. We have nothing but bacon, hard bread & coffee & a good deal of the time not so much as that.

§ JUNE 11 We left Washington abt 9 A.M. marching for Georgetown Heights 6 miles distant. We hired a team to carry our knapsacks. The day was hot and we made but one halt. The men began to fall out & sit down or lie down by the roadside before we had gone 2 miles. More than 150 men fell out before we got through. Two are reported dead but I am inclined to think it is a mistake. I saw one or two by the roadside who seemed to be dying but I believe they revived. We arrived about 12, got nothing to eat after breakfast except what we bought or stole. Everything cost double what it does at home. I gave a man 10 cts. & took what he asked a quarter for. He swore of course but there was no use of talking.

We did not get our tents till 10 P.M. I preferred to sleep on the ground rather than stop to pitch them. The provisions are poor & very scanty at that. We have had but one meal per day most of the time. We have to be very careful what we buy for fear of poison.

The men got hold of a Secessionist to day. They seized him,

---

* Haydon reports rumor here. As late as the end of June, when the first returns were made, the troops in and about Washington came to 52,700.

searched his house for a secession flag but found none. They would have killed him but for Major Williams who was obliged to place a guard around his house to protect him.

Our location is beautiful. The heights rise almost to the dignity of mountains. The Potomac flows at our feet. Arlington Heights are nearly opposite. Our camp ground is abt 100 ft. above the river & slopes toward it. The ground rises immediately in rear of it 60 or 80 ft. higher. Vegetation indicates a southern latitude. It is darker & richer than at home. The country does not seem in a thriving condition. Slaves come into camp occasionally. It is a very bad place for their owner to leave them. They hear very free & easy talk.

We are placed here to cut off the retreat of troops from Harper's Ferry. The enemy are scouting about camp & have a proclivity for shooting sentinels. Our men have a great desire to shoot them & will do so at the first chance. Guard duty will be severe but there will be less drilling.

§ JUNE 12 We got a reasonable breakfast this m'g & I feel much better. The dinner & supper both together were also good. I had eaten so little of late that I began to feel weak. We got beans, rice, bread, cheese, bacon & coffee to day.

The scenery along the Allegany Mountains is much the finest I ever saw. We rode for abt 20 hours among them. The road winds around on the cliffs following the course of the stream. There seems no end of the coal in this region. The sides of the cliffs are pierced in many places with holes which look like kingfishers holes a little way off. The rock where the coal is found is not hard & solid but a sort of slate or shales I believe they call it. The country produces little except coal & oil. There were oil wells in some places every half mile. There is in some places very fine timber but for the most part the trees are short, grow thick & are of a rich green foliage. They are however in some places scrubby & scattering. There are other places where for several acres the rocks are entirely bare. I saw more stones at a single glance of the eye than I had ever seen before in my life.

In some places the track runs so near the edge of the cliffs that one could easily toss a biscuit far enough so that it would fall 150 ft. before it would strike. In other places the ends of the ties reach quite to the edge of the cliff. The Secessionists could easily have finished the 2d Regt. here if they had run it off the track. I kept awake a great deal of time when I ought to have been asleep for the purpose of seeing the sights. I have now got too far behind to attempt to describe them.

§ JUNE 13 There was an alarm in camp last night. There were cries of murder just outside & a call for the guard. The drum beat & we all got on our accouterments & prepared to strike tents. The pickets sent out however soon returned with news that there was nothing more serious than an Irishman whipping his wife.

The enemy are prowling around nights as spies. Some of them will get tripped if they are not careful. There are picket guards out about 2 miles all the time to keep watch & fire upon anything which attempts to approach. After firing they are to retreat toward camp. The firing is a signal to fall in prepared for battle.

I have observed several things since I have been here. First, that all the women whom we see except our own go barefooted & I am sorry to say that some of them do not keep their legs any too clean. I further observe that there is a vast amount of stealing or cramping as they call it going on. The boys passed off 15 or 20 dollars of Allegan & Berrien County [Michigan] money to peddlers to day for 95 cts. on 100 & in some cases got silver for change. Our tent purchased a 10 gal. keg of beer for $3 of it, got it into the tent & had drawn about a gallon when the man concluded to return the money & take away his beer, which he did minus as much as would run out during the time it was in our possession.

Co's. A & K are sent up the river to day to work on entrenchments. Shoveling dirt is fine business for soldiers in this hot weather. I expect our turn will come soon. We drilled but little yesterday & shall not go out to day till after four. We have been taking things easy. Most of the men have been writing home. There is no card playing — they could not bring the implements. We have sold, given or thrown away *everything* not absolutely necessary.

§ JUNE 14 As expected we work on fortifications to day. The weather was cool this morning, an overcoat did not feel at all uncomfortable.

Four sentinels are under arrest for sleeping on their posts. Some of the men will have to be shot before the rest will learn anything. The officer of the day took away one sentinel's musket & he slept on for half an hour afterwards. He stared a little when he woke up but a guard was standing over him who cut short his meditations by marching him to the guard house.

§ JUNE 15 Co's. B & I were introduced to practical instruction in the science of field fortifications yesterday. I did the first work that I have done in a long time. I handled a pick or shovel all day, blistered my hands and am very sore & stiff. There is a long bridge [the Chain Bridge] about a mile above us across the Potomac. A battery of 12 pounders is to be erected at the end of the bridge to sweep men crossing it. It is 110 rods long & would be a very bad place to march. This battery is composed of stone & turf. The hill immediately in the rear of this is abt 100 ft. higher. On that is to be a battery, of 42 pounders, built of earth which will rake the bridge & the road beyond & keep clear the opposite heights.

The climate here is beautiful, the air is clear & pure & always cool in the morning. There are innumerable springs of good water along the river which flows with a rapid current over a rocky bed. The country just about here does not seem very well suited to agriculture. It is uneven & rocky in places. The crops are generally poor. Still their thriftiness in occasional fields shows what might be done with better cultivation. Near Baltimore we saw good crops & good farming. Everything was thriving. I do not see much evidence here of business of any kind.

§ JUNE 16 Sunday. On guard but as it is fairly my turn I have no cause to complain. Guard duty is more burdensome than heretofore. The number of posts is increased & much of the ground is rocky & uneven. It is a difficult task to get to the posts in the night. A scouting party was driven in to camp this m'g by the enemy. A brush is expected to day or to night with the troops retreating from Harper's Ferry. We need something to rouse the men up to a sense of duty.

The rations are passably good but there is still considerable scrabbling at dinner time. There is very little left of anything except bread & pork. The rice, sugar, coffee, vinegar & beef are eaten to the last particle & double the amount would be consumed if it were at hand. I cannot tell how many times I have heard men say to day that they would like to be at home to see what the folks are doing or that if anyone had told them 6 months ago that they would be here to day how surprised they would have been.

Four Co's. are at work to day on the batteries. We are beginning to lose all recollection of Sunday. We have not yet seen hard times enough to complain about. Somebody has said that "From all his ills the tired soldier makes a safe & sure retreat at last into the grave."*

The weather is very dry. There was quite a storm of wind last night but not rain enough to lay the dust. It seems a little curious sometimes to lie down with equipments at your head & your gun stacked at your side. A guard over the spring where you drink. A circle of guards all around you who will fire on you if you attempt to pass them or take you to the guard house if you halt. The guards themselves have to pace up & down with loaded muskets & at the slightest noise be on the alert to shoot somebody. There are 128 men on guard to day.

A drunken rowdy just fired off a musket through the side of a tent & came near killing a man. He soon after had his shirt off & was trying to get the snakes off his back. He is a young man of 22 or 23.

The 3d Regt. Mich. passed by us this P.M. moving to their en-campment a short distance above. We were right glad to see them, first because they are from Mich. & second because we may need their assistance. They are a good looking set of men but their uniform does not look very well. It was originally grey but has become very dirty & has now a dull lifeless appearance. If offers a very poor mark to the enemy but it has not the fresh lively appearance of blue with bright buttons.

§ JUNE 17 Guards will soon be discharged for this time. The night was quiet. One sentinel mistook a lightning bug for a dark lantern & fired upon it. Some of them are very much inclined to be scared. They would hang upon the Sergt. when he came around as if he were a sure protection. I should have slept well from 11 to 3 had not the officer of the day come around & called out guard rounds & called me to go out as Sergt.

Some rascal stole my belt & left a much poorer one in its place. This stealing is the greatest draw back on camp life. I had a first rate relief last night, the best I ever had. One man drew a revolver on the guard & was tied neck & heels & dragged to the guard house. Several others were arrested, cause whiskey in every case. There were no certain signs of the enemy.

---

* A loose paraphrase of Byron, a favorite author of Haydon's.

The 3d Regt. is encamped just above us. I was up to see them to day. They look better since they have washed. I went on guard at the right time and was excused thereby from a hard day's work on the batteries.

§ JUNE 18 The battle of Waterloo was fought on this day 46 years ago I believe. To morrow if I remember right will be the anniversary of the battle of Bunker Hill, 86 years ago.* This day has been a very quiet lazy one. There was a lazy company drill in the forenoon. I wrote a letter to the Kalamazoo Telegram after dinner & read a few pages in Hardee. Afterward put the corporals through the manual of arms.

The Capt. came blowing around at the Sergts. this m'g because the men were not out on drill, saying that there had not been a Co. drill in a month. There has been one almost every day, & further if he did but know it it's not the Sergts.' business to conduct Co. drill. The Capt.'s business is with the assistance of the Lieuts. to conduct Co. drill. He has never drilled the Co. an hour. If Handy were Capt. Co. I would soon be the best in the Regt. The Capt. does nothing, knows but little, thinks he knows it all. The Orderly [1st Serg. G. W. Crego] is a first rate fellow & knows his business but he is sick all the time. These two things seriously hinder our progress.

There was considerable skirmishing down about Alexandria last night. I am nearly out of money, 3 shillings is all that is left, and that cannot last long. I am not going to live poor while I have money. I guess Uncle Sam will afford us some change before long.

§ JUNE 19 I was a little sick last night but think I am all right this m'g. There was some commotion in camp last night. A corporal of Co. G got out, as report goes, robbed a house of $150, shot at a guard &c &c and without any doubt brought up in the guard house. Should all this prove true he will be shot.

One sentinel fired at somebody or something but I do not know what the trouble was. Two men from Co. K have deserted. A sentinel who was missing sometime since & supposed to have deserted now reported killed.

There was a most glorious battalion drill last night, our Capt. never did so well before. The Col. was delighted. He said in his

---

* Bunker Hill was in fact fought on June 17, 1775.

peculiar blunt old fashioned way that all we wanted now was a chance to put our drill into use. I believe he is as anxious for a battle as a school boy for his dinner. An officer came up from Washington yesterday & told him that an Ohio Regt. had been driven back from a battery which they attempted to take. How many men were killed asked Col. 15 replied the officer. Oh was that all said Col. R — humph — and they did not take the battery. It was well understood by all who heard the remark that if we had been there the battery would have been taken or very many more than 15 men would have fallen.

I believe there is not a better fighting man in the United States than Col. Richardson. I heard an officer of the Regulars say that he saw him kill 4 Indians in Texas with his sword in less than a minute of time. They were attacked by abt 100 Indians while out reconnoitering. The Col. knocked the first off his horse by a stroke on the head with the back of his sword, immediately mounted his horse & slashed the other three in quick time.

This is a very warm day as I have already found from an hours exercise at guard mounting. Col. R. said last night at drill that the neighbors complained that the cows which come into camp are milked & that if it was so it must be stopped as much as *possible*. The camp ground is an improved field which is seeded down & a part of it is an old orchard. There will be considerable fruit in the fall. The cows like to come on the ground to feed & the men take pains to feed them pieces of bread, salt &c.

§ JUNE 20 The m'g is warm. There is a prodigious sick list which might be reduced half by taking out the lazy & shirks. It is reported to night that some of our blue jackets are likely to be striped with red before three days. Gen. [Joseph K. F.] Mansfield was here in person with news that 75,000 men are advancing on Washington. Col. R. was so pleased that he could hardly contain himself. I could see him laughing to himself during the whole drill. I believe very little of all this but intend to be well prepared. Forty rounds of cartridges were issued to night to each man.

I have been Sergt. of the Police this P.M. I hate it like the duce. This ordering men about to rake up straw & chips, file stones, pick up scraps of meat & bread, cut down apple trees & drag them off, level down stumps &c while the rest are lying in their tents is a miserable business.

§ JUNE 21 A very quiet night. Our tent is quite convenient &

the inmates are very good. It is occupied by the 5 Sergts. & the Drum Major on one side and by stores & provisions on the other. The greatest difficulty is to keep a crowd of loafers out of it. Some crowd in to talk over the news & others to pick at the sugar & bread or at anything else they can get hold of.

The men are drinking too much coffee. I could with good relish drink a quart a day but I get along with a pint. I can easily see how the excesses of a soldier's life occur. When a man has been on beef, bacon & bread for a few weeks he seizes upon tea, coffee, liquor & a thousand other injurious things with an avidity which he never would have known had he have kept his usual diet. There is no doubt but soldiering begets a tendency to vagabondizing. This rolling up in a blanket to sleep whenever night overtakes one is a very free & easy life.

The 75,000 is reported a hoax just as I expected. I wish I had some books. The best I can do now is to repeat over & over such pieces of poetry as I have committed to memory. The day is very hot & I did not get off police till noon. There is a disturbance in Co. B, nearly all the men are under arrest. They say that the Capt. uses up the extra rations to support three whores which he keeps under the name of washerwomen. There are various other causes of complaint.

The 3d Regt. wanted our Col. to come up & put them through battalion drill. He said he would show them a few simple moves. He went up, called them out at 9 A.M. & drilled them till 12, more than half the time on double quick. They swore they never wanted to see him again. Their Col. was accustomed to go out & sit upon his horse half an hour during dress parade, say very little & do less. When they saw Richardson tramping up & down the field on foot, his great iron sword sheath hung to his side with chains, rattling like a log chain on a pole bridge, giving orders loud enough to be heard a mile & reprimanding the officers in a manner which fairly raised them off their feet, & keeping them on the jump by the hour, they thought the Devil had surely come. The man whom he talks to dont wait to be told twice.

§ JUNE 22 I was routed out 4 times last night, three times by the firing of sentinels. One of them shot at a dog. Two shot nearly at the same time at an unlucky wight [creature] who was belated & was trying to creep into camp without going to the guard house. The dog was killed but the man escaped. The third time one sentinel fired at nobody knows what & called lustily for the corporal's guard. Two others immediately fired for fear the corporal would not come quick enough.

Some of them are genuine cowards I believe. But be that as it may, they get so feverish from gazing in the dark still night at some one object which they cannot quite make out, that imagination readily converts it into a big Secessionist just ready to fire on them.

Once I piled out to strap up the tent to keep out the wind & rain. There was considerable wind & lightning but very little rain. On several occasions there have been like signs of rain but never more than a few drops fall. There has been no rain of any account since we came from Detroit. The weather is very hot to day. All the grass is drying up & dying.

We drilled on skirmishing about 2 hours this m'g & have done nothing since. The other Regts. drill less than ours.

§ JUNE 23 Sunday. A hot quiet day. I cleaned thoroughly & oiled my gun in the m'g then went & drew 3 days rations for the Co. Then read the articles of war aloud to them. I then went with Orderly Crego to the brook & had a good wash, put on clean clothes &c, dinner immediately after. We were called upon at 2 to go to church but as that is not compulsory I preferred to go to sleep. There was a fine battalion drill after service & immediately after came supper. We had fried bacon, bread & coffee for breakfast, boiled beef (fresh), soup & bread for dinner, bread, cold beef & coffee for supper.

The picket guard yesterday interrupted Capt. Beach [Co. B] very unceremoniously. He sprang to his feet, asked what in hell they wanted there, drew his pistol & ordered them to retire on pain of death. They retired (to inform the officer of the day) and the Capt. was pacified. He stands a fine chance to leave this Regt. very soon.

I have been drinking coffee since I came from home. I have been trying to leave off. I can do it but it comes pretty hard. I drink little more than a pint cup full per day. I could with a good relish drink 2 quarts. Many of the men drink near that amount. It is wonderful how strong the passion for drinks other than water becomes in camp. Our Surgeon says that so much coffee is highly injurious. Genl. Scott says the same. Men need to be very careful about drinking spirits or they will get habits which they can never break. No one could have made me believe without actual experience that I could ever acquire a desire for such strong, black, dirty coffee — without milk — as we have.

§ JUNE 24 We had a very quiet night. The sick list is large. The measles are in camp. Bread & rice for dinner. A first rate drill this m'g on skirmishing & bayonet exercise under command of Lt. Handy. No one else does anything for the Co. nowadays. The Capt. came out & looked on for about 10 minutes.

The guns are now mounted in the battery which we worked on some days ago. They have been firing at an old stone mill across the river, which has had the roof burned off. It was built in 1810 & the walls are still very strong. The 42 pound shot make the dust fly very smartly.

We see every day a balloon which is sent up daily to observe the movements of the enemy. It seems to be a very large one. It is let up ½ a mile or more & held by ropes to prevent it from drifting away. There is always a telegraph wire direct from the balloon to Gen. Scott's room. The men in the balloon by the aid of telescopes can obtain a good view of the country for 50 miles about. There are wires running out from the city to all the Regts. The enemies' pickets are said to be only 10 miles from us.

Some of the men of the Mass. 1st encamped just below were shouting & making a good deal of noise last night. Col. Richardson said when he heard them that he guessed they would have enough to halloo about in less than 10 days.

§ JUNE 25 Warm dry weather, brisk drilling, plenty of double quick, bread, beans & pork for living.

§ JUNE 26 Cloudy with some prospect of rain. The times in camp are quiet. There is a report that we are to go to Washington as home guards. It is called a post of honor & is in many respects a very desirable one. There will be no knapsacks to carry & there are many things in the city which are worth seeing & which need to be looked at often. We should get little liberty but I think I could get out at least once a week.

If we go there we shall of course be made a fancy Regt., well drilled & clothed & equipped. Col. R. may go on his wife's account. He would never do it if it were not for her. He would push us into Va. as far as orders would allow. It would be very pleasant to be in the Capital during the session of Congress.

A sentinel was decoyed off his post last night by a washerwoman & both bring up in the guard house this m'g. There are from Co.

I 20 men per day on guard & special police duty. Including the sick & lazy this takes near half the Co. Three of the Mass. 1st are reported poisoned from eating pies filled with finely pulverized glass.

The Regt. meets with a great loss to morrow. Lt. Col. Chipman leaves us for a captaincy in the regular army. He is a perfect gentleman & the strictest & most perfect disciplinarian in all the minutia of a soldier's education that there is in the Regt. He always gave great attention to the personal appearance & polite behavior of his soldiers. I mark a very favorable contrast in these respects between this Regt. & many others which I have seen. Politeness adds greatly to a soldier's appearance and equally so to their discipline & usefulness.

There was a smart shower of rain this P.M. Our tent was not quite prepared for it & leaked considerably. By gathering our things together in the middle & spreading our oil cloth blankets over them they were kept quite dry. The ground will be a little damp for sleeping but our oil cloth blankets are a good protection. They are an excellent thing to sleep on. I believe there is no one thing which contributes more to the preservation of health. The ground becomes very damp under a person sleeping on the bare ground.

§ JUNE 27 A fair pleasant day devoid of any unusual interest or excitement. There is a good deal of sameness about life in Camp Winfield Scott.

§ JUNE 28 Weather fine, nights cold, dews heavy. There are at least a tenth of the men sick with diarhea, bloody flux &c. There are hardly any who are not troubled more or less in the same way. It must be the water or change of climate.

There can be nothing about beef, pork, beans, bread & coffee which should make men sick in this way. I have been troubled by costiveness [constipation] ever since I have been in this camp, which is the case with all who have not diarhea. I feel the want of vegetables more than anything else. We seldom have more than bread, beef, or pork & coffee at one meal. The rations of beans & rice do not come oftener than abt once in four days each.

I occasionally hear these sick boys saying that if they were only at home once more they would bid farewell to soldiering. They undoubtedly feel most sincerely what they say yet half of them if discharged would reenlist within 3 months. A soldier's life is a hard one but those who have tried it once are the first to reenter the service. Whatever other things may be wanting soldiers are seldom without a good appetite. They take a tin cup & tin plate filled with their coarse food, drop down on the nearest log, stump or stone, or for want of a better seat the bare ground, & eat with a relish which men in better circumstances might well envy.

Our camp is kept very clean & neat. All the rubbish has to be picked up & the ground swept twice every week. I have 12 men at work under me to day at that business. The morals of camp are good. I think one could hardly find 1000 men assembled for any other purpose who behave better than this Regt. has at Camp Scott. There is some cramping but that among soldiers usually indicates very little real viciousness but merely the craving of a half filled stomach. They are temperate from necessity & most of them are clean & neat about their persons.

We have a secluded life knowing little of what passes outside. There is a general opinion among the men, & I think it is correct, that if we serve 3 years here we shall be worth very little for any-thing else when discharged. I can readily see that the veteran of 3 yrs would look with regret on the close of the war. No man likes to see his occupation spoiled & war may very properly be regarded as the occupation of a 3 yr soldier. When discharged their habits & ways of life are all broken up. They must seek occupations & associations which are in a great measure strange to them. It is not therefore singular that an old soldier looks with regret on the close of the war & hails with joy its renewal. In this view wars are injurious even to the victor & tend often to endanger the stability & security of the government they were waged to sustain.

Sergts. Crego, Benson, Major Underwood & self made a good breakfast this m'g. Benson, the only man who had any money, bought some butter, milk, and a cherry pie out of which with coffee & a good slice of beef steak made us as good a breakfast as could be wished. We did very fine drilling to night at parade. Col. Rich-ardson begins to think he has a Regt. worth commanding. All the officers who know their business like him. He blowed Capt. Beach sky high to night.

I am surprised that I do not hear from home. It is near a month since I have recd a letter. I am afraid something is wrong. I have to go on police again to morrow as I am informed. I dislike it very much. I find a good deal of trouble in keeping the ground dry &

good in the tent where I sleep. If you use straw it soon gets damp & mouldy & full of bugs & crickets & all manner of vermin. I afterwards tried cedar boughs. These keep the insects out but the ground gets damp & mouldy under them. I now sleep on the bare ground. If the tents could be struck every day or two all this might be avoided. This however is a good deal of trouble & men dislike to do it. Straw if used should be changed every day in warm weather.

§ JUNE 29 A rainy damp morning. Everything is very moist inside our tent. The reveille was changed yesterday from 5 A.M. to 4½, rather too early in the morning for personal convenience.

I have been figuring on the average height of Co. I. The tallest man is 6 ft. 1 inch, the shortest 5 ft. 4½ inches, average height of Co. 5 ft. 8.6 inches.

We had pork, bread & coffee for breakfast, pork, bread & rice for dinner, bread & coffee for supper. This living idle here in camp is becoming dull business. The Capt. will do nothing & spoils everything which others teach. Orders were given to drill on skirmishing to day. The 1st Lt. is sick & the rest of us do not understand it well enough to drill it to advantage. The Capt. was mad, swore he would hire some man to drill the Co. He forgets that this is his especial business.

§ JUNE 30 Orders were issued last night for the Regt. to be ready for inspection this Sunday m'g at 8 oclock. Accordingly we all brushed our clothes, cleaned & brightened guns, blacked shoes & improved our looks generally. Went out formed in column, stood in the ranks with knapsacks, haversacks & canteens on for 3 hours when it commenced raining before the inspection reached us. The roll was called & we marched back to quarters.

The enemies' pickets were within three miles of us yesterday. There is a great army collecting around Washington. Regts. arrive every day. We can hear the morning drum beat of a score or more, but there are only 4 in sight, the Mass. 1st, N.Y. 14th, Mich. 3d & the District Guard, numbering about 600.

I am going to read a chapter in the Testament when I get done with the day's journal.

4 oclock P.M. I find myself under a large old pear tree in front of our tent seated on a stone. This tree is one of a large old orchard, a considerable part of which we cut down to make room for battalion drill. 20 years ago I am told this field was part of a beautiful

estate. The ground is certainly fine enough & the location is unsurpassed. There are now 3 board shanties on it. It was abandoned because the land was run out. It looks to me as though it might be made to produce plentifully. It must certainly be good for grazing. And that where milk is 10 cts. per gallon & butter 25 cts. per pound in the most plentiful season of the year must be profitable business.

There is an abundance of cherries to be had over in Va. for the picking. A great many union families fled some weeks ago & since that many secession families have moved off. Their farms are left vacant & the fruit &c is going to waste. It is however so much trouble to get passed out of camp that few can profit by the opportunity.

We made a very good dinner & supper both at once on soup, bread & raw onions. Battalion drill comes off at 6 P.M. as usual.

§ JULY 1, 1861 I commenced the day with a violent headache which continues at 4 P.M. I drilled 3 hours this forenoon but was nearly blind. I began to feel bad 4 days ago & have been feeling worse ever since. I got some medicine of the Surgeon but it does not seem to help me much. I think when I get thoroughly physiced out I shall be all right again. I have eaten nothing to day & after washing thoroughly feel somewhat better.

It is a first rate day for fasting. Breakfast consisted of bread, onions & coffee, dinner of soup & hard bread. I think that much of our sickness is caused by bad cooking. Everything we have is cooked in 3 or 4 camp kettles interchangably, so that beef, pork, coffee, beans & rice are pretty well mixed by the time we get them. The provisions are not generally cooked long enough.

Many of the men have taken to doctoring themselves & have in several cases cured with the juice of boiled blackberry roots a diarhea which baffled the Surgeon's skill. The seeds of all this disease or at least the greater part of it were laid by the irregular & insufficient diet during the first week after we left Detroit.

We left the tent door open last night as usual & I could nearly wring water out of my blanket this m'g. The night air is frequently very damp.

I was rejoiced to day at the sight of a long expected letter from home. I have been fearful abt Father's health & the letter does not entirely satisfy me on that point. A letter from home is a very welcome visitor nowadays. Arthur's [his brother] brief account of things at home & at Kalamazoo brings up an abundance of pleasant thoughts & images of times past.

Our German neighbors of the Saginaw Guards & Scott Guards true to old habits are erecting each a pole & parallel bars &c for gymnastics. They seem to stand the campaign better than we.

§ JULY 2 Last night abt sundown came a very heavy shower of rain accompanied with thunder, lightning & strong wind which lasted for near an hour. The tents are pitched on a side hill & the ground being very dry & hard the water came down in torrents. There was a trench around our tent which was supposed to be more than sufficient to carry off the water. It however overflowed in some places & two or three smart little brooks came rushing down through the tent before we were aware of it. This was soon stopped but the tent itself leaked so badly that the ground was soon saturated. Our things were rolled up in the oiled blankets & kept dry.

After abt an hour during which time we were huddled up in the middle of the tent or were holding onto the poles & ropes to keep it from blowing over the rain ceased & we went out to view the premises. No serious damage was done save the upsetting of most of the cook houses & blowing down the trees which had been planted around the tents. The water poured through some of the lower tents in torrents. As soon as the water drained off the men laid hold of nails, poles, bushes or anything else which would keep them out of the mud during the night. I curled up on top of a box & passed the night comfortably.

Owing to a mistake of the commissary supper & breakfast to day like breakfast & dinner of yesterday consisted only of bread & coffee. Some meat has now arrived & dinner & supper to day will probably be an improvement over yesterday. The m'g was clear with high wind & cold enough to make overcoats very acceptable.

After dinner I induced Sergt. Whiting to ask Capt. for a pass out to get berries which as I expected was very promptly refused. Orderly Crego ventured to write us passes & sign the Capt.'s name to them. We put them in our pockets & went to a German sentinel who we knew could not read English, showed him some other papers, passed out & kept the passes in our pockets. Corpls. McGee & Mack who kept behind to watch our progress got out in the same way. We had a fine run over in Maryland, got all the black-berries & raspberries we could eat & a pan full to bring back & as many beets as we could carry, they being the only eatables we could find. I dont think I shall be kept as close in this camp hereafter as I have been.

§ J u l y 3 On guard. Day fair & warm. It was very cold this m'g, it must have been near a frost. I do not feel quite as well to day as yesterday but think I shall bring myself out right in a day or two. I have missed no duty as yet by reason of sickness & I do not think I shall. As long as we are well we lead a very comfortable life but a sick soldier is a very sorry looking object. He thinks too much abt home.

I was yesterday talking with 1st Sergt. of Co. K, a German who was in the German Revolution of 1852. He told me that for 3 weeks they were so near the enemy, in such constant fear of surprise & were on duty so much that they became so worn down that it was necessary during the night to send men around with raw hides to whip the sentinels to keep them awake. I have heard such things before but had always doubted it. I have however good reason to believe this man's story. I think it would not be a bad idea to try it here. Hardly a night passes but some of them are asleep. They will by & by get shot for it if they are not more careful.

What I have often feared seems abt to come to pass. Col. Richardson is appointed Brevet Brigadier Genl. of the Mich. 2d & 3d, Mass. 1st & N.Y. 12th. This will take him away from us half the time & when the Brevet is removed as I have no doubt it soon will be he will be gone entirely from the Regt. except in Brigade movements. The loss of 500 men would decrease the strength of the Regt. less than his departure.

§ J u l y 4 The glorious 4th. The night was quiet but for me laborious. I had a very lazy sleepy Corpl. & was called out to go the grand rounds soon after 12 p.m. It was 11 a.m. before I was discharged from duty.

The night was clear, cool & beautifully starlight. From 1 to 3 a.m. I had little to do save keep awake & watch the stars. There was no wind & the silence of the night was undisturbed save by murmuring of some half dozen little spring brooks as they went jumping down from rock to rock on their way to the blue Potomac, which was just distinguishable at the distance of 100 rods. The Great Bear moved with stately steps on his nightly round closely lighted by a fiery comet shedding as was once believed war, pestilence & famine from its blazing locks. Pleiades & Orion lent their beauties to the scene. When finally the moon rose shedding its silvery light over river & brook, gently undulating plains, steep hills & rugged rocks; but for the long rows of glittering arms in sheaf-like stacks & the dark ranks of men sleeping behind them, the scene would have been one for pastoral love or a fairy dance.

A closer view showed how hollow & uncertain was this scene of quiet & how quickly it might be changed to one of carnage & death. Beneath all this quiet & beauty of nature the struggling passions of men were but ill concealed. It sometimes seems as if men were constantly striving to mar the beauties & violate the laws of nature.

After guard duty is over I always repair at once to a large rock where the water pours over making one of the finest shower baths in the world & wash & put on a clean shirt, after which I take something to eat & feel well for the balance of the day.

For experiment's sake the non-commissioned officers asked leave to drill the battalion at the usual hour. Genl. Richardson readily granted the request & we appointed field & commissioned officers from our own numbers, filling up our places with privates. The officers readily lent us their uniforms & swords & many of them went into the ranks & acted as privates. Our Col. was selected because of good looks &c rather than military knowledge or ability to command. The consequence was that he made three mistakes to start on, which with some others which followed, detracted very much from the performance. Some of the movements were finely executed & on the whole we succeeded pretty well, at least Gen. R. said he wished some of the other Regts. of his brigade could do as well with their regular officers.

At night cannons were fired at the batteries & at the city & every camp had a bonfire. The Potomac was lighted for miles by their blaze. Bands played a few patriotic tunes & each camp gave 3 cheers for the flag & the union. Thus ends our 4th of July, 1861.

§ JULY 5 Was a day of little interest. Drilling as usual. Corpl. Card & self went out of camp in the afternoon. We picked all the berries we wanted & traveled around a good deal to see the country. Saw one handsome dwelling & only one. It was well shaded, tastily arranged but had an old & somewhat weather beaten look. It looked good homelike hospitable. I have seldom seen a more en-

ticing place for study & retirement. A man of education with a
good library might enjoy himself in such a spot. There was nothing
about it which looked like noise or business.

The country around is hilly, almost mountainous. The trees
thick, the foliage dense & of a very deep green. Three or four lazy
negroes were lying about under the trees & added to the general
laziness of the scene. The roads were so exceedingly crooked, wind-
ing around among the hills, that we came near getting lost. One
might start out on a road running the direction he wished to go
& before he had gone half a mile he would have described a circle
& all the angles laid down in Geometry. The scenery was most
beautiful to the admirer of nature but rather discouraging to the
agriculturist. I cannot deny that the country is a very pleasant one.
Perhaps it is in some degree from the thought that this region was
once the home of Washington & Jefferson & others whose names
lend an interest to the most desolate places.

Again such scenes are new to me. There is such a contrast between these hills & rocks and the oak plains of Michigan. I wish I
could travel about more to see the country. It is a rare thing to get
outside the guard lines.

§ JULY 6 Another inexplicable accident occurred to the commissary last night & we got no bread for supper or breakfast. Col.,
or as we are henceforth to say Genl. Richardson, sent orders to us
to do no drilling till the bread came. He sent for Mr. Commissary
to come to his tent at once. I can guess what passed there between
them. The bread came about 10 A.M.

I had a letter from Mr. Miller last night inquiring abt Homer
who has been making most bitter complaints to his father. I was
asked to write a plain letter & have done so. He offered to send
me $50 if I desired. I am glad I do not need to ask him for it. I
recd $10 from home to day which is an ample supply for all present
wants. I suppose that Uncle Sam, or Abe, will give us some money
very soon, it has been promised times enough. We shall lose all
patience if it does not come pretty soon. The 1st & 3rd [Michigan]
have both recd pay from the state.

I have read the President's message to day in which he asks for
400,000 men & $400,000,000 of money. I say give it if the work
cannot be done for less. I for one am ready to work & give if need
be all I am worth which is very little, till the last secessionist is dead
or subdued.

But 400,000 men is a great army & it will need to be well managed or it will not stop when its proper work is done. If it should continue long in the field it & its attendant consequence may work a great change in the habits & thoughts of the people. It will need to be closely watched or someone will be snatching for a crown before the work is done. I have no fears of such a result unless the war continues long enough to destroy the prosperity of the people & generally demoralize them. The day for that has not yet come. Still there may be great changes without going that length.

§ JULY 7 Sunday. A very fine morning, gentle rain last night. The air is cool & pure. I have got my bed arranged now so that it is pretty much out of the way of bugs & inundations. At home the soft side of a board is called a pretty hard bed but here men are glad to go half a mile for one to sleep on and bring it on their backs. I did so & have cut it in two pieces & put it on crotches making a very comfortable bed.

We (the Sergeants) made a good breakfast this m'g. Some potatoes, the first I have tasted in more than a month, found their way to our tent. We bought some meal which was made into pudding or rolled up in balls and fried. These two rarities were enough to make a glorious breakfast although we had nothing but salt to season them with.

There were only two men reported on the sick list this m'g & one of them is lame. A week ago there were from 12 to 15 every m'g. At six P.M. we were called out for battalion drill. The weather was very warm & Genl. Richardson gave us an hour & a half brisk moving. One man was sun struck & 3 others gave out. One hot day's marching would take off half the Regt. They talk of re-examining the men. A tenth of them would be thrown out. I have seldom felt better than I did to day. I could have marched 20 miles.

Orderly Crego & I picked a good lot of blackberries this m'g. A man in Co. F shot himself in the foot with a pistol this m'g. Another was stabbed in the hand at Georgetown.

§ JULY 8 I had the promise of going to town to day & got a pass from the Capt. but the Adjutant refused to sign it. The Col. [Richardson] says that we are liable to move at any hour. I was very much disappointed. I have not been out of camp except after berries since we came here. I wished to see Congress in session & to visit the Smithsonian Institute & Navy Yard. It was reported that we were to be quartered in the Navy Yard. It looks very little like it now. They have been giving us more shoes & clothing to day. We have more now than we can carry.

It is reported at 4 P.M. that we move to night. Two Co's. of the Mass. 1st moved up the river this m'g. We went down to the road and gave them three hearty cheers. We should have gone if we had have had wagons for our baggage. Old Mass. gives the whole hog, gives her troops teams & wagons not only for their usual baggage but for their knapsacks. I could walk forever if it were not for these cursed knapsacks.

There was fighting up the river yesterday & the boys have gone up to help. I regret to leave our comfortable quarters here for the uncertainties of the march.

§ JULY 9 A good hot day. We expect to move before night but I cannot tell where we shall go. We are loaded down with clothes & more are coming every day.

I had a fine bath this m'g down at the large flat rock over which the water pours in a clean thin sheet. I shall remember long these rocks, the falling water & the pleasant shade around. Many a good wash I have had & that little brook has done a great deal to preserve the health of the Regt. I also contrived to evade the guards & got out after berries. I clawed the blackberries off in double handfulls. I never saw larger or finer berries.

The Atlantic was welcomed to camp to night and two articles, "Ellsworth" & "Washington as a Camp" were read aloud in our tent. The latter article written by Major [Theodore] Winthrop was published after the poor boy was killed in the battle of Great Bethel. Both pieces possess unusual interest to us & were listened to with eagerness. There was a very heavy shower of rain just before dark but we were well prepared for it & came off well.

I have been trying to lighten my pack. I have made arrangements for one pr. of pants & a pr. shoes. I gave a powder flask to Lt. Handy & tried to trade my Testament given me by the Kalamazoo County Bible Society off for gingerbread. I could get nothing for it & put it in my pocket with the determination of carrying it along.

The bodies of some men passed down to day who were killed in the fight of yesterday a few miles above here. The sick have all been moved from camp & a considerable part of the baggage. We are all ready to move.

§ JULY 10 Is a most delightful cool m'g. There was a call this m'g for 9 men from each Co. to go up to Big Falls, the skirmish ground. All wanted to go but only a Corporal & 8 men were allowed to Co. I. On such occasions I feel the need of a better gun. If I only had a good Mich. rifle there would be fewer secessionists in the world before long or I am mistaken. Sharpshooting seems to be the order of the day. I should not feel sure of a man more than 15 rods with our guns.

We recd regular knapsacks to day which were very much needed on the march & will relieve much of the inconvenience arising from our old bundles. Two Co's. of District Volunteers whose time has expired passed down toward the city this P.M. They have done good service in a time when they were needed & should return with the thanks of all unionists. They were well drilled & finely uniformed. Two of the best Co's. I have seen.

Miller & I ate a blackberry pie & good one it was at the expense of a peddler this m'g. Miller was to treat so he bargained for the pie, handed it to me & I immediately set out for the tent. He remained to pay for it but finding the crowd large & the man very busy he concluded to come away without doing it. It was undoubtedly wrong to take the pie, nevertheless it was a great addition to our breakfast.

We have been drilling a little on bayonet exercise to day. The Capt., actuated by some new idea took up the notion of drilling us & therefore commenced on bayonet exercise. I was glad to see this although he knew no more about the drill than the man in the moon. He read it off out of a book, & it was much better than lying in the tent.

There is a good deal of change going on in military affairs. All the stiffness & unnecessary airs are giving away to a more free & easy mode of standing & walking. Common sense must have dictated this long ago & the introduction of the Zouave drill brought it into practice. Ellsworth had more to do with the reform than any other man.

§ JULY 11 There was a smart shower with high wind last night about sundown & the rain continued till after I went to sleep. It is quite pleasant to hear it pattering on the tent close by your head but to feel the cool streaks down your legs & body where it leaks through is not by any means so pleasant. Nothing however hurts a man after he has been in camp a few weeks.

There have been two deaths in the Regt. to day. The orderly sergeant of Co. F & a man named Vance from our Co. Vance has been sick of typhoid fever for a long time. He had a brother in the Co. who has taken good care of him. They came from Grass Lake & enlisted at Detroit when the call was made for three years men. They were intelligent young men, well brought up & the children of wealthy parents. He has laid down his arms early in the day. The flag is at half mast & trimmed with black. It will be so more than once before the 3 yrs are up. Deaths have not been more frequent in the Regt. thus far than should be expected.

I went after blackberries this P.M. I picked a large milk pan heaping full beside eating a great many. I never saw such blackberries or such briars before. I am scratched raw from head to heels. You could fill a pan with berries almost as quickly as with plums. One of them would make a good mouthful. I dislike to have such fine secession berries go to waste. I got very wet coming home. I took out a squad of men & we all together brought back abt 2 bushels of berries.

Co's. A & K marched to the skirmish ground this P.M. We have orders to all be ready in light marching order which means with nothing but a blanket, pair of socks extra, arms & equipments & 3 days provisions.

There are 35 men from Co. I out on guard & picket to day. We shall soon be off. As good as 4 Co's. have gone already. I would rather go than remain here. I wish for a little change. We never shall get out of here except on duty unless we do march. When we go after berries we are detailed with leave of absence of 3 hours.

We have been living duced poor to day. Pork, beans, hard bread & coffee. Beans at dinner, hard bread, pork & coffee for breakfast, hard bread & coffee for supper. I bought a pint of milk for breakfast & soaked some hard biscuit in it till they were eatable. I can eat salt pork nowadays. I could eat a great deal more than I do. I avoid it as much as possible. I hope we shall have some beef to morrow. We have hardly provisions enough to keep up our strength.

§ JULY 12 The night was cold & I slept cold. I had nothing around me but a blanket. I shall put on my overcoat next time. I carelessly left my good pants out doors last night to dry & some one punished my carelessness by stealing them. Sergts. Benson &

Crego & Major Underwood made raise of a pie & card of ginger bread, 2 qts of milk & some mush out of which we made a good breakfast. But for the articles we should have breakfasted on salt pork & hard bread.

One of the washerwomen committed the laughable mistake yesterday of trying to milk a he goat. She will hear about that as long as I shall about milking the steer calf. The Irish women who come around camp to peddle are the stingiest people I ever saw without any exception. The niggers sell at a much more reasonable rate. I think we manage to keep nearly even with them by diligent exertions.

There is a report to night that Genl. McClellan has gained a decisive victory at some place down in Virginia, God knows where. 'Tis said that the rebels are utterly defeated. The news was brought up by Sec. [of State William H.] Seward to night & we gave 3 rousing cheers when it was read.*

We were truly glad of the victory yet it cannot be denied that there was a strong feeling of envy & disappointment that we could not share in the glory. There is to night a general fear that it will all be over before we have a chance to do anything. There are very few in the Regt. who want to see Mich. till after they have smelled the enemies powder.

§ July 13 There was a long steady rain last night. We had a poor breakfast this m'g, pork, hard biscuit & coffee. I ate a piece of bread abt 2 inches square & nibbled at a piece of pork. Dinner would have been little better — pork, peas, soup, hard bread — if I had not succeeded in securing some corn dodgers for ourselves which made us a very fair dinner. The corn dodgers are made by rolling meal wet with water in little cakes like biscuit which are fried in pork grease. They make first rate eating for soldiers.

Genl. Richardson says he can preserve the Union so far as fighting can do it with his brigade alone if they will give him 6 hours a day for 2 weeks to drill them. We got mush & good beef for supper. The Orderly of Co. A. returned from up the river to night. He says they have killed 3 secessionists since they have been there. If

---

* Gen. George B. McClellan's victory was at Rich Mountain in western Virginia on July 11.

we had decent guns we should very soon be there. I recd a long expected letter from home to day.

Benson & Underwood sung so much last night that the rest of us slept very little. Underwood is the first musician & an excellent singer. Benson is a mate for me in that respect. It rained hard by spells to day & is very cold to night.

I find myself much stronger than when I first came here. It used to make my legs ache severely to walk up the long steep hill where we have to bring up the water. I can now run from bottom to top without any inconvenience. The heat does not trouble me at all now.

I saw an old school mate to night from the Ill. 21st. He was the dullest boy I ever saw in school. He is now Capt. of a Co. I dont have to serve under him. I bought the Atlantic yesterday & have busied myself with its contents to day. I saw Walbridge of Kalamazoo yesterday. He was out here with a wonderful pretty *niece*. He was pretty drunk & she had smelled his breath so much that her sensitive nerves were slightly affected.

§ JULY 14 Sunday. Good breakfast on beef & biscuits (hard). Crego, Benson & self went out with Lt. Handy & drilled on bayonet exercise 2 hours, came back & went after blackberries, got barely enough to eat. They had all been picked within range of our camp. Dress parade as usual.

We have been packed & ready to move on an hour's notice for more than a week. It is getting to be tiresome business. I hope we shall advance. We are as ready for fighting now as we shall ever be.

I went to the Little Falls to day just above the Chain bridge. The falls do not amount to a great deal but the rocks are worth a Michigan man's attention. The river is deep, I should think about 8 rods wide & falls 15 or 20 ft. in 100 rods. The weather this A.M. was very cold. Overcoats were in good demand.

§ JULY 15 On guard. Guard duty is very dull business, nothing to do but watch our own men & keep them from going outside the lines. 40 men at a time with loaded guns & fixed bayonets walk constantly with solemn & measured step around us, while 80 other men lie lazily on the ground, fully armed & accoutered to take their turn in six hours in the solemn procession. 3 Corpls., 3 Sergts., 2 Lieuts. & 1 Capt. oversee this monotonous parade. All this with much more is repeated every day with great precision & regularity. 129 men succeed in guarding from surprise a camp around which are encamped on all sides other Regts. three or four deep & to which the enemies pickets dare not come nearer than 15 miles.

The sentinels have ceased firing nights & do very little save go to sleep as quick as the officer is out of sight. The officers do little but seize on the unlucky ones whom they catch asleep & send them to the guard house after which they are compelled to roll stones up hill for a week. One man of Co. E was found dead in the canal to day. There is a prospect of a bad rainy night. Co's. A & K returned to camp last night. The camp has been as still & quiet as a church yard all day. So many men are out on other duties that very few are left for drill.

If report be true we yet stand a good chance of seeing the enemy. I was to day told by a reliable informant that we are the foremost brigade of the N.E. Division of the Grand Army & that the Mich. 2d is the foremost Regt. of the brigade. There is one Division ahead of us but they cannot do the work alone. If, as expected, there should be a great battle at Richmond we shall be there.

Genl. Richardson with abt a dozen men went within 2 miles of the enemy at Fairfax a few days since & had a fair view of them with his glass from a high hill. When he returned Genl. Mansfield asked if he did not know that he went much farther than his orders allowed. He replied that he did not read his orders & that if he had have had his brigade with him he should have taken the place. There were at that time abt 7000 men at Fairfax. Genl. Mansfield immediately informed him that if he had done any such thing he would have been court martialed at once. He would have been higher in command now if he had not fought two or three times in Mexico without orders.

Since writing the above the aspect of affairs has changed. We have recd news of two battles fought & victories won for the union.* We also have orders to march in light order to morrow at 3 P.M. Since those orders came the stillness of camp has been broken by the bustle & hurry of preparation. The rapid galloping of horses & the rumble of heavy baggage wagons as they were dragged with

---

* Further successes in McClellan's western Virginia campaign.

loads of provisions & supplies slowly up the hill or returned empty at full gallop. This looks like war. I hardly know what we should do for wagons if it were not for the Mass. 1st. They supply the brigade. Old Mass. is never behind when fighting is to be done. I knew before our orders came that something was going on when I saw the pickets hurrying in from all directions in little squads of from 3 to 8 each with a corporal.

Three

BATTLE ALONG
BULL RUN

Charles Haydon's introduction to combat came on July 18, 1861. Pressed by the administration to take the offensive against the secessionists, and aware that the term of his numerous three-month regiments would soon be up, Brigadier General Irvin McDowell put his field army on the march for Manassas Junction on July 16. In Daniel Tyler's First Division in the van was the Fourth Brigade, commanded by the 2nd Michigan's Israel Richardson. Haydon notes that the undisciplined troops plundered everywhere they went. On the eighteenth Richardson's brigade came under fire in a sharp skirmish at Blackburn's Ford on Bull Run. "The musket balls began to whistle around us," Haydon wrote.

Three days later, on Sunday, July 21, the armies clashed in the Battle of Bull Run. The 2nd Michigan was now in reserve, and Haydon witnessed the fighting from afar. Following McDowell's defeat, however, he was in the rear guard as the army fell back on Washington. "I confess," he wrote, "that I believed my chances of living through the day less than even." Subsequently, like many another Northerner, Haydon used the pages of his journal to ponder the causes of the Union defeat.

* * *

§ JULY 16, 1861 Contrary to expectations the night was fine. I got about 4 hours sleep but awoke feeling anything but well, in fact I was near sick all the night. I drank a glass of liquor & a

strong cup of coffee, ate some breakfast & felt much better. I went
& bathed & now feel quite well. One needs to be well when he has
the prospect of 3 or 4 days & nights marching before him on short
provisions. The tents are now all struck except such as are needed
for the baggage guard & those who are not able to move.

It is quite likely that this is the last we shall see of this camp. I
do not like the prospect of Manassas Gap with no water within six
miles but feel ready to advance to the Devil if need be rather than
stay here on expectation any longer.

At ½ past 2 P.M. our camp presents the most dirty & confused
appearance that it is possible to conceive. Old barrels, boards,
boxes, cast off clothes, hats, caps, shoes &c are scattered in every
direction. The blankets, haversacks, canteens &c are lying on the
ground promiscuously. The tents are all struck except a little circle
composed of one tent from each Co. for the guards' baggage. Our
things are packed in our knapsacks with the expectation that they
will some day follow us, which I think more desirable than certain.

I am sitting on the remnants of our home made camp bed &
looking around on the scenes amid which we have spent the last
5 weeks & which we have little expectation of seeing again. I am
already loaded with 3 days rations of biscuit & salt beef, plus a loaf
of fresh bread which I obtained.

Promptly at 3 we marched off by way of the Chain bridge & by
11 P.M. after many halts & delays occasioned by the time taken to
explore the country & prevent surprise we arrived at Vienna, a
distance of 11 miles. We should have been the 1st Regt. here but
owing to a delay of 20 min. 11 other Regts. & several batteries
passed in & encamped before us. 2 men were accidentally shot just
before we left camp, neither I believe were killed.

§ JULY 17 We encamped last night in a large meadow by the
road side & had I been on a bed of down I should not have slept
sounder than I did rolled in my blanket. I ate my supper on the
march as did most of the others, so that we threw ourselves on the
ground as soon as we stopped. The greatest trouble was to get
water. I was obliged to go to bed dry. The enemy are near us &
we all slept on our arms.

At the time of writing this I am lying on the ground in the high
grass talking with Lt. Handy & writing by turns. We can hear the
firing of cannon in advance which is supposed to be [William T.]
Sherman's battery engaged with the enemy who are reported

strongly entrenched a few miles ahead. It is now 8 A.M. The advance moved at 5 this m'g. Breakfast was rather slim, biscuit only. I had some salt beef but do not care to eat it because water is too scarce. We go half a mile for all we have & most of it is very poor at that. My feet ached badly last night but I am in good marching order this m'g.

This is the place where the Ohio men under Col. Shenke ran into the masked battery with the loss of several men.* We saw the spot & where the trees were cut up by the balls.

The boys have torn a secession grocery all to pieces & carried off everything there was in it even to the grind stones. They took tin ware & carried off a hogshead of molasses. Several of the men have clothed themselves with a new suit. Molasses & bread are all the go. The union men are following along after us returning to their homes which they have been compelled to abandon. There was in the first part of the march strong union feeling among the inhabitants & many friendly cheers & greetings, but they all ceased as we advanced. A disunion regt. passed over this road yesterday scouting & pressing men.

The enemy were entrenched at Fairfax 6 miles in advance of us & we expected a battle. The line was deployed & formed in line of battle something over a mile from the place & we advanced upon it but found nothing but the works & 6 cannon which they abandoned in their haste. The road all along was filled with fallen trees arranged in windrows to impede our progress & at which they waited for us last night. If we had been foolish enough to run into it they would have given us a sharp brush.

The road was strewn with provisions & clothes thrown away by the Secesh & our advance. I saw more than 2 wagon loads of blankets & jackets in one heap. The day was pretty warm & the road beginning to be dusty. Our line of battle was formed in a field of wheat in the shock & in a fine meadow of prime hay. The wheat was little injured, a few shocks being trampled down but the grass was wholly destroyed. All the fences for a mile square were torn down.

When we arrived at Germantown our brigade having passed Fairfax by a short cut without stopping, we found several houses

---

* An expedition on June 17 led by Robert C. Schenck, in which the 1st Ohio was ambushed by the 1st South Carolina.

in flames & the men of our brigade burned nearly all the rest before they left. It was but a small village & like most of the farm houses was recently deserted by the inhabitants. Some other buildings were burned during the day. A very neat breastwork intended to rake the road to Germantown was abandoned about two hours before we arrived. The enemies campfires were still burning brightly. The men here stole everything movable.

Near sundown we turned off into a large field & camped for the night. All the cattle & hogs & sheep that could be found were at once killed, in fact everything eatable was seized. The men would take bee hives off the stands & devour the honey & half the bees at the same time. Abt 20,000 encamped together. Several of our men were shot at here but none killed. We were roused up in the night by an alarm & heard for the first time the long roll.

§ JULY 18 We were up at 4 A.M., ate such provisions as we had & moved off at 5½, our brigade in the advance.* We moved on quietly till within 4 miles of Manassas Junction when we halted & allowed 2 batteries to pass, not long after which we heard cannonading in advance. Then moved on to ½ a mile of the cannon. Trees were thick & we could see nothing but could distinctly hear the whistling of the shot & shells.

After ½ an hour moved up near our batteries (light artillery) & filed off into a hollow behind them & remained for some time. We could see our batteries but not theirs. After some time we deployed out into the open field. There was immediately a very brisk fire of musketry on the left of our line & in front between our skirmishers & the enemy. Soon after our skirmishers came over the hill at a full run. Their batteries were 3 in number situated among sharp hills & rocks & were wholly concealed & about a mile off, as near as I could judge.

So soon as they appeared on top of the hill the musket balls began to whistle around us. We lay flat down on the ground & let them pass over us. After a short time we deployed to the right & afterward countermarched to the right. While passing along we saw one Co. A man shot through the arm & body lying on the ground stripped & under Surgeon's care.

---

* In Richardson's Fourth Brigade were the 2nd and 3rd Michigan, 1st Massachusetts, 12th New York, 1st United States Battery G, and 2nd United States Battery M.

As we came around onto the hill the batteries opened on us & we backed down abt 8 rods over the hill & lay down. They shot well & the balls coming on a curve just missed the top of the hill & would have hit us if we had been standing. Abt 20 or 30 six pounders struck in the opposite bank just behind us. Here Orderly Crego & several others were taken suddenly ill or were sun struck & fell out of the ranks.

There was sharp fighting on our left where the N.Y. 12th & Mass. 1st engaged the enemy in a piece of woods. They fought well but were driven out. The enemy were so situated that they could not reach them effectually. The rebels followed to the edge of the woods but came no further.

Finding that nothing could be done with our force (4 Regts., 3 batteries & 300 cavalry) we moved back a short distance & the batteries moved up again. The Mich. 2d was moved up to second them in case they were attacked. Co's. I & K were posted abt 2 rods behind the guns & in fair range of the enemy who now opened a brisk fire from their batteries. It was a very unwise move to place us just there but we stood the ground for about 10 minutes when we were ordered to fall back abt 4 rods further, which we did & laid down on ground a little lower than the batteries. The balls mostly passed abt 4 feet over our heads. One struck a man in Co. H abt 20 ft. from me shattering his arm & turning him over endwise. After some time we moved back still further. Here Miller fell down & was brought to with difficulty & carried into camp by 2 men at night.

The batteries had now used up most of their ammunition & we retired from the field in good order & fell back abt 2 miles on Centreville & encamped for the night. I was very hungry & dry & pretty tired. I got water, had some broken crackers, plundered some beets which I ate raw & helped to carry off a warm bee hive out of which I made a supper. There was a shower of rain in the night & those who had thrown away their blankets & jackets fared hard. I threw mine down with intent to abandon them several times but always took them up when we moved off & finally brought mine & Miller's into camp.

The men generally behaved well. I am not so certain abt the officers. The Sergents beginning with the 2d were the only ones who did anything on the retreat. I did not like the actions of some of the officers. The men appeared careless & would slip out of the ranks to pick blackberries when the cannon balls were plowing up the ground around them.

We expected an attack at night, slept on our arms & were very very wakeful. There were 3 alarms but no attack. I got thoroughly wet but slept well.

The day was hot & we suffered a good deal for want of water & some 40 or 50 men in the Regt. must have fallen from the effect of fatigue & heat. I stood it beyond my expectation. I was firmly determined not to give up as long as I could keep on my feet. I have no doubt that this determination would have kept me on my feet as long as there was a breath of life in me. I was not scared I believe but I did feel uneasy & mortified when I saw our troops driven back. The Mich. 2d except the skirmishers did not fire a gun. I cocked my gun when the enemy showed themselves on the edge of the woods but I did not dare to fire without orders, although the temptation was great.

General Richardson offered to clean out the battery with the bayonet but they would not let him loose. A cannon ball cut his horse's crouper strap off. His pretty young wife embraced him in a most distracting manner when he returned. He declared himself satisfied with our doings during the day. The men retired sullen & many of them sad from the field. I know I felt mad & anxious to try it again & afraid that some one else would get the start of us.

§ J U L Y 19 We were up at 4 A.M., breakfasted on crackers, honey & coffee & before 6 were on the road back to the battle field of yesterday. We moved back to ½ mile from the battle ground, 2 batteries took the position of yesterday & are supported by the advance of this brigade. Here we are waiting for the movement of other troops which are to attack the enemy flanks.

The dead & wounded have been gathered in & cared for. Our loss is supposed to be abt 60 killed & wounded & missing. From our Regt. one was killed & 2 wounded, none of Co. I were hurt.* Some of the dead were terribly cut to pieces by the cannon balls. The rebels bayoneted the wounded men without mercy.

Orders have been given which will effectually put an end to the

---

* Federal casualties at Blackburn's Ford would be officially reported as 83: 19 dead, 38 wounded, 26 missing; for the 2nd Michigan the count was one man wounded.

plundering & burning. This should have been done before, for the men have literally swept the country of everything eatable.

§ JULY 20 Co. I was marched out last night abt 100 rods to rear of camp to act as a picket guard. Abt ½ were out & the rest were a rallying point & protection for them. We slept well under the trees in ranks with arms in hand & all our things on. There was an alarm somewhere as often as once an hour. The men behaved remarkably well. They would spring from a sound sleep to their places in line all ready for battle in two minutes at the outside. There was a good deal of firing during the night but so far as I know no one was hurt. The enemy were very lively & our pickets could frequently hear their challenges. They evidently feared an attack from the amt of firing they did.

We had nothing to eat yesterday but hard bread. This m'g we got some bacon. The Commissary has been put under arrest for not supplying us sooner. We have not had more than one days rations since we left Camp Scott. It rained considerably last night but it did not disturb my sleep.

We know but little of the real state of affairs but everything indicates a great battle near at hand. The Mich. 2d has the right of the line to day & will see the first of the battle. I pray that I may have the strength & courage to carry me safely through or to die decently & in a manner becoming an American soldier. If I go goodby to all. The contest will probably come before night. Troops are pouring in on both sides. 40 Regts. came up on our side yesterday bringing 70 pieces of cannon. We are still waiting for the completion of other movements. There is a continuous row of musket stacks 4 miles long by the roadside back of us.

I have been down on the battle field or as near it as I could. I saw a secession flag & battery, troops & wagons moving & their picket guard distant out more than ½ a mile. I also saw the enemy out on the field picking up the coats & blankets which our men threw down. They would stick their bayonets through them & shake them at us with great satisfaction to themselves. We will arrange these little matters very soon & therefore care less about it than we otherwise should. I am very glad they can get nothing with my name on it. Benson left a jacket with $5.00 in the pocket.

I find we are strongly commended for our good behaviour on the occasion. Major Williams declares that he had no words to express our unconcern. I saw some actions which did not indicate remarkable coolness. Some of the men were well scared on picket duty last night & some of the others have had not a few hearty laughs over their sayings & doings.

There will be no fighting before to morrow. A drove of fat oxen came in for us to day. I begin to feel impatient at waiting here so long. I feel well although we have lived poor & drank very poor water since we left camp. I have seen men quarreling & fighting over puddles of water which were not fit to wash one's hands in. We can get no water for washing. There are plenty of good springs but the quantity of water is not sufficient to supply the army.

§ JULY 21 Near noon. We are lying by the roadside just back of one of our batteries which is firing slowly on the enemy. The Mich. 2d is in reserve to day. The firing commenced on the right abt sunrise this m'g & has been continued from right, left & center at a moderate rate ever since. There is as yet no return fire from the enemy.

We spent some time at breakfast & after falling in formed square & awaited an attack from cavalry which was expected on the left, then moved up to the present position. Genl. Scott is said to be in command to day in person. The firing is increasing gradually & the heavy guns are beginning to open. I have seen some laughable scenes but as I do not know into whose hands this book may fall I will not describe them. The night was very quiet but the day is rather noisy for Sunday.

Since writing the above the firing is becoming very brisk on the right, both of cannon & musketry. At abt 1.30 the cannonading on the right is not quite as heavy but the volleys of musketry are rapid & very heavy. The firing on the left has ceased. There are occasional shots of cannon & volleys of musketry just in front of us. We can see nothing & hear no news of the battle. The greatest anxiety prevails. The battle must be very desperate.

At 10 minutes later cannon shots are more rapid than at any time during the day. They follow each other almost as fast as one could count. Between 3 & 4 the firing was very rapid. I went out on the hills in front, could see very plainly the dust & smoke of the battle rising in great clouds. Reinforcements were pouring in to aid the enemy. The road was filled for more than three miles with men moving at double quick. Our batteries fired upon them but at a distance of 3 miles produced little effect. I did not like the appearance of affairs by any means.

Between 4 & 5 news came that the rebels were fleeing in every direction. This news was joyful, still no one dared cheer. At the time this report started it was true. On the strength of it I began to prepare for supper & dinner, having had nothing to eat for 3 meals except hard bread & muddy water. Before I got supper however the bugle sounded & we fell in quickly & were moving lazily across the road in line of battle under the good natured & easy orders of Major Williams.

There was now a heavy fire on our left. Just then Genl. Richardson came up behind us & shouted Battalion, in a manner different from everyone else, left face, double quick, march. This took us back on the road toward Centreville & we expected to file to the right to support the left wing. We had 2 miles of double quick in the densest dust I ever saw. I thought several times I should choke down & fall. We then filed to the right & commenced forming a line of battle with the brigade across some large open fields.

News then came that our men had beaten them on the left & Genl. Richardson told us to cheer as loud as we pleased. We gave 9 good ones and commenced moving back into the road when the former news was contradicted & we commenced the double quick for our former position in the fields.

After a great deal of double quick a line of battle was formed, our men lying behind a long stone wall waiting for what we have since learned was the approach of a victorious army. We could have inflicted great loss on them here but were after a few minutes ordered to fall back on another position by Genl. [Col. Dixon S.] Miles, a man who had been pretending to command this part of the division during the day in place of [Daniel] Tyler. He was now arrested for being drunk & suspected of treachery.

The whole command was now upon Genl. Richardson, who brought things into order in a hurry. We formed the line as occasion required, effectually covering the retreat. The enemy were several times near us but declined to give battle. Just at dark we moved up a short distance toward the enemy, stopped, stacked arms & laid down in a cornfield to rest. I found myself without blanket, coat or haversack & my shirt very wet with sweat & the night beginning to be cold & myself on picket guard. I posted the guards, cut an armful of fine bushes & laid them on the ground & another armful of coarser ones which I laid over me & slept from 9 to 12 as warm & comfortable as I ever did in bed at home.

It was not till we had been some time here that we fully understood that we were beaten & almost surrounded.

§ JULY 22 A little after 12 all the other troops having made good their retreat, we being the only Regt. not in motion & being abt a mile in rear of all the others, commenced retreating in the most perfect stillness and order. This is the first time that I ever believed our danger to be very great.

I confess that I believed my chances of living through the day less than even & accordingly made all the preparation I could for a good defence & made sure of the means of speedily finishing myself in case I should be disabled so that I could not fight. The rebels kill all the wounded & often in the most cruel manner, even shooting at & disfiguring the bodies of the dead.* This too at a time when their own receive from us the same care & attention as ours.

It was a terrible sight to see the wagons coming in last night loaded down with dead, cut, torn & mangled in every possible manner & the wounded running or hobbling along with arms & legs dangling or hanging by shreds or crawling on the ground & dragging their limbs slowly after them, crushed, broken or torn off entirely.

After marching abt 3 miles finding that we were not pursued the 2nd passed on and the Mich. 3d took the rear. For 3 or 4 miles the road was strewn with stores, supplies, ammunition, wagons, provisions, all of which fell into the hands of the enemy. For some unknown reason we were not pursued with any considerable force & there was no necessity of so rapid a retreat except an order which was given for us to repair to Washington at once. During the first part of the march the army moved in good order but toward the latter part of the march the Regts. mingled together promiscuously & some of the men threw away their arms.

At a separation of the road I became separated from the main body of the Regt. & marched to Ft. Corcoran into which I very foolishly went. Here they retained all the men who came in till they were all collected & called for by their respective commanders. As I had been marching all day in the rain with no protection but shirt & pants I did not like the prospect of lying out on the ground

---

* Such atrocity stories, quite unfounded, were widely circulated at the time.

all night in that condition & after trying in all lawful ways to get out I fell in with the Mich. 1st which wore the same uniform & marched out. The officer of the guard searched the ranks through & took out several men but did not detect me. Capt. Bretschneider was there with his skirmishers in arrest, also some 40 of our men.

I went to Washington, got something to eat & marched back 5 miles to our old camp where I arrived at 3 P.M. expecting to find the Regt. I was mistaken however as I was almost the first one in except some sick men who came in wagons. The women got me a fine supper, a good cup of tea & last I got some dry clothes. After a march of 25 miles was glad to rest.

§ JULY 23 I turned out at 7 A.M. feeling well all things considered. I bathed, cleaned up my clothes & gun. After which I made an excellent breakfast of which I ate too much & laid around the camp till abt noon & then came down to the city. Here I ate & drank beer several times. Bought a paper, read the news. Was glad to find our loss less serious than was at first supposed.

About sundown Orderly Crego & I set out to hunt up the camp of the Mich. 2d at Arlington Heights, which after a good deal of trouble & 3 or 4 miles travel we found. Our men were most of them lying on the ground many of them without either blankets or coats. I bought a coat in the city. I felt pretty well during the day except a general feeling of exhaustion & protracted weariness.

Six days of marching & sleeping on their arms & living on bread & water has used us up pretty much & we need a few days to recruit before we move again. Now that our Commissary is under arrest for neglect of duty I hope we shall get something to eat. I was so tired & uneasy that during the night I several times sprang up in bed & seized my gun which lay near me & began to prepare for action before I could make up my mind where I was.

§ JULY 24 I feel very stiff, sore & lame, generally used up. I still keep on eating & drinking & am getting pretty well filled up & have been sleeping a large part of the day. I have been thinking over the battles & the consequences & the instruction to be derived &c.

It is now well known that if Genl. Richardson had charged on the battery [at Blackburn's Ford] as he desired with his brigade none of us would have come out of the infernal gap alive unless we had been carried out as prisoners. The brigade numbered abt 3,500. If we had have charged it would have been down a valley abt a mile long, partly a cleared field & partly trees & bushes, having high hills on both sides the tops of which were perhaps a mile apart. The charge would have been for a battery of 6 guns directly in the center of the valley. With a fair chance we could have taken this & held it.

We now know that there was a battery on each side of the valley concealed by projecting hills both of which we must have passed & that there were 2 other batteries further on which would have fairly raked us both before & after we reached the one we were to storm. The hills on both sides were covered with woods & which were filled with from 5000 to 10,000 infantry. We should undoubtedly have been allowed to advance nearly to the battery without much molestation but should then have been fired upon from all directions & surrounded by more than 3 times our numbers.

Our defeat on that day was owing to Genl. Tyler's disobedience of orders & ignorance of the enemies position. The defeat of Sunday [July 21] was a matter almost of course. The enemy were more than double our numbers & in one of the most difficult positions to attack which can be conceived. The enemy can never be induced to fighting fair open battle. We could whip them to death if they would. They will keep around in masked batteries & skulk behind trees & shoot officers & bayonet wounded men. We must expect severe loss.

The next attack needs to be made with more care, with better preparation for a retreat if it be necessary. We should not have retreated on Sunday farther than Centreville. We need more good skirmishers & sharp shooters & all the men need better guns. The want of a more perfect military establishment is now seen. There are thousands of good & brave soldiers in the army, but there is a great want of competent commanders. The soldiers are far better than the officers. There is a hard job on hand & we have got to act with circumspection or we shall suffer still greater losses.

I have made up my mind that my chances of coming out of the war alive are less than even. The want of food I do not deem as serious as drinking mud. That more than anything else I fear will tell on the constitution. Very few men in the Co. have or can bear as much fatigue as I.

Be the result what it may I will not turn back on a good cause. I never have the prospect of a battle [but] I prepare myself as if I were sure of not returning. I enlisted during the war unless sooner discharged & I mean to stand to my bargain let the discharge come in what form it may.

Many of the commissioned officers will resign including I think our Capt. Our men have been lying in the open field all day without tents or shade. They had cold boiled pork & hard biscuit for breakfast, & for dinner & supper together boiled rice & hard bread & this is all. I had neither plate, spoon or anything else so I took my rice on a piece of board & ate it with a chip. Pork & bacon I cannot & will not eat in any amt. I have still some money & have had all I wanted to eat to day.

On the march there is no chance of buying anything. Everything is consumed & destroyed or removed, the country is abandoned & desolate. With the best of regulation the march of an invading or retreating army is accompanied with great loss & damage to the country. Virginia will be desolate before the close of the war.

I want to travel the road to Manassas once more & only once. I wish to pass through Manassas Gap or stop there. I never intend to give up till have been whipped more than twice on the same ground. It can & will be taken & I hope I shall be there. I feel sullen & mad about the retreat & the more so because it was unnecessary. We might have held Centreville.

All or nearly all that I have written concerning affairs which was stated on report or rumor has proved false. Hereafter I shall write little except what I know to be true. I have seen war in its most unpleasant forms & now have only to hope & wait for something better.

§ JULY 25 I was detailed with 28 men to assist in cutting trees over back of the river. They were slashed down helter skelter to prevent or delay the progress of troops. They are an effective defence for a short time & are of service for delay besides affording an excellent place for skirmishers. It was not my turn to go but Whiting was used up (ie lazy) & Stevenson is lame.

The battle of Sunday was a curious one. Our men are continuously swearing because they did not hold the field & the enemy are swearing because they did not take us prisoners. I believe there were never two armies so deceived in each other. The Mass. 1st I understand has left the brigade. Our Col. [Richardson] is too savage for them. I am sorry to see them leave, we shall not get a better in their place. I like their Lt. Col. very much. He was Police Justice in Boston before he became a soldier & is a man of rare abilities

& will distinguish himself in the service. I am not personally acquainted with him but was struck with his appearance when I first saw him.

§ JULY 26 A very warm day — pay day — men eating & drinking at a terrible rate. A good many of them drunk. I think I shall get to the city to morrow.

I cannot cease to regret & speculate on the affairs of Sunday. Our army is large & full of good material but it is loosely put together. Not one man in 50 ever saw a battle before this war. Not one in 10 knew the simplest elements of military drill. They are liable to be confused. Where rough & tumble fighting & personal bravery are needed they are great but for steady movements in line & on retreat they are not reliable.

I did not run in either of the battles except when I was ordered to & had no thought of it. Still when I go into another battle I shall do many things differently & some I shall not do at all. I begin to feel more like a soldier & there will not be so many new things to look after. The army will get beaten into discipline after a while if they are not drilled into it in any other way. If there were experienced officers the men would improve much faster.

Four

DUTY WITH
THE ARMY OF
THE POTOMAC

Although Haydon does not record the fact in his journal, July 27, 1861, was the first day of General McClellan's command of what he christened the Army of the Potomac. Two weeks later Haydon would write of the general, "There is a great improvement since he took command. The men begin to feel more confidence." Still, indiscipline remained a problem in this army of volunteers, and the period was marked, as Haydon describes, by incipient mutinies. He is equally candid in portraying those other army vices, drinking and whoring. The size of the sick list, he notes, was due in good measure "to contributions by the ladies down town."

Change came to the 2nd Michigan in the person of a new colonel, Orlando M. Poe, in place of the promoted Israel Richardson. Haydon judged Colonel Poe, accurately enough, as "one of the best in the service." For Haydon personally, two additional events marked the period. He was notified of his promotion to 2nd lieutenant, and then, during one of the picket line exchanges of these weeks, he was persuaded that he killed his first enemy soldier. "I am a little surprised myself," he wrote, "to see how cool I took it."

*   *   *

§ JULY 27, 1861 I went to Washington to day. Ate beefsteak &c, drank lager beer &c. I went to see Congress in session. Heard a good speech in the Senate by [Andrew] Johnson of Tenn. on Secession in reply to [John C.] Breckinridge. I listened to him for 2 hours & then went over to the house of Representatives & heard a part of an Ohio man's speech.

The men are drinking & gambling too much to day. Col. Richardson sent the sutler of the De Kalb Guards off the ground for selling beer in front of our camp. Three Dutchmen charged on him with their bayonets but he upset two & the other took to his legs. Col. R. had about a dozen of them arrested & closed up the establishment so far as beer is concerned.

§ JULY 28 Sunday. 30 men were detailed for chopping this m'g but they did very little & returned by noon. There was a sharp shower of rain abt six. The day has been quiet. There was a skirmish between our pickets & the enemy abt 4 miles out last night.

§ JULY 29 A pretty quiet day, boys spending their money faster than there is any need of. Our location here [Arlington Heights] is a fine one in many respects. We are nearly opposite Washington of which a good view can be obtained from the hills near by. Just in rear of us is Genl. Lee's estate.* His house and the surroundings make the most beautiful spot I ever saw. He is in the secession army & Genl. Mansfield occupies his house. If I had have had his estate I would have stayed at home. The house is not magnificent according to modern style, but is massive, strong & ancient. There is very little of the artificial abt the grounds. The beauty consists in the trees, the undulating surface & 3 or 4 of the finest natural springs I ever saw.

The weight of our defeat seems to be settling down pretty certainly on Genl. [Irvin] McDowell.†

In many of our men who are fine fellows now I can see the exact pictures of worthless drunkards five years hence. They are so surely on the road that nothing will stop them.

§ JULY 30 A warm day. All quiet in camp during the day, but some what noisy at night. It seems almost impossible for a man to go to town without getting drunk. Many of the best men disgrace themselves in this way. Capt. Lawson of Co. G has been drunk for a week & behaved worse than any of the soldiers. He will lose his commission.

---

* Robert E. Lee's Arlington.
† McDowell retained a divisional, then a corps, command.

If it were not for the sacrifice that it requires nothing would suit me better than this soldiering. I bought some butter this morning and have lived well on bread & butter. I can sit down with a small oyster can which I have full of beer & make a passable meal out of very little. As for liquor I keep clear of it as much as possible. There is a good deal of gambling among the men since they were paid. There is one fine thing about it, that is that the money will soon be gone. Liquor dealers & prostitutes will soon clean their pockets.

§ JULY 31 There was an inspection of the Regt. at 12 noon. Some close & very necessary inquiries were made about the Commissary Dept., the sale of provisions &c.

4 P.M. we got orders to move, packed our knapsacks & marched down the river ½ a mile & abt as much farther up into the country. We have gained by the change in most respects. We are now encamped in a clover field just beside the Arlington road. They are throwing up a breastwork to cover the road & have cut down a fine orchard & all a man's shade trees to give the guns fair range. We have a very fair view of the city from here. The Capitol, all the public buildings, the Smithsonian Institute & Washington Monument are in full view.

§ AUGUST 1, 1861 The excessive heat of yesterday was followed by heavy rain at night, which continued with little intermission till noon. I laid for some time last night thinking that our tent must leak dreadfully. Finally I waked up so as to know what I was about & found that the side of the tent had blown loose & that I was lying half my length outdoors in a heavy shower. The tent did in fact leak considerably but that troubled my slumbers very little.

Our rations are poorer than usual of late. Bread, pork & coffee, with beans at long intervals are the bulk of our living. Peddlers come around with ginger bread & pies but they are miserable worthless things, not fit to be eaten. It is hard to conceive of anything thinner, tougher or more tasteless than a Virginia pie. I want some good beef & potatoes but it is almost impossible to get them.

There is some fear of an attack at this place. I should be very sorry to have it come just now. It seems to me that we are in a very poor condition. There are men, guns & forts enough but very little order or arrangements for a vigorous systematic defence. I am afraid it would be too much like Bulls Run (or Calves Retreat as we now call it), a conglomeration of blunders from beginning to

end. The best officers of the regulars say that it is the greatest
wonder in the world that we were not all taken prisoners.*

The men continue their drunkenness & gambling almost without reproof. If we had a Capt. worth a row of pins he would change
some things & not allow men to stay in town 3 days on a pass for
6 hours. One fellow came back last night saying that he had stormed
a masked battery of one gun, spiked the gun & retired with but
little loss to either party.

§ AUGUST 3 The weather is still very hot. We have sharp battalion drill every night. A large sick list owing in some cases to
sleeping on the ground without blankets & in others to contributions by the ladies down town.

We made a very good breakfast this m'g on potatoes, bread &
a slice of fried pork in place of butter. I can eat pork sometimes
but bacon is too detestable for any Christian to put into his stomach.
Congress has passed a law prohibiting the sale of liquor to soldiers.
A better thing could not have been done.

We have a new Lt. Col., Sylvester Larnerd, a Detroit lawyer. He
takes hold of business as though he meant to do something. I am
glad he has come. We have been greatly in need of more field
officers. Col. Richardson cannot devote a great deal of time to us
& there has been no one but Major Williams, kind, good natured
& accommodating, to look after things.

I obtained the Atlantic yesterday & have been busy on it ever
since. The article "Concerning Veal" is a most interesting one.† In
a thousand places I can see its truth in my own feeling &
experience.

Several of our men will have to be discharged because of sickness
& incompetency. Some of them were the largest & strongest looking men in the Co. when we started.

There was a series of promotions to fill vacancies in Co. C last
night. This to [2nd Sergeant] Benson & I was partly a pleasing
& partly an aggravating sight. If [1st Sergeant] Crego had done
anyway decently Benson & I would both have gone up a step.
He might have been Sergeant Major as well as not but for some
unaccountable reason refused. He wont do even so much as to

---

* There follows a rough sketch (omitted) of the Manassas march, based on
misinformation.
† This oddly titled essay dealt with intellectual maturity.

stand out of the way. He has done next to nothing since we left Detroit, sick all the time. He could have exchanged his place for a much easier one higher in the line of promotion and of the same pay. Benson & I could lift him out of his present place in 3 days if we were a mind. We shall be very strongly tempted to do it if he does not stand out of the way when he has a good chance.

§ AUGUST 4 Sunday. Has been a hot quiet day. There was a regimental inspection of arms, accouterments, tents &c this forenoon & dress parade P.M. I have been acting as Orderly for 2 days. Crego is sick as usual & Benson is suffering from injuries recd in storming a masked battery.

I got to thinking abt home this m'g. I recd a good letter from Father & one from Arthur yesterday which may have brought such scenes more forcibly to my mind. The long rows of maples, the pretty round topped cedars & pines. The large drooping elms. The sturdy oaks. The old orchard behind the house. The green yards around it. The probable occupations of its inmates & all the familiar scenes around it which a thousand times I have seen with the sincerest joy from afar off when returning home, passed before me with all the vividness of reality. I paused for a moment & wondered whether I might ever see those cherished scenes & friends again.

There was a tinge of sadness about these reflections, still they were very pleasant. I was not sorry to be here. I never have been & never shall be now that the necessity of the times calls for it. May the curse of God light on the men who brought me here. I came here willing to give my life to the cause & with the expectation that it would in all probability be needed before the 3 years were up. As often as I escape a danger I consider it as so much net gain of duration of life & as an unexpected gain where death or wounds would be the natural course of events.

§ AUGUST 5 & 6 were so much like other days as to need no separate description.

§ AUGUST 7 There was an alarm in some of the camps last night but not in ours. I could hear the long roll & the cry "to arms, to arms" in some of the other Regts. The cry "to arms" sounds far differently when it bursts upon the ear of the startled sleeper at midnight than when it is repeated by schoolboys on exhibition days. There was some pretty heavy volleys of musketry abt 3 or 4 miles out. Our Lt. Col. took 30 men & went & stationed them as pickets in addition to the regular out posts.

This is a rich country in wild fruits & nuts. I never saw trees loaded as they are here with butternuts, black walnuts, beechnuts, chestnuts, persimmons, hazelnuts, to say nothing of blackberries, grapes &c.

I am acting as Orderly & thereby escaped guard duty to day. It is all very well except getting up before all the rest & routing them out in the morning. Benson & I begin at last to have some prospect of promotion.

Col. Richardson has had guards stationed around a large peach orchard just above here at the owner's request to protect them from soldiers. He was walking past there to day with his lady & went in & picked abt a dozen for which the owner who saw him charged 50 cts. The money was immediately paid but Col. R. turned to the guards & ordered them to their quarters. Peaches have since that been plenty in camp at a good deal less than 50 cts. per doz. or the peddlers price (20 cts. per doz.).

§ AUGUST 8 Weather is very hot. We are living well, working moderately & getting fat. The rations are good & I live somewhat beyond our regular fare.

Johnston whose wedding I attended at Detroit was made 8th Corpl. yesterday. He stands the third chance for the 5th Sergt. place I think. The time when he can take that step is not far off if they will only give us a little hard work. The Capt. is tottering on his legs, the 2nd Lt. detached from the Co., the Orderly has done nothing for six weeks & two Corpls. are little better than dead men. This looks very much as though Benson & I would become Lieuts. someday & Johnston would get a Sergts.' post. There is many a slip twixt cup & lip I have already found. With Miller's aid I think I could pass over Benson in the line of promotion. I do not wish to do this & will not if I can do it in any other way.

§ AUGUST 9 Six P.M., heavy thunder storm coming, white squall. Recd good long letters from Father & Arthur to day. I have sometimes had a presentiment that I should not see the end of this war. There was something not right. All that is changed. I now feel only that joy & eagerness for the conflict which for me has always foretold success. I am glad of this for I would rather, for many reasons, not go at present.

If we can ever see the day when our officers are equal to the soldiers we will have the best army the world ever saw. If the officers were better they could double efficiency of the men. A great many things have gone wrong with us. We were nearly all ignorant & showed our ignorance before the men every day. Such a thing should never happen. I could take a company of new men & have a different state of discipline. Some of the N.Y. Regts. are the poorest drilled men I have seen. I have very little confidence in some of them.

The whole army is as yet a great, green overgrown loose concern. The men who are to organize & consolidate it are not yet sifted out of the mass. I think one or two of them are pretty plainly visible — McClellan, [John Charles] Fremont, [Nathaniel] Lyon in the order they are written. Col. Richardson will do good service but he is too old to become a very prominent leader. He would do better if he had never seen his young wife.

§ AUGUST 10 Major Underwood & self went to town to day. I drilled 2 hours & after traveling around till 7 at night was well tired out. After the preliminaries of obtaining a pass & showing it 5 times to sentries we reached the city abt 9 A.M. & went at once to the Smithsonian Institute where we remained till noon. Of the beauty of the building & grounds & of the many curious & interesting things we saw it would be impossible here to speak.

Thence we went to a hotel & obtained a good private dinner to which we did ample justice. We then went & gave Mr. Walbridge a call who declared himself overjoyed to see us & I believe he was really glad. He immediately insisted on some iced brandy & sugar to which the day being hot we consented (the Major never refuses). The bar keeper said he dare not sell to soldiers so Walbridge told us to go back into a pleasure garden in rear & he at once ordered the waiter to bring him three glasses of brandy & sugar at the same place which was done without hesitation.

After this was disposed of he requested us to accompany him to the National Conservatory, a garden where all the different kinds of tropical plants & trees are raised, such as Oranges, Lemons, Bananas, Tea, Coffee, Palms, Cactus &c. I saw Palm & Banana leaves 8 feet long, 2½ broad. Not a coarse rough leaf but a smooth rich green handsome leaf. Most of the fruit bearing trees had fruit on them. There is hardly a tropical country or island which had not its representative. The "loved & lone acacia" was growing there luxuriantly.

After this Walbridge ordered 3 other glasses of iced brandy for himself after which Major & I went to transact the various little items of business which brought us to the city. On returning W. insisted on more iced brandy. I took the ice minus the brandy & we talked over the adventures of Bulls Run for 2 hours & then returned to camp.

§ AUGUST 11 Sunday. On guard. A very quiet time. Only 12 men in a relief. The Lt. Col. told us this m'g that the enemy were within 5 miles. There is skirmishing every day. We shall perhaps have a battle here before many days. McClellan is bringing the troops into pretty good order & discipline. There is a great improvement since he took command. The men begin to feel more confidence.

Abt 5 P.M. the rain came down in torrents & did not cease till sometime in the night when I was asleep. I got well soaked while posting the guards at 9 P.M. I returned & found a place to spread my blanket on a dry board under a shed where I slept well, except some interruptions, for near 5 hours. Habits change wonderfully with circumstances. Six months ago I should have hesitated to go to bed in damp sheets. I can now lie down out doors with clothes wringing wet & sleep all night without the least inconvenience.

§ AUGUST 12 We were in due time relieved after a very quiet guard. This day has been as monotonous as possible. I had a proposition to day to become a correspondent of the Detroit Free Press at the rate of $2 per column. I hardly know whether to accept but think I will. It will take up some time & may impinge on my study of tactics. It will at the same time be a very beneficial exercise & the pay is better than nothing. At any rate it will keep me from idleness which is one of the worst vices of a soldier's life.*

Lt. Handy is promoted Adjutant I suppose. Crego or Benson I presume will take the 2d Lt's. post. Crego will take it if he can. He ought not to have it. We will be almost without officers in that event. If he does not get it he will go home which is the best. It looks considerable as though I should bring up in the end at the

---

* Apparently Haydon rejected this proposition. He makes no further mention of it.

Orderly's post or at least at the duties. It is not a very desirable post but I am willing to take it. There is more work abt it than all the other offices in the Co.

§ AUGUST 13 Heavy rain, tent full of water. The weather became very cold toward night & some of the men who had no blankets suffered considerably. We came near having to charge bayonet on the N.Y. 12th last night to make them obey orders. They are a miserable Regt. I would like to charge on them just to see some good running. Major & I made a good bed yesterday & slept remarkably well.

§ AUGUST 14 I was very much amused to day to see the men clean out a green peddler's stock of cigars, ginger bread, pies &c. As he came up a soldier asked for a cigar. The peddler very foolishly let him get hold of a box to pick from. He had no sooner got it in his hand than some one hit the bottom of it and scattered the cigars in every direction. Very few of them reached the ground. The peddler then very foolishly left the wagon and ran to the Lieut. of the guard who was near by. He made grievous complaint but as he could identify no one no arrests were made. He then returned to his wagon & found it empty. He then jumped into it, plied the whip on his horse & went out of sight at a full gallop.

The N.Y. 12th is in open rebellion. I hope they will send them home. They are the most miserable, worthless set of scapegrace vagabonds that I ever saw collected in one regiment. They are a graceless set of cowards & not fit to be in any army. The morning was very cool. The living is good nowadays.

It seems pretty certain that Corpl. Miles H. Card has deserted. I believed him one of the best soldiers in the Co. & one ambitious of promotion. He was badly scared at Bulls Run & his health rather poor. I suppose he must have concluded that soldiering was not his profession. He is reported on the books as a deserter. All his letters are sent back with "Deserted" written under his name.

§ AUGUST 15 I wished yesterday that I might some day have a chance to charge bayonet on the N.Y. 12th. I came near realizing my wish sooner than I expected. I was this m'g ordered to take 10 of them confined in our guard house out for police duty. I drew them up in line, brought out 5 men to guard them. We all loaded our pieces just before them & informed them that if they offered to run they would be shot. I kept them making privies all day.

Gen. Richardson sent over orders to the [12th New York] Regt. this m'g to turn out for Co. drill. They did not turn out. He then sent orders to them to join us in brigade drill at 6 P.M. They refused. Gen. R. called us out, marched over & formed us just in front of their tents. He then ordered us to load & cap our guns, then to fix bayonets. This being done they were again ordered to fall in & they did it with wonderful alacrity. They marched out into the road & we moved along just behind them. Thus we moved out onto the parade ground. Two brass 12 pounders loaded with grape were placed out just in front of them & they were ordered to go to drilling which they also did & drilled pretty well too. Gen. R. was very kind & mild to their officers. We went through brigade drill, marched off in good order. They were ordered to turn out for Co. drill at 8 A.M. to morrow.

Sixty-nine* of the 2d Maine "having refused to do duty & having falsely alleged that they were no longer in the U.S. service" were sent to the Tortugas Islands, Gulf of Mexico, till they were deemed worthy to be received again into service.

The trouble has been that several Regts. have the idea that they were not legally sworn in & in consequence can go home at the end of 3 months. The Mich. 2d has been talking a good deal about it. They have stopped their talking. Tortugas opened their eyes. I have seldom seen anything produce such an immediate effect as the doings of to night. There would have been gay work if the 12th had refused to come out. I am very glad they did not. I am afraid we should have lost our Genl. in the affray.

§ AUGUST 16 Bright & warm. It has been cold for two days. This Regt. is improving daily. They form in when called upon with much more promptness, their dress & guns are neater. They behave better on guard. The camp is cleaner. The men are more respectful to officers & more civil to each other. Nothing does more to improve the appearance & behavior of soldiers than politeness among officers. Next after cowardice few things are more deleterious than rowdyism & buffoonary among officers.

Thirty of the N.Y. 13th were sent to Tortugas to day.† The [New

---

* The actual number was sixty-three.
† The trouble in the 13th New York (like that in the 12th New York) was handled without resort to the Dry Tortugas.

York] 12th say that we took them by surprise yesterday & that they will not go out again. Our Lt. Col. & Adjt. went over and took dinner with them to day and since that they say they will do anything that the Lt. Col. asks of them. They swear that Richardson can never make them go out again. They know he will probably never order them out except through the Lt. Col. (or Col. as he is supposed to be now). In other Regts. & Brigades they send for Col. [William T.] Sherman of the regulars to quell disturbances. Richardson says he prefers to do it himself.

§ AUGUST 17 We made out to live pretty well & considering the misty, rainy state of the weather that was about enough. We had a short Company drill & Brigade drill at 6 P.M. The N.Y. 12th came out without assistance.

§ AUGUST 18 Sunday. Twenty men & a Corpl. from each Co. are ordered out for chopping to day. I should have gone on guard again to day but induced Corpl. Mason to act as Sergt. in my place. The orders about the observance of Sabbath are very strict but somehow we do more work on that day than any other.

Gen. Richardson is lost to the 2d as Col. We shall probably always remain in his brigade & when we have hard work to do I have no doubt he will be near us. We are left with a pretty feeble lot of officers.

There was a temperance lecture P.M. by Merwin the State temperance lecturer, Michigan. The 14th Mass., a new regiment, came into Ft. Albany to day. They join our brigade. If they only have good officers they will make a fine Regt. some day. The N.Y. 12th would make a fair lot of soldiers in a month with Richardson to command.

§ AUGUST 19 Is a rainy day as every day since I can remember has been. It is hard keeping a camp or tent decent in such weather. The mud creeps in further every day & will soon overrun the whole tent if the weather does not clear up. The living has been pretty poor. No peddlers are allowed to cross the river to day. I have been studying bayonet exercise & skirmishing (or scrummagin as the Capt.'s darkey calls it). There is some talk of an attack here but no one seems to believe it.

Time moves on rapidly in the army as well as at home. My first summer under arms will soon be passed. I have learned a great many things during these four months of soldiering, some useful & some which are not so useful. I think I never learned such a variety of things in the same length of time. I have learned a good deal of the military, much of which ought to have been known by one in my position before I entered service. The State [College] has the start of us in that respect. Nearly every one there who receives the education in other things than I have understands tactics pretty thoroughly. I knew the School of the Soldier passably, a few things abt Co. drill, nothing abt battalion drill or movements in line or the multitudinous duties of camp & field aside from drill. Almost everything was new, blunders were abundant. I believe that I have pretty well mastered Co. & Bat. drill, can get through skirmishing & guard duties passably.

All this is very well for the soldier but how about the lawyer struck from the list of practicioners forever, I am afraid. I thought of all this before I enlisted & am therefore not at all disappointed in this respect. I see little prospect of being released from here before I shall have forgotten too much of my law & have advanced too far in life to recommence with any hope of success. I intend to leave the army with some few dollars in money laid by & with the experience picked up in soldiering I think I can hit upon some business which will carry me through. It takes one somewhat aback to have all his well laid & long matured plans for life changed entirely & so suddenly as mine have been. Not one thing which I relied upon six months ago now seems practicable. Beyond this war all is uncertain. The end of the war is unseen & till that comes there is little use of troubling myself about anything else.

§ AUGUST 20 Last night about sundown some of our men returned from the city saying that everybody was excited by fear of an attack on the city. Families were leaving by hundreds &c &c. They raised quite an excitement in camp. Others brought in the report that 15,000 men were known to have advanced toward us from Fairfax that morning. I believe there were really apprehensions — the guards were doubled, all the men required to examine their guns & equipments, to sleep with their clothes on & arms at their sides &c. Two drummers were stationed at the Adjutant's to beat the significant melody known to soldiers as the *long roll* & which means that the devil is to pay right off. The officers' horses were hitched at their quarters saddled & bridled.

It did look a good deal like business still I could not believe it. The Adjutant swore that he had reason to believe that there were

200,000 men in three hours march of us.* I thought that other things being prepared the best I could do would be to take as much sound sleep as possible before Jeff came. I went to bed but had been there but a few minutes when the rain poured down in such torrents that I was glad to bound out & roll up my bed in the rubber blankets. The old tent leaked like a sieve. After an hour the water drained off so that I went to bed again. The Major & Benson were so wide awake & jumped up so often that it was some time before I got to sleep. They were determined on an attack. The rain came down briskly all night but Jeff has not come yet. I slept well after I got to sleep & feel far better than the men who laid awake all night. I am glad they did not come for it was a very bad night to turn out.

§ AUGUST 21 We had a cold night but the weather has now become hot & oppressive. The night was quiet save some disturbances raised by our own men who were intent on extra rations, that is on making the war sustain itself. The enemy are near in force & an attack is expected hourly though it is presumed that it will be a mere feint to cover some other movement.

The 2d Lieutenantcy gives rise to a good deal of diplomacy in our Co. & to lying & intriguing beyond the bounds of morality & decency. Benson has said a thousand times that the Capt. is a coward but he now swears that there is not a braver man in the army. He tickles the Capt. who works hard for his promotion. Handy is Adjutant & works hard for Crego & both of them quarrel with the Capt. & Benson.

The same anxiety is felt among Corpls. as to the vacant Sergeantcy. Magee & Mason are the chief buglemen. The same trouble & anxiety exists with two or three privates concerning the next Corpl. I believe Benson (now 2d Sergt.) will be Lt., the 3d, 4th & 5th Sergts. will each advance one step, Mason (2d Corpl.) will be 5th Sergt. The other Corpls. will each move up one step to fill the vacancy. C. H. Butler will be 8th Corpl. If this calculation is correct [1st Sergeant] Crego I think will leave the Co. Self will take his place. There will then be but one step more to a commission. No one knows however what a day may bring forth.

---

* Such imaginative rumors were not limited to the rank and file. On August 19 Gen. McClellan wrote his wife that the enemy was 150,000 strong and poised for an attack.

We moved our quarters yesterday abt 60 rods to bring us more out of range of the cannon in case of an attack. I am on guard to day. Mich. 3d came up to day & encamped a few rods from us. The N.Y. 12th are quiet & are beginning to act & look better. Gen. Richardson gave their officers a severe reprimand yesterday attributing the disorganized state of the regiment to their laziness & incapacity. 1000 men from this brigade chopping to day. They are laying all the trees flat to the ground which are within range of our cannon.

The soldiers will eat up all the corn in the country before it is ripe — very little wheat saved & none will be sown this fall. The rail fences are fast disappearing for wood, the board fences, outhouses &c are all torn down for the sake of the boards. The whole country will soon approximate to a state of nature. The enemy make worse havoc than we.

The guard emptied 10 barrels of beer & whiskey which were brought up by peddlers on to the ground. The men have entirely emptied two or three peddlers' wagons of their contents in a tenth part of the time it took to load them.

§ August 22 A quiet night on guard. We lived well to day. I made good use of guard duty to secure corn & potatoes for dinner. Benson bought a couple of good melons, Sid Prentice a pound of cheese. We had good beef & bread & out of these we made a first rate dinner. They have very fine melons & peaches in this part of the country, but apples are worthless & very few in number.

There has been a new feature introduced into our camp duties, to wit a Provost Guard of 80 men & the necessary officers drawn from the different Regts. of the brigade. Their duty is to arrest soldiers who are more than ¼ mile from the camps without a pass. To prevent stealing from peddlers. To seize all liquor & beer which comes within their range. To keep prostitutes off the ground &c &c. They have no posts but roam about in squads wherever there is a probability of their services being needed. They took about 25 bbls. of liquor & beer to day which had in some way been smuggled across the river & also 3 women.

The N.Y. 12th leaves the brigade to morrow. The N.Y. 37th has come up to take their place. I do not believe we shall make much by the change. They are all Irish & a hard looking set. Their guns look pretty well & that is the only redeeming, soldier like thing I have seen as yet. The guard house has been filled continually with the 12th & I am afraid it will need enlarging now. The prisoners are kept at work from 5 A.M. till 7 P.M. Our camp is now arranged, with one or two slight exceptions, in strict conformity to military rules & requirements. We have never been before where the ground would permit of a strictly regular camp.

§ AUGUST 24 This day Genl. Richardson's Brigade was reviewed by Major Gen. McClellan, Pres. Lincoln & Sec. Seward. I had the best view of the Pres. & McClellan that I have ever had. I saw McClellan full in the face at 6 feet distance. I like his looks pretty well but he is not a man of very imposing appearance. His ways however pleased the men remarkably. He is undoubtedly the man on whom the United States are hereafter to lean as a military chieftain. Gen. Scott is unmistakably past taking the field. His advice is good but the field requires a younger man.

Gen. Richardson is a much more imposing man in appearance than McClellan. I have never seen a man who so nearly resembles Scott's picture of Roderick Dhu* as our Genl. He was very particular to recommend the 2d to especial favor. "Yes President this is the 2d, my Regt., that is the 3d there." "These men can be relied on." "We could have held Blackburn's Ford that Sunday if it had been allowed." This & many other things I heard him saying to recommend his pet. He finally got in with the Pres. & Sec. & rode off. Not however till we had two or three hours of drilling. We went out at 9½ and were gone more than 4 hours almost without rest. The slice of bread & molasses which was all I had for breakfast was all gone when I got back.

McClellan is taking a personal view of every Regt. in the army. He is preparing a great move which will soon be made. I have confidence in him & all our men think Richardson is almost God.

I am vexed every day to think what a Capt. we have and a Col. & Major who are hardly fit for a Corporal. If we *could only* have a Col. who knew his business.† The field officers make blunders at every step. The Regt. could do better without any officers. They are all good men & good lawyers but how it is that they learn so

---

* The Highland chieftain in Sir Walter Scott's *The Lady of the Lake.*
† The acting commander of the 2nd Michigan was now Lt. Col. Sylvester Larnerd.

slowly & make the same mistake so often is more than I can tell. I can swear that I could drill a battalion better before I had been in the service a month. There is not a Sergt. in the Regt. who cannot do better.

What troubles me most is that there is no Capt. who seems conspicuous & who can hereafter take their places. Bretschneider & Dillman are both good officers but both are Germans & would not on that account & some others be very acceptable. They are the only suitable men among the Capts. I think Dillman would make a good Major. We have now a good regimental band & it is a very desirable thing. One can certainly hear all the good martial music here which he desires. I presume the morning call of a hundred Regts. can be heard.

§ AUGUST 25 Night before last four pickets of the N.Y. 30th (I believe) were shot. A party of men went out with our Lt. Col. to day to reconnoiter the enemy. Kellogg the Orderly of Co. E was shot & severely wounded. Our men killed 2 Secesh. The enemy are near in considerable force. The long roll may come before morning. We have taken things very quietly to day. I mean to do the same till I see some cause to do otherwise. They cannot be allowed to remain here long. They must be dislodged.

Our Irish friends of the 37th [New York] prove to be a first rate regiment. We shared our breakfast with them the first morning they came & have gained their good will entirely. They were out in the rain without tents & we could do no less than all we could for them. Generosity is prominent among a soldier's virtues.

§ AUGUST 26 A quiet & very warm day. The night passed off without alarm. Kellogg it is thought will recover. He was married abt 2 weeks ago to a very pretty girl who came with us from Detroit.

§ AUGUST 27 I went out with a party of men to day to chop. The men have had a great deal of fatigue duty & Benson, self & three Corpls. volunteered to afford them some relief. I wanted to get away from camp & see the country out toward Alexandria. We went abt 3 miles on the Alexandria road. We had a good view of Alexandria, the [Potomac] river & surrounding country. We passed over the ground where Gen. Washington, I am told, fought a battle during the Revolution, to wit the Battle of Four Mile Run.* We did a pretty fair days chopping.

---

* Haydon was misinformed.

I visited the camps of the Garibaldi Guards [39th New York] & German Rifles [8th New York]. I am convinced that we have not yet learned the science of camp life. They enjoy more than double the comforts & conveniences on the same means that we do. I have never before seen camps so neat, so tastefully arranged, so convenient & so beautifully ornamented with trees & other decorations. More good eatables were to be had there for 25 cts. than at any place since I left Detroit. Several of our men drank such large rations of whiskey at night that they were pretty drunk.

We saw some commotion in camp as we were returning & just as we got in Benson came running to me & said h--l is to pay we are all cut to pieces. I asked him what he meant. He replied that there had been a battle out on the road, that all our men had gone, been defeated & nearly all cut off. I at once concluded that he was excited. It turned out that the enemy had commenced driving our pickets and a skirmish had ensued. The long roll had been beaten & 800 men from the brigade sent out to reinforce the pickets. I have to go on picket to night. I dislike the business, it is going to rain hard & I am tired.

§ AUGUST 28 The rain last night was of short duration. While we were waiting at the guard house a man was arrested as a spy. Soon after Genls. McClellan & Richardson and escort came in from a tour of inspection. Gen. McClellan asked us if we were "ready for a brush." We all replied yes & he said he "would risk the night with us." I do not like to see them exposing themselves so much. I know that if I knew of [Confederate General P. G. T.] Beauregard coming out in that way toward our camp I would try to shoot him. They go out in sight of the enemy every day. They went out again to day just after dinner.

I went out with the Lieut. of the pickets abt 2½ miles to where a detachment of abt 300 of our men were stationed. They were at a four corners & extended along the roads in front & on the right & left. We stationed our guards between them & our camp at short intervals, some in the road & others in the fields. There were some 1200 men stationed in detachments outside of our pickets extending out abt 6 miles. The night was quiet, a few shots were fired but there was no general alarm.

One of the men from Co. I brought in near a bushel of green corn. There has been considerable firing, both of cannon & musketry to day in various directions & all sorts of reports as to the result. I have heard little which I believe. Almost every day however there is unmistakable evidence of fighting in the shape of dead or wounded men brought along in the ambulances.

During the day our pickets & the enemies keep within sight of each other but at night generally fall back a little. Capt. Dillman is reported to have led in 200 skirmishers this afternoon. If that be true there will be sharp fighting.

The mosquitoes were so thick last night that I slept very little. We are not troubled with them in camp. The countersign was badly mixed last night by some one. It was in no less than 4 different shapes before morning. I think the Lieut. of the picket was partly at fault. He owned that he did not know certainly what it was.

§ AUGUST 29 Just at dusk last night as I was writing near the door of the tent I heard a gun which was immediately followed by one of those deep hollow unearthly cries which are never uttered except by men when seriously wounded. I stepped to the door & saw a private of Co. G lying on the ground. He had been accidentally shot by a comrade. The ball & three buckshot passed quite through his body. He was breathing with great difficulty. His chest heaved convulsively at every breath. He never spoke after he was shot & lived but about 10 minutes.

This m'g there was an order for 25 men from each Co. for pickets. Sergt. Stevenson & self had charge of ours. It rained hard at daylight & has continued to do so up to this time (2 P.M.). I am writing in the church at Bailey's Corners or Crossing 7 miles from our camp on the road to Manassas. The enemy are on our right abt a mile distant. They are on a hill [Munson's Hill] in full view. They have breastworks & two pieces of cannon which can be seen from here. We have abt 300 men & there are 20 cavalry & some artillery near by.

There are 3 or 4 houses here besides the church, which has been occupied for some time by our pickets. The walls are covered with ludicrous pictures of Jeff Davis & other secessionists as well as the names of our men & Regts. "Lakeman's Zouaves," "Irish Rifles," "The Mozart Regiment," "3rd Maine," "2d Michigan," "Col. Carrigan's N.Y. Irish Regt.," "N.Y. 37th Col. McCunn," "Gen. James E. Nye," "Patrick Murphy" & a host of other names decorate the walls in large letters.

I am wet to the skin & feel very dirty as indeed I am. It seems now rather doubtful whether the enemy will fire on us to day. A few well aimed shells would send us out of the houses in a hurry. If the pastor of this congregation could return to day he would find a full congregation but I doubt whether they would pay much heed to his preaching. His sacred desk is now occupied by four men who are engaged in a brisk game of euchre.

Abt 4 P.M. the rain ceased. The enemy are intrenching themselves on a high hill to the west of us. I suppose that we are here to busy them while everything is preparing to fall upon them from Alexandria & the Chain bridge. They have fired at our pickets several times to day but have hit no one. A rifled cannon ball was yesterday sent through the barn where we are quartered.

§ AUGUST 30 The night was quiet till abt 4 A.M. when six guns were fired in quick succession back on the road towards camp. We all sprang to our feet but as nothing further followed we did not form in line. Soon after breakfast firing commenced in the same direction. There were some 20 shots. We quickly formed & sent out some skirmishers. There was further firing soon after between the enemy & a small party of our men. One man of Co. D was slightly wounded & one secessionist was killed. Both parties retreated pretty briskly.

We are now drawn up in loose order in the graveyard just behind the church. I am sitting as I write on the grave of some individual who has made a safe retreat from the alarms of war. The enemy can be seen with a glass carrying in one of their dead or wounded men. Everything is now quiet. About 100 shots have been fired. I slept well last night on some straw under a tree. I was a little apprehensive that they might send some shells into the barn during the night. They have the range & distance & might have done so if they desired.

At noon we were ordered, ie. Co's. I & K under command Lt. Park into the wood on the right of the enemy as skirmishers. We deployed at abt 3 rods distant from each other along a fence & off into the woods forming a line abt 120 rods long. I was with the Orderly of Co. K on the extreme right. The trees & underbrush were there so thick we could not see more than 3 rods. All laid or sat down on the ground & waited in perfect silence for the approach of the enemy in case they should attempt to send out scouts or flanking parties. The day was windy & the rustling of the leaves & the motion of bushes kept us in a constant state of watchfulness which in the course of time became exceedingly painful. No one showed himself on the right. The next man on my left carelessly snapped his gun but it did not go. I did not know for some time whether it was our man or some one attempting to shoot at us. This kept us wide awake for a few minutes.

Soon a gun was fired on our left which was immediately followed by that cry of death which I have before described. D. S. Buck a boy of 18 from our Co. had killed his first man. He was still lying on the open field where he fell when we came away. One other man is supposed to have been shot. He fell among long grass & weeds & was not seen afterwards. None of our men were hurt though probably 100 shots at long ranges were fired at them.

The enemy commenced a practice of shooting at pickets & every man they could see on the first day we were here & we took it up yesterday for the first [time]. Three of them were shot in the road just between our quarters & their battery. One of them, an officer, was shot from his horse by the Major of the 37th (of our brigade).

§ AUGUST 31 The night was quiet till just daylight when a low whistle passed along the ranks brought us quickly to our feet & into ranks. It however proved a false alarm. The enemy have again commenced firing at such of our men as show themselves within range. All the officers dress exactly like the men to avoid being singled out. I yesterday pulled off my jacket which is dark blue, with light chevrons but when I saw where we were going I put it on again, thinking that my gray shirt might attract the fire of our own men sooner than the chevrons would that of the enemy.

There is brisk shooting with muskets to day most of it being done by the enemy. Our men return their fire occasionally. A man of Co. G was shot through the body this m'g at 100 rods by a secession picket. He will probably die. The living here is poor except what is gleaned from the country. Green corn & bread have been the principal diet till to day a hog & several pigs were taken.

1 P.M. A secession picket was shot a few minutes since by a N.Y. soldier who came out to try his gun. I would like to try mine but they wont let me. I have not yet fired a gun at a rebel. After all it is rather barbarous. Gen. McClellan is doing all he can to stop it but without very much success. It is strictly forbidden to us. I obey the orders myself but I have taken no great pains to stop the men. It is very provoking to have them fire without replying.

§ SEPTEMBER 1, 1861 Sabbath morning 9 oclock. I am sitting behind a bunch of oak bushes, near a rail fence, about ½ mile from Bailey's Crossing, on Picket Guard watching for the villainous Secessionists. I have the charge, overseeing or command whichever you please to call it of 18 men stationed along on a line in groups of 3 having about 20 rods between groups. One of these three men is to keep watch while the rest lie on the ground, sleep or whatever they please except leave their posts or make a noise. My business is to see that they attend to their business, to go up & down the line every 2 hours & see what they have discovered & what they are about. We are kept at this business for 24 hours. The Rebels shoot at us or not as they feel inclined & we return their fire if they shoot too close or advance.

About 10 A.M. another detachment came up from camp & relieved us. We set out for home, as we call it, but before we got there met Gen. Richardson who detailed us all to chop for the balance of the day. He has located a new fort on a spot which had escaped the attention of the engineers although it is said by McClellan to be the most important one in the line of defence. McClellan at once ordered him to have a fort constructed.

All the ground around about was covered with trees and it required some hundreds of acres to be chopped. We would go to the devil to please Richardson & as he asked us to chop with unusual mildness of manner & explained the whole thing we went willingly. One field of near ten acres which had once been ploughed & cultivated was grown over with scrub pines from 10 to 20 feet high & that too within sight of Washington, Georgetown & Alexandria.

§ SEPTEMBER 2 is a dull quiet day. We receiving our State pay.

§ SEPTEMBER 3 I was on guard last night. To day I have kept clear of fatigue duty. The man who was wounded at Bailey's Crossing died last night. We returned to day all safe except one man who had his finger shot off. They did a good deal of firing. One of the Secesh called to our men to know what Regt. they belonged to. He replied Mich. 2d. "By God I should think you did. Cant you stop firing for a minute" cried Secesh. Our men then asked who they were & were answered S.C. 2d.

§ SEPTEMBER 4 I find myself again at Bailey's Crossing. Co's. I & K were sent out this morning. All is quiet up to noon, no firing.

I was last night introduced to Lt. Col. Larnerd & informed that I was soon to be 2d Lieut. of Co. I. This was in many respects a gratifying announcement. I had been incorrectly informed that it would be otherwise & was not well pleased at the announcement.

It will give much greater opportunity for study & research. I can carry such books as I need & a sufficient quantity of clothes & shall not be obliged to carry them on my back. Benson & I will occupy one tent instead of sharing it with 4 others.* I can keep better company, enjoy much greater privileges, have nothing to carry but a sword & pistol and sometimes my eatables. I shall also get $103 per month from which I pay my own expenses instead of $17 with expenses paid. A step from 3d Sergt. to 2d Lieut. is a pretty good one. I am to day Sergt. of the camp guard or rather Lieut., Sergt. & Corpl. all at once.

A man of Co. K was dangerously wounded just at sundown last night. He carelessly left his post & went to a house near by to get a drink. When he was coming back to his post he was shot in the back by some one concealed about the house.

§ SEPTEMBER 5 The night was quiet, rain toward morning. I was up nearly all night & when not it was too cold to sleep much & I had no blanket. We are apprehensive of an attack.

Everything was so quiet during the day that we thought something must be wrong. I posted the camp guard as pickets after dark. Some of them showed the white feather badly. I would get them together in part & while looking for the rest some of the first were sure to sly off & hide themselves. I was more than two hours, & did an immense sight of swearing, in getting them out. One of Co. I's men, Louis Leonhardt, dodged off & hid himself so that I could not find him. It commenced raining about 8 this m'g & rained till dark. We were relieved about 10 A.M. & set out for home where we arrived in due time well wet & covered with mud.

All the men who are in the habit of it, as many of them are, got liquor enough to get drunk. They were of course noisy & quarrelsome. The Big Sailor & another quarreled in our tent. One suddenly drew a sword & the other a dirk & were parted with difficulty. We are in as much danger from our own men as from the enemy. Not less than 6 or 8 have been accidentally shot since we left Detroit.

§ SEPTEMBER 6 Fatigue duty, chopping for the whole Regt. Richardson seems determined that his brigade shall do all that is to be done and that the 2d shall do the most of that.

---

* Haydon's commission as 2nd lieutenant would be dated September 22. Benson was promoted to 1st lieutenant.

§ SEPTEMBER 7 The officer of whom I spoke as having been shot by the Major of the 37th proved to have been Col. Stewart of the rebel army. The enemy are known to be making an extensive move from Manassas to day but its direction is not yet known. Their tents were taken down this m'g as seen from balloons.

§ SEPTEMBER 8 A soldier of one of the Vt. Regts. is to be shot to morrow for sleeping on his post as a sentinel.*

We are to go to Bailey's Crossing again to morrow. I do not desire the job very much. It was interesting enough the first time but it is getting pretty dull business. We were all called out for fatigue duty this m'g but by a general order of Gen. McClellan prohibiting Sunday labor except in cases of strict necessity were excused.

Benson has gone to the hospital. He has already broken by excesses one of the best constitutions ever given to man. I have been acting Orderly for 3 days. I bought the Atlantic this m'g & have been reading that & distributing clothes & shoes to the Co. all day. I have a bad cold in my head but care nothing for it if it does not trouble my living. I would like very much to go to the city but it is impossible.

§ SEPTEMBER 9 Contrary to expectation the Co. was sent on fatigue at 7 instead of picket. We drew a weeks rations to day & I stayed in to attend to that. At 4½ P.M. we slung our things & marched to the crossroads for picketing. Arrived there before sundown & made all necessary arrangements. As usual Capt. May had me on camp guard as soon as we were within sight of here.

§ SEPTEMBER 10 The night was very quiet. Some shot & shells were fired yesterday but none during the night. Their shells were so badly constructed that not one which they fired exploded.

Hereafter there is no fatigue duty for the 2d but they have to do all the picket duty at this place. This is a little tedious but after all a fine thing. A third of the Regt. marches out every day. It gives them a march 5 miles out on one day & 5 back the next, a view of the enemy & a chance to exchange shots. All things considered it is an excellent school.

Two other Sergts. & myself stood guard on a post in front of the officers quarters. I was on from 11 till 2. It was a fine starry

---

* The sentence of Pvt. William Scott, 3rd Vermont, was commuted by President Lincoln.

night. I looked at the stars & found groups & images out of them till my eyes ached. Now & then a group came up which looked as familiar as the face of an old friend. It reminded me very forcibly of the time (some 8 years since) when a girl named Mary & myself used to recite Astronomy together days & sit up late at night to view the constellations. It is now a long time since I saw Mary. She has gone I know not where & I am here. Many a change in thought, feeling & prospects of life has come to both. The sky is just as blue & the stars as bright as then but neither would look upon them with the same interest.

One of our pickets yesterday stumped a Secesh to lay down guns & meet half way to trade newspapers, offering a N.Y. Times for a Charleston Mercury. The soldier was willing to do it but his officer would not let him. Two of our Capts. crossed the lines this P.M. & held a conference with a Major & Capt. of the Rebels during which it was agreed that the pickets should not hereafter fire on each other. They had a very friendly interview & talked over matters for near an hour. They were from the Va. 2d.

The man of Co. K who was wounded some days ago died yesterday. One of our men told the Rebels that he wanted to go over & look for a blanket which he lost on the 21st of July. They are bantering each other pretty freely to day. In the afternoon I went to a Secesh house & got a very poor dinner for a quarter. There was not a manufactured article in the house which was not made north of Secessiondom.

§ SEPTEMBER 11 We started last night abt 7½ P.M. for home where we arrived after a brisk walk at 9. I tumbled into my blankets at once. Several shots were fired at us at the Cross Roads just dark but they all fell harmlessly in the ground round about. There must have been some mistake about the arrangement made between the officers yesterday in regard to firing. I presume the men who made it had not authority or their command did not extend to the whole line of pickets.

At 4 P.M. we were ordered out to Bailey's again. It rained hard & we were well soaked before we got there. I was posted on what is called the center on the right of the road leading to the Secession fort. We were fired upon at the post where I was 6 times. All the shots passed over. As I was going into head quarters after the countersign a ball cut off a corn stalk abt 3 feet from me.

§ SEPTEMBER 12 Abt 7 A.M. I am sitting in a little hole in front of the Ft. I never passed a more uncomfortable night. Abt 11 P.M. there came a very heavy shower of rain which lasted with little intermission till near daylight. We were entirely without shelter save our little rubber blankets which did good service but could at best shield little more than our guns. We were all well drenched & felt the cold pretty severely before morning.

We have holes dug in the ground & the dirt thrown up in front & a rail or two laid on top & some corn stalks stuck up around. These are very good in dry weather but soon filled with water. In these holes we can stand & be entirely out of danger if we are careful. We do not however take any great pains to conceal ourselves.

They commenced firing abt 1 this m'g & kept it up briskly all the rest of the time till daylight, I suppose more for the sake of getting the damp charges out of their guns than from any expectation of hitting anybody. A few of their shots struck near our post but no one was injured. After daylight they did better shooting but still hit no one. My haversack rolled into a ditch filled with muddy water & spoiled the provisions. The rest of the men however had enough to supply me.

It was a positive relief to hear the firing commence last night. It was so dark, rainy & lonesome that it was cheering to hear men although you knew that they were firing at you. The sun came out warm & bright at last, dried our clothes & cheered our spirits.

Our 1st Corpl. McGee is in a difficult situation. He is anxious to play a prominent part in this war & is eager for promotion (wants to be a 2d Lieut.) but has a great dread of bullets. He is a tall raw New Brunswick lumberman, somewhat green but with frankness enough to own that he is a little afraid. I went out where he was this m'g a little after daylight. We stood talking together when a ball struck in the field some 30 or 40 rods off to one side with a sharp whizzing sound. He no sooner heard it than he threw himself down into the mud with such rapidity & violence that I thought he would have knocked all the breath out of his body.

The firing was kept up on their side all day but not returned by us. If I had have had a good gun I could have killed some of them. There were plenty of chances at 80 rods. We suffered almost as much from the sun during the day as from the rain & cold during the night. We however laid on the bare sand & talked & joked away the time as best we could till sundown when we were relieved. My friend Sergt. Wilkinson of Co. K who was on the left had a narrow escape. A minnie ball tore off the side of his cap, cut a clean furrow through his hair & grazed the skin so as to make it bleed pretty rapidly. Half the width of the ball nearer & he would have got his discharge. I had previously some cold & expected to find myself sick but am I believe none the worse for the wear.

§ SEPTEMBER 13 I am not on duty to day & am taking things easy. I forgot to mention that after Wilkinson was shot yesterday Co. K returned the fire & killed one man. We, that is Benson, Major, Butler & I had an extra dinner to day on sweet potatoes, oysters, broiled mackerel, bread & butter &c. Our men shot 2 rebels at Bailey's to day, so they say. Perhaps it is so.

§ SEPTEMBER 14 A fine warm day. We are going to Bailey's to night. An extra dinner is to be served to day as yesterday. I yesterday recd a letter from Arthur, one from Prindle & one from Miller. Two men were accidentally shot yesterday.

§ SEPTEMBER 15 Sunday at Bailey's. A very pleasant day, warm & bright. There is a good deal of firing on both sides but it amounts to very little. I have been all along the line of pickets making the third time I have been out to the line to day. When we went to the left near the barn they gave us a salute of 6 shots, the farthest off about 20 feet, the nearest abt 4. The two lines at this place are not more than 45 rods apart. They keep well concealed & seldom get a fair sight at each other. I saw the smoke of every gun that was fired at us but did not see a man. There are two barns & 4 or 5 haystacks where they are & it is impossible to get at them. There has been much talk abt burning them & it may be done.

Our men are getting pretty well acquainted with the Virginia troops. They are talking backward & forward all the time & do not fire very much at each other. The fact is they — Va. men — dont care a great deal which whips. The S.C. men are rabid. There are many words between them & our men but they are all very uncivil. They will fire at us and yell out "take that you d----d Michiganders." Ours will reply "go to h--l you d----d fools you cant hit anybody" and all the other abusive remarks they can think of.

A single 32 pds. rifled cannon shell fired by our men at the skirmish near Lewinsville a day or two since dismounted a rebel cannon, knocking it entirely off the carriage, killed 4 men & 2 horses & wounded 9 men.

The day is remarkably hot & the heat is more unpleasant than that of August. Brigadier Gen. Kearney [Philip Kearny] of N.J. who lost his left arm in Mexico & a Major Gen. whose name I could not learn paid us a visit toward night. There were a large number of officers present & some very fine looking men. We were relieved abt dark & made a rapid march home.

§ SEPTEMBER 16 Two N.J. boys were shot last night. We started at 4 P.M. for the Cross Roads where we arrived in due time. I disliked very much to go this time. I did not feel well & it was not my turn but the Capt. was gone, Benson thought he ought not to leave, Crego never goes, Stevenson was gone, Whiting was suddenly ill & could not be found when the time came, so that there was no one else left. As it turned out I did not fare badly. There being no one else I had charge of the Co. & in consequence slept at the house & had very little to do save distribute the whiskey which I made out to do in such a manner that no one got drunk.* This is quite unusual & cost much swearing on part of the men & a little on mine.

§ SEPTEMBER 17 I had another squabble over the whiskey this m'g but succeeded in obeying orders from headquarters & cutting them all short with one drink. Things have gone at loose ends in our Co. so long that it is not the easiest thing in the world to govern them. The Capt. is no better than a wooden man as far as discipline is concerned.

Major Williams blowed me sky high yesterday in behalf of the whole Co. because the quarters were not kept cleaner. My temper got up a little & I said about as much in reply as was prudent. Major finally concluded that he had said more to me than was necessary & went off vowing that he would attend to the Capt. as soon as he came back.

There has been considerable firing this P.M. I have some reason to believe that I shot one of them.

I went out to a post where there was considerable firing & took

---

* McClellan had instituted a whiskey ration for those on duty.

the best aim I could at one, with a minnie musket, off abt 80 rods.* He was standing in the edge of the corn & went down just abt the time the ball should have reached him. This of itself was nothing as we always do that, but as soon as he fell 5 or 6 others ran up to the place & bent down over what would seem to be the man I shot at. I am however by no means certain. The second time I know I did not hit anything.

All the commissioned officers except one have been two thirds drunk all day. Our pickets & the enemies' have been talking together on the left all day. They have exchanged buttons, tobacco, cards, whiskey &c. One chap gave one of our men the name of his mistress in Charleston & urged him to call on her if he ever went there. There was a heavy shower near night. I think the prospects of my promotion might be better.

I am confirmed in the belief that I killed the first man I shot at by the fact that a man was seen to be carried away from the place about ½ an hour after. I know he did not dodge the ball for he was not quick enough. I think I must have been made for the business or I have improved very fast since I enlisted. I am a little surprised myself to see how cool I took it. I went out to a post where they were troubling our pickets a good deal. I sat there a few minutes talking with the boys & seeing that the Rebels showed themselves pretty fair. I asked one of them to let me look at his minnie. I took it, looked at it for a minute, asked him a few questions about its shooting, raised the sight to the 400 yds. mark, placed the end of a board on the top of the little embankment in front, letting it slant back on to the ground, as I used to at home when shooting at a mark. I laid down on the board & did not wait more than ½ a minute before one showed himself. I took such aim as I thought ought to fetch him & I have good reason to believe it did.

§ SEPTEMBER 18   I slept well & feel well this morning. I saw an article on picket firing this m'g in the Chicago Tribune which meets my views. Much is said of late about the barbarity of the practice but there is nothing makes soldiers so fast. The first time they get sight of the enemy on picket the men are all excitement & half of

---

* Haydon fired a Springfield rifled musket, with a bullet designed by the French army's Capt. Claude Minié to take the rifling, at a range of about 440 yards.

them will shoot off their guns before they are within a mile. Let them be out a week they will shoot at one another with as little concern as they would at squirrels. They will sit & talk & joke when the bullets come within from 3 to 10 feet & some of them much nearer or swing their hats & tell them to try it again. They are not of course to go out & shoot as fast as they can load unless the enemy should advance but merely exchange 6 or 8 shots per man each day when the chances are favorable. The loss will not as a general thing be great on either side. There is nothing like it to keep pickets awake nights.

A trooper belonging to our brigade had the handle of a sheath knife shattered at his side by a ball while attempting to go to one of our picket posts yesterday P.M. Two of our men from Co. E were wounded to day, one it is thought mortally, the ball going in at one shoulder & out at the other, the other slightly. A picket of the Mich. 3d was shot last night, the ball going in at one cheek & out at the other. One of the Mass. 14th was shot last night by a sentinel of his own Co. whom he insisted on attempting to pass. Half his lower jaw, all his left cheek & his left eye were blown entirely away. He is still alive.

Another stand up fight came off in the N.Y. 37th to day. I ran over with all my might but the crowd was so great that I could only get an occasional glimpse of two "bully boys" & their seconds all stripped to the skin except pants. The crowd was so great there being no ring that they had but a poor chance. The crowd turned the officer of the day all ends uppermost & Frank Leslie's* reporter got his eye bunged.

§ SEPTEMBER 19 An arrangement was made yesterday between Gen. Richardson & the Rebel commander to stop all picket firing which will probably be effectual. They owned 13 men killed to say nothing of the wounded. The Co. has gone on picket but as I had been out every time I thought I would stay at home this time & let the rest of the Sergts. try a hand.

The 1st Corpl. has been swearing terribly, that is in a religious way, at the men who suffered from masked batteries in the city. Since then one of them induced him to trade drawers & in this

---

* *Frank Leslie's Illustrated Newspaper.*

way gave the 1st Corpl. the clap. I never laughed so hard in my life. I am rather sorry for him. I have seen too many men ruined in health already to rejoice at such things.

The Mich. 5th came over last night. They thought they could whip the Devil when they first came but after lying out on the ground last night for the first time & having little to eat except what we gave them, seeing a couple of wounded men which our boys brought in just after they came & hearing all the dubious stories with which our men delighted to fill their ears, the fighting 5th as they call themselves had a good many long faces. One of them asked me in a whisper this m'g if our pickets were driven in last night. They have gone up to Hunter's Chapel abt a mile out to camp. They were very anxious to know if they would be in sight of the enemy. Whether they probably would be attacked there right away. Wasn't it pretty dangerous to put them out so far. They are more than three miles inside the pickets.

We used to call ourselves the "Bloody Second" but that was all over long ago. We dont think nowadays that we can whip everybody as we used to, still we are willing to try anything which the occasion requires & will do far better fighting than the "Bloody Second" ever thought of. The Secesh have learned us at least. One of their pickets just stuck his head out from behind a tree the other m'g & cried out to one of ours, "Halloa there, where did you come from." "New Jersey" was the reply. "All right" said Secesh setting his gun up agt the tree, "I didnt know but it was one of them Michigan cusses."

§ SEPTEMBER 20 In camp. Nothing unusual. We had some oysters for supper. The weather is hot. I recd letters from Arthur, Miller & Father.

§ SEPTEMBER 21 I am acting Lieut. of the Guard & have a pretty busy day. Our guard is very much reduced. There are only 5 in a relief. The Corpls. act as such & also as Sergts. One Sergt. does the work of 2 Lieuts. & a Lieut. acts as officer of the day. I hope there will soon be some officers in the Regt. There is a fair prospect of it.

We have a Col. at last. 1st Lieut. [Orlando M.] Poe of the Engineers. I suppose he is a much better officer than we could reasonably expect, in fact one of the best in the service.

Five

SOLDIERING
IS VERY NICE
BUSINESS

The two months from late September to late November 1861 were the most pleasant of Charles Haydon's army career. As a newly minted 2nd lieutenant (September 22) he began to enjoy the privileges accorded an officer. Additionally, thanks to his civilian legal experience, he frequently found himself assigned to court martial duty instead of more demanding tasks.

In his journal Haydon thought often of fighting and how he would react to it. "We have an enemy before us," he wrote, "which respects nothing that is good; venerates nothing that is holy; hesitates at nothing which is damnable," yet his actual contact with that enemy continued to be limited. On September 28 the 2nd Michigan helped occupy Munson's Hill, west of Washington, after the Rebels abandoned it. On November 12 the regiment joined a reconnaissance in force along the lower Potomac near Mount Vernon that proved empty of result. Working conscientiously to improve his own efficiency as an officer, Lieutenant Haydon came increasingly to appreciate the vital role leadership played in an army — and how outstanding was the example set by his colonel, Orlando M. Poe.

* * *

§ SEPTEMBER 22, 1861 I passed through my first day & night as officer of the guard in a manner quite satisfactory to myself. I passed the night at the officers' guard tent. It rained very hard most of the night. I was called up 3 times in the night, each time a deputation was sent over from the 37th to our guard house & it was necessary to have them gagged & tied at once or there was no sleep. We got 12 of them, all drunk, during the night. The weather was cold this m'g. I do not know exactly how we shall fare during the winter if we do not move farther south.

Promptly at 4 P.M. we set out for the cross roads & arrived as usual. The Capt. was sick & I being the only Sergt. who could make it convenient to go had command of the Co.* Capt. Bretschneider who had command at the crossing was in high temper. The agreement with regard to picket firing was at an end. The enemy commenced firing & Capt. B. took a flag of truce & went up to inquire the meaning. The officer in command at the fort said he knew nothing abt any agreement. He came there to fire & was going to fire. Anybody was a d----d fool not to fire. He wanted nothing more to do with Capt. B. & he would have him arrested in less than no time unless he was off. Very well said Capt. B. "You want to fire I gives you enough of it. Good day Sir, I hope I meet you again before the war is over."

"Now boys, you waits till they fire once then you give them h--l. Shoot at the d----d rascals so fast as you can." The order was obeyed & considerable firing was done before dark. He scolded & sent a complaint to camp because no officers came with Co. I. He said he had no objection to my commanding it so far as one man could do it but it needed more than one. He had the men crazy for fighting in less than ten minutes.

§ SEPTEMBER 23 I passed a very comfortable night, slept well. Firing commenced at daylight briskly. There had been very little firing on the center till I went out to our pickets just after daylight.

There was a persimmon tree loaded with rich fruit abt 4 rods in front of the line. Its fruit had often been coveted by our men. I concluded to go & get some. I was busily knocking them off with a pole when a rascal fired at me, the ball striking abt 20 feet short & a little to one side. I grabbed up my hands full of persimmons & made no unnecessary delay in returning inside the lines to my proper place. After that there was a pretty steady fire all day, our Co. shooting about 20 rounds per man.

---

* Haydon's 2nd lieutenant's commission bore this date, but he only received it on the twenty-sixth.

Not less than 2000 shots were fired by our men during the day. None of them were hurt though several would have been killed but for the holes & little breastworks into & behind which they dodged. It is claimed & with much probability that 4 of the enemy were killed. An ambulance came down to the line 3 times & it could have been for no other purpose than carrying off dead or wounded. We had nothing but old blunderbuss [smoothbore] muskets. They shot a good distance but the ball traveled slow & was inaccurate. The balls fell patter, patter about us all day hitting trees, houses, fences &c but there was no loss except one cow which was shot in the road near our quarters.

In the afternoon the enemy burned 2 houses just beyond our lines fearing it is presumed that we would occupy them. Capt. Bretschneider sent me down to the left to see what was doing. The road was abt 40 rods back & nearly parallel to our pickets. The enemy shot over almost invariably. I think not less than 20 balls struck in & near the road while I was returning. I could frequently see the balls as they passed & could hear them long before they reached me.

An old man where our officers usually get their meals was in great concern. The balls were flying around the house & several of them struck it. His wife & family of small children were much alarmed. There were two large barns & five stacks of hay & grain from which they annoyed our men very much & they determined to burn them. They succeeded in firing one barn just after dark by means of red hot iron slugs shot from muskets & from this the fire communicated to the other barn & the stacks. Besides breaking up the haunt there was a loss to the enemy of a large amt of hay & grain. The barns were very large & well filled. It puzzled Secesh very much to know how it was done.

Our men begin to show an eagerness for conflict & which will soon become allied to ferocity. This feeling is terrible but sure to win. It needs to be educated to coolness & politic caution. There was very much foolish firing to day. Far more men could have been killed in a different way. I could get nothing but a musket to use & did not care to fire. If I could only have had a good Mich. sporting rifle I should have enjoyed it. They would throw open the great doors of one of those barns as soon as they found we were shooting muskets & a man would walk out into the open doorway & stand till he saw the smoke of our guns & then run

back before the ball would reach them. This was exceedingly vexatious. With a small bore rifle & quick powder I think I could have
stopped that business very quick.

There was brigade inspection at camp by Gen. McClellan, Prince
de Joinville & others & it was very late when the relief came.

§ SEPTEMBER 24   At one A.M. we were ready to turn in to blankets at home, having returned at 12½ from picket with empty
haversacks & bellies. Capt. Morse took command at the corners
last night & was trying to stop firing. It proved an easy job for the
rebels sent down a flag of truce from the Ft. asking that it might
be discontinued. The burning of the barns troubled them. They
think we crept up to them. We had brigade drill for 4 hours. It
was hot, dusty & tiresome.

We have a new Col. & a glorious good one he is. He was late
aide to Gen. McClellan & 1st Lt. of the Engineers. Orlando M. Poe
is the man. We shall not be able to keep him long but he puts life
into the Regt. while he is here.

Gen. Richardson had to brag stoutly about how his non-com-
missioneds drilled the battalion last 4th July. He declares that they
can beat most of the field officers drilling.

§ SEPTEMBER 25   was pay day & drunken night. I have stood
it very well till last night when it came into our own tent. Abt dark
Benson, Corpls. Prentice, Mack & Mason, Major Underwood &
North & Butler came into the tent & began to play cards for 2
bottles of ale. Orderly Crego soon joined. Two bottles being found
wholly insufficient to supply their wants 2 more were added &
soon after 4 others. After some further playing 12 more bottles
were found necessary. By this time they were all pretty drunk &
thought 6 bottles of champagne were needed. These were drunk
which together with some liquor obtained outside made them all
drunk enough to be very noisy.

At this point Mack & Mason quarreled & got into a fight in
which Benson, Prentice & Butler took part. They all tumbled over
onto the ground to rise as I thought no more for the night. Pretty
soon however they fell apart & Mason & Prentice came out with
black eyes, Butler & Mack with noses skinned & bloody & Benson
with some hard knocks in the bowels.

Mason then insisted on whipping the officer of the guard for
ordering them to make less noise. He was finally dissuaded from
this & he & Mack put to bed in their respective tents. Mack soon

spewed all over the ever unfortunate Hadlock who ran to the Sergts.' tent for redress. Benson & North at once seized him & rolled him all ends uppermost outdoors into a ditch. The Drum Major tried to embrace the Orderly & both tumbled over nearly breaking their heads. There were innumerable songs, speeches & mishaps which I have no time to relate. I was glad to get off by giving them a dollar & drinking one bottle of ale. The others spent abt $20 and lost $15 in the melee. Everything in the old tent was turned bottom side uppermost. I laughed myself nearly to death but got very little sleep.

§ SEPTEMBER 26 This day came Lieuts. commissions for Benson & I. I could agree to all [the others] except Bryan's promotion [to 8th corporal] to which I was opposed. I do not believe he can ever control a squad. Many of the men were drunk & there was much noise about camp.

§ SEPTEMBER 27 was a rainy day. Benson & I looked up our effects & made arrangements as far as possible for our departure from the Sergts. tent. We tried to get a pass to the city to make the necessary purchases but it was impossible. We all started for picket ground & at 4 P.M. the Lieuts. having few other things to carry paid more attention to their haversacks which were well filled with bread & butter, cheese &c. It rained very hard most of the way. Everything indicated the approach of Fall. The rain & mist driven by sudden & uncertain gusts of wind showed unmistakably that snow & squalls would some day follow. I got pretty muddy but not very wet. We had a good fire & a warm cup of coffee at the head quarters. There was little rain during the night but the wind was high & cold & severe on the men who were on posts.

§ SEPTEMBER 28 Hot coffee was sent to the pickets at daylight. No one was seen about the Ft. this m'g & about 8 A.M. it became apparent that the enemy had withdrawn their pickets during the night. Some 6 or 8 troopers are all who have been seen abt the Ft. up to 3 P.M.

A woman who came down past the Ft. this m'g with 4 children, a wench & some furniture & a one horse wagon reports that there are still 2 Regts. concealed in the fortifications on Munson's Hill & 6 Regts. not far beyond. We hardly know how to take this move but intend by care to avoid any trap which may have been laid. Scouts were out all day looking cautiously around, peeping into every accessible place.

Abt 4 P.M. Gen. Richardson & Col. Poe came out. After looking
around for a little while Gen. R. ordered Capt. Sherlock & self to
take 12 men of Co. I & occupy if possible a house abt 30 rods in
front of the enemies battery. We advanced, occupied the house &
scattered along a fence parallel to the battery. Here we lay concealed in the weeds for an hour & a half. As we knew nothing of
the enemies force or position & as we were over ½ mile in advance
of all our pickets we were rather anxious to know what was doing.
We took such precaution as we could to prevent being surrounded
& waited the progress of events. We could see abt 20 men around
their works who fired occasional shots at us none of which took
effect.

After an hour & a half abt 20 men of the 5th Mich. crept up
to us. Soon after as many more came through the woods & got
into a school house on the opposite side of the road & a little
nearer to the Ft. than we. Another party under Lt. Benson of abt
40 men came up the road even with us. We were all looking very
earnestly when someone I know not who it was cried out forward.
At this we all made a rush & entered the works on the run & found
them empty. A few of the men who had been there ran afoul of
our scouts & were taken. The rest disappeared.

Gen. Richardson & Col. Poe looked on not believing the works
were deserted. The Gen. swore worse than a Corpl. Benson & I
had neither of us had a chance to get swords & were armed with
nothing but pistols. I was fortunate enough to escape his obser-
vation but Benson caught it. "Is there another Lt. here" shouted
Gen. R. Yes Sir said B., I am. Gen. turned short around & looking
at him a moment said "Well by G-d you look like one. You'll kill
somebody yet. Where in h--l is your sword Sir, where have you
been? What have you been about: out on duty without a sword."
Here Col. Poe interfered in behalf of the paralyzed Lieut. & explained. Ah well said Gen., "can you get a sword Sir?" Capt. Whipple handed him his. "Do you see that barricade on the road?" Yes.
"Can you lead these men there?" Yes. Then without waiting a
second, "Come. Why in h--l aint you off Sir, what you standing
here for?"

When he saw the men running to the works he pretended to
be very much enraged but could easily be seen laughing in his
sleeve. "There d--n it Col., there goes one of them up to the Ft.
There goes 2 more. There by G-d goes the whole of them. Col.

all you have to do is to hold these men if you can till it is time to let them go."

We quickly hoisted the Union Flag & gave it three lusty cheers. Some other parties soon after took possession of a work just beyond. The N.J. brigade had already seized one on the left. When sun set we had possession of all the enemies works in that locality without loss. We had from Munson's Hill a fine view of Washington, the Potomac & toward the West the high hills to the right of Manassas were visible.

All the officers except Benson & I went back to the corners to sleep. We laid down with abt a dozen of our men on top of the hill. We had our oilcloth blankets under us & only one blanket to cover us. There was a strong, cold N.W. wind which when we awoke a little after midnight had chilled us pretty thoroughly. We got up & ran around till we were warm again & then slept well till daylight.

2 Regts. came up before 9 P.M. to help hold the works & when daylight came 6 others & 2 batteries were seen nearby. The Garibaldi Guards [39th New York] were among them & I must say that they can beat the world at stealing. All the N.Y. troops are great at that but I believe the Guards can beat them all. The country was soon plundered & houses which have been perfectly safe in our hands for a month were stripped by them in an hour & have been burned.

§ SEPTEMBER 29 At noon Sunday we were allowed to return to camp which were very glad to do.

§ SEPTEMBER 30 Benson & I succeeded after near a half days running in getting passes to the city & have bought swords &c.

We have been boarding for the last two days at a house nearby. Neither of us knew how to act. It is now 5 months since we have done such a thing before. Benson got to talking very busily with an officer's wife of the 37th & so far forgot himself as to seize his beefsteak in his fingers twice instead of making use of the civilized & Christian method with knife & fork. It really seemed very much like home to me to sit down at a table where there were ladies & everything was in good order. We have been so used to slashing everything with bowie knives & scrabbling up the pieces with our fingers that it is hard to restrain oneself at first.

We have each of us spent abt $75 for necessaries to day. Orders were issued for us to march to morrow with two days cooked rations in our haversacks.

§ OCTOBER 1, 1861 We have been picking up our things to remove from the Sergts. tent to the Lts. We expected to march this m'g & were all out at 7½ A.M. & stacked arms in front of quarters. Our things are all packed & we can march at 10 minutes notice. There is a rumor of battles up the river but nothing certain is known.

Night has come & we are still in camp but in readiness to march on short notice. Benson & I went on Dress Parade to night for the first time. It was new business to us & we knew that we should be closely watched. It was in no small degree embarrassing. If my heart had ever pattered when there was fighting to be done as it did when we marched out to the front I should have called myself a coward beyond all hope of redemption. I have been several times where I thought my chances of being shot in the next half hour were too good to be pleasant but my pulse was even compared with what it was when there was a chance of making a blunder on Dress Parade.

Benson came out in full uniform but I thought best to try it the first time in half dress. The Col. likes to see considerable style but Gen. Richardson's advice when we started for the city was "now dont go to getting any fancy things." We both of us succeeded in getting through without any mishap. At the first command "Order Arms" I instinctively threw up my left hand to my sword as if it had been a gun but I got it down so quick that no one could have seen it if he had been watching.

We are now nearly arranged in our new quarters & shall soon be accustomed to all the new duties. It costs something to be promoted. I spent yesterday as follows & have as yet not more than half an outfit.

A new suit of clothes	$21.00
Sword & belt	20.00
Navy revolver	20.00
Gold embroidered shoulder straps	3.50
Gold bugle for cap	2.50
Trunk	5.00
Military Dictionary	5.00
Share in mess chest	6.00
Gloves	2.00
	85.00

Beyond these are needed an Officer's Overcoat, say $25.00, a sash $15.00 to 20.00, a pair of boots $6.00 & other articles too numerous to mention. The pay however when it comes will be double what is needed for expenses.

§ OCTOBER 2 We have been living pretty well to day. Gibson of Kalamazoo is here & Handy usually eats with us & Gibson always does. Handy was a little mad about the promotions but he has come around all right of his own accord. Crego is still rabid.

We know nothing about the movement of troops. At night we have two or three Regts. beside us. In the m'g all are gone. No one knows where or when they went. At 9 P.M. an order comes to march. The men fall out without noise. There [is] a guide furnished who leads the way. Ask them where they are going. "Dont know, that man on the horse ahead there knows." They march on for a time. The guide says to the Col. pointing to some open field, you camp there.

A few weeks ago 4 batteries of artillery were encamped beside us. We heard their tattoo at 9 P.M. In the m'g they were all gone. No man of the Regt. knows to this day where they have gone. We go to bed at night with no one near us, in the m'g we may be surrounded by Regts. We have had our arms stacked in line ready to move for three days but we are still in camp, where or when we are to go we do not pretend to ask.

§ OCTOBER 3 A very warm day. Skirmish drill all the afternoon. Our new Col. is crowding things. He says that in 6 months the Mich. 2d is to be the best drilled Regt. in the United States. Our drills & parades already attract large numbers of visitors & are highly praised. He straightens men & officers to their places in a hurry.

§ OCTOBER 4 Benson was sent on fatigue duty this m'g & I went with the skirmishers. There has been a great itching among the men to get into a Cavalry Co. attached to our brigade. They were cured of it this m'g. Capt. Handy was out with the skirmishers, 30 in number & invited them [the troopers], about 65 in number, to charge them. They came down at full gallop till abt 4 rods off. The men who had formed in a square fired on them with blank cartridges. More than 20 men were hit by the wads & were scattered in every direction. They rallied again & came down to about 10 rods when the horses began to break. The men fired upon them again. This time they scattered worse than before. Two of the men were thrown. It was impossible to bring them up again. If the guns had been loaded not a third of the troopers would have escaped. These men have been drilling 2 months & are called a fair Co.

The skirmish drill is one of the finest in use. Whether you view them stretched out in a long line, 5 paces between the men, or rallied in their pugnacious little groups of fours, with a bayonet at each corner or in their stronger groups of sections or platoons they are active, self reliant, sharp, mischievous fighters. It is a curious sight to see them when firing. They are as I said before deployed one in a place having a space of 5 paces between each 2 men. They are then numbered off from right to left 1, 2, 3, 4 &c. At the command, commence firing, the odd numbered men run forward 10 paces very quickly, throw themselves down on their bellies, fire, roll over on their backs & commence loading. While these are loading the even numbered men run up 10 paces beyond them, throw themselves down, fire & commence loading.

By this time the odd numbered men are ready again in turn & advance 10 paces beyond these & throw themselves down as before & so they keep going. You will see either nothing but the smoke when they fire or their heads peeping up above the weeds & grass except when they advance. This when near the enemy is always done by an oblique or zig zag movement. Good marksmen in this way make bad work with little loss to themselves. They are of course to seek the shelter of all the trees, logs, ditches & inequalities of the ground which are at hand.

It is said that we are to move to morrow.

§ OCTOBER 5 I have been on fatigue duty to day with Capt. Bretschneider & 100 men at Ft. Richardson. The trenches had to be deepened. It is slow work. Soldiers hate to work. The ground was hard as a stone wall. Every shovel full has to be picked up. The earth had to be raised abt 20 feet. It had all to be handled over from 3 to 5 times. It is to be a pretty fine work. It will mount abt 20 32 pdrs. It has 2 underground magazines. It commands every work on this side of the river which is within 2 miles as well as the river itself.

§ OCTOBER 6 Sunday. We were out at roll call at 6 A.M. By a recent order all the Co. officers are required to be present. We then went out to guard mounting at 8. At 10 came Inspection, here we were detained near 2 hours. Next inspection of quarters.

Then came church for such as desired to attend. Dress Parade at 5 P.M. & an hour spent in listening to orders. This occupied most of the day.

Our new Col. is getting stricter every day. The weather is very hot. Gen. Richardson came out yesterday with a new uniform hat on.* He did not know what to do with himself. It had a large silver eagle on the side which he tore off the first pass. He then came into the room where Capt. Norvell his aide was. He took hold of his chapeau with both hands & lifted it off. "Capt. Norvell" said he with great deliberation, "what do you think of that hat? It had an eagle on but I thought the hat would do without any eagle, so I took him off." He then jammed on the hat & went off nodding & shaking his head.

It is astonishing what influence he has over this Regt. There is hardly anything possible to be done which they would not do or attempt at his command. It will do for a Brigadier Gen. to tear the eagle off his hat, but if a Lieut. under our Col. comes on Dress Parade without all the uniform which belongs to him, boots blacked, white gloves on & not a speck of dirt about him he would be sent back to his tent. This style is pretty hard on me, I must admit. I never spent so much time on dress before. Col. Poe sent 10 men to the guard house this m'g so quick they did not know which end they stood on because they did not move quite as quick as they ought. When not on duty we have a good opportunity for reading, study &c. We are clear of all the hangers on except the inevitable Sid Prentice who can no more be got rid of than one's shadow.

§ OCTOBER 7 The weather is intensely hot & is beginning to be very dry. We had skirmish drill this m'g. The sweat poured off me in streams. Capt. May has now been gone 2 days. He is going to recruit for the Regt. but more especially to work for his appointment as Lt. Col. of the 10th [Michigan] Regt. May God have mercy on the country if May is to be Lt. Col.

The most alarming feature of the whole war is to see the men who are placed in such responsible positions. Our Capt. is not in truth qualified for a Sergeant's place in one of our Co's. He might,

---

* Richardson's brigade, assigned to Samuel P. Heintzelman's division, now consisted of the 2nd, 3rd, and 5th Michigan and the 37th New York.

if he would work, make a very good Capt. for a new Co. Look at Kellogg of our own state. It is no better than manslaughter to send men into the field with such a man. No man at the very least ought to have command of a Regt. who has not seen a year of active [service] & studied diligently all the time. There is not more than one in a Regt. as a rule who would be passably qualified in so short a time.

The Col. makes the Regt. If Ellsworth had lived the Fire Zouaves would have been the best Regt. in the army. As it was they were little more than an armed mob. They fought well in one battle [First Bull Run] but never rallied afterward nor would they if they had been victorious. Gen. Richardson or Col. Poe could make a good Regt. out of almost anything. Major Williams would spoil the best Regt. in the service in 3 months.

§ OCTOBER 8   Last night came a terrible storm of rain & wind, wet everything & drove some of the men out of their tents. It is very cold this m'g. Col. Poe gave the 1st Lt. of Co. H a sound berating this m'g because he did not have the men in better shape at roll call. I saw him coming in time to put mine in good shape. They think it awful to be made to stand around as they do of late. It is in reality easier & better for them in all respects aside from its benefits in a military point of view. If our Capt. had have stayed till this time he would have been lifted quite off his feet if he had not moved more circumspectly.

I nearly laughed myself to death last night to hear Corpl. Galpin of Co. C. He is a fellow with large eyes, large mouth, full of gab, impudence & nonsense, always trying to shirk his guard duty & generally by means of family relations or pretended good breeding & abundant brass succeeding. There is some real wit about him & on the whole there is many a worse fellow in camp than Corpl. Galpin. We chanced to speak of Col. Poe while Galpin was by. Said he "did you ever notice that Col.? He is the most wicked looking man I ever saw when you get close to him. My God there is not one spark of human feeling or sympathy about him. If you could have seen how he looked at me the other morning you never would have liked him again." All of which & much more was told with a long face & great solemnity of manner.

We know Galpin so well that both of us guessed at once what the trouble was. The truth of the matter was that Galpin left his guard duty at 10 P.M., went to his tent & slept well after 7 next m'g. He swore upon honor that he was so sick he could not stand on his feet. The Col. excused him but informed him in very decided terms that he knew all about him & that if he was ever absent in that way again he would reduce him to the ranks.

Benson is on guard to day for the first time in his life. Capt. Dillman is officer of the day. Both are wonderfully alert for fear the Col. will be after them. Dillman comes out abt every hour & inquires of Benson what he has done, seen & heard since last visit: whether the Col. has been around &c &c. The Col. has gone to town & Benson is very much afraid that he will come into camp from the back side or some other unusual way & find something amiss. He has a man posted well down the road to watch for him & give timely notice.

Our Col. as well as the whole Regt. are in remarkable good health. If you except about 6 professional invalids who will soon be discharged there is hardly a sick man in our Co. The balance have become thoroughly acclimated to camp life.

§ OCTOBER 9 I waked up this m'g with the painful impression that I had slept till after roll call. I scrabled on my shoes without stockings & pulled on my overcoat without stopping to button my pants & rushed out expecting to see the Col. "clothed in thunder"* because no officers were present at roll call. I was happy to find that the Orderly was just falling the men in instead of dismissing them. Skirmish drill in the forenoon. The weather duced cold all day.

It costs terribly to keep house. I shall be disposed to quit it very soon. We have too many boarders. Handy comes around to dine with us abt twice a day. He is such good military authority & so full of fun & jokes that we can not demur to his presence. Gibson has been on a visit boarding with us for a week. The ghostly Prentice is still hovering around, all of whom together with Benson, self & servant eat a large amt of provisions during the week. We could get fair board for $3.50 per week at a neighboring house. It has cost us thus far not less than $6.00 per week.

I have to go on fatigue duty to morrow. There seems no end of building forts. There are already some 30 or 40 around Wash-

---

* Job 39:19.

ington & 4 new ones have just been commenced. We have done a large share of the work on 4 of them besides doing near 1000 acres chopping. To day we broke ground for a fifth one.

§ OCTOBER 10 The weather continues cold & rainy. We have no fire in our tents & have to resort to an increase of clothing to keep warm. We had a very interesting skirmish drill to day. Three Co's. were out together, drilled with the cavalry a part of the time. They & the skirmishers drill together every day.

There was one of the 37th put in the guard house last night. He sent for his Capt. who came. Said he "Capt. O'Connor help me out of the guard house." "No I'll not do it" said Capt. O'Connor. "Go to h--l you d----d lousy son of a b----" replied the prisoner. Capt. O'C. left. The prisoner turned to the Corpl. of the Guard who was standing near & said "Corpl. you must excuse me. I wouldn't have talked to him in that way only he's my brother."

I have been reading the Atlantic. I shot at the mark this P.M. with my revolver. At 10 paces I put one ball in the size of a dollar, another within 2 inches, the other 4 varied from 4 to 7 inches. This is the first shooting I ever did with a pistol & expect to do better after a little. I have one of Colt's best Navy revolvers. It will shoot accurately 20 rods & at that distance throw a ball through a two inch plank. It weighs about 4 lbs & Capt. May of whom I bought it would not carry it because it was so heavy. He would have thrown it away coming from Bull Run if he had not found a man to carry it for him. I know very little about swords but I think I can hold my own on shooting.

§ OCTOBER 11 We had a skirmish drill A.M. & afterwards divided 2 Co's. into platoons & had a battalion drill on our own hook. Orders came at 7 P.M. to move at 8 A.M. to morrow.

I have always liked this camp & have become so used to seeing the morning sun reflected from the white walls of the Capitol, the public buildings & the straight handsome shaft of Washington's Monument, the many tasty brown spires of the Smithsonian, the tall black chimneys of the Navy Yard & the Potomac which at a distance is a pretty stream that I shall miss them. Not less familiar is the sight of some dozen forts & batteries nearby, or of our neighbor Johnson's flock of 8 or 10 little contraband blackbirds all of a size & always in a huddle when outdoors. Bare headed, half naked, half human in looks they point clearly to Va.'s chief source of wealth.

Benson would insist to day on making a bedstead, to wit, on driving some crotches in the ground & laying some poles & boards thereon. I reluctantly helped to do this but when I found that he was on a general cleaning up spree I bolted flatly & went off & read in the Atlantic, "Concerning people of whom more might have been made," by the Country Parson. That writer has beyond all others a faculty of getting hold of the secret thoughts & feelings of men. "Oh the unutterable sadness of the thought of what might have been,"* yes & of the unutterable gladness also.

To morrow we move again our wandering home. I would not be surprised if we saw fighting soon. Four Regts. of Cavalry & a drove of fat cattle a mile long passed us to day on the advance. I always feel sad at the approach of battle but at the same time there is an impulse, I know not what, which drives me on with ever increasing eagerness as the hour approaches. Sadness is easily concealed by light jests & reckless remarks & I have quite too much pride to tell anyone of its existence. It was thus when I enlisted. I hated to go yet nothing could have prevented my going at the first call. It would seem as if there were some impulse which I am always striving against yet always obeying at its first call.

§ OCTOBER 12 There was a terrible storm of wind & rain last night which nearly upset our tent. Reveille beat at 5 A.M. & we had breakfast before daylight. The m'g was cold & clear. All the effects, except the arms, of our Co. (95 men) were packed in 2 wagons & promptly at 8 A.M. we started by the river road via Alexandria for our present camp.

The Mass. 14th came down to the road & gave 3 cheers for each Co. as it passed & its band was ready to give us a farewell salute. The roads were pretty muddy but the air was so cool & fine the march was very pleasant. The country is very fine. There are many interesting points both in view of the scenery & of the historic associations. Our band or that of the Mich. 3d played us lively tunes all the way. The men had nothing but their guns to carry &

---

* Haydon appears here to be paraphrasing Whittier in "Maud Muller": "For of all sad words of tongue or pen, / The saddest are these: 'It might have been!' "

in the midst of so many new things & the jokes, story telling &c the journey was made almost before we were aware of it.

We passed through Alexandria to the tune "In Dixie's land I'm bound to travel." It is a quaint, old looking place but some parts of it possess considerable beauty. The ladies were out in goodly numbers waving their hkfs. as they always are. I know not whether it is because they are so patriotic (I guess it must be) or because they are so fond of soldiers or are simply attracted by the novelty of the thing & speak fair to all while present. Some of them I am sure were handsome, or at least I know they looked so to me. Anything that wears petticoats (& hoops) looks pretty well to a soldier who has been in this respect for a long time fasting.

The Mich. 5th & N.Y. 37th came down from Munson's Hill & have joined us here. I am sorry the Mass. 14th could not have remained with us. We agreed remarkably well. The Mass. 1st did not like us. They would never tell why but I suppose they were mad at Gen. Richardson abt something. I dont believe there was ever a poor Regt. went out of Mass.

§ OCTOBER 13 A clear, bright cold Sunday. I am on guard. There is another Lt. with me & we do not have a very serious time. The 37th held mass this m'g & every man in the Regt. not on duty was out. All knelt down in a huddle bare headed for more than an hour.

§ OCTOBER 14 There was a sharp frost last night & men on guard slept but little. I was up till 1 A.M. & had a very fine time for star gazing. We came off guard at 8½ & went on battalion drill at 9. It was one of Major Williams' characteristic drills. He marched us a mile & a half onto the top of a high hill where we went through all manner of movements many of which no one ever heard of before. It was well worth the journey however to have so fine a view of the country. We could see Alexandria, Washington, some 10 miles of the river, Munson's Hill and the camps of 45 Regts., some of which were more than 10 miles off. Washington is abt 9 miles, Alexandria abt 3. We are near the river between Alexandria & Mt. Vernon.

Benson is on picket for 2 days & I am acting Capt. I would like right well to go to bed but must stay up till 9 to report the Co. I had my first experience in command of a Co. on battalion drill to day. All went in a satisfactory manner. Two Corpls. were reduced to the ranks to day for neglect of duty.

We have mail but twice a week here & no one is allowed to go to Washington. We can purchase all necessaries in Alexandria which place by the way used to be a great slave market. Niggers are so thick there now that one can hardly get through the streets but there is very little sale for them.

§ OCTOBER 15 A very pleasant quiet day. Benson returned from picket abt noon. He was highly delighted with the place — it is near Mt. Vernon. I am going on picket somewhere to morrow. All the Regt. except the pickets have to march at daylight for some place unknown with one day's rations.

Sid Prentice says to Benson just now "Come Benson direct an envelope for me to my sister." "Well where is it?" "I dont know" says Prentice, "I haven't any." It struck me that it was an ingenious way of asking for it. We have not a suitable supply of rations for to morrow (that is B & self). "We are just so d----d careless" as Sergt. Stevenson said abt his brother in law when he s--t his breeches.

§ OCTOBER 16 Capt. Handy, Benson & I went late last night to the sutler of the 37th & procured a large stock of provisions for to day. At half past three this m'g reveille was sounded. We of course all sprang out & set abt getting ready. The roll had just been called & the cooking of breakfast commenced when the order to march was countermanded. This remanded me to picket duty again. We were to have gone out into the country abt 8 miles to carry off some hay. We marched at 7 for picket duty abt 4 miles in a south west direction. Mt. Vernon can be seen in the distance.

Our Capts. (Dillman's) head quarters are at the home of Col. Mason of the rebel army. The Col.'s young wife, slaves & property in general are in the hands of the Yankees. The lady does not seem in any very great tribulation. I have no doubt she receives many kind attentions & is well cared for. The Col. has a very pretty place. Like most houses in this country the Col.'s is abt ½ mile from the road. It is a very old estate. Some grave stones in the dooryard bear date 1771. There is none of that new, fresh, brisk business look which we see at home. There is an old look abt everything which is almost allied to decay. I presume it is so to some extent in all old settled countries. More beautiful springs of water, natural groves, distant scenery can hardly be found. The house would be called shabby in the North. It is so on the outside but is well furnished within. There is the usual amt of little curly wool heads, all of a size as usual. There must have been a wonderfully prolific season some 10 years since. The crops are to be good or at least the corn. The timber is of alternate belts of oak & chestnut and of scrub pine & cedar.

There is no enemy near here. We are posted to cut off communication & to give timely notice of any advance. It is pretty dull business. One old lady with her colored servant were the only persons seen during the day. There is an interest abt these hills & fields which were once trod by the Father of his Country which is felt in no other place. His footsteps have sanctified the ground on which he trod. There is not a half hour in the day that I do not have his presence associated with the surrounding scenery. I hope to visit Mr. Vernon but it is very doubtful whether I can. It would do us all good to spend an hour at the grave of Washington in tears over the fate of our country.

§ OCTOBER 17 The night was very quiet. There has been heavy firing down the river at times for 2 days. There were several very heavy guns abt midnight. I slept under a large chestnut log which hung on the stump. I filled upon the back side with fine bushes & in front also except a hole large enough to crawl in. I never had a better sleep.

A man from Co. K told me this m'g that he would see me d----d sooner than go on guard when I told him to. I had him on the road to the guard house before the words were fairly out of his mouth. I dont stand any such talk as that. We set out for home abt 9 A.M. I beat the men shooting at 15 rods they using muskets & minie rifles & I my revolver. When we arrived at camp [at Hunting Creek] I found the tent admirably arranged by Benson & a good allowance of oysters ready for dinner. Oysters are plenty here at 50 cts. per bushel in the shell or 40 cts. per qt.

§ OCTOBER 18 There was a heavy shower last night. I go on fatigue duty to day.

§ OCTOBER 19 Abt 2 P.M. yesterday while on fatigue an order came for Co's. A & K to return to camp for an expedition half an hour later, for three other Co's, soon after for all of us. This was hailed with joy, anything to get rid of work. Soldiers would rather march all day than shovel an hour. We were soon ready in light order with rations for one day. We marched off briskly at 4 P.M.

down the river on the Richmond road. The day was clear & bright but exceedingly hot & muggy.

We marched with few halts till 8½ P.M. The moon was nearly full and a pleasanter time could not have been asked but for the road which was very muddy in places. The Mich. 3d was in our rear & between us & them 2 6 pdr. rifled cannon & a 12 pdr. howitzer. We had gone 10 miles when we halted. We could here see fires off to our right which were supposed to be those of the enemies' pickets. News came in from the scouts that there was a considerable body of the rebel cavalry in our rear & also that there was a large camp in front. The fences on both sides of the road were immediately torn down, the artillery moved out into the open fields & everything made ready for action. After ½ hour having seen & done all we came for we faced abt & started for home.

Whether there was any camp in front nearby I do not know but it is certain that their scouts were in our rear in considerable numbers. We reached camp at 1 very muddy & pretty tired by our march of 20 miles. Benson went to the city yesterday & did not return in time to go with us.

I had a good deal of trouble coming back to keep the men in their places. Some were determined to go ahead & others determined or unable to keep up. There were but 2 Sergts. along & they were so tired that they did nothing. I succeeded in keeping them from going ahead of the Co. but could not prevent some of them from falling behind. Eight fell out & slept by the roadside & some have not yet returned. I have reported them to the Col. I feel none the worse for my journey this morning. It rains quite hard. There is heavy cannonading down the river while I am writing. It is quite possible that we may be needed in that direction soon.*

§ OCTOBER 20 Sunday. The men came out to Inspection looking finely this m'g. Col. Poe & Genl. Richardson both said that there was only one Co. in the Regt. which looked as well as ours & none which looked better. I inspected the guns of the whole rear rank without soiling white gloves. Gen. R. called Capt. Handy aside

---

* The cannonading Haydon reports in these days was between the Federal navy and Confederate batteries along the lower Potomac.

after we got through and says "Adjutant, what are the names of these new Lieuts. of Co. I?" The rest I did not hear. Benson & I were not a little gratified at the result and the men were equally well pleased. They begin to have a soldierly pride about their appearance & the condition of their arms. If the Capt. will only stay away we shall soon have them well trained.

Benson & I took dinner & supper with Lt. Eldred of Co. K. We had stewed oysters for dinner & fried ones for supper after which we told so many stories that I laughed myself nearly to death. On the whole we did not pass an unpleasant day. I was well pleased also that we could have a social day without any one getting drunk or even drinking anything.

I feel the want every day of a military education. What a fortunate thing it is for me that Col. Poe came into this Regt. I am learning rapidly under him. I shall get knowledge enough if he remains for some time so that I can obtain a commission in the regular army if I desire. I would not like to leave the Mich. 2d so long as that remains in the field.

A man can fight better if he has nothing else to live for. Let fighting become a sort of necessity of his existence. One who has hopes beyond the war, labors to perform & dear friends to greet will sometimes be struck with the thought "how much I should hate to die to day"; "how great a loss it would be to me & to others." This will be forgotten in an instant when the rush comes, but when one has only to stand still and wait, the thought is sometimes almost sickening. Therefore it is that the genuine soldier should have no thought or hope beyond success on the battlefield.

There is one view in which the thoughts of home, friends & the attractions of life are a stimulus. It is when one can conceive that all these are dependent on the success of the battle. There is much of that feeling in the present war. But after all I think that in most cases pride sustains men at the beginning of the contest which is soon followed by excitement & rage which so completely occupies the mind that there is no chance for anything else.

§ OCTOBER 21 A cold windy day preparing for a long rain I think. We are well prepared for it. The camp has been well cleaned & ditched to day. We have a good stock of provisions on hand & if we are not ordered out on duty can pass a storm very satisfactorily. I have to act on Court Martial to morrow.

§ OCTOBER 22 has been a cold rainy day. I had to take out a

party of 25 men to chop wood for cooking. I was out only about an hour. I went out after dinner to fire my pistol & slid down a long hill on my ass with my best trousers on. As if that were not bad enough on the pants, I went out after dark & ran into a hole full of dirty water up to my knees. I must have some boots. These shoes are a very fine thing in fair weather but when the water is more than 3 inches deep they are of no account.

Benson & I have been examining accts. We find that it has cost us $27 to live 22 days besides paying $15 per month to a servant. We conclude that this will not do. We have accordingly made an agreement with the servt. to furnish the eatables for $7 per week. This improves matters a little but Benson feels very economical to night & swears that the servt. must be paid less or nothing. He is from the Co. & is now getting pay & clothes as a soldier besides his board & $15 per month from us. I agree that he must work for less or quit. Benson declares to night that he will spend no more than $25 per month. If he gets along with less than $75 he will do better than I expect. I do not believe I can do with less than $50 per month, which will leave a balance of $55.50. We shall know better after awhile about all these things.

Major Underwood was in but a short time since very drunk & very sentimental. It's lamentable that a man of his ability should be the slave of drink. He is certain to go back into the ranks within 6 months if he does not stop drinking. Col. Poe is a very polite obliging man to any one who minds his business and keeps his place but those who do not, think him worse than the general adversary of mankind. He never has lectured me but once & then only in a mild form. It is providential however for the most part or was at first. I happened to find out early that there was a storm coming & have since kept my eyes open when he is around. Since the time Gen. Richardson took me by the arm at Cantonment Blair I have been wonderfully circumspect in his presence.

The Court Martial intended for to day was deferred till to morrow.

§ OCTOBER 23 On Court Martial as Judge Advocate. Tried two cases. Sent one chap 20 days hard labor & a fine of $13 for swearing at a Corpl. Another for 10 days hard labor for not standing at attention on Dress Parade. I have been trying to make up the record to night but the wind blows the light out every 10 minutes. It is deuced cold.

§ OCTOBER 24 Court Martial again but as it saved me from going on picket I am satisfied. We gave the man from Co. H whom I arrested the other day 20 days confinement at hard labor. If Col. Poe had been on the Court he would not have escaped less $50 pay & 3 months.

The men have hereafter to drill every day with all their things on, i.e., in heavy marching order. This looks like moving. I think we shall leave here soon. There is a grand review to morrow of 20 Regts. The Mich. 2d takes the post of honor. The right of the line. Gen. Richardson takes good care to look well after us.

There is a damnable report in circulation to night that Gen. McClellan is taken prisoner. H--l if that is true: well, I have no words to express my shame, sorrow & indignation. He has often been too careless. I cannot believe any such thing. I supposed our cup of disasters must be full by this time. God knows it has been bitter enough without this. Even the thought of the thing almost paralyzes me. I'll say & do no more till that miserable falsehood is contradicted.

§ OCTOBER 25 The morning was fair. I laughed at myself for ever being troubled at the report of the night. McClellan however is all the time running all over God's creation with only one or two men with him & such a thing is not impossible.

The grand review came off to day. We went down to Washington Valley, in sight of Mt. Vernon where there is a succession of open fields abt 2½ miles broad. Here we formed the line, 13 Regts., 2 batteries & 3 squadrons of Cavalry. Gen. Richardson acting as Major Gen. Marched in review & then marched home again.

It was as usual a very fine sight for lookers on & a great bore to the actors. We were pretty well covered with mud, burrs & dust when we came back. We had no water to drink for near 6 hours. If there had been any chance I should have been tempted to play the game Sid Prentice did one hot day while we were marching through Georgetown. He wanted something to drink awfully but had no means to procure it. Finally he threw himself down on the side of the road pretending to be sun-struck and laid there till they poured abt a pint of whiskey down him, when he slowly recovered & went on.

Gen. Richardson is to be Major General some day if the bullets let him alone. Relating this fact makes me think of one Sid related one night when we were on guard. It happened some time ago when Sid was thought by most people to be a fine, promising young man. Two or three very aristocratic young ladies came from New York to Kalamazoo. Sid was out with them & some others riding on horseback. One of them proposed that they should run a race, which was accordingly done. After some conversation one of the N.Y. ladies turned to Sid and said: "Mr. Prentice did you ever do any leaping?" "Yes: I've done a great deal of that" says Sid. "How many bars did you ever leap?" "Oh . . . bars . . . I never counted them" says Sid. He relates that she never recognized him afterwards.

§ OCTOBER 26 I am in command of the Co. to day & shall be to morrow. Benson is on picket. We have a pretty good thing, Capts. Whipple, Handy & self, in this Court Martial. We are excused from all other duty till the Court is dissolved or we adjourn for at least three [days] at a time. We sent up the record to the Col. for approval this m'g. It suited him so well that he said he should not dissolve the Court at present. We meantime will meet every morning & adjourn till the next. Good by guard, fatigue & picket till Col. dissolves the Court. I have to day made out charges agt two Sergts., a Corpl. & a private of our Co. which will be preferred on Monday. Half this Regt. will go to State Prison in 6 months after they are let loose.

Gen. Richardson has always kept a bodyguard from this Regt. till abt a week ago he came to Col. Poe saying "Col. I guess you'll have to take this bodyguard back. I'm afraid they'll tear my house down if I keep them any longer." They have such a passion for boards to make floors in their tents, for bricks to make ovens, for straw to sleep on, for something to cook in their ovens when built, in fact a passion for everything which is movable. I must say in their behalf that I have never known much wanton destruction of property by them. What they are unable to carry off they generally leave in as good condition as they find it. They will however carry off a good sized house, barn, stack of hay or anything of the kind in an hour if it is near camp & no one happens to see them.

§ OCTOBER 27 Inspection as usual. [Michigan's] Gov. [Austin] Blair present. Col. said that the Co. was in fine condition, had improved very much within a few weeks. Gov. Blair & Gen. Richardson have gone to Mt. Vernon. The day is very fine.

At 1 P.M. 200 men from the 2d & 200 from the 5th [Michigan] had permission to go to Alexandria to church, to a church built by Gen. Washington it is said. They point out the pew in which he used to sit. It is a large square pew different from the others & situated near the centre of the building. The church is brick & looks old on the outside. The inside I think must have been repaired for many parts of it are certainly of modern date. We had a very good sermon by a man old enough to have been an acquaintance of the builder of the church. There is a small graveyard around the church, all the stones which I saw bearing date previous to 1800, one was dated 1772. They are nearly all of a coarse gray color except where covered by moss.

For some reason I did not feel quite as solemn & contemplative as it seems to me the occasion required. I believe I should have felt different if I had left my sword at home. Somehow I could not get the idea out of my head that I was on duty. The church is not generally open. Each Regt. quartered near by is however given an opportunity of attending service there once.

I believe that I saw more than 2000 "niggers" at one time when we were returning. They made it so dark we could hardly see the road. Several of the streets were well paved & there was an abundance of grass growing between the stones. There are some wicked secessionists there. I did want to slash some men whom I saw. There was so strong a look of hatred & contempt abt some of them that I could hardly pass them peaceably.

There were present three Brigadier Gens. & several quite distinguished officers of the navy. I had the satisfaction of seeing Gen. Richardson occupying the right of Gen. Washington's old pew. So far as fighting is concerned he may be as good as many of its former occupants but in point of morals ———. Not by any means that I wish it to be understood that Gen. R. is not a good moral man as the times are nowadays.

§ OCTOBER 28 Cheering news from Mo. & western Va.* The North is alive yet. We shall advance on them soon from here I think. We are fully able to do it if other parts of the army are in as good condition as this.

The men are fairly settled down to soldiering and take things as a matter of course without grumbling as they used to. They are learning the art of soldiering so that they fare much better & make

---

* Union gains at Springfield, Missouri, and at Romney in western Virginia.

themselves more comfortable with the same means. They are full of mischief, still they obey orders as a rule remarkably well & are civil & respectful to their officers. The poor corporals however fare hard. There is but one in our Co. (Johnston) who has any control over his squad when they are in the tent. I am going to have some of them reduced to the ranks if they do not attend to business better.

Sid Prentice swears that he dare not stir in his tent after abt 8 in the evening. He is however seldom there at that time. He says that after they all get in at night they "pass" at least one man "in review" as they term it. This performance consists as near as I can learn in stripping a man & passing him two or three times around the tent all ends uppermost & in no very gentle manner. The tents are pretty large, designed for 20 men & it is no small affair to be "passed in review." They always seek first to get a man from another Regt. or Co. or tent at least, but take one of their own if they cannot do better. They usually lie in wait near the edge of the tent and grab some luckless passer by the legs & pull him in. Sid has a terror of this "passing in review."

§ OCTOBER 29 To day Court Martial was in session. We had up 2 Sergts., a Corpl. & a private from Co. I for being absent without leave. The private got off by means of one of Benson's perennial passes. We have scared the others badly & shall punish them a little.

Lt. Col. Larnerd says that Capt. May let the Co. run wild so long that they were pretty much disorganized. This is true. After we left Detroit there was no order or organization. It took the Sergts. ½ hour to get the men out for roll call in the m'g & they would have to go into every tent at that. They would then stand in all manner of shapes & places, in not less than 5 or 6 ranks. It would be a hard case to get them still enough to call the roll. There was never a commissioned officer present & not more than ½ the privates.

If they are not out and in ranks now & without being called upon either within 30 minutes after the drum stops beating they are put on extra guard or sent on some extra labor. They have to stand at attention in ranks well dressed & preserve the most perfect silence.

§ OCTOBER 30 Brigade drill to day. Major Williams spoiled everything. Col. Poe was gone. The Major reads so many books all at the same time that he really knows hardly anything for certain. Gen. Richardson was after him to day. "Now Major Williams, this is too bad. G-d d--n you Sir, if you ever do such a thing again I'll have you Court Martialed." So said the Genl. when Major spoiled one of his movements. No one could doubt who saw him that he meant all he said. He looked blacker than a thunder cloud & savage enough to eat the Major up at about one mouthful.

Gen. R. cannot give up the idea that he could have carried Manassas on the 18th of July. I heard him say yesterday that with the loss of 300 men he could have cleared the place and been in Richmond two months ago. I am sometimes strongly inclined to believe it. They were terribly frightened on that day and I have little doubt that a spirited attack from our brigade together with the supposition that it was supported by a large force near at hand would have driven them headlong & ended the war by this time. The golden opportunity was lost, hence Bull Run, Springfield, Lexington & God knows how many valuable lives and certainly not less than $500,000,000 are lost.

§ OCTOBER 31 Inspection & muster. We were out nearly all day and without dinner. We have a first rate fireplace in our tent which keeps us very comfortable. We dig a hole in the ground and run out an underground chimney. Gen. Richardson has been instructing us. He lived for 14 years in tents all the time.

I was talking to night with one of [William] Walker's filibusters. He was with him abt 5 months till he got a chance to desert. He got on board a steamer and was trying to work his way home as a coal heaver. The passengers took pity on him & paid his passage or he would never have seen the Mich. 2d. He had $400 in Nicaraguan scrip but could not get a penny for it. He came off in good health which he attributed to eating no meat & drinking no liquor. Col. Kerrigan & Billy Wilson were there at the same time.

Benson & Billy Mack have been trying to make the pay rolls. After making them over twice they are abt half right. Col. Poe has promised to shoot the first man he sees stealing from the inhabitants. I have little doubt that he will do it. The men believe it. He is the best looking man in the service at a short distance off. He does not look so well near by. He looks coarse and rather green when you are near him. He has a very piercing almost wicked looking eye. He is I should think about 26 years of age. He dresses in full, rich uniform. He was out to day with a $40 hat & $75 epaulettes. He & Gen. Richardson have both very pretty young wives who come out to Dress Parade in fair weather. It is very gratifying to look at them even at a distance.

I was weighed to night & balanced 142 lbs. being 6 lbs. more than I ever weighed before.

§ NOVEMBER 1, 1861 I went to Mt. Vernon. I am not going to try to tell how I felt or what I thought. I spent abt 3 hrs there. I went through the house, saw the rooms, the fireplaces, the pictures, musical instruments, much of the furniture, and many of the ornaments in the same places where Washington left them. There was his compass which he used in surveying & the great key of the Bastille given him by La Fayette who said he knew no other person who could so safely be trusted with an instrument which had so long aided the hand of oppression.

I went through the garden, looked at the plants & trees planted & cared for by the hand of Washington. There was a Century plant which had been growing for 60 yrs and had yet 40 yrs to tarry ere its first and only blossom. There were oranges, lemons, pomegranates & ripe figs hanging on the trees & also a fine variety of tropical plants & flowers. There was the summer house from which you have a fair view of the river for 7 miles above & 9 miles below. The river is very beautiful at this place. It is a mile & a quarter wide, free from weeds & with high & handsomely wooded banks.

The new vault in which the remains of Washington & his wife rest is abt 10 rods from the river. They are contained in 2 large stone coffins which are placed in a large arch in front of which is only a high iron railing. The vault is grown over with vines. The trees & ground around are still in the state of nature. Near the vault are the graves of a few of the family and what is very remarkable but in strict keeping with the character of Washington the inscriptions on the tomb stones were temperate & sensible. I remained here an hour, picked up 3 or 4 leaves which had fallen from the trees overhanging the grave & went again on my way.

No American can stand by the grave of Washington at any time but with hushed breath & a soul filled with emotion. Even as I gazed on the last abode of the greatest of men, on the holiest spot on American soil the sacred silence of the place was broken by the sound of the enemies' cannon. This is no time for words. We have an enemy before us which respects nothing that is good; venerates nothing that is holy; hesitates at nothing which is damnable. Till that enemy is humbled or annihilated American youth should know no pursuit but arms, American age & American women no aim but to support and cheer them. Are there hopes of an honorable future, are home & friends dear, hath beauty its charms, all these are the reward of victory. The loss of these is an inadequate punishment for any defeat short of death.

We need more energy & tenacity. With a little more dogged determination never to give up even if beaten we might have kept the field for an hour longer at Manassas & the day would have been ours & rebellion would have been crushed. In that hour the reserve of half a dozen fresh Regts. could have gone to the aid of the gallant but exhausted right wing. We could have fallen on their centre with 4 fresh Regts. while [Col. Thomas A.] Davies could have reached their right which there is little doubt might have been carried if the enemy had been vigorously pushed elsewhere so that they could spare no men to reinforce it. Even if this had not been done we could have stopped at Centreville in a position so strong that the enemy would not have dared to attack us. We could have renewed the conflict next day with 20,000 fresh men. It is time that soldiers realized that their best means of safety is in the vigor of their attack & the obstinacy of their defence. Of course I do not mean by this a bullhead obstinacy which leads men to rush at everything they see regardless of consequences.

§ NOVEMBER 2 It commenced raining last night abt dark & by twelve midnight it blew terribly on the tents, making so much noise that it was impossible to sleep. Our tent is new & of the heaviest ship duck. It did not blow over or leak. The rain striking against sounded like shot falling on a floor. The "fly" would flap down agt the main front every few seconds with a noise as loud as a gun but not so sharp. The rain & wind continued steadily till dark to day. The rain still continues but the wind has abated.

The tents are nearly all old. Some of them have blown down entirely & many others have split into ribbons. Not more than half of them are inhabitable. The men have scattered in all directions where shelter can be found. The wind is from the East & the water is driven into the bay below so that it has raised it here more than 3 feet in the river. It is over the top of the bridges across the creek to Alexandria. A boy & horse were drowned in attempting to cross one of them this afternoon.

I have fears for the great naval expedition.* The loss of that at this time would be a terrible blow. It was almost impossible to stand on the open bluffs near the river. The wind took one of the Chaplain's tents fairly out of the ropes & carried it more than 30 rods. Although ours did not leak the water blew under it & through the sides & in at one place or another till it was pretty wet. It was impossible to have a fire. The wind would blow even the wood out of the fireplace.

I saw abt noon yesterday that there was going to be a storm. The air was not misty nor smoky but seemed to thicken gradually. At 4 P.M. there were no clouds in sight but the whole sky was of a dim dirty color abt half way between yellow & brown. At sundown it had thickened up so that it [was] dark almost immediately & it began to rain soon after but did not blow much till some 4 hours later. The weather is warm. Such storms are common here at this time of year. They are made upon the Atlantic.

Harry Hopkins of our Co. died night before last & I went off to Mt. Vernon without knowing it. He had not done a month of duty since he enlisted. It was the grossest injustice to him & to the country to allow such a man to enlist. I knew the moment I saw him that he would give out. He might perhaps have held out for 5 or 6 years at home but it is a matter of surprise to me that he had lived here so long. He had no constitution or strength. I think he had will & courage enough to have made a good soldier. [Across this entry Haydon later wrote, "This is a mistake so far as his being dead & buried is concerned but I presume it will be true before long if his discharge does not come." He afterward noted that Harrison Hopkins was discharged on November 7, "cause permanent dilapidation."]

§ November 3 A fair day. The men had their things out early to dry in the sun & by fires & did their best to repair the damages of yesterday. Gen. Richardson's urgent letter of yesterday brought [Michigan's] Senator [Zachariah] Chandler over here early this m'g. Gen. R. took him around & exhibited to him the ragged tents & the old muskets which are our only arms & poured out some very urgent & emphatic complaints.

---

* A joint army-navy expedition directed at Port Royal, South Carolina. A transport and a warship were sunk in the storm.

Gen. R. always very attentive to his pet 2d is more than usually so at present. At brigade drill the other day owing to a misunderstanding the Regt. did not come onto line exactly where it ought. Gen. was impatient & ordered us to abt face & march back where we started from. We did so & when we got there he wheeled & twisted us into such shape that we hardly knew which way to go or what to do next. "Now see if you can get onto the line as you ought to," said he & rode off & left us. We got onto the line after a while but not till all the other Regts. were on there & laughing at us, disgraced for the day.

He blowed Major Williams who was highly indignant & Lt. Col. Larnerd likewise. They made bitter complaint of all sorts but the Gen. did not seem troubled in the least. Till finally Col. Larnerd who being a lawyer is pretty full of expedients told the Gen. how much the 2d thought of him & how they would willingly follow him to death &c & withal how bad they felt that he should disgrace them in that way before the other Regts. There was a great deal of truth as well as some fiction in all this. "Well, well: I dont know but I was a little too fast. Col. I'm sorry I did that." The Gen.'s eyes 'tis said came near getting a little watery over the matter. He at once declared that the 2d must have new guns & new tents as soon as they could be had. Last night he sent down two gallons of whiskey to each Co. to keep them from taking cold & went himself to look up barns for those to sleep in whose tents were blown down.

§ NOVEMBER 4   Was a very quiet day with little interest.

§ NOVEMBER 5   After breakfast I went out with Lieut. Eldred & another officer whom I do not know & shot at the mark with pistols. I beat them badly, put 3 shots inside their best, drove the centre once at 20 paces. Taking all the shots together however my shooting was nothing extra. I never till to day fired a shot with it which would have missed a man at 20 paces. One shot to day might have missed at that distance.

The Court Martial has finished its business & will be dissolved to morrow. Sergt. Whiting forfeits $10 of his pay for going [to] Mt. Vernon, Sergt. Mason $6 for the same offence, Corpl. Mack $4 for staying away longer than his pass allowed. Col. Poe was determined at first that they should all be reduced to the ranks but finally at our urgent request consented to spare them this time.

The news came to night that Ft. Sumpter was retaken & that Gen. [William S.] Rosecrans had defeated the rebels at Gauley Bridge. There was one prolonged cheer went up from three miles below Alexandria to the Chain bridge. Hail Columbia, Star Spangled Banner & Yankee Doodle could have been heard from 50 Regts. at least. I hope it may be true as to Charleston. I have however been soldiering long enough already to be careful abt believing first reports. I hope if they have taken it that they will not leave one stone upon another. There is no place that needs purification so much as this mother of nullification, secession & treason.*

§ NOVEMBER 6 Brigade drill went off well. Col. Poe said he was entirely satisfied and that there was not a Regt. in the army that could beat us drilling when we attended to our business.

§ NOVEMBER 7 Court Martial which came near being dissolved was reanimated & continued in session this m'g. Fined one man $6.50 and 20 days hard labor for telling a Sergt. to "kiss his ---" &c and other disrespectful language. I was detailed for officer of the guard to morrow but a new case came for the Court Martial & I go clear of guard for another day.

A sentinel of the 63d Penn. Regt. shot two of his own Co. last night at one shot. They had been outside & were trying to creep in unobserved.

The Col. got after me a little to day. They divided the Regt. in 8 Co's. because it was so small. This brought me down among some d----d idiots of Co. E. I happened to turn my eyes off them for a moment & one of them was gaping in all directions. Col. Poe, unobserved by me, was passing along the rear. His quick eye instantly perceived the puddinghead staring around. He tapped me on the shoulder & asked whether "if I was to exert myself I could not keep that man's head to the front." I touched my cap with great deference & replied Yes Sir. That man did not catch it much after that.

§ NOVEMBER 8 Court Martial again to day. I went to Alexandria after dinner. I walked around the city a little. I saw the building in which Washington was made a Mason. I saw also the steam

---

* There was an engagement at Gauley Bridge in western Virginia, but the retaking of Fort Sumter and the capture of Charleston was a false rumor.

frigate Pensacola (24 guns) all new & bright just from the yard. She is gay. The city is dull & shamefully dirty.

§ NOVEMBER 9 Just now I heard some man down at the tents repeating some [of] Capt. May's extravagant expressions at Bull Run. One can judge how ludicrous they must have been to be remembered so long by soldiers.

I can see him now with both arms stretched out, pistol in one & his sword in the other screaming "I will be obeyed," "Now or never," "I'll blow you through if you do not mind" and the men all gaping at him motionless with amazement. Sid Prentice swears that the Capt.'s actions scared him worse than all the "Secesh" he saw. He thought as he says "h--l must be out 'for noon" somewhere or the Capt. would not make such a fuss. The only trouble was the Capt. did not know what orders to give and when he gave one he would word it so incorrectly that they did not know what he meant. There never was any men more willing to obey orders if they could have heard any to obey. If there had been no other Co's. there I believe the Capt. would have scared ours out of their wits.

It is a cold rainy night but the wind does not blow & the tent is warm & comfortable. Benson is on guard & has to stay outdoors all night. I am sorry for the boy. Law does even a soldier some good for by means of what little I know I have escaped all these rainy nights for some three weeks. I have everything as comfortable as one could wish. I have a new work on field fortifications, the Atlantic & one of Scott's novels for reading matter & have just partaken of a good supper of oysters & crackers, that being about as cheap living as the country affords. Soldiering under these circumstances is nice, very nice business. When a man is out all day in the rain & lies down on the ground at night without a dry thread on him & only one blanket to cover him it is different in some respects. Still one feels glad enough when the sun comes out warm the next day to make it all up.

I do not often lose my temper but yesterday morning I went out to look for an orderly for the Court Martial and a meddlesome impudent chap from Co. K came after me & kept crowding & pushing against me & talking all the time some nonsense. I had had about enough of his foolery on other occasions. I told him twice that I wished he would keep away but he paid no attention.

Finding that he paid no heed to what I said to him & not caring to be troubled longer I turned suddenly round & gave him a slap on the side of the head which brought him down on to his hands & knees. He has not troubled me since.

§ NOVEMBER 11 I amused myself a little at Benson's expense to night. 1st Lieut. of Co. D had just been excused from the service of the United States because he could not pass examination.* This terrified Benson a little. In the evening I asked him a series of questions on tactics, many of which never had any answers and therefore could not very well be answered. He did not know this and was greatly concerned abt his inability to answer. He would scratch his head, strike the table with his fist, and swear often that he would study out these moves if it killed him. Occasionally I would tell him an answer which was usually as ficticious as the question.

Benson is a man of considerable resolution & self reliance yet a moderate influence constantly pulling in the same direction but never hard enough to attract his attention will draw him almost anywhere. I at first thought that I would let him go his own way & break at the examination as he would be pretty sure to do, but on further consideration I believe it will be better to have him pass pretty well & get the Capt.'s place which will soon be vacant. I should then probably be 1st Lieut. If he were to break, perhaps I should be no more than 1st Lieut., with a worse Capt. It is not impossible that I might pass over him to a Capt.'s place now but I do not care to try, at least not at present.

§ NOVEMBER 12 I kept up the catechism of Benson last night till after ten, later than I usually sit up, and was well paid for it. At 12½ A.M. when I was just in the sweetest of slumbers & dreams the bugle at the Gen.'s headquarters began to sound the assembly & immediately every bugle & drum in the division was in use. I was out of bed in quick time. Major Williams just then came around & ordered us all to be ready to march at 3 A.M. to attack the enemy at Pohick Church. By which he evidently must have meant that we would attack them if we could find them which proved no easy matter.

---

* McClellan had established military boards to examine officers' qualifications in the Army of the Potomac.

Promptly at 3 A.M. we were formed in line & ready for march in light order with one day's rations. The Mich. 2d or Gen. Richardson's "Pet Lambs," as some of the Regts. call us were as usual in front. It was a fine cool starlight m'g, roads somewhat muddy but not very bad travelling. All things considered it was a very fine time to march & by daylight we had reached our further pickets who were out abt six miles. About ten miles out we forded the Accotink Creek 5 times where it was abt knee deep & most d----d cold. At 8½ A.M. we reached the church 12 miles out.

The enemy had *just* been there but were all out of sight then. There were 8 Regts. of us & with 18 cannon the line was immediately formed & scouts & skirmishers sent out in all directions. We could see the enemy dodging around on some hills off a mile & half but did not dare to go for them till there was time to look into the woods & hollows round about.

The skirmishers went out with a will in all directions but could get sight of nothing save an occasional man all of whom except one ran so fast that they could neither catch or shoot them. One young "Secesh" got lost among the hills, ran the wrong way, and in consequence came back to camp with us. There were some scattering shots fired at our men but no one was hurt. The cavalry ran afoul of a party who fired on them from the woods & killed three & wounded one. Two or three others it is supposed were taken prisoners. We stayed at the church till after 3 P.M. when we set out for home where we arrived a little after 8 P.M. We marched abt 25 miles in all. Some of the Regts. marched as high as 32 miles. Each man carrying abt 4 lbs. ammunition, a day's rations, a blanket & canteen.

Pohick Church is a brick building built in 1773. Gen. Washington contributed to building it & was a frequent attendant. It has a very ancient look & one would suppose that it might be sacred enough to be secure. I have long known that the Mich. 2d had no fear or reverence as a general thing for God or the places where he is worshipped but I hoped that the memory of Gen. Washington might protect almost anything with which it was associated. I believe our soldiers would have torn the church down in 2 days. They were all over it in less than 10 minutes tearing off the ornaments, splitting the wood work of the pews, knocking the bricks to pieces & everything else they could get at. They wanted pieces to carry away.

I do not believe there is a civilized nation on the earth which has so little appreciation of the beautiful & sacred as ours. In the madness of the French Revolution mobs not one in a hundred of whom could read or write, not a man of them was known to injure a work of art or violate a place sacred by association. A more absolute set of vandals than our men can not be found on the face of the earth. As true as I am living I believe they would steal Washington's coffin if they could get to it. What else can you expect of men who will steal even from an enemy family pictures, daguerreotypes, family bibles, records and such like articles.

We heard the cannonading of what is said to have been a great battle at Falls Church. It was steady & rapid for near ten hours.

§ NOVEMBER 13 I feel none the worse for my journey yesterday. The firing at Falls Church is very heavy this morning. The volleys of musketry can be distinctly heard at the distance of 9 miles. Our men are all in a fever to move for the scene of action. I would like it very much but suppose there is no chance of our getting there. I presume they dare not take us away from here.

9 P.M. the great battle proves to [be] only men shooting at a mark.

§ NOVEMBER 14 Court Martial to day, two men convicted of disobedience of orders & sentenced. Major Underwood was drunk last night. He was in our tent after "taps" telling us a great story about Crego wearing his pants out the night before & losing his suspenders. Asking if we supposed that he could sleep with such a man any longer &c. He went out as he said to find a place to sleep. Not being very clear on points of compass he ran afoul of the sentinel in front of the Quartermaster's tent who immediately called "Corporal of the Guard post No. 4." In about 2 minutes we heard the Corpl. coming with his guard. Major saw them & ran lustily but in passing our tent his foot caught in the ropes & he went down amongst them becoming so tangled up that he could not get out. He screamed and swore stoutly but the Corpl. seized him & took him out. Finding who it was he took him to his tent & advised him to stay there.

§ NOVEMBER 16 I went to Alexandria, bought a pair of long legged boots, looked around awhile & then came home. The wind is very high. It is almost impossible to keep a tent warm or indeed to keep it standing.

Court Martial is dissolved. We have tried eleven cases convicting ten. I am on guard to morrow. There is some prospect of going South on the fleet. I put my name down to night to go. It is rascally cold. I would like to look for warmer weather.

§ NOVEMBER 17 I missed guard to day but go on to morrow. Gen. Richardson is using every means in his power to go South with the fleet. Col. Poe has leave of absence for 2 weeks to try to arrange something abt it. Gen. R. says he "dont know what to do with the 2d while he is gone unless he takes command of it himself." "That d----d Major Williams will spoil it before Col. Poe gets back." "The 2d knows too much for him." It is indeed wonderful how quick the "Pet Lambs" begin to take liberties with the Major. Let him have command for a month & I dont believe he could march them along a straight road. When he is trying to drill them they will begin in ten minutes to sprawl around, lop over to one side, talk & laugh & raise the d---l generally & it is almost impossible for the Co. officers to keep them in their places. In the midst of all this let them hear Col. Poe's voice & they will jump as if they were shot.

§ NOVEMBER 19 I have at 8 P.M. just got quiet. I went on guard yesterday at 8 A.M. & I have been on the jump ever since. The guards have to be trained on the regulations & that keeps one man busy all the time. They have not been so strict heretofore & it seems impossible almost to beat anything into some of the block-heads. Some of the Sergts. and Corpls. are not better than wooden men. I had one first rate new Dutch Corpl. but he talked so funny that the men had to laugh all the time. "Upport Arm" was his word for "Support Arms."

It was too cold at night to think of sleeping & I traveled around most of the time. I had one prisoner who pretended to be sick & I allowed him a little liberty. In fact allowed my good nature to make a d----d fool of me. I was told by the officer of the old guard that he was sick & he brought a paper (which he forged himself) from the Surgeon as it purported saying that he was too sick to be closely confined. As I said I gave him a little liberty & the consequence was that he gave me the slip & I have spent nearly all day trying without success to recover him. I will chain the next prisoner I have to a tree I think & see if I can keep the d----d rascals in that way.

There are few things surer than that I shall be arrested if I do not catch him & it is very probable that I shall be in any case. Major

Williams the dear good soul tried to tell me how to get out of it when he ought to have sent me to my quarters under arrest. If Col. Poe had been here I should have carried my sword to him & told him I came to be put under arrest. My request would have been granted much quicker than made. I was to blame, there is no doubt of it.

The idea of meeting Col. Poe bothered me exceedingly for awhile but I can do it now with a smooth face & touch my cap after it with as much deference as if he had called up to compliment my good behavior. It may however be a little different inside. Major Underwood was released from arrest to night. I do not like to try it very well. Sid Prentice's old lady love is just married & he swears that he will either go into a battle or get drunk within 3 days.

§ NOVEMBER 20 Just as the sun peeped over the Maryland hills this m'g we started out to go to Bailey's Cross Roads to the grand review. Well we went & have returned. We traveled 15 miles & were on our feet 13 hours. I suppose there were about 30,000 troops on the ground & the sight to those who had a fair chance to see it must have been a very fine one. There is an improved plain abt 2 miles long by one broad. All the fences and buildings have been burned off by the soldiers. The field is nearly level & was covered all over with cavalry, artillery & infantry. Major Williams says that there were 45,000 men. I could not see them to very good advantage.

There were a large number of spectators present, President Lincoln & a host of other great men. I never saw Gen. McClellan look so well as he did to day. The men think they have the gayest leader in the universe. He was on his newly imported horse & was dressed in the full uniform of his rank. The country around there looks rather different from what [it] did when we used to lie there in the dirt on picket. We have now a fine fort on Munson's Hill. I am too sleepy & tired to write any more to night.

§ NOVEMBER 21 The grand review must have been exceedingly interesting to the President. Gen. McClellan of course went ahead & the President next. They rode along the lines for abt 4 miles, the Gen. on his new horse sitting up as straight as an arrow, with hat in hand at a full gallop bowing to & waving his hat to each Regt. as he passed. The Regts. presented arms & sent up cheer upon cheer which might have been heard to Manassas.

The President's case was different. His horse had to go at a keen run & then could not get nearer than 4 or 5 rods to the Gen., one hand hold of the bridle, the other convulsively clutched in the mane of his horse which never relaxed its hold except for a moment to crowd his hat further down over his eyes. His long legs were well clasped around the body of his horse, his hair & coat tails horizontal. He looked as though he was determined to go through if it killed him but would be most almighty glad when it was over. I would gladly have given $10 to have been loose so that I could have seen the whole spectacle.

As I stood in the line looking around on the blue masses which covered the field in every direction a very strange thought occurred to me. It was this. What would be the consequence of having as many women collected in that field (providing it were possible) and no men among them. I confess that I was wholly unable to come to any conclusion though I thought of a great many things which might happen. He would be a venturesome man indeed who would dare go into such a crowd alone.

The idea was so very singular that I had to communicate it to several of my comrades. Our discussion of the subject occupied an hour. All were of the opinion that if such were the case they would venture themselves among the throng whether they were to come out alive or not. The ladies are always very kind to soldiers who in turn are willing to throw themselves into their arms on slight provocation & without conditions. God knows I would not fight any longer if it were not for them but such an ocean of love as is supposed above, the eye of mortal man can never hope to behold. If Mohammed be a true prophet we may see such sights some day.

It turns out that there were abt 75,000 men at the review yesterday instead of 30,000.

Six

IN WINTER
QUARTERS

*Concluding that his forces were not sufficiently prepared for a fall or winter
campaign, and preoccupied with his additional responsibilities (since November 1) as general-in-chief of all the Union armies, General McClellan
put the Army of the Potomac into winter quarters. Haydon's 2nd Michigan
took post at what it called Camp Michigan, in the southernmost section of
the lines guarding Washington. To the west, Joseph E. Johnston's Confederate army (also called the Army of the Potomac) was posted at Manassas
Junction and Centreville.*

*Haydon himself was preoccupied with his responsibilities as 2nd lieu-
tenant of Company I, and with his impending promotion to 1st lieutenant,
a post made vacant on December 16 by W. H. Benson's accession to the
captaincy of the company. Haydon, and apparently the rest of Company I
as well, had been greatly relieved by the resignation of Captain Dwight
May. As the year 1861 came to an end, Lieutenant Haydon took increasing
pride in his command accomplishments — "The men," he wrote, "are beginning to be soldiers" — and in his personal adaption to army life.*

* * *

§ NOVEMBER 22, 1861 This has been a pretty quiet day. Battalion drill P.M. & a part of the Co. were paid. Benson & I are both
dead broke, worse than penniless. We shall replenish to morrow.

Benson told me to night how Sid Prentice first got on the downhill road. He was engaged to be married to a girl in Kalamazoo. Benson coaxed her away from him and that was not the half of it. One would hardly think that any great affair for Kalamazoo but Sid took it to heart. Benson soon left her & Prentice would have been glad to take her back but she would not come. Sid took the road downhill & was very near the bottom when he enlisted. Benson is moderately sorry for what he did & has succeeded in keeping Sid straight most of the time since his enlistment. The girl married well abt two weeks since and her father sent Sid information of the fact in a sympathizing & encouraging letter full of moral precepts and good advice. Benson swears that Sid is going to reform permanently but I do not believe a word of it. He might possibly reform morally in part but physically it is out of the question.

§ NOVEMBER 23 We were paid to day. I went to Alexandria after dinner & tried to get some things but could find few that I wanted. 10 men from each Co. with a noncom. officer were allowed to the city to day. The most of them came back pretty tight.

I had the pleasure of seeing the countenance of my old acquaintance Charles Boren, the prisoner who escaped from me some days since. I was much more pleased to see him than he was to see me. I heard yesterday that he was confined in the Central Guard House at Washington. I had him sent for at once. It is no easy matter to escape from here unless you go toward "Secesh" & you want to be very careful in that case or the pickets will blow you through.

Our servt. Noble came home pretty drunk & full of gas. Private Charles Butler whom I sent with the Corpl. after Boren was a little upset, but very solemn, confidential & wise, expressing great fear that some of the boys would get drunk & make fools of themselves.

I do most certainly believe that there will be an advance from here within ten days. Private Clark Conrad went to town on a pass & has not returned. The battalion order making him a Corpl. was written but will now be torn up. If he had behaved himself he would have stood second for a Sergt's. place which will soon be vacant.

§ NOVEMBER 25 Monday m'g. Benson has gone to Washington. 11 men from each Co. have gone to Alexandria. They are buying boots, underclothes &c to keep them safe agt the cold weather. It was cold last night. The ground was frozen hard this m'g & covered with the first snow of the season.

Capt. Handy was in our tent last night & he & I talked over military matters for three hours. He would give $100 to be Capt. of Co. I.* He would make an excellent Capt. for us but would be very much in the way of the two Lieuts. I think we must keep him out. Co. I notwithstanding how they have been bamboozled by their Capt. is & always was composed of the best material of any Co. in the Regt.

Benson & I talked (jokingly) last night of a way in which we could soon get rid of our present Capt. but partly because of the wickedness of the thing & partly because we did not know exactly what the consequence would be, concluded not to try it. It was this — the Co. comes out on Sunday m'g now looking as neat as boys rigged for Sunday school. On the next Sunday m'g after Capt. returns we could bring them out without his knowing the difference looking so that they would be sent off the ground & he into arrest. Benson & I would of course have to be either sick or necessarily absent abt that time. The men would willingly lend themselves to the plan. Col. Poe has a very poor opinion of Capt. May now & one such exhibition as that would make his stay here very short.

Capt. Handy & I were considering last night the very singular turn our affairs had taken since we first met. He was then a clerk in a gift bookstore, I a lawyer's clerk at $5.00 per week. Rather peaceful occupations for soldiers. If Capt. H. had a little more of combativeness, vindictiveness, the genuine spirit & essence of War about him he would make a most excellent officer. He is good now, first quality everywhere except in the battlefield and that is saying a great deal. Such men are of great service in an army. I believe he thinks however that this killing men is very hard business after all. His father is a clergyman & his early education may have some influence on him in this respect, though very little in any other. Benson's father is a Presbyterian Deacon.

I find that near half the Regt. have gone to Alexandria. They will no doubt most of them return with what Prentice defines to be "side arms," to wit "a bottle in one pocket & a syringe in the other." I have some little fear that we shall go into winter quarters

---

* Handy had been made captain of Company B.

here but I hardly believe Gen. McClellan dare risk his reputation in such a move.

§ NOVEMBER 26 On picket guard abt 7 miles out on the Richmond road. I have command of the out posts. They gave me only 27 men to take the place of 90. The posts are badly arranged. There are no posts either to our right or left & there is nothing to hinder the enemy from coming around to our rear & cutting us off.

I supposed this m'g that we were only coming out about 2 miles & therefore did not bring my pistol. I miss it very much. It is exactly the right place to use it. I was always very partial to firearms. With that I should feel pretty sure of a man at 10 rods & entirely so at 6, while with a sword I am not at all sure of him at 6 feet. I think however that my two days will pass off without needing it.

§ NOVEMBER 27 The night was very keen. I went the rounds twice & slept very well during the rest of the night. There was nothing seen or heard along our line. Signal lights were seen further to the left.

Our shanty of pine & cedar bushes set up in a circle with a little fire on the inside is quite comfortable. We have to keep very small fires & have them well screened from view or otherwise we could be as warm as one could wish. The night was so cold that the men on post were very wakeful. Abt 8 A.M. it commenced snowing but it soon changed to rain which continued nearly all day. The roof of our house leaked badly but the fire soon dried the ground & kept us comfortable.

A little black boy came from a house nearby & brought us some very good pies & other eatables which he sold at a fair price. He said his brother ran away 2 years ago & went North & he would be darned if he didn't believe he would do so some day. He wanted we should give him some newspapers. He could not read them but knew a boy who could.

§ NOVEMBER 28 Last night passed off quietly. The cavalry got sight of some "Secesh" out abt 6 miles yesterday but they did not come near. Four men (all French) were sent up from the 5th [U.S. Cavalry] last night to stop with me until m'g. Also two French troopers for orderlies. One of them served in Africa & the Crimea. He is now in the service 9 years. He swears there is no better life than a soldier's. I am sure I would dislike to have him after me with his sabre 3 ft. 4 in. long & sharp on both sides. I believe he could be a match for any 10 of our new cavalry, either for fighting or endurance.

7 P.M. home again, returned abt 3 P.M. It is raining & snowing & is much pleasanter in our good tent than in a brush picket house. A Capt., Lieut., 6 noncom. officers & 65 pvts. of the 63d Penna. came out abt 11 A.M. & relieved my 27 men.

Capt. Handy offered me $25.00 to night if I would make him sure of getting in the Co. again. I think I cant do it unless the time comes when we must do that or worse. No man can live in it as Capt. if we are inclined to get him out. It is understood to be Thanksgiving in Mich. to day & nearly all the officers in the 2d, 3d & 5th Regts. are drunk on the strength of it.

I had a very sympathetic & affectionate epistle to day from the mistress of my friend Mr. Boren. She resides at present in Washington & seems to have great anxiety abt the fate of her "dear Charley" as she calls him. I can very certainly assure her that it is his fate to be prosecuted for desertion if something very unexpected does not happen to prevent my doing it. It will take more than the prayers of one prostitute to save him after the nice scrape he got me into by trying to favor him. He has a very pretty, intelligent & wealthy young wife in Mich. for whom I am sorry. She has probably learned by this time that a traveling showman however good looking or smart by nature makes but an indifferent husband.

As the rain comes pattering down on the tent I cannot but again thank the good fortune that brought me back to camp just at the right time. Tents are not quite home in all respects but no one who has not tried it knows how glad the tired soldier feels to find himself once more inside his own canvas house. Saving the presence of friends, no home however gorgeous ever gave greater joy. All toils & troubles are forgotten & he is mindful only of the cheerful warmth of his mud fireplace, the hearty greetings of his comrades eager for the history of his adventures & neither last nor least the contents of his mess chest. Those who are in camp are always sure to look well to these things ere the return of the absentees & as for the adventures they are generally none the less in narration than in reality.

It was very dark last night but I made my usual rounds at 10 P.M. & 4 A.M. to assure myself that the pickets were doing their duty. They were very much exposed & I was very anxious that none of them should be lost or driven in while I had command.

The ground was rolling & was bordered all the way either on one side or both with a thick growth of scrub pines among which one could move without the least noise. The posts were full 50 rods apart, & I could approach within 20 feet of any of them without being seen or heard. The men did their duty well but anyone could have shot every one on the line with perfect safety to himself.

While going along the path one day I found the little piece of poetry which I have pinned into the forepart of the book.* The only safety for pickets in such cases lies in frequently & noiselessly shifting his position. In this way a lurking enemy while looking for him in one place is pretty sure to be seen by him from another. It needs a keen witted fearless wide awake man for a good picket guard on a dangerous post. Our position was good enough to prevent the approach of large bodies of troops but worth nothing as to small parties who knew our location.

In warm weather I like picket guard but on cold nights it is hard keeping still enough. Cold interferes with the catlike stealth & secrecy of the movements. It however exhausts one rapidly. I hardly ever sleep sound enough not to hear the slightest noise & start up at everything unusual. I think likely one would become accustomed to it after a while but the constant attention of the mind to one thing for two or three days & nights is rather painful & makes me nervous.

§ NOVEMBER 30 Camp near Ft. Lyon, Va. I went to Washington yesterday, purchased some necessary articles for winter wear, had my picture taken &c &c. I saw at Brady's [photographic gallery] two pictures, "graphs" or "types" of some kind, of Harriet Lane.† I think she is a more beautiful woman than I ever saw. She is not one of the ethereal angelic kind nor one all smiles, love & voluptuousness nor of the cool, intellectual platonic love style but a most glorious combination of the whole. She has kindness, intelligence & good sense in every look, form & feature, perfect & full of life & vigor. She is not only beautiful now but bids fair to be 40 years hence. She has a modest, chaste, virtuous look but the tide of life in her veins is too full & rich for her ever to forget that she is a

---

* This poem, "The Picket Guard," records the ambush and killing of a sentinel.
† Harriet Lane, the niece of James Buchanan, had served as White House hostess for the bachelor president.

woman and being such was made for love. She knows that passage of Scripture which says "there is a time for all things"* and wont be sorry when the time comes.

As we came down the river last night they were practicing at the Arsenal with some small rifle cannon. They fired along side of us till we were off abt 3 miles for the purpose of seeing whether they could hit a vessel at that distance if disposed. The balls struck generally from 6 to 8 rods to one side & most of them just abt even with the bow. They sent up a nice little cloud of spray. I do not think one of them would have missed had they been aimed at the boat.

I found the Capt. here when I got back. He has returned only for the purpose of settling up his affairs & resigning. There was never a boy on his first night away from home more homesick than he.

Soon after he came a cold storm of wind & rain set in; the ground was very muddy & the tents damp & cold beside his rooms at home. He & I slept together in my tent, which flopped & slapped around so that he could not keep quiet for a minute — the bed was hard, the clothes too thin. He was so uneasy that I got very little sleep. Every 15 minutes he would punch me in the ribs, "Haydon, Haydon by G-d this tent will blow over." "Dont you feel how the wind comes through the canvas." "How damp it is here, I shall take more cold." In short the place which I had 2 days ago boasted of as one of the coziest in the world seemed to him the most wretched abode on the face of the earth.

Capt. May is a good lawyer & when he is disposed a fine man in private affairs and always an exemplary citizen but a most miserable soldier. I was going to punish a man this m'g for wasting some ammunition but he interfered saying "damn it all what is the use, let the poor chap go." He said "d--n it all what's the use" till his Co. was nearly ruined. He has a great dislike of Col. Poe, says he dont see what in the world they ever wanted to get such a d----d "critter" into this Regt. for.

It is hardly credible how soon & how rapidly men begin to get sick & die off where discipline is slack. I have never seen it fail in a Co. or Regt. & I have already noticed at least a dozen cases. I

---

* Haydon was perhaps thinking of "To every thing there is a season, and a time to every purpose under the heaven" (Ecclesiastes 3:1).

never perceived how sadly deficient Capt. May is in military [ability] till he came back. I suppose it is because there have been such great changes with the rest of us since he left.

One who visits Washington now will find three numerous classes of people, well marked & easily identified. Besides these there is a promiscuous lot of all sorts & kinds conglomerated who I suppose might be called the citizens. The first & most numerous class is composed of soldiers of every rank, hue, nation, uniform & branch. The other two great classes are politicians & prostitutes, both very numerous & abt equal in numbers, honesty & morality. A comrade said to me there yesterday that he used to dote a great deal on some day marrying a virtuous wife but had concluded that if he could find one who hadn't got the ---- he would not look any farther.

It is more interesting than a play to sit at Willard's or the National & watch the passing. I notice & learn all that I can from such scenes. I have enough to do to look out for my own affairs & do not worry myself greatly about the fortunes of the crowd unless there be something very unusual.

There are many things which I would like to write in this book which I dare not because it is so liable to fall into other hands. I think sometimes that there are very few things to be surprised at in these times save virtue in woman & honesty in man. "Whatever is, is right,"* they say & in this view of matters I laugh a thousand times where I feel inclined to cry once. I know there are some good, honest & virtuous men & women in the world. I wish there were more & that I was more zealous in imitating their examples. I am not disposed to judge anyone's faults but hope that all "may so live" that they may approach their end "like one who wraps the drapery of his couch around him & lies down to pleasant dreams."†

> *"These struggling tides of life which seem*
> *In wayward aimless course to tend*
> *Are eddies of a mighty stream*
> *Which moves to its appointed end."*

§ DECEMBER 1, 1861   I learned last night that one of our men died Oct. 15th at Georgetown Hospital. We learned the fact by

---

* Alexander Pope, *An Essay on Man.*
† William Cullen Bryant, "Thanatopsis."

way of his Father who wrote to find whether there was any pay due him. This dying off without our knowing it is what ought not to be. We expected to see him returning every day for duty.

I learned pretty nearly my standing in the Co. last night by accident. It was nothing new to me. I knew what it was to be when I recd my commission. I have no desire to have it changed.

I was passing quite late one of the tents & heard by chance one of the boys instructing one of our new recruits in the mysteries of soldiering. He had just finished it seemed a description of the Col.'s ways. "Now" said he "the next thing is to look out for that 2d Lieut. for he is a d----d sight worse than the Col. He'll give you h--l without mercy if you dont mind your business when he is around." I passed on & did not hear any more. His last sentence at least was true. I will not be run over by any set of men whom I am entitled to rule. They have got to mind their business & keep in their places. I give them fair warning & have no cause to complain in our own Co. but sometimes have a little trouble outside.

I would do as Lieut. Col. Burke of the 37th did to one of his men if I could not be obeyed in any other way. There was no order in his Regt. No Col. to appeal to who would do anything. He ordered a man twice to fall into the ranks. The second time the man openly refused & the Col. shot him through the head in less than 5 seconds. I saw him when he fell. He was never called to account & should not have been.

I hope the Capt. will soon be gone. He & I have been talking over old law matters. I began to feel as though I wanted to be back. I could see so plainly the kind, sober face of judge Graves, the familiar features of all my associates in the profession & especially the honest, good natured countenance of my best friend & partner Joseph Miller that it seemed for a moment that I must be there again cost what it might. God only knows how much I loved the Law & how hard it was to give it up. It was for a moment only. I stifled the thought ere it had a chance to gain a permanent hold. I swore to bear arms till the war or I was done & I'll not break my oath.

More than one tempting vision has presented itself to lure me away. I'll put this down as I have the others. I know the Law which I loved so much would have killed me. Here I can stand anything that any one will share with me. In an office I should work alone. I know that the labor & the unwholesome air of the court room would eventually have overcome me & broken my health. If I should fall during the war I shall be sure of having turned my life to good account. Though I would gladly do more still if I knew this were to be my lot. I would not complain. Perhaps it were better to grasp that certainty, if the choice were given, than to try the uncertainties of life in hope of making a better & more honorable end. At any rate the choice is not so great but that I can take the first alternative, I hope, with decent composure.

I think however it is full time for me to quit speculating as to how I could stand being killed myself & turn to the most approved methods as described in the best authors of killing others. [Dennis Hart] Mahan says that a 6 lb. shot at fair distance will cut in two abt 24 men. I call that pretty good work if the shot goes from our side. Fragments of shell will frequently scatter over a circle more than 200 rods in diameter & make very dangerous wounds, says the same author. There are nowadays a great many ingenious & philosophical ways of killing men. No one need die for love unless he prefers that way.

Benson is on picket. I have read the Atlantic nearly through to day.

§ DECEMBER 2 We had a brigade drill this P.M. during which we fired abt 50,000 of blank cartridges. The weather is cold & it is snowing to night. Col. Poe has returned. Capt. May is officer of the day. The Capt. has said a great deal abt Col. Poe putting on airs & that he did not care for him or discipline. He & I were talking together this m'g when he chanced to see the Col. coming. Capt. looked suddenly over toward the Guard Tent & not seeing many of the men there who were not on duty, started off in great haste swearing he would have every one of them arrested. He never did such a thing before and such an idea would not have entered his head then had he not seen the Col., whom he did not care anything about, coming.

§ DECEMBER 5 I was on guard yesterday. I was pretty busy & had one very pleasant interview with the Col. I had been to visit the out posts. He visited the guard while I was gone & thought he had caught me nicely. I met him when I was coming back & we had quite a conversation abt guards &c in which he found very little fault but after all I was not sorry when it was over.

It was tedious last night. The ground froze deep & hard. I slept not more than 15 minutes all night. I sat down on a pole which was stuck up near the fire & was soon asleep. I was dreaming that I was in the warmest and downiest bed imaginable and God only knows what other charms would soon have been added if I had not tumbled off the pole & burned my new trousers. It was a pretty long night & required a great deal of walking to keep from freezing. I got through however & feel none the worse to day.

I had two very interesting periods of conversation with the Col. to day. He was not after me this time but was, as he always is on such occasions full of politeness & good nature. He directed me to prefer charges against my friend Boren, which I have done under the following head: Desertion. Volation of the 42nd Article of War. Conduct prejudicial to good order & military discipline &c.

Col. Poe had a talk with Benson to day who was more courtier like and politic in his answers than I ever knew him before. He is apt to explode when things dont suit. Col. called him out & said to him "I think it proper that I should inform you that I have sent in a recommendation for a 1st Lieut. of this Regt. to be Capt. of Co. I. I wish to know how you feel abt it." Benson with a long face informed him that he had often thought and always said that he would not serve if any Lieut. in the Regt. was placed over him. He had always thought that there was no Lieut. in the Regt. more capable of looking after the welfare of Co. I than himself but said he "Col. if you have found one, I can only submit to your experience and better judgment."

He added several sentences in the same becoming tone of military subordination when I should have supposed he would have broken over all bounds and damned things sky high. When the conversation was nearly over the Col. began to laugh & informed him that he was the man. He had watched he said the conduct of B. & myself since our promotion & was pleased with it. There were several officers who were our seniors & better entitled in many respects to promotion than we but considering the manner in which we had managed the Co. he thought it would be unjust to place anyone over us. He had determined in short that Benson should be Capt. & I 1st Lieut. I am not at all displeased at that but shall wait for my commission before I congratulate myself too much. Many slips between cup & lip.

I guess I shall go clear on the Boren affair but one must keep his eyes & ears wide open all the time in these military affairs or he will find himself minus his commission some fine morning. Provided always that he has a wide awake West Point graduate to watch him.

§ DECEMBER 6 Is as warm, pleasant day as one could wish to see, very much like a warm day in May. Capt. May showed himself in a new & some respects interesting view, at least it was instructive & laughable. It was penuriousness personified. He figured up articles to the amt of $95 which he seemed to think Benson & I must buy or be the most mean & ungrateful beings on earth. There was hardly an article for which he did not ask more than it cost him. He made up his list & then told us that he would aid in our promotion, evidently thinking he could wring the money out of us in this way. When it came to a final settlement we gave him $28 for a part of them. He got very mad because we would not buy them all.

We had given up our own tent & bed to him & he had lived abt a week at our expense with the exception of some Michigan butter which he brought along. He charged us with the balance of it (abt 2 lbs.). He said he was going to give us an old brass candlestick worth abt 10 cts. but when he found we would not buy all his things he carried that away. He tried to get three old pewter teaspoons out of the mess chest which he said he had not sold but Noble would not let him have them. A little more would have induced us to have kicked him off the ground.

N. W. Foster, one of our best men died at the Regt. hospital a few minutes since of typhoid fever. He leaves a family. He took a severe cold at Cantonment Blair & has never been very well since though he did good service a large share of the time. There is not a great deal of sickness in camp but it is more than usually fatal. Typhoid fever is the most dangerous. Very few recover from it so as to be worth much for duty.

There were three good promotions in our Co. to night. Two of them, Johnston & Southworth, I have long desired & they would have come before if I could have controlled matters. I think that Johnston will be 2d Lieut. in case I am promoted. He is in all respects a gentleman & a soldier. He comes of good English fighting stock, near half his male relatives on his father's side having fallen in battle. His grandfather was Gov. of Canada when our Revolution broke out.

Our Sergt. [Johnston] had the misfortune to quarrel or fall out in some way with his father some six years since. Both allowed their temper to get so high that they parted for life, at least such was their mutual vow. If the father is like the son it will be kept. Since then the boy has worked his own way & married a very pretty wife. Both are poor & need the increase of pay which he will now receive. So much he told me and no more. His father lives in Canada & is a man of wealth, rank & influence. I wish they could come to an amicable settlement. I have done my best to aid his promotion and have done all I could to secure him my present place if I should leave it.

§ DECEMBER 7 We presented Gen. Richardson to day with a sword & sash which cost $75. It was a present from the officers of the Mich. 2d. If I could have had my way I would have waited till another pay day & then have bought a better one.

The Gen. knew nothing about it till we came in on him. He acted as funny & embarrassed as a boy with a new hat. He expressed his thanks in his usual dry blunt style & called on Col. Terry who was present to help him out by a speech which he did quite handsomely. Gen. said he desired to bring on the wine but unfortunately had none on hand. So he concluded to call us in at another time.

We took him entirely off guard. If so many secessionists had have come in & summoned him to surrender he would have been less confused. Anything like speech making is a terror to him. He has never been known to talk for more than two minutes consecutively since he joined the Regt. He likes to do things without ceremony if we may judge from the way in which he got married. When the Regt. first went to Detroit he was engaged to be married to a lady at that place. When he determined to go for three years she objected. She said she was willing to marry him and go with him for a three months' campaign but she thought that 3 years in camp was too much. Indeed she could not consent to it.

"Very well Madame there are others who will. Good day." The Gen. called for his hat, crossed the street, offered himself in less than 10 minutes after to a girl whom he had never seen but twice before, was accepted & married within two weeks.

Senator Chandler & a number of other Mich. men were here to see how we were getting along to day & we had a review & drill for their edification. To morrow we bury (or "plant" as Prentice calls it) Foster who died last night at the hospital.

§ DECEMBER 9   More lovely weather than that of the last 3 days no rational man could ask for. It is like the warmest days of Indian summer in Mich. only not so smoky. There is hardly any frost nights.

Foster was buried yesterday. A large number of men from other Co's. were present. With an appropriate discourse it would have been a very solemn funeral. Chaplain May's sermon was abt as appropriate and interesting as the dryest chapt. of Coke's Commentaries would have been. A military funeral when properly conducted is a very solemn & impressive scene. Its effect is far different from that of other funerals. Nothing sounds more sorrowful than the slow prolonged wail of martial music. The perfect silence & regularity of the procession, the measured tread, the inverted arms, and sober looks all increase the effect.

Soldiers always look very sad on such occasions, more however as a matter of discipline & duty than because they care a great deal about it. In truth after they have been 6 months in the service the death of a comrade makes very little change in their conversation or thoughts.

At Dress Parade to night came orders to move at 9 A.M. to morrow. I suppose we are going abt 3 miles down the river to Washington Valley. We shall undoubtedly winter there or at least go into winter quarters. One of the most important things for a soldier to learn is that he has & can have no home, no fixed place of abode which can be improved or beautified beyond the mere wants of the day. As often as he gets well to living the order comes to move, he packs the most necessary of his articles, abandons the rest & travels to another place. As a member of 1st Kansas hath written "he covenanteth with the credulous farmers for much poultry, potatoes &c to be paid for in ten days & lo on the ninth day his Regt. moveth to another place."

We shall be 3 miles nearer the enemy but with no more prospect of active service. I dislike to be cooped up there all winter but I suppose I can stand it at $105 per month. Our things are all packed & we have only to strike our tents & we are ready for the march.

Gen. Richardson gave Benson & I each a photograph of himself to night. It is a good picture & I prize very highly as coming from him in person. God knows I like the man & so, I think, does everyone in the 2d unless it be Major Williams. If the "Secesh" ever touch him they had better keep out of the way of the "Pet Lambs."

§ DECEMBER 10 Sundown finds us in the woods 3½ miles S. of our former camp. We are trying to camp among the trees. There is not a house or cleared field in sight. The ground is in its original state with hardly the mark of an ax on the trees.

I used to say that the Garibaldi Guards could beat anything in the Army of the Potomac at stealing, but Col. Poe says the 4th Brigade* has the highest reputation in that line at headquarters & everywhere else where they are known. The guns were barely stacked to day when the worthies of the 2d began to run up to the top of a hill a little in front of us to look around. At a little distance they spied a board fence abt ½ miles long & nearly new. They ran back in great haste to inform their comrades. In 20 minutes there was not a board left on the posts. Col. Poe got wind of it & rode to the place as fast as possible. He yelled at them as soon as he came in sight. Slap, crack went the boards on to the ground & the men scampered in all directions. He not knowing the men personally they all got into the bushes & escaped before the guard arrived. As soon as he was out of sight you might see them creeping out & snatching away the boards one by one & hiding them in the leaves.

Our Co. tents did not come till sundown & before there was time to put them up we were all ordered out on picket. We went out abt a mile to watch a number of old roads & cow paths which lead in toward our lines.

§ DECEMBER 11 The night was warm & I slept well with a single blanket & a pile of pine boughs during such parts of the night as were not required for patrols &c. Charley Godfroy shot at a man who was coming along one of the roads but missed him. He made wonderful time into the bushes. The night with us was very quiet.

In camp they were called out at 3 A.M. by a report that the enemy were advancing. When we were within abt 80 rods of camp coming in some Devil instigated me to fire off my pistol. I came so near getting into hot water for this that there was no fun in it. At any

---

* That is, Haydon's own brigade as it was initially numbered.

other time no one would have taken any notice of [it] but just then they were very wide awake. If I had have known that I should most certainly not have fired. It is all over now so far as any action in the matter is concerned. I would be very glad if it had not happened.

We all worked very briskly till noon leveling the ground, felling trees, putting up tents, digging wells, building log huts &c. Just as we were at dinner an order came to strike tents & be ready to move in 2 hours. Col. Poe had examined the ground with the critical eye of an engineer & had found that half a doz. guns might be so planted as to render our retreat to the main body impossible. In short the 4th Brigade would see Richmond sooner than they desired unless they were able to take the battery. Gen. Heintzelman did not like the place too far out.

At two oclock the tents were down & we were on the move again, the band playing "Aint I glad to get out of the wilderness." I *was* glad to get out, aside from the danger of being cut off the place possessed few advantages. It was warm & there was plenty of wood. We marched back half way to the old camp & there halted on an open field where we had no sooner stopped than the men began to make arrangements for camping. After abt an hour we moved ½ a mile further to the right, halted, stacked arms & abt ⅓ an hour later moved once more a short distance & stacked arms for the night. It was now near sundown. Gen. Richardson thought our first stopping place too cold so we brought up finally in a snug valley.

Few of the tents came & we nearly all prepared to bunk on the ground. Benson & I were fortunate in this that our things being the last to arrive at the first ground were the first to come back. Thus our bedding was at hand. We spread it on some boards & lay down for the night. Not however till we had told so many stories & joked so much that I nearly laughed myself to death.

§ DECEMBER 12 I slept well last night though the weather became very cold abt sundown. When we waked up in the morn the frost on our blankets was more than a half inch thick. The steam & vapor from our bodies had frozen on reaching the cold air. The ground froze hard enough to bear a horse. One feels fresh & lively when he rolls out of his blankets into the open air an hour before sunrise.

§ DECEMBER 13 The men are very busy at work fixing up

quarters, building log huts &c. I doubt whether we shall remain here long. I cannot see why we should not advance at once & make an end of this business. We shall be no better prepared so far as I can see 3 months hence than now. The men would rather advance in snow knee deep than go into winter quarters. There has not been snow enough yet to cover the ground. In two days moving with all due caution we can arrive at the place where the whole thing can be decided.

Would it not be better to go through Manassas at the point of the bayonet with a loss of 5000 to 10,000 men than to delay any longer? Many will say that would be cruelty. Indeed it would, that is a necessary consequence of war. Armies are raised for that very purpose. True the final object is quite different but such is the immediate consequence. The cost of waiting both in life & money must also be calculated. Every hour of delay is a positive gain to the enemy in most respects.

Gen. Richardson was around this P.M. to warn the men not to carry off any more boards. "It wont do to hook any more boards around here. They are making a devil of a fuss about it at head-quarters. They're goin' to arrest a lot of officers of the Mich. 3d." It must be said that he never stopped the boys from "cramping" till he was obliged to. His orders always were that such things "must be stopped as much as possible." Which was understood to mean that the men should not steal anything unless they really needed it. The men from this brigade have torn down a church abt 2 miles from here to day & carried it all away. They tear down barns & outhouses in presence of the owners & in some cases they have taken the doors & blinds off their houses.

§ DECEMBER 14 Benson who is a perfect monomaniac on the subjects of log & board shanties commenced one of the latter day before yesterday. He pulled down the tent yesterday & was so much afraid someone would steal his boards that we had to sleep out doors on top of the pile last night. I swore pretty roundly not that I cared any thing abt sleeping on the board pile but because I hate the muss & trouble of building the shanty. I swore I would never pay a cent toward it but that made no difference with him. I threatened to dissolve partnership but he declared that if I would live in it with him he would pay all expense. I think it is best to let him have his own way & I will pay a part of the expense or not just as I see fit hereafter. He has a great desire to do all the domestic duty & I have a great desire to let him. I never think of sweeping the tent, making the bed, building a fire or anything of the kind when he is here.

§ DECEMBER 15 Co. I looked gay at Inspection this m'g. Col. Poe commended their appearance very highly. They had all new coats, clean white gloves, boots well blacked & guns with few exceptions as bright as a new dollar. They were clean & neat enough in all respects for the parlor. There are some of them however of whom you can no more make soldiers than poets.

There was a battle 'tis said at Springfield Station abt 5 miles from here yesterday P.M. We could hear the guns & see the smoke very plainly. The firing was for an hour very rapid. I know nothing as yet of the result.* It seems as though *we* should never see any more fighting.

The men are beginning to be soldiers. You no longer hear a continual grumbling abt officers, living, clothes, turns of duty & every imaginable thing. When anything is to be done they turn out & do it as they ought. There is indeed less cause than formerly. How I used to pity the regulars when I first came down here. Poor fellows I used to think you are laced up in a straight jacket & imprisoned without hope of relief for the next 5 years. After all I could not help noticing that they did not seem to feel very bad about it & that they looked a vast deal better than we. Times & thoughts have so far changed that nothing pleases men or officers more than the thought of being made into regulars.

I on the evening of the 15th Dec. 1861 bet the oysters with Corpl. Mack that one of the 6 persons then present (Lieuts. Benson & self, Corpls. Prentice & Mack, privates North & Noble) would be killed in battle before this night 1862. A foolish bet perhaps but it is made.

§ DECEMBER 16 A very fine day. It is reported that we are to go to Ft. Pickens [in Florida]. I would not be surprised if some such thing would be the result of all this stealing. I do not care very much whether we go or not. It would be a change & that is usually reason enough for a soldier. It would be very pleasant for the winter but not so pleasant for the summer which we would be sure to encounter. I am beginning to be soldier enough to be pretty

---

* No such engagement is recorded for this date.

much passive as to where I am stationed and am ready to go wherever they see fit to send me, without question or regrets.

We have another 2d Lieut. in our Co. to night. The appointment was recd by the men with 3 groans. I do not understand some things in connection with the matter. I dislike it in this that it bars the promotion of men in our Co. who are far better qualified than the one appointed. I do not understand why he or I were not apptd. 1st Lieut. Till I know the reason of this I shall not feel quite certain as to the future. There are some things which can be done & some which cannot. I dont like the arrangement. I shall wait for the sequel.

§ DECEMBER 17 I am officer of the guard to day. "The officer of the guard must not leave his post except for his meals & for the necessary rounds" so says the Regulations & Col. Poe emphasized it this m'g. This confines me for 26 hours. The day is very warm & fine. Benson is officer of the day.

§ DECEMBER 18 It requires no small degree of patience to sit through a 26 consecutive hours guard duty. It has been done however. North swears he thought last night I would win the oysters (see Dec. 15th). He was on picket with abt 20 others just in the edge of a piece of woods. A volley of abt 50 guns was suddenly fired at them. No one was killed but one had a vest button shot off & a good sized hole made in his shirt. The boys returned fire once & then fell back on the reserve in quick time. The enemy did not follow them beyond the first posts. They took there 7 blankets, a few haversacks & 3 or 4 loaves of bread. This is the same place where I was apprehensive of an attack the last time I was out. North declares that his legs did their utmost to ruin for that time the chances for my bet. The boys only fell back a few rods & returned to their posts in abt 15 minutes.

The Col. solved my doubts abt promotion last night. He says that it is through mistake that my commission as 1st Lieut. did not come. I began to suspect that I had pulled the wrong string somewhere. It is rather unlucky in this that if my comm. had come when it ought I should have been senior to 2 1st Lieuts. & therefore outranked them, who are now senior to me. Col. says the papers will be along in a few days.

I well remember the first time I ever talked with Benson abt the some day when he would be Capt. of Co. I & I would be 1st Lieut. It was the day after the battle of Blackburn's Ford. We were lying just on the back edge of the field expecting every minute that the shells would be dropping in amongst us or that we should be called on to go down into the valley where we were peppered the day before. The Capt. was very pale & sick, some others higher in rank than we did not seem at all eager for the conflict. Benson was on the right of the Co., I on the left. Seeing him a little apart from the rest I crossed over & told him that some day we would command that Co. He was of the same opinion. We called out the two Sergts. next below us & instructed them in some few things that they might not be wholly surprised should such an event happen on that day. If there had been a sharp engagement our precautions would not have been lost.

§ DECEMBER 19 5 minutes past midnight. Half an hour ago we were called up & ordered to be ready to move in an hour with rations for one day & in perfect silence. I was sensible when I went to bed at 8 last night. I did not sleep a wink night before but have made sure of three hours of the best for to night. "God bless the man who invented sleep." Sancho Panza.*

If I could but hear a word from Kalamazoo to tell me how my brother fares with the measles I should be more at ease. It is a very dangerous disease for him. I fear its effect on the lungs. One's hopes & expectations for this life hang on a slender thread. A small thing may make the future worse than blank. I hope for the best.

It is surprising how prone to jokes & levity soldiers become even in the midst of the most serious & solemn things. I cannot refrain from jesting with Benson & the others abt our bet & with Prentice in particular who has recently been apptd. Corpl. of the Color Guard. Prentice has considerable Falstaff abt him. I think he would fight well enough when the time comes but he is not very anxious for the time.

Nine A.M. we are still at Camp Michigan. It seems that we were only called up to act as reserve to some other troops which had gone down toward Pohick. There are not two happier men in the army than Benson & I. "At every festive board there sits a ghost." Assured of one thing I would be as contented as I shall ever expect to be. Give me the assurance that all is well at Kalamazoo & I ask

---

* John Godfrey Saxe, *Early Rising:* " 'God bless the man who first invented sleep!' / So Sancho Panza said, and so say I."

no more. Benson & I have now a Co. which we like & which likes us as well as we like them. We are both, as to ourselves & it, in good favor with both Gen., Col., Major & the world in general as far as we care to be.

There was Division Review at 12 instead of a march. It went off well. 12 Regts. with the Cavalry & Artillery attached are as many as can be seen to any advantage by a spectator. I believe we shall move soon.

It was reported that Heintzelman said to Richardson that the 2d was the worst Regt. in all respects that there was in his Division. If it had proved that he said so I believe the boys would have murdered him. They went to Gen. R. forthwith to find out. It proved to be exactly the contrary. He & our Gen. sometimes like to chafe each other & I did not know but it might be true.

If Gen. R. could only ride on horseback decently he would be one of the finest looking officers I ever saw. He will always take hold of the mane with one hand to keep from falling off. He says he used to ride pretty well when he was in Mexico & can ride well enough now to suit him but the boys in the 2d laugh a good deal abt it. Col. Poe cannot be beat in the army in this line but the Gen. goes jolting along like some clumsy old farmer.

I believe the Col. is working to get this Regt. away from this brigade & from Gen. R. It would nearly break the hearts of the "Pet Lambs." I should dislike it very much but if I had to choose I should follow the Col. I like Gen. R. very much but after all Col. Poe in my opinion is the "coming man." Gen. R. will undoubtedly be a Major Gen. before the war closes but Col. Poe is too full of lightning for him in the long run. He could do far better with this Regt. if it were away from the Gen. The Gen. was a glorious good Col. but not equal in many things to Col. Poe. He must I think be 45 to 50 years of age, Col. Poe 28.* There is nothing like young men for war. It is a hard matter to make the 2d do anything that Gen. R. did not require.

§ DECEMBER 20 "Gay is the life of a soldier man" so sings Sid Prentice but our junior 2d Lieut. did not think so this morning. He was detailed with Benson & another officer for picket. He is a good young man, a distant relative of the Secretary but with not

---

* Richardson would turn forty-six on December 26; Poe was twenty-nine.

quite enough original sin for a soldier.* He has been in the Quartermaster Department since he came into the army. He knows abt
as much military as the man in the moon. Benson says he shall
have a Corpl. drill him.

But to return, he was detailed on picket. He had never heard
bullets whistle, never been on picket or anything of the sort. Never
was on guard, slept on the ground, or short of rations. Benson
loves him & took great delight in informing him how he must
conduct. He told him that he must not sleep a wink (2 days &
nights), must visit the posts 4 times each night, must be very careful
how he traveled around in the night or he would get shot, must
keep his hands on his things so as to be able to take them off at a
moment's notice in case the cavalry should come down, must be
in good condition to run but at the same time must not run except
in extreme cases.

The result was that he became so excited that he could hardly
sleep at night. He went off & bought provisions enough for ten
men — 4 lbs. cheese, 4 loaves of ginger bread, 2 lbs. sweet crackers,
2 loaves bread, 3 lbs. sausage & a number of other articles all by
Benson's direction. When they came to pack he found that he
could not get half of them into a haversack. Benson assisted him
in this crisis by filling his own haversack & thrusting the balance
dexteriously into our mess chest. He was then told how very cold
it would be nights. He strapped an overcoat & 2 blankets on his
back, not however without inquiring very seriously whether it was
really necessary to make "such a d----d pack mule of himself."

It would be just his luck to blunder around & get shot. I believe
Benson would care very little if he did provided there was no other
way of getting rid of him. I do not wish him quite as bad as that
but I did my best to help terrify him.

§ DECEMBER 21 I am afraid there is going to be a muss in
camp. Gen. Richardson was down here before breakfast this m'g
to inquire whether I had heard anything abt the 2d Regt. moving.
I was sorry he asked the question. I answered it with due readiness
but with a good degree of caution. I told him what reports I had
heard & that I did not know where they originated; that I knew

---

* The reference here is to 2nd Lt. W. H. Seward, related to Secretary of State
  William Henry Seward.

nothing abt it myself. He inquired whether they wanted to go. I told him no & by all means no unless they could return to his command in the spring. He then asked the more unpleasant question as to whether I knew of anyone making application to have the Regt. moved or whether I had heard any such thing. I replied that the impression among the men was that Col. Poe was trying to get the Regt. moved till the spring campaign opened. The Gen. at this gave his left shoulder a terrible shrug & commenced chewing his under lip. I knew that there was a storm brewing. "Well I'll go to town to day myself & see abt these things."

If he & the Col. quarrel one or the other must leave. They can never live in sight of each other. The Gen. looked as savage as a mad bull this m'g. The truth is I want to go if we can return in the spring — in fact I think I do anyway. If Col. Poe gets the Regt. fairly into his hands we are pretty sure to be kept for the 3 years whether the war lasts or not. There are 2 things which trouble the Col. exceedingly & which he fears can never be remedied in the field. 1st stealing, which in reality had always been encouraged by Gen. R. though in such a manner as to render him entirely safe. 2d negligence in guard duty, which has existed so long that it seems impossible to remedy it unless the men can be brought within close walls.

If we are discharged in 3 months I shall come out of the business with almost empty pockets. If we are kept 3 years I shall have some spare money. The expense for the first few months consumes nearly all the pay & leaves one with only a lot of military clothing, equipments & ornaments which are of little value for any other purpose. I like Col. Poe & if I could be under him where he had absolute control for 3 years should become a pretty thoroughly educated soldier.

In our present position if there is any fighting we shall see our full share & see it well done but there are a great many things for soldiers to learn besides that. They are perhaps on the battlefield 4 or 5 days in a year but on all the other days there are duties & important ones to be performed. I very much dislike that there should be anything ungrateful in the matter toward Gen. R., which would injure his feelings or in any way detract from the honor which is justly due him. He made us perhaps as good a Vol. Regt. as there was at the time in the army. Col. Poe has improved us & would make us the best Regt. in the army, regulars included. I suppose the Garibaldi Guards are as good & perhaps better than the 2d but I doubt whether there is now another Regt. of Vols. equal to it.

§ DECEMBER 22 Sunday really seemed considerable like home. I suppose it was because I washed & put on a clean shirt & did my own shaving. The business of Sunday is about this: inspection, guard mounting, dinner, reading newspapers, letter writing, euchre playing &c.

I was told some rather encouraging things by Capt. Norvell, aide to Gen. Richardson, formerly 2d Lieut. of our Co. He heard Col. Poe tell Gen. R. that he was glad Capt. May resigned when he did as should otherwise most certainly have been obliged to request him to do so; that when he went home our Co. was in the worst condition of any in the Regt. except B. That now it was in the best condition of any except A; that there were no two officers in the Regt. who had discharged their duties in a more satisfactory manner than Benson & I.

We have both got into good standing at headquarters & I believe we know pretty well how to profit by it. It dont pay for one to butt his head agt everything that comes toward him. Benson & I have both had several chances to put on airs & spoil all this if we had done as some others have. Nothing has been required of us which was not right in a military point of view & when we have been reprimanded (as both of us have more than once) we have received it (d----d hard work sometimes) as it is required a Co. officer should from his Col., with the most respect, deference & attention & have replied in as few words as possible avoiding all rhetorical flourishes & figures of speech and saving all the swearing till we were alone.

There is nothing humiliating in this nor in any way inconsistent with manliness or self respect. Anything like that is carefully avoided. Everyone, & especially those with no more military experience than we, is liable to be mistaken on points for which he will be sharply corrected. Nor is it always easy when you know your duty, to discharge it to the letter. It frequently depends on the action of many others & of those who are not under your immediate care.

The old officers were inclined to oppose the Col. in many things, were full of suggestions & arguments & frequently disposed to be obstinate. Many of them finding themselves sadly mistaken have resigned. There is not more than 4 of them who stand well in the

Col.'s estimation. It is almost impossible for a man of 40 years of age, who is naturally fit for an officer, but has had no experience, to conform to the rigid requirements of military rule & discipline. You can put such men into the ranks & drill them down after awhile. They know there is no escape, while the officer flies for relief to the loophole of resignation.

§ DECEMBER 23 I am on picket to morrow. There is a nice prospect of being up for the next two nights on short rations & very little fire. It has been raining & snowing all day in heavy squalls.

I would rather go on picket than be on guard here. There are 16 prisoners with no safe place to keep them. Some of them are almost sure to escape. They do not often get outside the guard but they are liable to & it requires a great deal of labor & trouble to retake them. They are a desperate set of fellows & need constant watching from the officer of the guard. If there was a good guard house which you could shut & lock them into or if there was a good solid ball & chain to put on them they might be kept.

I think these troubles are nearly over for the present. We all signed a request to be sent into some fort during the winter to drill on Artillery. Col. Poe says we are going without doubt. I like it. I like the winter quarters. I want to learn the drill. I want to see the Regt. under Col. Poe's control.

The only drawback is the disappointment & regret of Gen. Richardson. I do hate to leave him. It will nearly break his heart. He has been to McClellan & the President to prevent it but, it is said, cannot succeed. He was down to our tent to day & stayed some time but made no allusion to our moving. He has been traveling around among the tents nearly all the afternoon looking as if he hadn't a friend on earth. I swear I nearly cried to see the old veteran. I was almost sorry I signed the request.

Some of the officers allege as a reason for going that he is always in a quarrel with his superior officers & in that way getting into trouble & keeping us back. It is true he is very apt to quarrel with others but he never quarrels with the 2d. I would be glad to help fight out, if it were necessary, all his quarrels, provided we could stay with him. We shall not find another man whom we shall like or who will like us as we do him.

§ DECEMBER 24 On picket. I have command of all the pickets from our Regt. to day. That ought to secure me better headquarters than I have. There are quarters nearby which are good enough if I dared occupy them but they are so close to the line that it is not safe — cant get out of a house quick enough. My Christmas will have to be spent here. This may be the last of picket guard for this winter. I wait with patience for the development of affairs. Our camp can be plainly seen from here but is more than 5 miles off.

§ DECEMBER 25   The night passed off in perfect quiet. I made the rounds soon after dark, abt. 1 A.M. & just before daylight. It was a keen frosty night & the men were wide awake. They kept small fires, but well covered, swearing they would rather be shot than freeze to death. I stayed with the boys of our Co. till after 1 A.M. on post. When I had completed the rounds it was 3 oclock & I went up to the general headquarters & slept for a short time. It is abt. the first time since I enlisted that I have attempted to sleep in a house & it made me sick this time. I presume it was the warm close air. I was very sick for a short time but soon felt better as soon as I got into the open air.

I dont believe I can ever learn to live in a house again. I was always rather inclined to the Indian style of living & soldiering is an excellent way to cultivate such a propensity. It seems impossible for me to take cold do what I may.

There was a Regt. of the rascals came up within ½ mile of the 37th last night & carried away some things from a house. I heard their skirmishers but did not at the time believe it was them.

I have been around to all the houses in this vicinity to see the ladies. Poor set. I only saw 2 who looked decent. One reminded me very much of an old acquaintance whose name I will not now mention. The other — Jenny — had thus early (at the sweet age of 16) been unfortunate. She went to Alexandria to live where some sad rascal in the short space of 3 hours, as she says, stole both her heart & virginity, while she did not even so much as learn his name or business. She never had the luck to see him afterwards. The consequence was that abt the time the soldiers came she enlisted a recruit in an independent Co. of her own. When her mother had done scolding & her father done swearing at her ill luck, they, being poor, took her home & took care of her.

The soldiers will ask occasionally where her husband is & she is foolish enough to tell them she never had any. They however take a great liking to her boy on account of the unpopular way in which, without any fault of his own, he became a citizen of the

Old Dominion. I believe the bits of money which the soldiers give him more than half support the whole family. Jenny was unfortunate in her company once & she might be in a safer locality than she is now. Soldiers soon acquire a wonderous free & easy way in all things & war is pretty sure to relax the morals of everybody it comes in contact with, officers excepted.

I find on further examination that Jenny's case is too common to be accidental. There are two other cases very similar which have come to my knowledge since, all within a circle of 3 miles. Either morals are lax or this is the worst country for accidents that I ever heard of.

The pines will someday, not far off, conquer Virginia if we do not. There are the densest growth of scrub pines I ever saw on what not many years ago were cultivated fields. The pines are all scrubby & seldom go higher than 40 feet. In thickets where the trees are 6 inches through you can still see the marks of the plow & the ridges thrown up along the rows of corn can be distinctly traced. In going through these thickets one will occasionally find the remains of fences so rotted as to be almost indistinguishable. There are some fields but just abandoned & in which the trees are not more than 4 feet high but just as thick as they can stand.

§ DECEMBER 26 6 P.M. at home once more. I got in at one P.M. I have not been more fatigued since I enlisted. I have had no real sleep for the last two nights & have been on my feet the greater part of the time for 56 hours.

I arrived to find all things unsettled. The Col. & Gen. have quarreled. Both have been to Washington most of the time for several days. The Col. started to go again this m'g. The Gen. could not go this time so he issued an order forbidding Col. Poe to leave camp without his permission.

Lt. Col. Larnerd is at Washington as I am told striving to prevent our removal.* I know the officers of the Regts. in the brigade & Gen. Heintzelman are all working agt it. The latter expects that we will some day do hard fighting enough to win him great credit. The former like to have us to go ahead in all the hard places.

We are called the best Regt. in the service for picket duty & the others say themselves that they like to have us along to lean on.

---

* At issue was converting the 2nd Michigan to an artillery unit.

Lt. Col. Beach of the 5th Mich. told me this last night, adding that they all very well knew that we were the most steady & reliable Regt. in this part of the army & that the removal of it would be felt more or less by all the troops in Va. In short that he deemed it would be a great injury to the public service.

I fear the quarrel will get so high that we shall lose our Col. God save us from that. I should feel like wearing my sword bottom upward during the rest of my life. It is also reported that Gen. Richardson is soon to be Major Gen. If this be true I should think & I do in fact believe that he will be pacified & consent that the Col. go where he pleases with us.

Col. P. went to him yesterday to have him sign a paper laying the whole matter fairly before them at headquarters. "I wont sign your paper, when the 2d leaves I am ready to go home." So said Gen. R. Col. P. is pretty full of vindictiveness & obstinacy but he dont go it blind. He artfully suggested to Gen. R. that he was soon to be Major Gen. & would be so much removed from the Pet Lambs that he would hardly feel the difference between their presence & absence. Gen. did not believe that but concluded to sign the paper.

It is a hard case to be called on to choose between Col. P. & Gen. R. but I have taken the former. It would not be a small thing for Benson & I to be under a Major Gen. who would come to our tent two or three times per week & stay half an hour at a time & to be also as we are on the most desirable terms with his staff. We could hardly ask more than would be given if the suit were pressed with a little dexterity but at the same time with modesty & bashfulness of manner. This is a great thing to leave but nevertheless the matter is decided. All this I propose to give up when the time comes for the polished science, the severe accuracy, the keen reprimands, the rare but merited compliments, the cool, steady, philosophic courage (almost fierceness) of our young Col.

I found also on arriving that they had the comfortable report in camp that I got three bullets through me the night before. Sid Prentice expressed great sorrow, saying he hoped I was not hurt but that I would get every rag of clothes shot off me. He guessed "that would take some of the wickedness out of me."

§ DECEMBER 27 A cold, raw, windy day. I came off picket in good time. We have a good joke on Benson. He gave Jenny $5.00 for the privilege of naming her boy. He called him Sid Prentice.

Jenny seemed greatly pleased with the name but changed it as soon as B. was gone & called it after him. Benson swears he will kill the young one if she does not change the name again.

Our 2d Lieut. [Seward] is on guard to morrow. He will have a joyful time. We do not dare send him down to the Co. alone for fear they will raise the d---l with him in some way. I have not been very well to day but am going to be to morrow. I recd a letter from Arthur, at home. All is well & I am well content.

Benson had a letter from Capt. May to night in which he says that it is ten to one that he whips Handy the next time he sees him. He & Handy have fallen out in respect to their bravery, each accusing the other of cowardice. Till we have seen sharper fighting than we (2d Regt.) have yet, I look upon an officer's bravery very much as I should on a woman's virtue. When much is said of either I look upon it with suspicion. It seems to me if they had known or thought how quick men are in times of danger to detect the slightest word, look or action which is doubtful they would both have been more careful. They are both likely to tell considerable truth which might not otherwise have become public.

§ DECEMBER 28 Weather warm & pleasant. I rather pity Seward. He is on Camp Guard to day & a deal of trouble he has.

At guard mounting he gave the order "Inspection Arms" while the guns were at shoulder. Inspected arms as badly as possible; took his post after inspection two paces in rear of the front rank; "Officer of Guard will take his post" roared the Adjutant. He then neglected to present arms to the officer of the day when he should. The guard stood at present [arms]. Adjutant shouted "Officer of Guard present arms!" He either did not hear or was too scared to obey. "Officer of Guard present arms!" roared the Adjutant fairly black in the face. Seward made a dive with his sword as if he were trying to spear apples off a tree with a pole & if it had been sharp would have cut a drummer's head off with it when he brought it back to a shoulder. As it was however he only knocked him down on to one knee.

At noon he swore he was nearly ready to resign & at night he was quite. He says he will either go to a convent or become a detective policeman. He told all the guards this m'g that they must not leave the guard tent without his permission. In less than 10 minutes they were all gone but one. Seventeen prisoners asked permission all at the same time to go after some necessary article.

At supper time 2 prisoners had escaped. He was fairly crazy — had been on the jump every minute, was nearly tired to death, supposed he would be arrested &c.

Nine P.M. Seward has just been here swearing the most horrible oaths. Boren has just escaped & 3 others with him. He swears that he would give $100.00 for the privilege of shooting half the prisoners or he would give $10.00 to any man who would insure their presence in the morning. I dont believe there was ever a man on the rack in more misery than he is. He says he believes they must know that he is green.

§ DECEMBER 29 3 P.M. Weather very fine. The Chaplain is preaching to the prisoners over opposite our tent. The only way he can get a congregation is to take those who are under arrest. He threatens to have the whole Regt. arrested & brought to divine service. He says it is utterly devoid of religious enthusiasm. Seward came off barely alive this morning.

Mason & Slidell are to be given up.* I presume it is right & the best thing that can be done in our present situation. As soon as this is over I would however pluck John Bull's whiskers till he would roar. I do not believe Bull would have dared to fight. If he had I think Russia & U.S. could have divided his possessions in N. America in a manner which would have reminded him of 1776. It is better perhaps to end this affair which we have already on hand. When this [is] over there will be a great army of soldiers who will be ready for almost any enterprise.

I obtained quite a notoriety among the privates of this Regt. when on picket last time by making a soldier pay $4.00 for stealing a pig. They swear it is the hardest thing they ever heard of. They pretty much all know me now & swear awfully abt me when I am gone. I notice however that they keep in their places pretty well when I am present. Co's. I, A, K & most of H like me but the rest of them hate me worse than the d---l. Col. Poe says that Benson & I are the only officers who try to live up to their duty & we dont more than half succeed. It is pretty hard work — uphill business for us when we are alone but when we happen to be on duty together we can make things go to suit us. Co. I goes like a clock.

---

* On November 8 Confederate diplomats James Mason and John Slidell had been taken off the British mail steamer *Trent* by a Federal cruiser, inaugurating a period of saber-rattling in London and Washington.

I would rather like it if he & I could take some of these Co's. for a week or two. We are going to have it arranged if possible so that he can be officer of the day & I officer of the guard at the same time so that we can train the guards & prisoners. We are not oppressive by any means & do not go an inch beyond the regulations of the regular army nor do we intend to stop an inch short of them. It is far better for officers & soldiers that the regulations should be enforced.

There has not been a man of our Co. in the guard house for more than a month & I do not believe there will be in 3 months. They are kept the strictest of any Co. in the Regt. Co's. where things are at loose ends have from 3 to 5 in the guard house all the time. The sooner men make up their minds that they are soldiers & not citizens the better it will be for all concerned.

It rather surprises me that Benson & I ever agreed. We disliked each other or at least I did him when we came into the Co. at Ft. Wayne & Camp Scott, for more than 3 weeks we never agreed well till we both got mad at Crego. After Bull Run we agreed still better. We had then a common object to work for — commissions. When these were obtained each for a time needed the other's assistance to sustain him in the many new duties & not few troubles which at once devolved upon us. We have neither of us found it as yet convenient to labor apart if the thing was possible under our present circumstances.

That he possesses in a high degree the qualities of an officer cannot be denied. His natural good qualities, strengthened in early life by an exemplary education have not been wholly obscured by the bad company which he has since kept for a large part of the time. He has improved in conduct & company very much since he enlisted. I believe he will reform entirely. He has a father & many other relatives of the highest respectability & abundant wealth. He has only to behave himself & he can have every advantage which heart can wish.

I thought once that I would *at least suffer* him to go his downward way so that he might be out of my path. I might have hastened his journey very much. Before I had really made up my mind to do this our relations brought us in nearer contact. I found that he liked me better than I did him, he might be a useful friend, he is a younger man than I & I could assist him, in short, matters might so turn (they have) that it would be for my own interest to assist him. I resolved to do it for a while at least & the longer I did so the more inclined I was to continue. We have helped each other on more than one occasion very materially.

There are some wide differences of opinion between us, we occasionally get vexed at each other, but on the whole there are no two officers in the Regt. who hang to each other & who like to be together on duty as well as we. We have both been 50 times on the point of quarreling but always concluded that the necessity of the case did not demand it. He is exceedingly obstinate & I dont like to yield, consequently the danger of a quarrel. If I were sure that I could thrash him I think it would have come long ago. I would not hesitate to accept it if he would commence but he wont & I hardly dare to on any of our small differences. Furthermore it would be very foolish & we would both get court martialed.

Benson left home 8 years ago without his parents' consent, came to Kalamazoo, was there 4 years in the employ of a man who did a large business, but was a rascal & took pains to instruct others. During that time he stood high & moved in the best society. He then joined a Utah expedition & spent 3 years on the plains as a govt. express messenger &c. Here he fell into hard company; it had been none too good in Kalamazoo. He then returned to Kalamazoo, fell into still worse company. He went into a drinking & billiard saloon — general gambling house & great resort for prostitutes &c &c. The good company he once kept at once turned their backs on him.

This drove him still deeper down. He took to boxing & once got so far as to go into training for a prize fight. This lowered him in the estimation of all to the level of the class with whom he associated. He felt the degradation but seemed to have no thought of remedying it by reformation. At his stage of affairs he enlisted.

He never drank much, not at all now, seldom gambles. In fact leads in every way a respectable life. All that is necessary is for him to keep away from those d----d holes & he will be what he ought. He has a remarkable degree of control over himself & can do so if he will. He assured me with the utmost sincerity not 3 days since that he would never return to such business while he lived.

§ DECEMBER 30 They are practicing at Ft. Lyon to day with 32 pdrs. Although it is 2 miles off I can hear the balls whistle & strike the ground very distinctly. Our servt. Noble went to Alexandria to day, got drunk, & has not yet returned. We have been obliged to pick up our living as best we could.

§ DECEMBER 31 We were out at daylight this m'g for muster. The whole affair was over before 9 A.M. & we were back to our quarters. Noble has not yet returned. I think we shall have to send him back to the Co. again. He has gotten to be a man of more consequence than we can afford. I sent by him for the Atlantic & I care more abt getting that than anything else. I presume Noble is shut up in the Slave Pen by the Provost Guard. If so he may lie there. We have kept him more as an oddity than anything else.

I might go home on recruiting service for 6 months if I desired. I dont care to go. All other things being equal I would rather be picketing on the out posts than any place I have yet found.

Benson is officer of the day. I wish I was on with him. He has done what ought to have been done long ago, to wit, got 4 of the prisoners tied to trees. Tie their hands behind them & then tie the rope fast to a small tree. In this way you are pretty sure to find them if you have to go away a few minutes, when you come back. I proposed to have a chain put around their necks & fastened to a tree but I think this is as well. There is no sufficient place to keep them & they are getting exceedingly troublesome.

This is a most beautiful & romantic country. Still there seems something decayed, neglected, mournful about everything. Perhaps if I could have seen it at another time it would have looked different to me. Everything is so unlike Mich. Everybody lives away off the road & seems to have done all that they ever expect to except going through the mere formula of living. The idea of anything new or business like strikes one as exceedingly out of place, a great innovation on customs immemorially established.

I have not seen a new house since I came into Va. They have all those monstrous chimneys at one or both ends which I have so often wondered at in picture books. The house may burn up or rot down but the chimney remains firm as a tower. These chimneys standing alone are often all that is left to mark the spot where was perhaps a happy home, monuments alike to the departed joys which once clustered around them & to the general decline of the country where they are found. At each plantation you will also see a strong old building of brick or stone arranged with loop holes for musketry as a precaution against the possible workings of her peculiar institution.

One on taking a walk here has much the same feelings so far as regards the country as if he were in a grave yard, subdued, solemn thoughts of the many things which have been, not what is or will be. This may be called the classic ground of America perhaps & the memory of the statesmen & orators, warriors & patriots which are here buried lend a sacredness to the place which nothing can destroy. This is about its only claim to respect. Its high rocky hills, its pure crystal fountains, its clear healthful air, its distant & enchanting scenes would all point it out as a country where health & courage of body should be united with mental vigor & large share of taste, poetry, eloquence & refinement. From our own camp we have a most enchanting view of the Potomac for more than fifteen miles.

Benson & Goebel (1st Lieut. of Co. A) had a glorious time last night. They are both good men & they had business enough from taps till 2 this m'g. Goebel got so mad at his own Co. that he did not know which end he stood on. He was trying to arrest some of them when one tried to tap him on the head with a stick of wood. He knocked him down with the hilt of his sword & kicked him abt 10 rods down the hill into a brook & then took him to the guard house. By this time Benson came around & called out the whole of Co. I & marched them down to A's quarters with loaded guns. He and Goebel then went for them, "py Yesus I cag & puck (gag & buck) every man in the Co." They begged & pleaded in all sorts of Dutch, German & French to be let off but Goebel swore that if "Yesus" himself was there making a muss he would "cag & puck him py Got."

They finally took 4 to the guard house, tied & gagged them & let the rest go. They then seized 4 or 5 Corpls. & Sergts. of Co. C & arrested 2 Lieuts., Turner & Shearer, and made an effort to arrest some men of Co. B who threw stones at the guard while they arrested A's men. At 2 A.M. they had succeeded in quieting all the noise & Co. I returned to quarters. Corpl. Mack was the only man of our Co. who was riotous. He will get straightened.

Seven

COMPANY
OFFICER

⌒◡

Charles Haydon's commission as 1st lieutenant, dated February 7, 1862, put him second in command of Company I, 2nd Michigan Infantry, a posting he had been filling unofficially for several weeks. He devotes a good deal of space in his journal in these first months of 1862 to a description of what he took to be the duties of a conscientious company officer, and no other Civil War journal is more informative on this important topic. Haydon also continues to be thoughtfully descriptive of wartime Virginia, in particular its notorious wintertime mud and the war's effect on its population. In mid-March came the long-awaited order for the commencement of McClellan's spring campaign. The 2nd Michigan prepared to embark for the Peninsula.

* * *

§ JANUARY 1, 1862 A lovelier New Year never gladdened the face of the earth. The sun is warm & bright. The wind is just strong enough to be pleasant. A light blue mist hangs over the Potomac & around the tops of the distant hills. It is one of those dreamy, lovely, trance like days when life & animation seem half suspended. There is an absence of pain & trouble but after all no real, vivid, lively pleasure such as accompanies action. One feels very lazy & is willing that the world & mankind generally should journey on after their own sort. I would like to spend a few hours of this day with the dear good folks at home.

I find out some interesting particulars abt Benson's & Goebel's adventure which they did not relate. When they went to the 1st tent of Co. A the men blew out the light. Goebel & a Sergt. of A went into the tent & Benson was just getting in when his hat was shoved down over his eyes & he landed abt 10 ft. in front of the tent. Goebel & the Sergt. followed close after & both got their posteriors well booted as they came out. Goebel used some choice language abt that time & I believe Benson was not slow.

Capts. Benson & Handy, Lieuts. Crego, Seward & self mess together. We had a good roast turkey & so far as dinner was concerned it was good enough for anybody. With our dinner we each drank a quart bottle of champagne. I was not exactly drunk but I was nearer to it than I care to be again. I could walk straight enough for all common purposes & knew what I was doing so far as not to allow myself to get very noisy or nonsensical. Poor Seward had to be put to bed & Crego put himself to bed soon after. I have felt most wretchedly mean ever since. Benson & I gave the Co. 6 doz. bottles of ale to drink with their dinner.

Just at dark I saw the body of a man from the 5th [Michigan] who had a bullet put through his forehead this m'g while on picket. Also a Lieut. of the 5th whose cheek was furrowed at the same time. Five other men of the 5th & 2 of our Regt. are reported wounded. Several of the enemy were killed. The Adjutant has just been around to inform us that they are apprehensive of an attack on this brigade before morning. The wind has commenced blowing very hard. The noise & darkness of the day makes the time very suitable. It would be impossible for us to hear firing at the out posts & they might approach near us before it would be known if they moved with rapidity.

§ JANUARY 2 The order transferring the 2d to the Artillery needs only Gen. Richardson's signature & that he has refused. Good bye Mich. 2d if that be true. Richardson Major Gen., Terry* Brigadier Gen., Col. Poe resigns & the 2d Mich. is defunct for all practical purposes.

I have to go to Court Martial at headquarters to morrow in Boren's case. Billy Mack is heart broken, his lady love has "soured"

---

* Henry D. Terry was colonel of the 5th Michigan.

on him, as Sid Prentice says. The boys nearly ran over Seward to day on drill.

§ JANUARY 4 For the last 2 days I have been attending the general Court Martial at headquarters to give evidence in the Boren case. He however pled guilty & I was not called upon to testify. It was a very good move on him to do so & I am afraid that by it he will get off with but a slight punishment. The officers comprising the Court are all from the volunteers & have but little idea of the real requisites of a Court Martial.

Gen. R. serves this Regt. most confounded mean. His signature is all that is needed to put us into the Artillery, into good quarters, a more honorable position &c &c. Instead of that he keeps us here with the poorest camp of any in the brigade, with double guard duty, camp & picket, and all this after bringing us from good grounds because he quarreled with his superiors. We left Arlington because he had a quarrel with McDowell. The 2d day after we reached here he quarreled with Heintzelman. I have no doubt that he likes this Regt. but it looks as though it were going to be a very unprofitable liking for us. It looks now as though his love would be the death of the Regt.

Terry will be Brigadier Gen. when Poe will of course resign. He likes the Regt. & would gladly stay with it if he can have it where he wants it. It is no matter of necessity with him. He can have other places which will be more pleasant for him & full as profitable by asking for them.* If he leaves we have a miserable stick for a Col.† — a good man at home — and half the officers resign.

I am determined not to leave the service but God knows that in such a case I would feel that nearly everything was lost for us. I should be entirely disheartened. I did not think when we used to build forts days & stand picket nights to gratify the Gen. that this would be his return. An honor & a benefit has at last been offered us from headquarters & he takes it away. He undoubtedly thinks there will be a chance to work on forts again in the spring. We only got 6 weeks extra fatigue duty by coming here from Arlington.

---

* Haydon assumed Poe's influence at headquarters from his previous service as McClellan's aide.
† Lt. Col. Sylvester Larnerd.

§ JANUARY 6 Snow fell last night abt one inch deep & remained all day. I had a most wretched toothache last night but it ceased abt 12 & has not yet returned. I was rejoiced to hear from home to day. This is the first news from there for a long time.

The subject of artillery still agitates the Regt. Gen. Richardson has submitted an argument, 8 pages of foolscap long, opposing it. Col. Poe is going to write an answer which will probably end the affair. There is considerable chance of success. I was detailed on picket yesterday but the pickets were recalled & I did not go. Benson has gone to Washington to day.

§ JANUARY 7 Snow abt 2 in. deep, weather moderately cold. There is some prospect that we may be transferred to the Artillery. Over 600 Pvts. signed a petition to that effect. Fred Eames of Co. K who is in the Brigade quartermaster's department tried to circulate a counter petition thereon & came near being mobbed. The men drove him off the ground.

There is one draw back abt all this. I am afraid that should there soon be an advance we shall be left behind in our fort. I should not like that. If I am to be in the Artillery I want to be where there will be something done. The idea of being shut up while the rest of the army is on the road to Richmond is very unpleasant. I think there is little danger of that however.

Seward is on guard to day. When the prisoners saw him coming they commenced punching one another's ribs & winking. "There comes that Seward, we'll have fun to day." They are all gone but three.

I would rather let the Artillery go than miss the great battles which I believe will be fought at Centreville & Manassas. I want to visit those places once more. If the war is of long continuance we shall gain by the change but if it closes soon we shall lose. If we could come out in the spring as light artillery it would be a most glorious thing but if the army advances soon we have only to look on & curse our ill luck.

The reported treason of Adjutant Gen. [Lorenzo] Thomas makes a great stir. It is said that but for that we should have been on our road this m'g for the "land of cotton." There was it is said to have been an advance on the whole line.

The probability of my remaining in the army seems to increase daily. We are all in a whirl & no one can tell where we shall rest. At least I shall do what I can to prepare myself. I think there is little doubt that my practice of law is among things past. Good bye law: I am sorry we had to part so soon. The necessities of the times however demand it.

We are not the only friends who part in these times not to meet again. I came to the war just at the right time for my own interest. It is much better to serve 6 months as a Sergt. than not if one knows nothing of military, infinitely better than to be obliged to buy commissions like the lieutenants who enter the service now. Two of my acquaintances in Mich. have spent $1100.00 trying to get men enough to secure them commissions but have not as yet succeeded.*

North went home on recruiting service this m'g & thereby saved his legs for a time. He has always had a presentiment that he is to come out of the war on wooden legs.

§ JANUARY 8 Brigade drill P.M. It rains to night. The report of Adjutant Thomas' treason is contradicted. I hope it is not true. There is a bad leak somewhere. We have been obliged several times of late to change our countersign because the enemy had learned of it by some means.

Benson came home last night. A little child of love at Washington took all the strength out of him. He is nearly used up. I made a good thing exchanging guard turns with Seward. It was my turn to go on to morrow but I was detailed for Regt. Court Martial to night & consequently by means of the exchange go clear entirely. We picket by Regt. now & have only to go 3 days out of 36 leaving an interval of 33 days between each tour. We shall not have to go on more than twice before good weather.

Col. Poe was to day asked the question whether soldiers did not by long service acquire a love of obedience, become more respectful & easily governed &c. He replied that such, like most others, were good, very good, very respectful & obedient so long as the iron hand was upon them but not one moment longer. The moment it was relaxed they were the worst of any. I believe it. There is not a more intelligent, more moral or better educated Co. in the Regt. than ours nor is there any which is held as strict when Benson & I are with it. The moment our backs are turned they begin to step over the lines little by little cautiously at first but soon with

---

* That is, the practice of raising new companies (rather than recruiting the strength of the old ones) by paying enlistment bonuses.

bold strides. They changed officers in the Co. for drill to day & they came under the charge of Lt. Morton of Co. G. They very soon found how matters stood & there was not a Co. in the Regt. acted worse than they.

§ JANUARY 10 I have had two tiresome days on Court Martial. We have tried 8 men, 6 Pvts. & 2 Corpls. The men have already been 40 days in the guard house & we concluded to let them all off with a fine of $8.00 each.

Richardson & Heintzelman are both down on this Regt. most woefully. Never mind the 2d can take care of itself in any place where drilling, fighting or stealing is to be done without any help from either of them. It was always the worst used Regt. in all respects except praise. There never were any Regts. in the brigade with which we agreed except the Mass. 14th & the N.Y. 37th. Our men & the 37th have some spats but on the whole agree remarkably well. Yesterday one of their sentinels got after some of our men who were trying to steal a straw stack. "Out wid ye" said Pat. "Ye d----d Division thaves, ye're stealin' the whole wurld up & it's all laid to us. Ye've burned up all the rails in two miles of here & now you want to carry off the ground too, dont ye?" I am glad he did his duty so well. The men had to pay a dollar for their rascality.

The weather is foggy & rainy. The ground is plastered with mud knee deep. We can have no drills or parades & can hardly stir out of our tents. There is no knowing whether we shall get out of this. I do not care a great deal if Col. Poe will remain.

Benson is lecturing Prentice about drinking. Sid has been taking a sly nip. Sid comes back on him as the cause. The argument is in sober earnest & there is reason enough for it. Benson lectures him severely on his evil courses. Prentice retaliates by reminding him of the time he coaxed away his woman & seduced her. Benson comes back with the inquiry as to who first piloted him into a house of prostitution? The scores seem pretty near even but Benson is a cool calculating wiry chap who can tend to all such matters when he likes & leaves them when he likes, but Prentice is one of those constant confiding fellows who goes it blind & once on the downhill road can not easily be turned.

Corpl. Coleman's dignity met with a serious reverse last night. There was a row in the cabin & the Corpl. got up in his shirt to command silence & restore order. He had no sooner struck a light than two of the graceless rascals made for him, one with a red hot poker & the other with a red hot shovel. They brought these in close proximity to his bare legs & commanded him to dance — he did so. They then commanded him to hold up his right hand & swear eternal fidelity to his squad. This too after some delay was done. He was then commanded to stand on his head. This for a while he stoutly refused but the hot pokers & bayonets had by this time so multiplied around him that there was no escape. This last feat being performed he was allowed to retire to his bunk.

It is a big thing to be a Corpl. when none of the officers or Sergts. are present to keep the men in check. No man that we have ever had, Johnston excepted, could govern a squad without a great deal of assistance. The men think "The dignity which doth hedge a Corpl. round" is no great thing.

§ JANUARY 11 A man of the 5th [Michigan] Regt. was killed on picket yesterday. A Minie ball struck him in the forehead which shattered his head all to pieces nearly taking the top of it off. Those Minie, Sharp, & Enfield balls tear a terrible hole. Their weight & velocity is so great that bones stand a poor chance. Out of any given number of men who are shot in battle it is said that twice as many die who are struck by these balls as among those who are hit by the ordinary musket balls. It is reported that the 5th killed two of the enemy.

We finished up 8 Court Martial cases to day & sent them in to the Col. The offence were all absence without leave. Two were Corpls. whom we reduced to the ranks. The privates had been in the guard house 40 days & we let them off with a fine of $8.00 each thinking that sufficient to pay for a drunken spree of one night.

Corpls. Ball & Coleman will be reduced to the ranks to morrow for long continued neglect & ignorance of duty. They have done no one very serious thing but have been deficient in a number of small ones. They could not desist from talking & laughing in the ranks, had to be spoken to every day or two about standing at attention at roll call. These things are not to be allowed in a private, & in a non-commissioned officer, who is expected to be perfection itself in all the minutiae of military affairs, it cannot be endured.

Again they had no control over their squads. They were rolled & tumbled about at the will of the men. Disobedience to Corpls. is the germ & fountainhead of insubordination in the whole army. Sergts. quartering apart from the men & being less familiar with them have less trouble in sustaining their authority although they have really very little more power. If I had command of some of these Co's. I would have all the non-coms. in them standing on their heads before one day was past.

§ JANUARY 12 Very warm with high wind. The Col. complimented the Co. highly at Inspection. The Pensacola went down the river last night & there was very sharp firing between her & the batteries. A man of Co. D has sent a written complaint to the Col. agt Benson for punishing him while on guard. I think Benson will now Court Martial him for the same offence.

A large number of officers of this Regt. are drunk full half the time & some of them all the time. Col. Poe is lying in wait for them & a few of them will find some day that U.S. has no further need of their services.

Capt. Benson's house 8 P.M. Prentice took an inventory of his personal property a short time since & found it to consist of one pr. drawers, one hickory shirt, one Testament on lids of which were pasted 3 recipes for the cure of private diseases & 2 for making cooling drinks. These with some old letters constituted the entire stock. The men are very careful at all inspections to have their Testaments in some very conspicuous part of their knapsacks.

But to return to Capt. B.'s house. It is a board house 10 by 12 feet with 2 windows, one of 4 panes, the other of 6 & a stately door which I am told (God forgive the sacrilege) was once a part of a church & probably would have been now if the 2d or the Garibaldi Guards had never seen it. As it is however it constitutes the greater part of the front of Capt. Benson's house. On that door is a lock the key of which the Capt. very dexteriously extracted from the door of a Secesh house where we went after a drink.

The furniture consists of one table, two shelves, 4 stools, one bed, one trunk & one stove mounted on a cheese box filled with dirt. Three swords with very bright mountings, two of them pretty sharp & one (Seward) very blunt (so as not to cut his legs off when he brings it down or his arms off when he brings it up) hang agt the wall. Beside them are 2 of Colt's best with boxes for ammunition. Such ornaments are too heavy for Seward. On the walls also hang some coats with a great many bright buttons & shoulder straps said to be gold, all clothes even to shirts, caps &c of true Union blue. Two heavy crimson sashes & some other military fixin's make the sum total of this department. On the table are Army

Regulations, Military Dictionary, Field Fortifications, out post duties &c &c and the Atlantic, some newspapers, writing material, a fine tooth comb, paper of pins, diamond polish for swords.

Prentice who is our constant attendant & who is fast become indispensible reclines at full length on the bed talking to himself abt the propriety of "drowning sorrow in the flowing bowl." The Capt. will not let him go out of camp unless he or I are along to see that he does not get overcome by that "flowing bowl." There are no bottles in the Capt.'s tent & no liquor is drunk there except sometimes by visitors who think they are *ill used* if not *well treated.*

Contrary to military custom in this case the Capt. & one Lieut. to wit myself always room together. This is in reality incorrect. The Capt. should be alone but we prefer to have it otherwise & no one objects. The rigid distinctions of rank are carefully preserved between us when on duty or in presence of our Co. but inside the house there is a very large share of the free & easy.

§ JANUARY 14 Benson has the blues to night. I have them sometimes. He has been a little that way for 3 or 4 days. He said to me to night that he did not see how he could have acted as he has. His father had a very pretty ward, who had $30,000 in cash at her disposal. She lived at his father's & was engaged to be married to our Capt. when he went from home. She waited for him over 6 years. Benson got in bad company, forgot for the time his lady & forgot likewise to write to her for the space of 10 months. At the end of that time he made up his mind to go home if all was right. He wrote to the girl first to find out. In due time the answer came with information that she supposing that he had abandoned her & knowing nothing of his whereabouts had — in short — been married a week when his letter came. She was exceedingly sorry that it did not come sooner, liked him a great deal better than the man she married & a great many such consoling things.

Benson's good resolves were knocked in the head. He lay drinking for 2 days, got sober, felt ashamed of his drunkenness, cursed himself as the biggest fool on earth. He has felt sorry about it ever since but never could quite make up his mind what is the next best thing to do. I think he will go home after the war if he does not go to his other home before that time. Swindler alias Prentice says he knows all about such things. "Twice ye have kroased by paith" as Prentice's theatricals say. He repeats this often to Benson.

The 2d Regt. has *Enfield rifles.* [Haydon later inserted here "mistake."] Gen. Richardson says they were intended for us but seeing we are going into the Artillery we wont need them. We can tell him what he very well knows — that we could *take* them if we were a mind to. He had better be a little careful. It would not have taken much to have regained their good will before but now it will be a hard matter. They are a harder set than I want to have down on me. Col. Poe is not a man either to be fooled with. He can beat Gen. R. badly in the end.

Col. says that we shall have our guns before long. I dont want any quarrel with our old Gen. & I think that he will find his "Pet Lambs" rather unpleasant enemies. Gen. McClellan says that he prefers to have this Regt. remain as Infantry for the present because he has some work for us.

§ JANUARY 15 A most lonesome unpleasant day. The snow is abt 2 ins. deep & it has been raining & snowing all day. There is a hard crust & everything is covered with ice.

This will be a used up country when the war is over. The niggers all say they are going to leave before the army goes. They generally behave pretty well but they know a great deal too much. This war is the certain destruction of slavery. If they are not liberated they will behave so bad that they will have to kill them all.

§ JANUARY 16 Pay day. I put $212.50 in my pocket for the last 2 months service. It was all in treasury notes. They are bright, fresh, have very good pictures of Abe Lincoln on them & pass pretty well. One cannot help thinking some times of the paper currency of our Revolution & the Assignats of the French Revolution.

I sent $80 home. I am going to try & have a little money on hand if possible when I come out of the war. There is no knowing how, when or where that will be, but so long as one has a little spare change he can get always almost anywhere.

Corpl. Mack will get sent to the ranks I think. If I had commanded the Co. he would have gone long ago. His faults have been far more serious than those of Ball or Coleman. I was truly sorry for those two. They had not the slightest idea of such a thing till the order was read on Dress Parade. They went back to their tents & commenced ripping off their stripes & chevrons while the big tears were rolling down their cheeks. They did not say a word but I know it cut them severely. They came out next morning in the list of privates & in private's uniform. If they behave well I shall do all I can to have them restored after a while.

We start in the morning for a 3 days tour on picket. The snow, water & mud are full ankle deep. The whole Regt. goes. I am not very well. I have not been free from a headache since the champagne I drank on New Years. It will be a long time ere you get so much of the cursed stuff down me again. There is a good deal of noise & drunkenness in camp to night.

Col. Poe says he dont see why my comm. as 1st Lieut. dont come. I dont either & should have got $4.00 more pay to day if I had had it. I do not like this always acting as something which you are not. I always acted 2d Sergt. while I was 3d & have acted 1st Lt. ever since I was promoted 2d.

§ JANUARY 18 Yesterday we were off for picketing at 8 A.M. The ground was frozen hard & the walking was very good. The Regt. reached headquarters abt 10 A.M. & by 11 A.M. our Co. was posted next on the left of the Telegraph Road. The shanties are comfortable & Capt. & I have a comfortable log house for ourselves & reserve. By the time we were posted the roads began to be very soft & before night the mud was ankle deep. I made the rounds at nine but the mud was so deep I went no more during the night. The men should regularly be called up every m'g an hour before daylight. We have however our own men & non-comd. officers & know that they need very little watching.

The night was quiet as anything could be. Weather warm & foggy with some rain. This m'g there is considerable rain. Abt noon raining hard, came an order to advance the pickets 2 miles. We set out & marched a mile toward Accotink when we were ordered to halt. We remained there in the wood abt 3 hours after which we marched back & picketed along the Accotink road back to the general quarters at Potter's.

The pickets now run from the river to Accotink village, thence diagonally along to Accotink road to the Telegraph Road near Potter's. From the Telegraph Road a little below Potter's in a circular line around to the Orange & Alexandria R.R. which is I believe the extent of our Div. line. Thence the line runs around to the Potomac at a point abt 10 mi. above the Chain bridge. It requires abt 4 Regts. to fill the line. From the Accotink to the river the line is now 2 miles advanced from the point where we found them.

The headache troubled me a little yesterday but it is all gone now. It was the result of too little exercise & too much eating, as diseases usually are.

I think it a great piece of good fortune to Benson that he enlisted as he did. A more favorable opportunity could not have been found for lifting himself above the associations & companions with whom he was surrounded. He has improved & has so well succeeded that I think he will never return to them.

§ JANUARY 19 Pickets being posted & all arranged Capt. & I took quarters at our old house again. It was quite late in the afternoon when the men were posted but they fell to work with a will to build shanties. There was a fence opposite a part of them & they very soon had comfortable places. Some others found a deserted house & by taking the doors and all the boards they could tear loose soon made themselves good shelters.

There was an attack apprehended owing to our advance & the men were on the alert. I started on the rounds at 10 P.M. When I was near the furthest end of our Co. pickets I heard a gun farther down the road. I gave the men their instructions in case of attack to deploy a little to each side of their posts, lie down on the ground, behind trees if possible, & watch till they came near enough so that they could be sure of them & not back from their posts till they were forced to it. I then went along Co. H's line toward where the gun was fired. As I came near their 4th post — whang — went another gun abt 10 rods ahead of me. I snatched my pistol, stepped behind a pine tree of which were a plenty nearby & waited to see what would be the result.

After abt 2 minutes & not seeing or hearing anything more I went up to the post. It seemed they had heard something & thought they saw a man lurking among the pine trees, therefore they fired to venture. They were excited & as I supposed fired hastily. They had a sergt. with them who is reported a cool, discreet man but on this occasion he did not do the best. When he had notice of the noise he should have silently got his men out into safe positions where they could see without being seen & then have crept cautiously toward the spot either alone or with one man. In this way if there was anyone there he would have been pretty sure of a good shot at them & if not he would have saved a false alarm, the occurrance of which is always more or less injurious to the reputation of all connected with it as well as the safety of the line.

It has been raining now for several hours. There was no further disturbance during the night.

§ January 20 Home once more. Thank God. Last night was one of the worst nights for picketing that I ever saw. There was a drizzling rain & dense fog all night. The dripping from the trees at every gust made a noise very difficult to be distinguished from footsteps. You could see but a few feet & the fog caused everything to appear 3 times its natural size. There was a nearly full moon or it would have been impossible to see anything. The 2d Lt. of Co. H was shot at just before dark while passing along the line. Some of the enemy were seen lurking around the hills not far off, all of which together with the gloom & uncertainty of the night produced some effect on our men & a very decided one on Co. H.

I passed along the line between 12 & 1 & again just before daylight. I confess that I more than once took hold of my revolver & slid it up & down in the case to see whether it was exactly right although I well knew that it could not be otherwise. I found the men very wide awake & on one or two occasions all of them on the lookout at the same time. At several places they were very sure they had heard men walking & had heard them talking in a low tone. It may have been so but I doubt it.

It was easy to tell who was scared. Those who were cool & knew their duty, when they heard me as all could at a good distance, splashing along through the mud & water, would step noiselessly behind a bush or tree & the first I would hear or see would be a short low firm & fearfully distinct *halt,* and the muzzle of a loaded & cocked gun not 2 feet from my breast. Those who were weak in the knees would roar out h–a–l–t at a distance of 10 rods in a voice whose tremulousness was perfectly apparent even at that distance. There was only one shot fired on our line, that at a stump. The fog drifting along in streaks now dense now thin gave to objects an apparent motion. There were 4 men of our Co. who showed cowardice badly, the rest were firm. It was almost impossible to keep a part of Co. H on their posts.

One of our men went off after provisions without leave yesterday noon & has not been seen since. I fear he was shot by the same men who shot at the Lt. of Co. H.

We reached home abt 4 P.M. to day perfectly covered with mud. We fairly wallowed in mud for 3 days. There were full 72 hours of rain during our tour of duty. I was wet & tired not having had off my clothes, boots or belts during the time. My feet & clothes have not been dry for 3 days.

§ JANUARY 21 A very stale weary life we have at present. The weather is like the worst of springtime in Mich. We have no drills, parades or anything else. They can hardly get provisions here from Alexandria. The mud is knee deep all the time.

§ JANUARY 22 I made out to get Dickens' "Great Expectations" from town to day & also some good military maps all which afford me great pleasure.

There has been a good deal of drunkenness & absence without leave. To morrow we are going to have some of them sitting astride a pole all day. I have commenced giving a course of instruction to our Corpls. They need it & I cannot better employ a few of my leisure hours. We have a most glorious lot of Corpls. & they will turn out some good Sergts. & in turn Lieuts. if well instructed & encouraged. There is nothing like knowing how to stimulate ambition & soldierly pride & emulation among non-comd. officers. It tends wonderfully to lighten the duties of the officers & give promptness & activity to the Co.

I am still on Court Martial. Corpl. Mack is reduced to the ranks & Charley Butler appointed in his place. We have done sending men to the guard house for drunkenness. We just tie their hands & feet, gag them & put them to bed till they get sober.

§ JANUARY 24 There is to night one of the worst storms of the season — rain & snow. Benson has gone to the city. I have been getting ready to drill the Co. on skirmishing & bayonet exercise but there is no knowing when the weather will permit. Handy & Crego were both very drunk to night. I thought I should have to send them both out doors but finally succeeded in persuading them to pay the Sergt. Major a visit & thus escaped them.

Crego has just returned from the city where his pocket was picked of $100.00. Court Martial still in session. I have been on camp guard but once since we came here.

Benson talks of getting a set of boxing gloves to day for Seward's amusement. Benson is a good boxer & I know very well that he will serve S. as he used to Prentice at home, viz coax him into his room, lock the door & not let him out till he puts on the gloves & then punch him till the breath of life is hardly left in him. S. is very enthusiastic but has never tried them. If his ardor is not dampened by the time both arms are black & blue to the elbow, ribs so sore he cant draw a long breath, eyes black & nose knocked down, as they will be in a very short time in his case, I am very much mistaken in the man. I have had a taste of these things & relish it immensely in others & do not object to it myself very seriously.

§ JANUARY 25 It is an ill wind that blows nowhere. Now that we have finally settled down on the facts that we cant get into the Artillery & that we are on bad terms with Gen. Richardson, Heintzelman has taken a wonderful fancy for us. He & Col. Poe agree remarkably. Gen. H. tells him to take no further notice of Gen. R. or his staff but to draw all our stores & supplies direct from headquarters. This chance of showing our independence is not lost. Gen. Richardson has been down twice lately looking through our camp as he used to, but I could not see that he spoke to anyone or that anyone took any notice of him.

I could never have believed that Regimental pride ran so high with us as it does if I had not seen it. The likes & dislikes, more especially the latter, of soldiers are very strong. I dont believe there is a Pvt. in the Regt. who would not go ½ mile out of his way to get rid of saluting Gen. R. A month ago there was hardly one who would not have laid down his life for him. Our men would today rather shoot or bayonet one of the 5th Mich. than a Secesh.

The other Regts. of the brigade have all new Austrian rifles. They sent up Minie muskets for us but they were not new. The men would not touch them till they were assured by Col. Poe that they were better guns (which is indeed true) than the Austrian rifles. They are an excellent gun. They carry flush up 40 rods with level sights & have a raised sight which brings the ball with a good degree of accuracy up to 165 rods.

§ JANUARY 26 A lovely morning. Co. inspection by myself. All in good order. Co. looks well. Guard mounting was well done this m'g for the first time in a good while. The ground is so bad that we never can have a good guard here.

The Quartermaster's wife came out to see guard mounting. She took post on the hill back of our quarters. I thought the men would go crazy at the sight of her ankles. She is a very pretty lady & has indeed as pretty a pair of ankles as I ever looked upon. They are a great deal too nice to exhibit in that way to the aggravation of soldiers. I swore when I saw them that if I ever got out of the war

I would seize on the first pair I came to if they were half as enticing as hers. I dont know whether she knew what a sensation she created. She would be pleased to know it though she would pout over it in company.

This is a joyful life-like spring day full of hope, energy & aspirations. One feels full of confidence, courage & enterprise on such days. Everything is exhilarating, strength-giving — no blues, no sad thoughts of the past nor forebodings of future ills. No thought of troubles, difficulties, lapses or misfortunes. All low mean thoughts are laid aside. The soul wild with enthusiasm grasps at nothing, sees nothing save unalloyed pleasure & perfect success in life. Amid the sweetest of surroundings everything moves with a flood tide toward victory.

This soldiering at times is the gayest life in the world — what a pity so many fine fellows must needs be killed by means of it. Or as North used to say, get their "toes turned up."

We have now a most excellent Co. of men. I have worked long to make them what they are & am doing something every day to improve them. There is the best lot of non-comd. officers in the Regt., two of them all fitted for commissions, yet I would not be surprised if before another year is past I should see half of them with legs or arms off or without heads or with bodies in two pieces or torn or mutilated even worse than that. Then my good soldiers will hear no more reveilles, the perfect Sergts. will get no commissions, my handy work is lost & mourning is in many a home. The hands which were strong in their country's cause are motionless, their pale calm features turned heavenward, the blue jacket faultless in its neatness is dabbled with life blood, the heart but now full of gay hopes, love, hate & the wild patriotic zeal of the battlefield has ceased to beat & the faithful soldier (there is not a truer man on earth) has joined his many millions of comrades who have gone before him. God grant their many toils & hardships may find some kind reward at last, not only for them but for those who have given their all to a sacred cause.

§ JANUARY 27 A long skirmish & bayonet drill.

§ JANUARY 29 The 37th [New York] are on picket. They had 2 men killed & 4 wounded this m'g. They stood to it well, brought off 2 prisoners & it is reported killed & wounded several of the enemy.

The weather has been fine to day. We had a most glorious skirmish drill. The men are enthusiastic & very eager for anything new in the line of drill. We fired at a mark yesterday P.M. with good success. We shall drill actively every hour when the weather will permit until the time comes for moving. I have been drilling the non-comd. officers on bayonet exercise to day & Benson [is] to night. I fear the weather will be bad to morrow.

There was a great deal of heavy firing down the river last [night]. This for some reason is almost invariably followed by rain within 24 hours. I have noticed it in many cases & have never known it to fail. Whether it is caused by the great concussion of the air or by some quality of the gas engendered by burning large quantities of powder I cannot say.

It seems for the last few days as if I never wanted a better business than soldiering. One gets such eagerness & enthusiasm after awhile as makes him half wild. A good officer on the battlefield will take no more notice of the bullets than a man all absorbed in a game will of the idle talk of others whom he does not even hear. He is as eager & watchful of every move & chance as an ardent chess or checkers player. He sees nothing & thinks of nothing but the best movements for the men before him. I think a private soldier often needs a higher degree of courage to sustain him than an officer. He may have nothing to do but stand waiting while his officer's mind is so busily employed as to shut out every thought of danger.

The ladies are very kind to soldiers while they are present & some of them when they are absent. There seems however to be a pretty general disposition to "go back on" these 3 year soldiers. More than half our Co. were engaged to be married when they left home. There are not more than 3 or 4 whose ladies have not already (to use one of Prentice's expressions) "soured on them." They for the most part take it with soldierlike fortitude. It goes very hard with some of them for a few days but they soon to all appearances swear it off. There are some reasons for all this. The soldiers are very free & easy with everything that comes in their way. It is a very discouraging thought to them no doubt. It is perhaps as well that they should look elsewhere. Many of them will never return & many more will forget them. It is as well that both should go where they please, seek their mates with freedom.

We, that is Capt. & I, have a boy 13 years old for waiter. He came from Detroit with the 5th. He had been employed there in the theatre for 3 years. He is a smart boy but about the hardest case in some respects that I ever saw. He will not steal (ie, from us) nor get drunk but he will do almost anything else. He is well enough drilled for a Sergt., learns very rapidly, and spouts Shakespeare ad libitum but he is the wickedest chap I ever saw.

§ JANUARY 30 It rains hard & did nearly all night. No drill to day. It is very lonesome & tedious. I have been quite sad during the day for some reason — because I was so idle I presume.

I finished reading "Great Expectations" to day. It is a singular book. Like most of Dickens' works it requires great patience to get through the first two thirds of the story. He seldom gets beyond what is rational & credible. Such things might happen without an unreasonable stretch of imagination. The story amounts to a good deal in the end but one must live on the wit & satire which are for the most part independent of it till he begins to think there is no story at all. I do not think there is that liveliness & vivacity about it that characterizes his earlier stories. His best days are past.

They are trying to reduce the pay of soldiers. It is a very bad policy. The pay was so low before that the army could not retain its best men. It is hardly supposable that, so long as the Govt. can pay, such a class of men as the officers of the army are or at least shall be, will willingly incur all the dangers & hardships of the war for their mere subsistence.

It is now near 10 months since I enlisted. I have spent no money foolishly & but little which was in any sense unnecessary. I have thus far barely $40.00 to fall back on in case I should leave the army minus legs or arms or as many will with broken constitutions & ruined health. I can live on less than I have. When the country is poor & exhausted I will serve it still for ¼ what I now get or when the worst comes for nothing & do it willingly. The country is now rich. It can pay all that it does. It hurts me that it should begrudge the miserable pittance which can now be saved beyond bare subsistance.

There is another feature which displeases me still more, viz that our pay is to be cut down by men who loll away more time in houses of public prostitution than they spend in legislative duties. Let them cut down their own pay to begin with or before they talk about reducing ours let them lie out in the mud & rain a few days on picket.*

§ JANUARY 31 We had a very energetic skirmish & bayonet drill to day. Benson is on fatigue & there is no one but I to drill the Co. The men are eager for drill. I have never seen them so full of enthusiasm. They are getting vindictive & bloodthirsty, willing to drill the whole day long if they can thereby be made more sure of success. I stimulate these feelings by words & actions as much as possible. A word at the right time often fills a soldier with a zeal & ambition which will be life long. I miss no such chances.

This spring will open with great events. It will be such a summer as never was seen on this continent. I await its coming with high hopes. No one knows whether he sees its end. I hope to but if I do not I have little doubt that there is some reward in store for the soldier who does his best in his country's cause. Meanwhile I will do all that lies within my limited sphere to ensure success. So far as those under me & myself are concerned I will leave no stone unturned which can contribute ought toward victory.

I recd with much pleasure letters from Arthur & from home.

§ FEBRUARY 2, 1862 Corpl. Godfroy came in with the gloves from town to day. The first pass we set two big 6 footers, stout as bulls, but who had never boxed a blow, to work with them. They went in with might & main & in abt 2 minutes one of them went over "cafummix" on his seat. He sprawled out both hands & stared around the very picture of astonishment, a stream of blood as large as a pipe stem flowing from each nostril. They concluded to dispense with any further amusement of that kind. I nearly laughed myself to death. Seward is sick & can now take no part. There has been quite a general round. Corpl. Godfroy appears to be the champion of our Co. The weather is fair but it being Sunday we have no drill.

§ FEBRUARY 3 The snow is now 3 inches deep. This is the deepest of the winter. The weather is warm. It is very certain that we cannot leave here unless it be on a fleet for several weeks. I shall be glad to see spring & activity. We are shut up in a little valley where we can neither see or hear anything or anybody.

§ FEBRUARY 5 I put on the gloves to night for the first time

---

* Congress made no cut in military pay.

with Capt. Handy. We went easy & he being a very weak opponent I came off without being touched. There is a great deal of boxing in the Co. & there is considerable talent in the crude state.

Corpl. Godfroy is the instructor. He has the genuine fighting build — a square solid head, a neck like a bull & though only 5 ft. 7 in. high weighs 170 lbs. without being fat. He is French & cares no more for pounding than for the wind blowing in his face. He is one of the real old Detroit French, a nephew of the man who used for years to buy all the fur in our country. The family at Detroit are wealthy & he is said to have some very pretty sisters. He is himself well educated & an excellent Corpl. but has heretofore led a very hard life. He has spent a great deal of time on the Mississippi river & in places generally where there was any prospect of a muss.

I have been drilling the non-comd. officers on bayonet to day. Benson is building a log guard house & must need be excused for when he has a log shanty in view it is useless to talk of anything else. I hope he will have it done soon.

Handy is disposed to have a little strife on whose Co. will come out ahead on the bayonet drill. He has a Lt. to help him & as I have no one at present it goes much slower than it ought. He has become so jealous already that I cannot get a word out of him nor will he let me look at one of his books. I am glad to see that. It is a favorable indication. I can get all the books I want with ease & without his assistance. If Benson was one half as good on drill as on log houses we could beat him to death.

§ FEBRUARY 6 Rainy. "E'en as a herd of bustling swine in Brentford town a town of mud are pricked along." So do we wallow abt in mud up to our knees. It is pretty dull business but we can see the end of it I think. We shall have to go on picket once more at that place but only once I think.

The health of the Regt. is remarkably good & that of our Co. is almost all that could be asked. How in the world it is kept so good is more than I can tell. The men are in the mud all the time, feet wet a great deal, the ground in the shanties damp & often clear mud, far less attention given to cleanliness than at home, beds frequently wet. They have little to eat save meat, bread, beans, rice & coffee yet most of them are so fat they can hardly see out of their eyes.

§ FEBRUARY 7 Our expectations of picketing were realized

much sooner than we expected. At 9 P.M. last night an order came for us to go out this m'g at 9 A.M. We had to take the place of the 5th for some reason. I understand 300 of them have the measles. The men dislike to take their places. If it were any other Regt. they would have cared less. We have only a brush shanty & evidence of a coming storm is apparent. The mud in many places for rods was full 10 inches deep on the main road.

§ FEBRUARY 8 I got orders last night to go beyond the lines a short distance before daylight with a few men & look about. I accordingly set out at 4½ A.M. with 13 men. It was very dark but we worked our way along toward Pohick Church as well as we could. We scared 2 rebel horsemen who were watching on the Centreville road but one makes so much noise that it is hard getting near them.

As we drew near the Church I sent Corpl. Russell with 4 men around to the right to take them in the rear in case anyone was there. We proceed cautiously along both sides of the road & keep a close lookout for ambuscades. We do not proceed far when we hear 5 shots abt 30 rods in front & soon after 7 others. Corpl. Russell has missed his way & came back on to the same road. He saw some videttes of the enemy & fired on them. We take the double quick & are soon near the spot. We see some men run across the road (it is still dark) at abt 10 rods distant. We are in doubt who they are & fearing a trap withdraw abt 4 rods on hands & knees to a thick line of bushes where it will be more difficult for them to get to our flanks or rear.

We lie still for a moment to listen & then whistle the signal which is answered & we again advance. We look cautiously around but finding no one hurt on either side we go on to Pohick & examine all the houses & rummage the place generally. The boys were pretty ravenous & punched pretty much everything with their bayonets in which there was room for a Secesh. They however took nothing & injured nothing. The people had just turned out of their beds which were still warm & tumbled. The men were all gone except one or two old ones, in fact the place is mostly deserted except for the negroes.

After searching abt as long as we thought best we started for camp, met a part of Co. G & some Cavalry who were coming to reinforce us. Two of the men were absent but they are always running off & we left them. Soon after we came in they came all out of breath & badly scratched by running through the briars. They report that they saw a Co. of Cav. & were near enough to them to hear them talking abt the G-d d----d Yankees.

When we had been back a short time came a report that we had fired on some of our own Cav. Of course we could not swear positively as to that but I knew very well that they had no business there at that time of night. Major Williams however gets things confused so badly that I was afraid something might be amiss. I was still more confirmed in this by an order abt 11 A.M. to report myself at headquarters forthwith. Although my [scouting] orders did not specify any particular distance to which I might go I at once concluded that something was wrong & as my orders were not in writing the one who issued them would try to save himself by leaving me in the lurch.

My orders were from Benson, his from Major Williams. As against anyone else B. would do anything in his power & spend his last cent to save me, but as between himself & me the case might naturally be quite different. If Major had done wrong in not limiting the distance it was very probable that he would make or try to make Benson or I shoulder it.

I started for headquarters fully prepared for arrest. I knew I had done nothing wrong & had confidence that I could stand it through somehow. If my flanking party had gone right I should have known who the Cavalry were. As our energetic Lt. is always singing, "Life is so checkered you never can tell" &c. I found at head'qrs that they were veritable "Secesh" whom the men fired on & that I was summoned to receive a commission as 1st Lieut. instead of being arrested.

I got around to our quarters & found a good stock of fresh beef. I immediately laid hold of a good chunk, put half of it to roasting & while that was cooking ate the other half raw.

§ FEBRUARY 9 Sunday. I think there is very little doubt that they were our own men whom we shot at yesterday. If so it is the fault of those who sent us. They had no business in front of our line & I ought not to have been sent out without knowing of their whereabouts. A body of a dozen men which runs upon another in the night knowing nothing of their number & in a place where they expect to meet the enemy cannot be expected to make any very extensive inquiries as to who they are. Someone was to blame but we had no share in it. I am very glad we did not kill any of them. One of them was cut through the coat over his shoulder & another on the side & one of their bullets struck a tree behind which one of our men stood.

I believe there is not a braver man in the Regt. than Corpl. Russell. He stands next Johnston & Stevenson among the non-comd. officers. I had to work a long time before I could make Benson believe that there was genuine stuff in him but he now has to acknowledge it. I opposed Bryan's appointment but could not prevent it. I knew he would never be a good Corpl. Benson now acknowledges it. We have both to acknowledge that we were greatly mistaken on Corpl. McCullum. He is a good man & will do his individual duty but he is a poor hand to make others do. Prentice will have to be the next Sergt. to satisfy the Capt., not because he is worthy of it.

Sunday has been a very quiet day. The men when not on the watch have been lounging around on the straw in their bush shanties or roasting beef on long sticks at a large fire in the center of the circle. Some speculate on affairs at home, some tell stories or practice jokes & drives on each other. Indeed we lead a very lazy but not unpleasant life. A few have letters & papers to read but most are employed as above or sleeping to make up for last night's watch. The weather has been good which is fortunate as our house is all walls & no roof. This post is the reserve & being interior we can keep as large a fire as we like. There is a large quantity of dry cord wood near by & we use it without stint.

§ FEBRUARY 11 We were relieved late yesterday, after 1 P.M. & did not reach home till abt 4 P.M. I was somewhat tired but feel none the worse to day.

I saw one of the cavalrymen yesterday whom I have no doubt (though Major Williams still denies it) we shot at the other morning. He had a bullet hole through his overcoat shoulder & the opposite ear was very red & nearly blistered. I presume the ball did not pass an ⅛ of an inch from it. It is from no good judgement of the Major's that half of us on both sides were not killed.

I had target shooting & bayonet drill this m'g & a bayonet drill after dinner. I have added one bar to my shoulder straps which makes no change in duty or feeling. Benson's still at work on the guard house. Prentice has been sick for 3 days bleeding at the lungs. I am afraid he cannot live long. There is too much mercury in his bones & bad whiskey dregs in his system.

§ FEBRUARY 12 We have news of great victories to night & are jubilant.* The war cannot last a great while at this rate. I have been practicing bayonet exercise & am too warm to write much. Things look encouraging. The weather is very warm to day. Spring & activity will soon be at hand.

I would like a month for drill before we start. With that length of time Co. I could enter the field, not perfection, well drilled in all that can be required of an infantry soldier. Men will get tired & lazy. If they would work as long as I would work with them a great deal might be accomplished. Benson is a good Capt. but he sometimes lags. He is very energetic but he lets up now & then.

What I like is a constant determination which never lags or falters or seeks for excuses. I cannot say that I have this. I aim at it. I *wont* give up the ship is what wins. It will carry one through everything. One can live on it for years when without it he would have died in a day. Have an object and pursue it with an eagerness which cannot recognize defeat or hear words of discouragement, not blindly but with the most vigilant watch for everything small or great which may aid your course, drag them all to you & force them to pave the way toward success.

It may often be necessary to seemingly abandon this object but this is only with that part of yourself which the world sees & knows, ie, the counterfeit man, the other part which is indeed yourself. The real man knows no change. There is a vast difference frequently between the man whom the world sees & calls by your name & the one you see & call yourself. I am not now speaking of that peculiar class, with whom self esteem hides all other faculties. They believe themselves something which others know they are not. I am talking of those of whom the world believes something which they themselves know they are not. In one case the man deceives himself, in the other he deceives those around him. I would rather be the latter but would much prefer to deal with the former.

§ FEBRUARY 14 We had brigade drill in the forenoon. Co. drill P.M. & at dress parade a little of everything. Major Williams ought to be Court Martialed & yet there is no way to reach him. First he

---

* Presumably Federal victories at Roanoke Island, North Carolina, and Fort Henry, in Tennessee.

put the Regt. on double quick for a while then deployed them for bayonet exercise. He did not know how to give the commands & most of the Co. knew no more how to execute them than if they had been ordered to write a poem. Those who knew the moves would not stir because the commands were wrong so the whole thing was a dead failure.

Then must come double columns at half distance, double quick. The men started with a will all yelling like demons. This over he ordered a charge down a steep hill at double quick. The men paid no attention to any one but ran just as hard as they could & many of them did not stop less than 100 rods. We brought them together again & marched off the ground notwithstanding Major's orders to reform the line. "Major says the men were really so full of the d---l that he could do nothing with them." "It was all wrong in a military point of view but still he had to laugh so hard that he could not give the order halt." It is exceedingly unmilitary & wholly wrong for a field officer to allow himself to be trifled with in that way or even in the slightest point.

The Devil must also show himself in the form of a call for 600 men from this division to man gun boats.* Two thirds of the Regt. were anxious to go. I began to fear our whole Co. was broken up. They came almost in a body to our tent but finding we would have nothing to do with them were going away when they cried simultaneously, rally on the Major & in less than 5 minutes he was surrounded by nearly the whole Regt. First they gave 3 cheers for the Major, declaring that he must go with them to Gen. Richardson to see about it. Off they went taking Major with them. Every time he said anything, which was often (he being a great talker) some of them would propose 3 cheers for the Major.

Major had sense enough to know that he was making a very ridiculous appearance. He formed them in four ranks thinking if he once got them in order they would obey him. It all went very well till he tried to run away from them, when they all broke after him yelling like devils, seized him & put him on their shoulders till they were near the place when they let him down on his promise that he would not try to run away again. The Gen. told them none

---

* This directive was aimed at finding crewmen for the gunboats in the western theater.

but sailors could go & thus ended the excitement. We tried to pass off some scapegraces for sailors. They were very eager to go at first but as soon as they found we wanted to get rid of them not a man would enlist.

§ FEBRUARY 16 Sunday eve in camp. I am not very deeply impressed with the solemnity of the hour or occasion. They are singing church music at the Orderly's tent & there is mingled with their harmony the voice of woman (yes, of a virtuous? woman, a sight rarer to soldiers than were good men in Sodom), which naturally brings some recollections of past scenes, of times when I was very different, no doubt better than I am now.

There is nothing like church music & the solemnity of divine service to carry one back to other days. Faust refrained from the poisoned bowl & wept when he heard the Cathedral bell, though he was before & after ready to barter his soul with the devil. The solemn mysteries of religion are salutary. The vague terror which they inspire in childhood can never be obliterated. It brings to me thoughts of my mother with whose memory none but thoughts of purity can mingle. It carries me back more especially to that best of all villages, Kalamazoo, that being nearly the only place where I voluntarily attended church. One never regrets having done so. One at the thought of it is constantly led to say, as did the ruined Margaret "how different was it with you then when all innocence thou knelt before the altar."*

It is near a year since I can properly be said to have attended divine worship. I would go to night if I could. I felt reckless when I began to write on the first page but some good spirit changed my tone for the moment. That devil's imp Sid Prentice must here needs relate to me some worthless adventure which he never met & the thoughts of days well spent are lost in his not over chaste recitals.

Drawing here the curtain between what goes before & what follows, I will say with all candor that he is abt the most inveterate whoremaster I ever knew. A man of good form & figure, considerable talent & of the most peculiar look of any one I ever saw. He has a very large head, light yellow hair, white eyebrows, light

---

* Haydon's thoughts here are still on Goethe's *Faust*.

blue eyes very large, a long & very red face, nose scarlet & of ample proportions, ears & mouth very large. The first thought when you see him is that he has the most face of any man you ever saw. I must say for him that he has naturally a kind, generous & confiding heart. Notwithstanding his extraordinary appearance & manners not less peculiar, he was always a favorite among the ladies. His bleeding at the lungs or more probably from the stomach has slightly dimmed the strawberry hue of his nose but not in the least his desire to relate his wonderful adventures.

Benson has during the last three months played the coolest & most consumate game on ex-Corpl. Billy Mack that I have ever seen. He has taken pains to have all the outlines & most of the details paraded before him all the time & yet he could not or at least did not see it till it was too late to be of any use. When he finally opened his eyes the work was done & it was too late to secure any positive proof of it.

He has acted as mediator in a lover's quarrel & by a skillfully written series of letters has settled the whole affair very much as the monkey did the famous cheese case by taking the girl himself & leaving Billy only a valuable experience to console him for his loss. I forsaw long ago that the end would not be otherwise but concluded it would be more prudent to let Billy find it out himself than to get the ill will of both by telling to one what he would not believe & what the other could easily & would deny.

This was the coldest morning of the winter. Snow melted considerable during the day. If I had my journal here I would rewrite it. It is now a most wretched mass of confusion & non-sense.*

§ FEBRUARY 20 The time has passed off in various not un-pleasant ways since the last. We had a very fine bayonet drill this m'g. A most glorious battalion drill P.M. Col. Poe was in command. He makes the difference. With him the Regt. is all life, vigor & attention, without him it is all indifference or deviltry. He com-plimented Co. I as being very prompt on drill.

I have been trying for two or three days to instill into Seward's mind & fists the art of boxing but have met with only moderate

---

* No doubt Haydon is referring to the previous volume of his journal, which he had sent home for safekeeping; he had just started here a new volume.

success. On the first day I knocked all the breath out of him by an inconsiderable punch in the ribs & since that time I have been obliged to be so gentle with him that we make slow progress.

I put the gloves on with Capt. [Benson] to day for the first time. He pretty soon gave me a smart blow over the left eye which I returned on his nose. I was afraid of him & my blow being rather unexpected & a little harder than I intended he was pretty cautious. After a little while he caught my left hand & gave me a smart punch in the head which I promptly returned in the ribs. After that we were both so careful that there was no hitting on either side.

We induced Gus Goebel 1st Lt. of Co. A to put them on this m'g & sent him off with a very black eye after a few preliminary flourishes. I was right sorry for honest, jolly, free hearted, plump, rosy Augustus but he could hardly expect to be initiated short of at least one black eye. I have seen many a one who did worse & did not do a great deal better myself when I first tried it. The pain is nothing but to be the butt for the jokes of all your comrades & the fear of being called before Col. Poe for any purpose is very unpleasant. The men are apt to look with very inquisitive eyes on such things.

§ FEBRUARY 21 We had a long bayonet & skirmish drill this forenoon and at half past 12 were called out for brigade drill. The 2d platoon under my command came near running the 1st platoon through this m'g. I had been skirmishing & was coming in at a double quick. The 1st had guns stacked & were standing in line. I put the 2d on the gymnast step & ordered charge, supposing of course that they would either stop or throw up their guns when they came to them. Instead of that however they made for them on a dead run. I roared halt & they stopped with bayonets not more than 2 feet from their breasts. One man did get a bayonet through his coat sleeve.

The brigade drill was very severe. Gen. Richardson put us in where the mud was very deep, in a corn & potato field. We could sometimes hardly move. Our feet looked as though they were muffled. Corpl. Southworth in addition to all this got the men out & drilled them more than an hour after supper on bayonet exercise. He took only such as volunteered. He is proficient. There is not a Corpl. in the Regt. who is a match for him. It is a great mistake that he was not promoted sooner. He should have been a Sergt.

long ago. There are only two better non-comd. officers in the Regt.

I wish I had the power to advance men who deserve it. To look around & see the miserable worthless pudding heads who hold commissions in many of our own Co's. & especially in other Regts. & then look at some of our own non-comd. officers competent to drill a Co. or a Regt., I lose all patience. I would like it very much if I could by any means get commissions for abt three of them.

§ FEBRUARY 22 There was no drilling or exercise of any kind to day except a dress parade at which a part of Washington's farewell address was read. Salutes were fired at all forts & by all batteries.

§ FEBRUARY 23 Sunday damp & misty. Benson has been on the sick list for two days. I am afraid he will have to go to the hospital. There was no need of his being sick if he had done as I told him.

I am detailed as officer of the guard to morrow. Court Martial has served me a good turn for the last two months but it is played out at last. Two months' relief in mid winter from guard duty is no small thing. I am not over partial to police guard. Picket does better. If we could once more have a glimpse of fair weather it would be a great consolation. We must it is thought roll in mud for one month yet at least. If the weather were good we could not long be here. I am in good bodily health but do not feel very blythe in spirits owing I suppose to the bad weather.

§ FEBRUARY 24 I went on guard as I expected. Just before noon came an order to discharge all the guards but 3 & to be ready to march with one day's rations. I had barely time to lay off my sash & seize my haversack & overcoat & run. We marched 3½ miles to Windsor Hill running a large part of the way in mud from 3 to 10 inches deep. I was on the point of throwing away my overcoat when Col. Poe overtook us & ordered a halt. When he came up the Regt. was scattered out abt 30 rods wide, ½ mile long through woods & fields trying to find solid ground to travel on. They set up a tremendous cheering when they saw him & all made for their places in line without orders as fast as they could run. The Col. well knowing how he was at one time disliked by the men seemed well pleased at the change.

We waited here till near sundown. Six rifled cannon came up soon after us. We came back to camp soon after dark. The 37th [New York] had been attacked on picket, one man killed & 2 wounded & it was feared from exaggerated reports that they would be driven in or cut off by a heavy force. We went out to be in relieving distance if needed. I went back to guard duty as soon as I returned. There was a heavy shower of rain this m'g & there has been such a wind ever since that one can hardly stand. A great many of the tents are blown down.

§ FEBRUARY 26 Taps. It is raining steadily. This Division has just recd orders to be ready to move at an hour's notice. We are to have no baggage except what we carry on our backs, provisions the same. A blanket, overcoat, one shirt, one pr. stockings will make my outfit.

I am glad to go although the difficulties attending a move at this time are great. We are to have only 4 wagons per Regt. The mud surpasses anything I ever saw & we have rains as often as every other day. We shall neither at day or night have anything but the one blanket to protect us from the mud below or the rain above. It is however all important for us to follow up our recent victories. We shall I presume go to Occoquan which place is now occupied by the rebels, but will I think be deserted on our approach. I hope that we may not be called upon to go to night. We could not march more than one mile per hour.

§ FEBRUARY 27 We are to turn out for muster at 7 A.M. to morrow morning & march for picketing at 9 A.M. We have to take the place of the 5th [Michigan] again. The 5th has lost 7 men by disease this week. We have to go to Pohick Church now & the line is lengthened so far that it requires 2 Regts. I presume that we shall move before our tour is over. I hoped that we should avoid picketing at this place again. It seems otherwise however. To wallow 8 miles & back through the mud & spend 3 nights & 4 days in bush shanties as you can find them makes war appear more like a reality than it does on dress parades & reviews. I can stand it very well, in fact remarkably well, still I much prefer fair weather & good roads for such business.

§ FEBRUARY 28 On picket 2 miles below Pohick Church. I marched 10 miles yesterday & was somewhat tired when we finally brought up. Co. I was posted on reserve at a passably comfortable place but this being a blunder of Major Williams we were ordered after dark to take new posts. The line we were to occupy was 1½ miles long & ran through a thick pine forest without road or path. It was abt 9 P.M. when we were posted.

The walking yesterday was pretty good. The ground was frozen hard in the morning & did not thaw very much during the day. Last night was I think the coldest of the season. This winter has been unusually mild. The Potomac has many times been frozen so that teams could cross on the ice. This winter it has not frozen at all. I make my headqrs at a house on the line. I slept very little last night, it was too cold & there was an infernal dog under the floor which barked all night not 6 inches from my head. I could not coax him out & I was afraid to go under after him.

I lay half dozing, at one time thinking myself the unfortunate gentleman we read of who lost his money purse & killed his favorite dog thinking him mad, while in fact he was trying to induce his master to return for his money. Again I was Lord Llewellyn & had just killed Beth Gelert.* Again I saw myself lying on the floor bathed in blood because of not heeding the dog's warning. Again I was very carefully looking around for a crack in the floor where I might spear him with my sword. Last of all I waked to the reality that I was very cold & that the dog being beyond my reach would bark till he was ready to stop. The old man who lives here keeps 4 dogs but is so poor that he can sell us nothing to eat. The Confeds carried off all his hay & grain last fall which was in fact but a small amt.

This man like ⁹/₁₀ of all the men & women you see here is ignorant & simple beyond conception. He has lived here 57 years, never been in Washington but once, never been over 30 miles from home, knows the distance to only 3 places, Occoquan where he goes to mill, Alexandria where he goes to trade & Accotink where he goes to fish. He wanted to know last night if I had heard abt that murder in Washington. I asked him what one. "Why abt that — that whats his name — Sickles, who shot a man (Keys) the other day." He overheard some of the pickets talking abt it & having never heard of it before concluded it must be a new thing.†

§ MARCH 1, 1862 Sunday. It was warmer last night. I slept in a bush shanty & rested finely. The night was quiet, one or two

---

* "Beth-Gêlert or the Grave of the Grayhound," a ballad by William Robert Spencer.

† In this notorious 1859 incident, Congressman Daniel E. Sickles shot and killed his wife's lover, Philip Barton Key, son of the writer of "The Star Spangled Banner." Sickles, acquitted by reason of temporary insanity, now commanded a brigade in the Army of the Potomac.

shots were fired but none on our line. Everybody in this country I find drinks. A very pretty girl at a house where we get our meals put a canteen of whiskey to her fair lips, took a smart drink & offered it to me. Coming from her I could not refuse. I think she is the prettiest girl who makes any pretention to virtue whom I have seen in Va. Her lover is in the "Secesh" army but she is not beyond the reach of consolation.

Capt. Whipple is one of the most remarkable men among the ladies whom I have seen since Horace Mower died. There is an old maid there whom he will insist on calling Auntie. This vexes her very much but his lavish compliments in other respects console her. Besides this he keeps her half drunk all the time & the old man who owns the house in about the same condition.

Sergt. Johnston is out on a scout with 4 men & I am a little anxious abt him. The Va. women know altogether too little to banter with soldiers.

§ MARCH 2 Abt 9 A.M. it began snowing very hard & by 4 P.M. it was 3 inches deep. Prof. [Thaddeus S. C.] Lowe was up in his balloon at Pohick Church during all the clear spells. Sergt. Johnston returned abt 3 P.M. He was lost during the storm. Fitzgerald the jolly Irishman & Buck a boy of 18 but one of the best & most reliable members of our Co. became separated from him & I fear will get in trouble. He saw the rebel pickets on the other side of the Occoquan. They started to get to a house out in the open field to inquire their way. When within abt 20 rods of it they saw 5 cavalry come out & mount their horses which were behind a barn. Our men threw themselves down on the ground among the weeds & grass before they were seen. They were in doubt whether to fire on them or not but being near a rebel camp & not knowing the way home they wisely concluded not to raise the alarm. Doubtless more than one home is the happier for that. Towards dark it became misty & rainy. Our picket line is now on the north bank of Pohick Creek. The line along where we are is mostly through pathless pine woods.

§ MARCH 3 It rained more or less all night & everything was damp & slushy this m'g. Fitzgerald & Buck came in abt 8 A.M. They wandered around till they came out suddenly at Occoquan village within abt 15 rods of 40 or 50 rebels just on the other side the river. They thought at first that they were at Accotink but just at that moment one of the rebels called out, There comes some more of the d----d Yankees and they immediately gave them a volley. Jolly Jimmy escaped without a scratch. One ball glancing from the ground struck Buck in the leg but being nearly spent did not penetrate the flesh but bruised it considerably. Two other balls passed through his coat but did him no harm. The boys made good time out of that & after traveling some 3 miles through the woods came to the house of a lady whose husband is in the Secesh army. They however made themselves so agreeable that she took them in & cared for them well during their stay which was till m'g.

We were relieved by the 63rd Pa. & were ready to start for home at 2 P.M. The roads were exceedingly bad. Col. Poe gave orders to march in by Co's. & to keep them together. It was declared by several to be impossible to bring in Co. I in a body over such a road. Straggling on the march was always their worst fault & that of the whole Regt. likewise. The Co. has never been brought in more than once or twice from a long march as it ought to be. The men were in heavy order having expected to advance instead of returning to camp. After marching 2 miles right in front I found them straggling badly & that several of the smaller & weaker men were already badly blown. I halted, picked out these & put them on the lead & made the large strong men march in the rear. The little ones soon freshened up, recovered their wind & marched so fast all the way to camp that I was obliged to halt them 3 times to let the rear close up with them. It is incredible to those who have never tried it how much easier it is to march in front than in rear.

We came in at 6 P.M. with the loss of only Lt. Seward, who lagged, in the midst of a drenching rain, all the men whistling Yankee Doodle & marching as if they were at a review. We marched 9 miles in a little more than 3 hours, each man carrying an average of 40 lbs., on a road where the mud was rarely less than 3 inches deep. I believe I can march a Co. farther in a day than any other man in the Regt. if they will give me my own way.

It rains terribly & right glad I am to see the men & myself in good quarters, beneath a tight roof, with dry clothes & a plenty to eat — ie *at home*. Not our real home but our soldier's homes & right dear good ones they seem & are to us. The Col. had hot whiskey prepared for them all as fast as they came in. The men have found him out at last & love him far better now than they once hated him. He will do thrice as much for their comfort & safety despite his severity as Major Williams with all his milk & water ill timed mildness.

I do like our Co. as I never liked a lot of men before. They like me as well now, though they disliked me exceedingly at one time since my first promotion. I know the change in my conduct as Sergt. & Lieut. was great, Capt. May's departure made it still greater & I was very little surprised at the wish which I knew was more than once expressed that the next battle might be the cause of my exit. I also well knew that in our own Co. & far more often among the men of other Co's. who from time to time fell under my command the determination was expressed to help me off the stage if the Secesh did not do it. It is unpleasant to know that such a feeling exists. It came near driving Col. Poe out of the Regt. at one time. I never had any fear for myself but I was really at one time afraid they would shoot him.

The fact is when the hour of danger comes the men are glad to cling to anyone who acts as though he is competent to carry them through. They think far more abt their own welfare than abt shooting someone who sent them to the guard house or Court Martialed them a month before. There is only one way in which an officer is sure of being liked by his men. Live right up to the rigid severity of military law without fear, favor or affection, be careful only that you punish no man who does not deserve it & that you let no one escape who deserves punishment. Keep partiality & ill timed mercy out of sight. Look well to the wants & instruction of your men, be careful of their health & welfare on every occasion.

You will be abundantly cursed & hated at first but be certain that no course will in the end secure so high a degree of favor or retain it so long. Never allow men to take liberties with you. It is well to laugh & joke with them at times but always commence it yourself & know how to shut them off when they have gone far enough. Some think it a fine thing to be very familiar with their men. I could never see it in that light. Always be open & attentive to all their proper questions & inquiries but be careful to be so polite to them that they will never presume to be otherwise to you.

5 men of the 5th [Michigan] were buried yesterday & 14 died last night of measles it is said. They have the Surgeon under arrest,

are investigating the matter to day. It is time. Men ought not to be allowed to die in that way.

I got quite a passable kiss from a couple of Secesh girls to day. I also learned some interesting facts from the father of one of them abt social affairs down South. First I learned that a large number of people were living together as husband & wife who are not married. He cited three cases among his neighbors. I further learned the important fact that it is considered no very serious thing for a young lady to have a baby or two before she has a husband. One of his sons had married a girl with a like start in life. He was himself courting for his second wife a girl of 21 who possessed a fine boy of two years. He called her a very upright young woman notwithstanding. He said there was no use of talking, women are all liable to make mistakes.

He is a remarkably honest candid old gentleman & I have no doubt expressed correctly the feeling of the community in these particulars. I thought such being his opinion it would certainly be no harm to kiss his daughter as soon as he stepped out if I had never seen her before. The old man did not seem to understand the idea of making such things a profession. It was several times very broadly suggested to him but he did not understand. When told by Capt. Whipple how great would be the profits if anyone cared to engage at the outposts he only understood that the money was to be made by selling "pies, cakes & such like." Va. will be a different state after the war. The people are learning very fast.

§ MARCH 4 The Col. has been around to day. He arrested a Sergt. & Corpl. of the guard & 2 sentinels. The latter one for relieving, the other for allowing himself to be relieved when no non-comd. officer of the guard was present. The Sergt. & Corpl. for allowing it to be done.

§ MARCH 5 A fair day. Co. drill in the m'g. There are to be some promotions soon I hear. Our Orderly [William Noble] is to be Qr. master, Sergt. Johnston Orderly. Prentice Sergt. & somebody Corpl. I am glad of this. Prentice does not very well deserve his advancement but it is the Capt.'s will & that is conclusive or at least so near it that I shall not try to change the programme. I dislike to lose Stevenson [to Co. K] but still am glad to see him rewarded for his faithful services & competency for the place. Johnston richly merits his promotion. It will also add $4.oo per month to his pay which his pretty wife needs. They will both have commissions before many months & when that comes the 2d will have two as good Lieuts. as have often been promoted from volunteer ranks. I wish Corpl. Southworth could be the next Sergt. instead of Prentice.

All the sick men were sent to Alexandria to day. We may move to morrow. I am quite ready. I have on the whole passed a very pleasant winter. I am now entering on a spring full of adventure. I doubt not there are many stirring scenes before me & it is very uncertain where my next winter may be spent. No one knows what a day may bring forth, still I have high hopes.

We are going to leave a bad hole behind us, viz Alexandria. There is not a hotter nest of treason in all the South. Our men are very anxious to burn it & it is quite possible they will do so. If it were not for the Govt. property stored there it would have been done long ago. The inhabitants say openly that they will burn it if we whip the rebels at Manassas so as to destroy our depot for supplies. I think it ought to come down.

§ MARCH 6 Every thing is rapidly preparing for the advance. The detail of 3 men per Co. for pioneers came to night. Fatigue parties are at work constantly on the roads. I bought 4 doz. combustible paper cartridges to day (expense $2.00) for rapid loading. I have a good supply of the most approved ammunition & have my sword well ground.

A Capt., the Qr. master, & a private of the 63rd Pa. were killed on picket yesterday & one man was wounded. This was allowing to the d----d milk & water idea of taking men prisoners instead of shooting them. A scouting party of 50 of our men almost near enough to 30 Confeds. to touch them with their bayonets must needs jump out of the bushes & try to take them prisoners. Consequence 3 of our men, one of them the best Capt. in the Regt., were killed on the spot, another badly wounded & the rebels all escaped unhurt. $9/10$ of them might have been brought down at the first volley.

This idea of taking so many prisoners is often a very poor one. Men who are under arms it is always supposed are ready to be shot at unless they make demonstrations to the contrary. I shall never ask such whether they want to surrender or not. If they dont want to fight let *them* say so.

§ MARCH 7 The report to night shows very little prospect of moving. Prof. Lowe from balloon observations reports that 80,000 men have moved up & encamped abt Occoquan within 3 days. I doubt whether McClellan will move from here at present if there is a prospect of a heavy battle at Manassas or Occoquan. I think he will reinforce Burnside,* take Norfolk & make a demonstration in the neighborhood of Winchester before he makes any general move from this point, unless the enemy should fall back. Such a course would be full as sure of success & be attended with far less loss. If it be true that the enemy have 80,000 men at Occoquan they will give us a very warm picket line on the Pohick. It is the place where their line ought to be in such a case. I would not be surprised if our line was withdrawn inside the Accotink abt 3 miles this side of the Pohick. I think this will be necessary unless our line is strengthened.

§ MARCH 8 I have been out with a fatigue party of 50 men to day bridging the Accotink. I am very tired.

§ MARCH 9 The Co's. of this Regt. have been rearranged to day according to rank of Capts. They all retain their original letters but the place in line is changed, viz C 1st, K 2d, H 3d, E 4th, F 5th, I 6th, B 7th, A 8th, G 9th, D 10th. Hereafter every promotion of a new Capt. will change our places in line. The promotions in our Co. please me although I dislike to see so much of the fruits of our labor going into other Co's. They infuse new life into them & make it much harder for us to keep in advance of them. They know all our ways & are zealous imitators. Stevenson went up to a commission sooner than I expected. I did a fine thing in sending Johnston scouting when we were on picket. He made a good report & acquired much favor on account of it. He is 1st Sergt. now & is sure of a commission very soon.

§ MARCH 10 Weather warm with occasional showers. Although no orders have as yet been recd we expect to march to night or in the morning. All is bustle & enthusiasm. Our men are reported in Manassas. [Gen. Joseph] Hooker has pretty certainly crossed below us. The centre is in motion. We cannot stay much longer. I eagerly await the hour when we shall once more set our faces in earnest toward Richmond.

§ MARCH 11 A beautiful stand of colors came to us this m'g from the War Dept. Chaplain May made as usual a woefully dull

---

* Gen. Ambrose Burnside had seized a foothold on the North Carolina coast.

speech on the occasion. Battalion drill A.M. & P.M. under Col. Poe, very interesting & instructive. It seems as if all the devils in hell were conspiring agt us. This Div. is to be held in reserve.* It is true the best & most reliable troops are always taken for reserve, still who wants to lie here idle or to go tagging along three or four days behind the rest of the army. I would like far better to be as we were before the leading Regt.

§ MARCH 12 The past 2 days have been the most lovely that can be imagined. We had a long battalion drill this A.M. & Co. drill P.M. I never saw such a change as there has been in the Regt. in the last few days. Col. Poe has been here. It never did such drilling before. Lt. Col. Williams will mix it in half an hour so that he cannot tell whether the men are standing on their heads or feet.† The prospect of anything worthy of effort seems to grow dimmer every hour. This is all that Gen. Richardson has got by quarreling with Gen. McDowell. If we had stayed in his Div. we should have been in Manassas now & should have done far less labor.

Things look gloomy. The war cannot last much longer & we are already 30 miles in the lurch. I begin to doubt whether we shall ever get out of sight of the Potomac till we turn our faces homeward. It may be that the rebels will make a stand in the cotton states. It would seem that they could not hold out much longer. Still they are pretty desperate & determined to do all the mischief they can.

The country is suffering terribly, as is always the case, from the retreating army. It is the doom of the country to be plundered, burned & ravaged. It may as well be thoroughly done. The country is worth more to us in a native state than when peopled by a rebellious population. They used to say "let the curse of slavery be upon us" & I say let it fall, so long as it comes from their own hands.

Benson has some not very unpleasant news from home. The man who married his lady love is dead & she has gone back to his father's. He will at once renew correspondence.

I suppose we must submit to our damnable fate with soldier like

---

* The 2nd Michigan was now in the division commanded by Charles S. Hamilton, in Heintzelman's Third Corps. Gen. Richardson was transferred to the Second Corps.
† Lt. Col. Larnerd had resigned, and Maj. Williams promoted in his place.

indifference. If I was in the army for life I would care less about it. I should then be passive as to where I went, caring for nothing except the wants of the day & a creditable discharge of such duties as were assigned me. Our Col. is trying to bring us to this as fast as possible. He does not allow us to drill with our own Co. but shifts us around from one to another every day. This is the case in battalion drill but not in Co. [drill]. He intends to keep changing us around till we lose all like for one Co. more than another, to break up all friendship or intimacy which now exists between officers & men. It comes pretty hard on us, still it is right. If I were to enter a strange Co. I would never speak to one of the men except in a business way. One must bring himself to see all soldiers alike in point of personal feelings.

Our white tents are conspicuous in this bright moonshine but all seems a reproach to us so long as we lie idle here. Our camp looks very neat now. The streets, or at least ours, are swept very clean every day & everything is as tidy as a good house wife's kitchen.

Eight

YORKTOWN
BESIEGED

The Third Corps, of which the 2nd Michigan was now a part, led the Army of the Potomac to its first field of battle in General McClellan's grand campaign. Haydon's regiment reached Fort Monroe, at the tip of the Virginia Peninsula, on March 19. One of his first sightings in Hampton Roads was the ironclad Monitor *(which he described as "a most ridiculous looking craft"), fresh from her historic duel with the* Merrimack *ten days earlier. Haydon found the countryside in this part of Virginia inviting, but discovered that bivouacking within sight and range of the enemy was less inviting. For a month the Federals besieged John B. Magruder's (and then Joseph E. Johnston's) outmanned Confederates at Yorktown. On the eve of McClellan's planned grand assault, Johnston evacuated Yorktown. The Yankees had gained the first step on the road to Richmond, but the Rebels had gained a month's time in which to gather forces.*

* * *

§ MARCH 14, 1862 At 10 last night came orders to move. Nothing was said as to destination. We expect to go down the river on transports. The camp was noisy all night & everyone was up by 4 A.M. I had a wretched toothache all night but it is not quite so bad now. The air is very damp & cold. We have accumulated a vast amt of baggage but a very small portion of which goes with us. All are joyous.

We reached our old camp ground near Ft. Lyon abt 10 A.M. Here we learned greatly to our dislike that the boats were not ready & that we should be obliged to lie there on a bleak cold sand bluff for the next 24 hours. This gives promise of an unpleasant bivouac. Our shelter tents are pitched for the first time. They consist of two oilcloth blankets with eyelet holes to fasten them together with a string. The edges are pinned down. There are no ends but they answer all purposes for this weather & save at least a dozen teams per Regt.

The troops are rapidly congregating abt Alexandria. The hills as far as you can see are covered with them. It may be three days before all are embarked. All our baggage, except what we carried on our backs & one satchel for each officer, was left at camp under charge of a guard. It has since been sent for & taken away. A few men from each Co. were sent back & have burned nearly everything which could not be carried. Our good old board shanty was by our orders together with a large amt of furniture & Co. property burned. The waste in breaking up such a camp is very considerable even when it is done deliberately.

§ MARCH 15 Passed the night tolerably well though there was considerable rain. The m'g was very damp & misty. Rain commenced to fall abt 8 A.M. & continued till late in the night. The shelter tents stood it very well till abt 11 A.M. when the rain came down in torrents & the wind blew hard & soon filled the tents with mud & water. They were useless, not being properly pitched. The men began to scatter in every direction & by night there were not over 400 of the whole brigade left in camp.

Abt 3 P.M. they sent Capts. Whipple & Brownell, Lts. Hodskin & I to Alexandria to send the stragglers back to camp. It rained terribly. But of course that did not delay the matter. We went down taking especial care to go on streets where there would be very little probability of finding any of our soldiers. Our first labor was to get a good supper & drink as much brandy as we could stand up under. I then went out & found 9 of our men, ordered them to return to camp, which I well knew they would not do.

I returned abt 9 P.M. The tide was up & the water on the bridge was abt 2 ft. deep. I got into the house at headquarters & dried myself partially. I kept pretty warm but so many were crowded into the room that there was very little chance of sleeping. I slept abt 2 hours. On the whole I think it was as hard if not the hardest time I ever saw. I believe I never saw the time when I would have given as much for a good night's rest.

I feel better this m'g than I expected. I am somewhat hoarse but otherwise am quite well. The weather is better this m'g, very little rain. The men are slowly returning. Four Regts. came into Alexandria after dark which had marched that day from Centreville (25 miles) in heavy order. The streets were full of men who had lost their Co's. & were wandering around in the rain & darkness looking for shelter. Many of them were scarcely able to stand. They after a while collected in squads & forced their way at the point of the bayonet to good quarters. They became so desperate that it was impossible for the patrols to do anything with them.

H--l is to pay somewhere among the officers. Gen. Richardson leaves us & takes command of Sumner's Div. Gen. Hamilton takes this Div. & Terry is trying to be Brigadier Gen.* Poe & [Samuel B.] Hayman of the 37th in that event it is said will resign. It would be nearly the destruction of this Regt. if Poe were to leave it. With him it is one of the best Regts. in the army but it is rather too talented for anyone else.

§ MARCH 16 The weather has been cold to day but not rainy. On the 14th 1st Lt. R. H. Eldred of Co. K, Signal Officer of the Brigade, died at Georgetown Hospital of brain fever. He was a young man of great promise both in a military & civil point of view & one of my most intimate friends. No one need shun death on the battlefield when such as he so young & full of strength & hope fall by disease.

§ MARCH 17 Orders came last night to move at 10 A.M. this m'g. We at once commenced to collect our scattered Regt. & when we started I think there were not more than 6 absent. I have a severe cold & am so hoarse I can scarce speak a loud word. We marched in excellent order to the city, the 2d ahead as usual & were the first to embark on the great expedition bound for parts to us unknown.

The 2d & the 37th are well stowed away on board the steamer

---

* Richardson was put in charge of Edwin V. Sumner's old division, in Sumner's Second Corps. Richardson's old brigade (2nd, 3rd, and 5th Michigan, 37th New York) had Col. Terry of the 5th Michigan as acting commander until replaced by Hiram G. Berry. The division of Heintzelman, now Third Corps commander, went to Charles S. Hamilton.

Vanderbilt. The wharves are crowded with boats & the troops
rapidly embarking. We unexpectedly lost the best of Orderlies
[William Noble] last night by promotion. I am sorry to have him
go & yet am glad. He is now sure of a commission very soon. Col.
Poe has things to suit him now, i.e., he makes his own promotions
& the Governor confirms them & forwards the commissions at his
leisure. This removes political influence from the affairs of the
Regt. as Poe cannot & would not promote anyone outside & the
Gov. does nothing in the matter except fill out & sign the papers
as directed by our Col. I believe ours is the only Regt. from the
State which controls wholly its own promotions.

§ MARCH 18 Abt 9 last night our boat & all the others which
were loaded swung out into the stream & anchored. The 37th stole
a barrel of whiskey & all got very drunk & noisy & were fighting
all night.

Gen. McClellan was down yesterday overseeing the movement.
He talked with our Col. abt an hour & was heard to promise him
good active times for the 2d. The Gen. looks thinner than when
I last saw him. He was very plainly dressed & but for a yellow sash
which occasionally was visible from underneath his overcoat no
one would have guessed his rank. Our Col. is much the best looking
man of the two & in ability may not be very far behind him.

I got into a room last night, slept well & am much better this
m'g. Big Louis got in a quarrel with a lot of the 37th this m'g,
broke his gun all in pieces over their heads & then went for them
with an ax. He was however stopped before he did any further
damage. The men now they are so crowded together are fighting
continually. Some of the 37th were foolish enough to go for Col.
Poe last night but he quickly ended the performance by knocking
3 of them down the hatchway & kicking 2 others after them.

We are now anchored abt 2 miles above Matthias Point where
we are to remain I think for the night. We left Alexandria abt
noon & a pleasanter ride I never had. The weather is bright &
fine, the scenery beautiful. The river has gradually widened from
1 mile to abt 3 miles. The banks are high, steep & thickly settled.
We saw several Rebel batteries, all deserted, and saw small bodies
of men. They supposed we would land at Aquia Creek & had
accordingly fired a long railroad bridge & wharf at that place
together with all the buildings. Only abt 2 Co's. were to be seen.

The boats of this part of the expedition are mostly North [Hudson] River steamers & are as far as I can remember the Elm City, Vanderbilt, John A. Warner, John Brooks, Wm Kent, T. V. Arrowsmith, Champion, Canonicus, Pioneer, Catskill, Naushon, Wissahicon, &c & a large lot of tug boats &c. The boats keep near each other & there are frequently 4 or 5 abreast. The gun boats are now exploring the river on the lookout for concealed batteries. A few shots would do terrible execution on these crowded boats.

§ MARCH 19 We moved down the river during the night & entered the bay soon after sunrise. I saw as soon as I looked out this m'g that we were on salt water. The boats rode higher & there was a broad thick sheet of creamy, snow white foam in our wake such as I have never seen on fresh water. The bay is covered with vessels. The shores can just be seen on each side.

At abt 3 P.M. we are in Hampton Roads. There are some 20 of our war steamers & gun boats anchored here. There is one English war steamer & one French, the Gassendi, for whose benefit our band played the Marseilles hymn as we passed. There are abt 100 vessels anchored in the Roads.

The Monitor is here & a most ridiculous looking craft she is. She has a flat open deck perhaps 2 feet above water but over which the waves wash continually if there is any sea at all. Abt the middle of this there is a round cylinder perhaps 10 ft. high & 20 to 25 ft. in diameter. Add a flag staff & a small steam pipe & you have all that is visible of the famous Monitor. Make a raft 120 ft. long & in abt the shape of a pumpkin seed & put a cheese box in the middle of it & you will have a good picture of this novel invention. Fort Monroe looks abt as I expected. There is considerable sea running, a good many of the men are sick.

§ MARCH 20 It rained most of the night & nearly all day. We landed abt 1 P.M. & marched abt a mile & half out into an open field where we arrived abt 3 P.M. Our shelter tents were put up in the midst of a heavy rain & on the whole the prospect was dismal. There was a pretty heavy growth of dry weeds around & in half an hour they were all picked & piled into the tents.

The usual quiet of the place was soon troubled by the characteristic propensities of the 2d. There was no timber or wood within a mile but a man with a 4 horse team & large load of wood, not knowing what he was coming to, attempted to pass on his way to the Ft. As soon as the men saw him they ran & seized his horses

by the bits, helped him down from the wagon & in a very quick
& dexterous manner unloaded the wood of which they soon disposed while the man put his horses to the gallop till he was out of
sight.

Their next move was to seize 3 or 4 oyster boats which had just
landed, throw the darkies out of them & carry off the oysters. Next
they drove a lot of darkies out of their shanties & took possession.
Next they nearly drove some regulars crazy who were trying to
guard the Hampton bridge. The boys were in 20 minutes across
the river to the number of 50, & in short the fame of the 2d had
spread through all the country round about before dark to such
an extent that early in the m'g Gen. Wool honored us with a visit.
He gave out the news that any man who was again caught at any
such performance would be quartered at hard labor for 3 months
on the Rip Raps.*

§ MARCH 21 The day is warm. The men are around in their
shirt sleeves & some are barefooted. Peach trees are in bloom. All
are very lazy. This is a very pleasant place. The country has a far
more prosperous look than we have before seen. The distance of
100 S.† is visible in the changed appearance of vegetation &c. We
here see the live oak for the first time. Pine is the most conspicuous.
The timber as seen from our camp seems good. The leaves are
full 8 inches in length.

We find the soldiers here & the people generally a good deal
frightened since the affair with the Merrimac. This pleases our
men immensely, they not believing any such thing. The stories they
have told to the regulars are truly astonishing. The regulars were
disposed to put on airs at first but when they heard their intolerable
lies & witnessed the assurance with which they were told they were
quite overcome.

The ruins of Hampton are just across the river. I have not been
there but judging from appearance it must have been a place of
great beauty. It was one of the oldest villages in the country & was
rich in historic associations & the romance which always clusters

---

* Maj. Gen. John E. Wool commanded at Fort Monroe. The Rip Raps was a
fortification offshore in Hampton Roads.
† 100 seconds, or 1⅔ degrees of latitude, the distance (some 125 miles) that the
army had moved southward.

around old places. The burning of it was one of the most wanton & unnecessary acts which has disgraced the Rebel cause.*

I must although at a late day mention the kindness & generosity of the N.Y. 26th to our Regt. when we were lying on the bare sand at Ft. Lyon in that long cold storm of wind & rain. They took in all their tents would hold & would even have slept out doors themselves to give our men a place if they would have allowed it. Their kindness knew no bounds & will long be remembered. I also pay the same tribute to the kindness of the Mich. 1st last night. It is a satisfaction to know that we have done what we could for others in the same line on previous occasions.

§ MARCH 22 The warm weather of yesterday brought a heavy thunder shower last night & a cold windy morn'g. The troops [are] coming in rapidly but we shall not move it is said till the force is increased to 80,000. I hardly understand why an advance was not made direct for Centreville instead of from this point but have no doubt it is all right. It is however known to be a dangerous business to advance from so many different directions on an enemy posted at a central point. Our forces are so numerous that it is now less dangerous.

The Monitor is a small unseemly looking craft but without its presence no vessel would feel safe in Hampton Roads. The towering 74 [*Minnesota*] has to look to her for protection. She is a hard customer. There is not a man to be seen & there is no opening visible except when the guns are to be fired. The port opens just long enough to allow the gun to be fired & then closes of itself. There is nothing to be gained by getting on the deck for it can be swept all over by steam & scalding water. If they should escape this there is only one place where she can be entered & that only by one man at a time & they can let steam enough onto him to scald him to death in a second.

§ MARCH 23 Sunday. Inspection as usual. The weather is cold & unpleasant. [Fitz John] Porter's Div. is landing at the wharf. The living is very poor. Among the new trees which I have seen are cypress & holly, both very pretty especially the latter. The men are mostly engaged in playing ball & pitching quoits or are down at

---

* The Confederates' John B. Magruder burned Hampton on August 7, 1861, in response to a rumor that the Federals were going to settle runaway slaves there.

the shore wading after oysters & clams of which they find an abundance. The enemy are in force at Big Bethel abt 8 miles from here, where [we] were once defeated & where Major Winthrop & Lieut. Greble, two very valuable young officers, were killed.* Their pickets are abt 4 miles out.

I have been down to the shore & had a good view up the Elizabeth River toward Norfolk & also some 15 miles I should think up James River. Sewell's Point, Craney Island & other familiar points are plainly visible as are also several Rebel camps.

§ MARCH 24 It rained moderately last night. Abt 9 A.M. we picked up our effects & moved across the neck into what used to be Hampton, thus on till we made abt 2 miles where we halted, stacked arms &c. We are on the road to Richmond via Big Bethel & Yorktown.

Hampton is said to have been one of the richest, laziest, handsomest villages of its size in the Union. The houses were all brick & surrounded with trees & very neat yards. The chimneys and corners are all that is left standing. All the farm houses out this far are burned.

Seward declared with great sincerity & emphasis to day that he thought soldiering "was played out" and that he wished he was at home. It does not agree with him. He says "the rain will get through the interstices of the shelter tents." He would starve to death if the boys did not take care of him. He never has anything in his haversack, has no cup, no canteen, no shelter tent nor anything which he needs.

I am on guard to morrow. Capt. & I have a small tent. Living is poor — hard biscuit, salt meat & coffee are the principal articles. The troops are coming in pretty rapidly & I hope we shall move on soon. Col. Poe says if we lie here 10 days longer we shall get whipped. I think it pretty certain that we shall see considerable fighting.

Seward's remark abt the rain coming through the interstices reminds me of Lt. Tolson C. Barden's remark to his Co. on drill "that if the cadence of the step was not more accurately observed the drill would be indefinitely prolonged."

---

* Maj. Theodore Winthrop and Lt. J. T. Greble were killed in the clash at Big Bethel on June 10, 1861.

Major Underwood has always been very bitter on the Abolitionists but to night he worked more than 3 hours in water up to his waist to help 20 contrabands across the river & on their way to their Paradise at Fortress Monroe. He said they looked so frightened that he had to help them.

§ MARCH 25 There was a hard frost last night. Several Regts. have moved forward this m'g for the purpose of driving in the enemies' pickets & giving more room for new Regts. which are constantly arriving. One learns much abt soldiering by moving abt from place to place.

I have seen some very fine looking troops here. Max Weber's German Zouave Rifles (20th N.Y.), a Regt. of Phila. Zouaves [58th Pennsylvania] quartered in Ft. Monroe & the Mich. 1st are all richly dressed, much better than we, and are well drilled. They are better in the minutiae than any Regts. I have before seen. They have always been quartered in nice clean barracks & had nothing to do but drill. We can kill them in the field in a month, do more work of any kind & form a line of battle as quick & do all they can & do it quickly but not so perfectly. We ask little odds in drilling save on small points which make a Regt. look very pretty & are to be desired but which are unattainable by one which is constantly on active & arduous duty in the field. They will cut short on all that is not absolutely necessary.

The 1st, 2d, 3d, 4th, 5th [Michigan] Regts. and Stockton's Independent Regt. [16th Michigan] are all here together. Mich. is well represented in this part of the army. The Ellsworth Avengers [44th New York] are quartered near us. This Regt. is probably composed of the best material of any in the army. There is one man from every town in the state of N.Y. & he is the best one the town afforded. All are picked men.

One of Major's contrabands died last night. Twenty two of them started from Richmond. Eleven were shot by the Rebels, one died last night & 10 remain.

§ MARCH 26 An idle day for us. A heavy storm is evidently coming on. I took a stroll through the ruins of Hampton this m'g. I visited the ruins of one of the first churches built in this country. Nothing reminds one more forcibly of the utter desolation than the ruins of this venerable building, the tombstones overthrown, the walls broken down & the place where the dead have quietly rested for 150 years laid open to common.

Gen. McClellan will be down to night, also Gen. Richardson & his Div. They are unloading artillery & stores as fast as possible at the wharf.

§ MARCH 27 There was a light flurry of snow last night but the day has been very fine. [William F.] Smith's and Porter's Divs. advanced this m'g & are reported in possession of Big Bethel. We had Co. drill this A.M. & Battalion P.M. Quite a number of the men are sick with bowel complaints. All are very anxious to advance.

§ MARCH 28 Drilling same as yesterday, weather warm & fair, living hard crackers & coffee. This is a very good diet but there is a great deal of sameness abt it. They will take nothing but gold & silver down here & that is something we dont get. Furthermore they will not let us out of camp to buy anything. Military law is strict & it is too dangerous to get provisions on ordinary occasions without pay. I have indeed no great amt of money & the rest have none at all. There is a promise of pay in a day or two.

Our troops were 5 miles beyond Big Bethel yesterday, killed 3 men, took 1 prisoner. Troops are still rapidly coming in. The almost perfectly level country around here offers a strange contrast to that around Alexandria & Washington.

§ MARCH 29 I am on Brigade Guard. There was a storm of rain & high wind last night & the m'g was very cold & raw. It commenced raining abt noon & a very cold driving rain with occasional hail has fallen with slight intervals till now 8 P.M. when it is raining hard. I had the gloomy prospect of lying out all night without shelter. Col. Terry comdg Brigade sent orders to dismiss the guard & I thank him for that. There was no use of keeping them on. The outlying pickets will protect from the enemy & no one will leave camp in such weather. The 7th Michigan landed this P.M. & will have a sorry time.

Our men have learned to keep pretty comfortable in shelter tents. They are made open at both ends but they tie 4 of them together & close up one end with sods. In this way they are expected to hold 4 men & with a little crowding 5 men.

§ MARCH 30 I came off guard in due time & went shivering around wet & cold till abt dark when we succeeded in building a small fire in our tent. We soon dried our feet & the tent became warmer. The damp ground was in a measure made wholesome & our personal comfort was soon greatly increased.

§ MARCH 31 The weather was fair. My bowels are turned upside down & the contents are running out at a double quick. Benson is on the sick list but I will not give in as yet. In fact I am better to night. I had Co. drill A.M. but am now detailed on general Court Martial.

§ APRIL 1, 1862 If I had not been on Court Martial to day I fear I should have been obliged to go on the sick list. I got some medicine this m'g which stopped the diarhoae but I have vomited no less than eleven times to day. I have nevertheless discharged my duty at the Court Martial & thus save myself from a list which I have never yet been on. The wind is cold & there is another storm coming. One can never believe reports in these quarters. I supposed McClellan was here long ago but I doubt whether he has yet come. The Provost Guard & Court Martial will make hot work with the "crampers." The 2d will have to restrain its propensities.

§ APRIL 2 I think Gen. McClellan is surely here at last in as much as an order came from him at noon countermanding a review ordered by Gen. Heintzelman & saying that he had other business for us. I am still unwell but not so bad as yesterday. I am determined to get well before the advance which I think will soon be made. I am going to start with the Regt. if I die by the roadside the first day. I attended Court Martial as usual. The weather is cold & raw but the expected storm has not yet come.

§ APRIL 3 I am better to day but not entirely well. Four of our best men were sent to the gen. hospital this m'g. This lying on the ground all the time is similar in its effects & the diseases it produces to those caused by moving into a new country. In the latter case the air is more impregnated with disease but the exposure is less.

I was on Court Martial as usual. The Qr'master is sick & Seward is acting. He will do well in that place & I wish he might retain it. I suspect we shall advance to morrow. I know nothing positively but have good reason to believe such is the case. I sincerely hope it is. I think numerous things abt the conducting of this war which I will not now speak of.

Just as I write this the Adjutant comes to inform me that we move at 7 A.M. to morrow. 10 P.M. Far as the eye can reach the sky is bright with the glare of camp fires, of soldiers preparing rations for to morrow's journey. Yes, to morrow at 7 we once more advance, I suppose, on Richmond.

§ APRIL 4 We were informed this m'g that we had a Brigadier

Gen. (Berry) [Hiram G. Berry] & were right glad to hear it, fearing it might have been a worse man. We left camp at the appointed time & are now 10 P.M. 2 miles beyond Big Bethel. Our march has been through a country in many respects pleasant but the water is very bad. It is all nearly stagnant & covered with green scum. The land is perfectly level & at high tide not more than 10 ft. above the ocean.

The march was slow & tedious. Halts were frequent on acct of difficulty with baggage & artillery. I saw the spot [at Big Bethel] where Major Winthrop & Lt. Greble were said to have fallen. We stopped at sundown & ate supper, made a cup of coffee &c. Moved forward one mile abt nine, I presume we shall advance again before m'g. We shall fight to morrow if the rebels do not run.

Some of the Regts. straggled so badly & many of the men threw away their overcoats, blankets &c. Our Regt. marched in good order & picked up more than they threw away. Col. Poe had a fracas with a lot of Quartermasters abt a train of wagons & marched 2 of them off our grounds at the point of the bayonet.

§ APRIL 5 We were up at 3 A.M. but did not march till 7 A.M. & then did not go more than a ½ mile before we halted. Five Regts. of Regulars & above 100 pieces of artillery have passed us. There was a very hard shower of rain while we were waiting. We left abt 11 A.M. & now at 5 P.M. find ourselves near Yorktown.

We have marched abt 11 miles over a very bad road. Firing opened pretty briskly abt 9 A.M. at Yorktown & Wayne's [Wynn's] Mill & has been continued to this time. We are abt ½ mile in rear of a part of our batteries. The enemies' shot & shells fall near us, occasionally within 10 rods or such a matter. I have seen 1 man who was killed & 2 who were wounded. I would not be surprised if we got shells into our camp before m'g.

§ APRIL 6 The m'g opens very bright & fair. I slept pretty well last night. Our baggage did not come but I took the precaution to pick up a good blanket by the roadside & found it of great service. I have washed, eaten my breakfast, filled my canteen & made sundry little preparations for whatever the day may bring forth. Our balloon is up nearly all the time viewing the enemies' works. There has been no firing this m'g except a few shots by the sharpshooters.

Noon. Not more than a half doz. cannon shots have been fired to day. Three of our pickets were shot this m'g. Cattle, sheep &c have been driven in from the country around & we have plenty of meat but no bread. The men are eating raw corn as substitute. There is a swamp between here & Big Bethel through which the road is almost impassable. Whether we are waiting for some 150 pieces of artillery which are still on the road or out of respect to the Sabbath I cannot tell. A wounded man was just carried past.

Virginia towns are far larger on the map than in reality. We passed Little Bethel without seeing it & found only one house at Big Bethel. There was formerly another but it is now burned.

Sundown. There have been a few cannon shots since noon but none very near us. I saw 4 men brought in who were either killed or wounded. Abt 5 P.M. there were some very heavy volleys of musketry abt 2 miles to our left. We fell in but having no orders to move soon broke ranks again & prepared for supper which indeed is no great affair inasmuch as it consists of nothing but muddy water & beef without salt. I have often been without anything to eat but hard biscuits & fared very well. To have nothing but fresh meat is more unpleasant. By reason of having the junior Div. Gen. of the Corps & the junior Brigadier Gen. of the Div. we are the rear brigade of the rear Div., in consequence our wagons are the last to arrive.

§ APRIL 7 The m'g is cold with a raw east wind. Several of the men were sick last night from eating too much warm meat without salt. There were at one time last night abt 200 musket shots fired in quick succession. I presume the rebels were firing at our pickets or to find by a return fire where they were posted. All is quiet this m'g. I am told we are getting heavy siege guns in position & making various preliminary movements. 4 P.M. Only a few scattering shots to day. This delay is irksome.

There is still great trouble abt rations except beef. There is no bread of any acct. Some of the Regts. are boiling wheat. There are plenty of rations at the mouth of the [Poquosin] river 10 miles off & teams are trying to get through with them. It takes 2 days to make the journey & 6 mules cannot draw more than 1200 lbs. I think they would do better to pack the provision than to draw it. A great many mules are killed by the present mode.

There is a heavy, cold, east rain falling but all the tents (shelter) are pitched & we are comparatively comfortable. We need only bread & coffee to be well off. Crackers 3 inches square & of the usual thickness would sell readily at 5 cts. apiece but there are none for sale. The man who has one looks on it with miserly eagerness

& holds it tight as if afraid someone would take it away. There is an abundance of meat but it does not satisfy the stomach. The Capt. got 2 potatoes this m'g & had them cooked but they were stolen before he could eat them.

I presume however that our hardships, which indeed are not serious, must be light compared with those of our Revolutionary Fathers at this place. If they could endure so much to found the Govt. surely we can with light hearts bear the small privations necessary to defend it. The general impression is that the battle will be severe but there is evidently a determination to die sooner than retreat.

This Regt. is far different now from what it was at the battle in July. Then they were alive with curiosity & excitement the moment firing commenced whether it was near them or not. Now unless it be unusually heavy it is hardly noticed.

§ APRIL 8 It rained hard all night. It is very cold & the rain lacks little of being snow. The clay mud is everywhere full 2 inches deep & very slippery. Many of the tents were flooded & the men driven out because they could not be properly drained. It was one of the worst nights we have ever seen. And one can hardly expect a more disagreeable day. There is no fighting to day. Each man recd 5 hard crackers this m'g. All are very impatient for action.

Four P.M. It takes little to make a soldier happy. The teams have arrived bringing a pound of biscuit per man & report that coffee & sugar & salt will be here to night. This, although the mud is still deep, the weather cold & misty & wood scarce, has made the men to all appearances as happy as larks.

A soldier misses his coffee very much. I will myself bear testimony to its virtues here though I rarely drank it at home. After a toilsome day or a night of cold & exposure nothing seems to revive men like a cup of hot coffee. Give as much & as good food as you please they do not feel like themselves without their coffee. I obtained a good cup abt an hour ago. It was the first since yesterday m'g & did me more good than all I have eaten during the time. I have no doubt that in large quantities it may be injurious & I have just as little doubt that a pint for breakfast & the same for supper, especially when there is marching or other labor to be done, prevents disease & is a desirable & necessary stimulant. If I were home again where I could get good water & fruits & a variety of food I should drink but little of it.

9 P.M. The coffee & sugar have come. The storm is still pelting us without mercy but the camp is well ditched & the men have bark & boughs enough in their tents to keep them off the damp ground. One of the luckiest hits imaginable was the purchase of the Atlantic for April just before I started. Last night & to day I have read it nearly through. I should have had a lonesome time without it.

I cannot get the idea out of my mind that we are in some danger of surprise on these stormy nights. It is certain that we have a numerous & desperate enemy, perhaps 75,000 in number before us & not much more than 1 mile distant. It is so very dark & so much noise is made by the wind & storm that it would be impossible under any circumstances to get a Regt. into line without some delay & confusion, which of course would be increased by a sudden dash of the enemy. In 10 minutes after the first alarm they could be in our camp.

§ APRIL 9 The storm still continues with little intermission. The sun has not shown once since it commenced. The air is full of fog & mist. The smoke from a thousand fires drifts along the ground & almost stifles & blinds one. Mud, mud surrounds us on every side. There is not a foot of hard ground anywhere. We are abt the dirtiest lot of men I ever saw. Those who have been used to camping out in small parties do not understand our difficulties. I could take 6 men with our blankets, go into the woods where there are bushes & fuel in abundance, pick our place & build a great fire & pass such a storm as comfortably as anyone could wish. We have to go onto the open field, take the ground as it comes & carry our wood from ¼ to ½ a mile on our backs.

The enemy tried to disturb our pickets last night. They brought out a Regt. & kept up a steady fire for near an hour. The pickets wisely lay close & did not return the fire. The enemy unable to find where they were did not advance any farther. One of our men was slightly wounded. This Regt. has not yet been on picket here. I should like [it] in good weather.

Some men seem born to be shot. I saw one killed by a shell to day who was walking alone in the open field more than 30 rods from any other men. There was only one shell fired in that direction during the day & that of course not at him. As his ill luck would have it he was just under it when it burst & a fragment struck him in the head killing him almost instantly.

Only a few scattering shots have been fired to day & those merely for amusement or to ascertain ranges. The works are too strong for our field artillery & we can do little till the siege pieces are in position. This will take some days. Col. Poe is assisting in this work & the engineering generally. The old battlefield of the Revolution is in full view a little to our right & nearby.

§ APRIL 10 Last night we had a very pleasant episode & one common to besiegers. It was learned in some way that the enemy intended to surprise us. Abt 1 A.M. an order came to form as soon & as quietly as possible. In a very short time we were in line & marched to the supposed point of attack, without a loud word being spoken by anyone. The other Regts. of our Div. were soon on hand together with 24 field pieces. All were posted so as to be concealed as much as possible. The pickets were ordered to give way without resistance. The enemy came with a heavy force into a piece of woods near the picket line where they remained for abt an hour. After looking abt them they very cautiously withdrew without further demonstration, much to our regret. We after being out 2 hours in a very cold wind & rain were not sorry to regain shelter, after we found the enemy had fallen back.

This m'g we had several squalls of snow but abt 11 A.M. it brightened up a little & the sun is out at intervals. We moved our camp back abt ½ mile into the woods to day. We shall here be out of the reach of both wind & shells. Some of the pickets of the 4th Maine were so chilled when they were relieved that they were unable to walk & were brought in on stretchers.

§ APRIL 11 The wagons came in last night with crackers & coffee. The men had good quarters & plenty of wood & were unusually jolly. Weather fine but a hard frost last night. We were kept pretty busy P.M. There were quite a number of shells thrown, mostly by the enemy. The long roll was beat twice & we came out in line of battle each time. The pickets were driven back at several points & 2 of the 63d Pa. & 1 of the 5th Mich. killed. There was skirmishing along the whole line.

§ APRIL 12 Our Regt. came on picket last night. Only 2 shots have at this time (8 A.M.) been fired by us. There are 3 forts & 2 rifle pits within ¾ of a mile of us but we are screened from their view. Some sharpshooters have just been sent to the front & I presume we shall soon hear from them. They make such warm work for the gunners in the forts &c that they now compel the darkies to do all the loading.

9 P.M. We are relieved & together with the Maine 4th have the credit from Gen. McClellan of keeping the best line of the siege. There is no doubt that the conduct of the 63d Pa. & N.Y. 87th on the day before was cowardly in the extreme & a disgrace to both officers & men.

§ APRIL 13 I might have shot a rebel picket yesterday but it being agt orders of course did not. Indeed I am not sure whether I would have shot him anyhow under the circumstances. He was off abt 30 rods from me standing by a tree looking very earnestly toward where he undoubtedly supposed our lines were. I having crept up behind some fallen trees outflanked him unawares. He had a sort of innocent harmless look which would have made it a little hard to shoot him though I have not the least doubt he would have shot me if he had have seen me.

I would like above all things to belong to the sharpshooters. I am sometimes almost tempted to throw up my commission for the sake of joining them. I know that with a good gun I could shoot on the average of a half dozen men per day during this siege. Three good sharpshooters will often render a line more unsteady than a battery of artillery.

I feel well to day. We have matters so arranged that we can get provisions. I believe this is the first day since we left Hampton that I have had enough to eat.

I have great faith in Gen. McClellan, still there are matters abt which I have my own thoughts & speculations. I do not believe Napoleon would have spent so much time in preparation. Indeed everybody knows he would not & knows equally well that he would have succeeded. Would Gen. [Henry] Halleck or many others we can mention have waited so long & if not would it have been better or worse for us? Might Manassas & Norfolk have been taken last fall & Va. cleared of the Rebels? Was it more expedient to wait till after they were beaten in the west? Is our present delay a part of a great plan for overwhelming success?

We all know that as a rule delay means defeat to the invader & victory to the invaded. Knowing this, seeing our delay without knowing the cause, it is but natural, in view of the vast expense, the dangers of foreign interference & the unexpected misfortunes to which every nation is liable, that many should feel anxious & some should have serious misgivings. I wait with confidence but not without emotion the perfect vindication of our much honored General's plan of operations.

So far as we are personally concerned we are very impatient of delay. I feel perfectly prepared for my fate in the battle, whether to see the glorious old flag floating mid shouts of victory over Yorktown or to die on that field where in times of old better soldiers than I have given their lives for their country. All I ask is strength of hand & heart to bear me honorably to the end which is appointed for me. For the 2d Regt. in particular I hope a high & honorable part in the action. They are in all respects deserving of it. None but soldiers can know how sensitive the men of a good Regt. are of its reputation. Insult or reproach are insufferable.

Provisions are now landed at Railroad Point only abt 4½ miles from here & are easily obtained. A large part of the road had to be crosswayed from 3 to 4 times but is now quite good. I recd a good long letter from Arthur this m'g which with its welcome news of all well at home made this Sunday a very pleasant day.

You cannot get out 20 men of this Regt. to divine services unless it be a funeral. They will play cards &c all day on Sunday, almost to a man swear beyond anything I ever heard elsewhere & steal everything they can put their hands on. Still there is a large amt of a certain kind of rude religious feeling. Perhaps it is more allied to superstition yet such as it is I have no doubt there is more of it than ever existed with the same men elsewhere.

§ APRIL 14 I have been engaged at the Court Martial to day. Weather very warm & fine. We have lived well this day at least. Our light batteries have thrown abt 100 shells to day to keep the enemy off some new works which they are attempting to erect. The enemy succeeded during the night in cutting down a small piece of woods which obstructed the range of their batteries. We took 7 very ragged prisoners to day. None of our men so far as I can learn have been hurt.

§ APRIL 15 A light shower of rain in the m'g but the day was warm & fine. I was on Court Martial. There was considerable firing by light batteries on the left & by gun boats on the [York] river. Regt. went on picket at dark & I got permission to go along.

§ APRIL 16 Weather very warm & fine. Brisk firing by light

batteries on the left to all which the enemy replies. We cannot see the guns of either party but can very distinctly see the shells explode. One stray ball struck in the woods near us but did no harm. Abt 9 A.M. we changed our position a short distance to be more out of the way. Soon after that a 12 lb. shell struck very near us (Co's. F & I on reserve) but did not burst.

At 1 P.M. there is little firing though it had been brisk till after 12. Abt 11 A.M. Sergt. Bishop of Co. F was killed while standing near our battery. He thought himself too sick to go on picket last night but came out to day in disobedience of orders to see the artillery practice. In consequence of going when & where he ought not to be he was cut entirely in two by a ball from the enemy. Not a man abt the battery has been hurt. He was a fine young man & in most cases a good non-comd. officer. He had long had a presentiment of his fate & though a young man was tired of life & often expressed a wish that the appointed time would come. Yesterday m'g he said he knew he should be killed soon & twice repeated the wish that the time was at hand. This m'g he went out & was almost immediately killed. We wrapped all that could be found of him in his blanket & buried him under an old chestnut.

I saw one of the 3d Mich. pickets with both legs shot off. No other accident occurred to the pickets. From abt 8 A.M. till sundown from 150 to 200 shots per hour were fired on our part from light guns. Nearly all the barracks of the enemy on the left were burned by our shells & several of their guns dismounted. For more than an hour the shells dropped one after another into one of their forts just like clockwork, not one missing. The men inside could be seen running, creeping on their hands & knees & crouching in every nook & corner trying to escape them. They flew around like a flock of chickens when a hawk pounces down among them.

Gen. [Erasmus] Keyes engaged the enemy at the extreme left & toward night there was very heavy cannonading & great volleys of musketry. The battle must have been severe. A few heavy shells burst to the right of us probably thrown from mortars. They burst at the height of 1000 ft. & the fragments made a great whizzing.

Our balloon has hung all day like an evil spirit over their doomed works. It must be very aggravating to have a man just beyond their reach looking down on every move they make and telegraphing it as soon as made to Gen. McClellan. They have a balloon but for some reason it will not stay up more than 2 minutes at a time &

must be more vexatious than useful.* Seward declared when the shells began to fall near that he longed for the peace & quiet of his Michigan home.

§ APRIL 17 The cannonading which was continued at intervals during the night opened vigorously at sunrise. It slackened abt 8 A.M. but continued moderately all day. A heavy rifled gun which the enemy put up yesterday drove one of our light batteries off the field just in front of us in quick time. A fatigue party of 600 men was detailed to work on the intrenchments. I went along. The enemy however shelled the spot where we intended to work in such a manner that it was thought best to keep off it during the day. There are all sorts of reports abt yesterday's work but they are so uncertain that I will record nothing but what I know to be true.†

9½ P.M. It seems pretty certain that we lost 100 men killed & wounded yesterday. A work toward the left was taken by our men & 9 guns spiked but it could not be held. There is still some firing on the left. It sounds wonderfully distinct in the stillness of the night.

§ APRIL 18 At 11 P.M. we were all waked up & ordered to be prepared to fall in on the shortest notice. Soon after midnight there was considerable musketry on the left & we all turned out in line. It lasted abt 10 minutes & just before 1 A.M. we went back to quarters. Abt 3 A.M. musketry again at same place & we turn out & in again as before.

Three men, Myers, Winnie & Drake concealed themselves in their tents & tried to escape going out. I dont know what the Capt. will do abt it but I would put them in a way at least to serve the balance of their enlistment in the District Prison.

One of our guns on the left (a 32 I think) has been firing at intervals of abt 5 minutes since yesterday m'g with remarkable regularity. No satisfactory acct can be obtained of the fighting last night. The story of the battery and 9 guns is more likely to be something else. There is no certainty that we were not badly repulsed.

There are not a few things here which displease me. Many of our officers are tired of war, want to be home. They have not the

---

* This was a hot air balloon, which sometimes stayed aloft somewhat longer than Haydon indicates. The Federal balloons used hydrogen for their lift.

† This fighting on April 16, at a site called Dam No. 1, was a sharp Union defeat.

right spirit. The sight of those 3 rascals skulking away from duty exasperated me beyond all measure. It was hard indeed for me to keep from shooting one of them on the spot. Things move slowly & there are many vicissitudes. I learn also that there were some 3000 to 4000 skulking cowards at the battle of Pittsburgh.* There is no way, only to carry out the army regulations & shoot every one that can be identified.

§ APRIL 19 The Regt. went on fatigue to day & I went along although I might have remained by reason of the Court. We are building a military road along the bank of a small stream. The banks are high & by following them we approach near the enemy under cover. There is an old military road built by Gen. Washington on the opposite side. The road is 24 ft. wide & costs not a little digging & chopping. It is to be level as a railroad & with its branches will be 4 or 5 miles long. There were 3 old rusty cannon shot of the Revolution dug up to day. Four Regts. were at work.

We were at night within ½ mile of one of their batteries. Seward was wandering around & not knowing that we were already up to our pickets started to go to the enemies', supposing them to be ours. They were foolish enough to shoot at him before he came very near & in that way missed him. He made excellent time back to our lines. I am glad he got off but I believe I should have laughed myself to death if he had been taken. They fired one shot over where we were at work but not being able to see us could do no damage.

They also threw an 80 lb. shell over our camp to day. It struck a little beyond the camp & plowed a furrow in which a log 2 ft. in diameter might have been concealed. They may give us trouble here with that gun. There was no cannonading last night & but a few straggling shots from pickets. There have been but few cannon shots to day. It is pretty certain that in the musketry affair of the 16th we got by far the worst of it. It rains hard to night.

§ APRIL 20 Sunday. The Regt. has not been on duty to day. Weather moist. The firing of small arms has been pretty brisk along the lines. Our Regt. goes on picket at 4 to morrow m'g. I am on Court Martial & shall not be able to get out with them.

---

* The Battle of Shiloh, or Pittsburg Landing, was fought in Tennessee on April 6–7.

I have read an account of the battle of Pittsburgh which is in many [ways] very disgraceful. No pickets, camp full of women, 5000 cowards &c. The whole affair shows a most disgraceful ignorance or neglect of duty, a great want of discipline in one part of the army.

§ APRIL 21 Court Martial A.M. adjourned sine die. It was a dark rainy m'g & the Regt. barely succeeded in getting into line at the appt. hour 4 A.M. & per consequence Capt. Benson & Seward as well as all the rest went off without breakfast. As a punishment for not getting up earlier the Col. would let them have nothing to eat till 3 P.M. It is no small job to get a Regt. out at that time where no drums or bugles are allowed to sound except for alarms.

§ APRIL 22 I rather verdantly, the weather being fine, concluded to join the Co. I did so. It rained horribly nearly all night. I got well drenched, was very cold toward m'g & never but one more unpleasant night on picket. There was not a gun fired & nothing relieved the monotony of rain & darkness from dark till daylight. At four several times I sat down on a rail, leaned up agt a tree & patiently waited for sleep. I each time got an uncertain doze of abt 15 minutes & to pay for it had to walk industriously for an hour to get the chills & cramps out of my legs. I had only my overcoat. With a blanket I could have slept very well. We were within 200 rods of a rebel fort & fires of course were not to be thought of except in fireplaces at home & other places equally distant. I had to laugh over Seward's lamentations, still I was sorry for the poor fellow. He says by God he has no desire to be distinguished in war or anything connected with it.

Our men with their usual desire for conversation opened on the rebel pickets yesterday & soon found them to be from a Georgia Regt. which they often met at Munson's Hill. They talked for more than an hour & finally some of them laid down their arms, met & shook hands on middle ground. They before parting agreed that being old acquaintances & in as much as each knew the other could shoot if he was a mind to, they would mutually refrain from hostilities while opposite each other. I dont like such meetings for various reasons. They take all the spirit out of war.

The weather has been showery all day. At 12 noon to day I had been 1 year in the service.

§ APRIL 23 We went on fatigue at 7 A.M. building another road. The men worked well. A few shots were fired at us when we were returning. A 6 lb. rifle shot & a heavy shell struck near us but no one was injured. A raw recruit in Co. F rushed up & down the line several times in great trepidation not knowing exactly what ought to be done but evidently of the opinion that it was no time to be idle. We have 2 luckless fellows who have come down to take their first lessons in soldiering. We have not taken them out yet.*

Yesterday was the anniversary of my enlistment. I cannot say that matters with me have during the past year been very adverse. Many things have been different from what I expected. Nothing was more remote from my thoughts a year ago than becoming a soldier by profession. I then looked forward only to 3 months in the service, now I rarely attempt to look through the uncertainty of my future. The army has so soon become a home to me. I often think, 'tis true, of friends & other scenes but cannot determine when, if ever, I shall see them again. That sort of tremulousness & quick beating of the heart which I once felt, at the sound of bullets, has gone. I feel as though the destined one is pretty sure to come sooner or later & have no more anxiety abt the particular time than I have abt the approach of death by any other cause. When it comes I will try to meet it decently & till that time I will indulge in no vain fears or idle speculations.

§ APRIL 24 For some reason unknown to me we were all called up at 3 A.M. & stood in line till after daylight. Such things are becoming far more common than pleasant. I met my quondam friend Dave Briggs to day. His Regt. came up last night. He wears a very doleful disconsolate look which he attributes to hard crackers but I more than half suspect that the peculiar music of shells which he hears in close proximity for the first time is a far more fruitful cause of his melancholy. He declares he would much rather be back in Mich. again at work for the Squire.

I went on fatigue at noon with 80 men. Gen. McClellan came where we were at work. We were engaged in throwing up a redoubt within abt ¾ of a mile of 2 of the enemies' forts. They neglected to cut down the woods & under their cover we work unseen. Five hundred men will work day & night till it is completed. Shells have been falling haphazard over the country round about in small

---

* Several officers of the 2nd Michigan — Capt. Dwight May of Co. I, for example — had returned home to recruit new men for the regiment. In March 1862 Haydon made a note of fifty-five such recruits to date.

number but no one was hurt so far as I could see though there were several narrow escapes. The paymaster, a very welcome visitor, to night handed over the needful for Jan. & Feb. I was reduced to $2.00.

§ APRIL 25 Weather cold & unpleasant. Nothing in particular has happened except that we have lived a little better than usual. Seward (alias Swiveler) is detailed to go on fatigue at 11 P.M. to remain till m'g. He was a little tight at the time & repeated emphatically that he was devoid of ambition in all warlike affairs & as for Country the last syllable spoiled the word for him.

§ APRIL 26 Seward had a rainy night but returned in very good spirits. He was just near enough to a smart little skirmish to hear & see all that was doing without being in any danger himself. He had very glowing accts to give of his narrow escapes. A Mass. Regt. took 15 prisoners with a loss to themselves of 3 killed & 9 wounded.

The Monitor & Merrimac I see are making a great stir in the world. The latter gives the army here much more trouble than we would willingly acknowledge. The fear of it creates not a little uneasiness. If it was outside the Roads our communications at Ship Point would be destroyed & our operations much embarrassed.

This is a cold, dismal, rainy day. All the occupants of our tent save I have rolled themselves in their blankets & gone to bed to keep warm. I have not tried that way but find it very cold sitting up.

§ APRIL 27 Sunday was spent on picket. It was abt the old story, a little musketry, some solid shot & shell all of which produced no effect so far as I know on our side. Some heavy shells from the gun boats made a great scattering at their works. Our first parallel is nearly completed & a general bombardment cannot be far off.

§ APRIL 28 The night was cold & damp but the m'g is fine. The lines were quiet except a few shots from the gun boats. The rebels threw several shots at the working parties this m'g but without effect. A shell burst near my contraband yesterday when he was bringing out a pail of coffee & frightened him terribly. "Cant stan dat zur, cant stan dat zur. I didnt want to drap de pail but if any more dem fellers come I hab to fling her." I dont dislike the animals so bad as I used to. They are very convenient to have around & I have more hearty laughs out of mine than from all other sources.

§ APRIL 29 Weather fine. We were called out at 3½ A.M. &

remained in line till after daylight. The scurvy is beginning [to] make its appearance but rations of potatoes & onions are now issued once in two days which will soon arrest its progress.

§ APRIL 30 We all went on fatigue at 4 A.M. & remained 12 hours. There was a cold drizzling rain from the east & it was in consequence a very bad time to dig trenches. A considerable number of shells were thrown abt ½ mile to our right. I saw a Lieut. & 2 Privts. of 105th Pa. wounded by the explosion of one but know of no further damage. Our gun boats replied from the river below. I am very much surprised that they did not fire on us as we were in plain view of their works & not over 1000 yds. distant.

We returned to camp abt 5 P.M., were mustered for pay. Supper was very acceptable after 13 hours' work on hard crackers. As my good fortune would have it, after much trouble I succeeded in getting the "Atlantic" for May. In this I read till ten oclock.

§ MAY 1, 1862 The weather is cold & misty. Atlantic storms are by no means so agreeable as Atlantic magazines. We were not called up last night & although the cannonading was very heavy at one time I enjoyed unbroken rest till breakfast. The Rebs fired pretty briskly P.M. from batteries on the right. I find that I now weigh 148 lbs., being 6 lbs. heavier than when I left Camp Mich.

§ MAY 2 The Rebs kept up a regular but moderate fire all night. We are guarding the trenches near where we used to picket. One of the 38th N.Y. was killed here last night. I see by the way the trees are cut off by the bullets & the shanty in which I slept, when last on picket, is knocked to pieces that there has been some brisk work since we left. The firing this m'g is slack on both sides, not more than a half doz. shots per hour. We are well protected in the trenches but for which many might be hurt. Abt 8 A.M. the firing became more lively & abt 500 shells were thrown by the enemy without return. Very little harm was done so far as I know. We were called out at 3 this m'g.

§ MAY 3 We came off guard soon after sunrise. A very quiet night we had. No one from the 2d or 3d Mich., which Regts. now go out together, was killed or wounded, but one of the 3d had his trousers near all torn off him by a shell. They fired 8 & 10 inch shells most of the time & with very accurate aim but we were very careful & thus escaped. The whizzing of the shells was very much like the rapid tearing of a stout piece of cambric. In the night they were plainly visible from the time they left the gun. The firing to day has been less active but several shells have fallen near our camp.

Gen. Kearney [Philip Kearny] of N.J. now commands our Div. Gen. Hamilton remonstrated so strongly abt our being compelled to work so hard that he has been arrested & sent to Washington. He asserted that all things considered we were worked beyond human endurance.

When we first came here a great number of cattle, sheep, hogs &c were killed all about the woods & fields, the offal of which with dead mules & horses as well as the necessary accumulations of filth abt large camps all combine to render the air unwholesome & sometimes at night & m'g the stench is almost insupportable. This is made still worse by the low marshy nature of the ground, the heavy rains & hot sultry days which invariably follow. There is not much sickness yet but it can hardly fail to come.

Nine

ONWARD
TO RICHMOND

From May 4 to June 24, 1862, McClellan's grand campaign edged forward to and across the Chickahominy River to within sight of the spires of
Richmond. Four battles were fought during this advance — a sharp, savage
fight at Williamsburg on May 5; a lesser action at Eltham's Landing (or
West Point), where the Pamunkey and Mattapony rivers join to form the
York, on May 7; at Hanover Court House on May 27; and a major battle
at Seven Pines (or Fair Oaks) on May 31 and June 1 in which the two
armies between them suffered over 11,000 casualties. One of the wounded
at Seven Pines was General Johnston, who was replaced by Robert E. Lee.
  Although Lieutenant Haydon's company, the Kalamazoo Light Guard,
had been under fire at Blackburn's Ford on Bull Run in 1861, and had
afterward experienced numerous picket line skirmishes, Williamsburg on
May 5 was its true baptism of fire. Haydon carefully analyzed his conduct
there and was satisfied. "I believe that all I did was as well done as I could
do it," he confided to his journal. The 2nd Michigan was continuing to
benefit from outstanding leadership — Colonel Poe at the regimental level,
Hiram Berry at brigade, and Phil Kearny (whose name Haydon consistently
misspells) at division. And Haydon, at least, was also persuaded that the
Army of the Potomac was in good hands. "The confidence of the army in
McClellan is at this time unbounded," he wrote on June 14.

* * *

§ MAY 4, 1862 Early this m'g came news that Yorktown was evacuated. Our troops at once commenced pouring into the works & 8000 cavalry were put in pursuit. I am on Brigade Guard. The Guard is now dismissed & the tents struck & we are (at 3 P.M.) ready & eager to march. Just before we started the bands struck up a national air. It was the first music we had heard since we left Hampton & the men burst spontaneously into cheering.

At abt 4 P.M. we left & moved out through Yorktown. It was no small gratification to enter those works which had held us in check for a month. They are very formidable, far surpassing any of our works on the Potomac. There were a large no. of guns still mounted & the fields were covered with tents & hastily abandoned stores & baggage. There was a large amt burned but only a small part of the whole. New made graves were abundant. The stench abt the camp was intolerable. The ground, roads & in fact every place were filled with torpedoes [mines]. Several men were killed by them. Signs were posted & guards placed all around to warn agt them. We camped 2 miles above Yorktown.

§ MAY 5 We were up at 3 A.M. at which time it commenced to rain. We moved off at abt 8 A.M. Rain continued till midnight without intermission. We moved on rapidly over the worst road I have ever seen. It is no exaggeration to say that I was many times in the main road in mud to my knees. It required great exertion to urge on the men & to keep them in the ranks. There was considerable cannonading in front. Aides were every few minutes coming back to urge us on.

When we were within 3 miles of the battlefield the men all took off knapsacks & everything not absolutely necessary for the fight. We pushed on the most of this distance at a run. There was hardly a man who did not tumble headlong at least once. They looked as little like human beings as any men I ever saw. All were drenched with rain to the skin & cased with mud to the waist at least. The troops we were to relieve had been fighting five hours & were tired & nearly out of ammunition, hard pressed & held their own with difficulty.* So rapid was the march that we had not more than 800 men in line when we arrived.

Co's. F & I were at once sent into the dense pine woods to sup-

---

* These were troops of Hooker's division.

port the 5th Mich. The firing was heavy & we had not advanced
a rod into the woods when Col. Poe was wounded in the hand,
Capt. Morse of Co. F fell shot through the leg & an aide to
Gen. Kearney who attempted to show us the way was instantly
killed. Having discharged this duty we moved to the right across
the road & deployed as skirmishers & after abt ½ hour we
moved forward into a thick pine slashing in which the fight was
raging.

It was full of our men & great caution was necessary in firing.
The men of course all concealed themselves among the brush,
logs, treetops, &c. We saw what we supposed to be the firing of
the enemy in front. I was just abt to give the order to commence
firing when one of their officers rose up, waved his cap & cried
"for God's sake dont fire on your own men." This he repeated 3
times & we desisted from firing. During all this time they were
pouring into our men in another direction.

A Co. of the 38th N.Y. now gave way & fell back hurriedly on
our line. The Rebels supposing that the whole line was retreating
at once rose to pursue. Abt 20 of them, "grey coated chaps," started
to come down a little open space toward us. Our men fired on
them at abt 20 rods killing 7 including one Sergt. & a Lt. The
others immediately dodged behind the logs & abt 20 minutes of
very sharp firing from perhaps 200 on a side ensued. During that
time more than 30 balls struck within 5 feet of me & several within
a foot.

The enemy then fell back & we pursued them across the road
led by Gen. Kearney to the edge of the slashing. The enemy then
opened on us with shot, shell & canister from a light battery which
they had taken from us in the forenoon. We lay down on the
ground & I saw only 1 man killed by their fire. The shots nearly
all passed from 5 to 10 ft. over us.

We lay here till after dark. I had, as well as most of the men,
by this time become so chilled by the rain & exhausted by our
exertions to arrive on the field in time that our legs & arms were
cramping so that we could scarcely use them. We had now driven
them entirely out of the woods & were determined not to give
them a chance to come back. The Regts. & Co's. were all mingled
together in the woods & slashing. Lt. Young of Co. F with 2 Sergts.
& 11 men & I with five of our men were all there was of the Mich.
2d at that point. There was a motley crowd from other Regts.

at one time under our command but as it became dark they all crept off but our own men.

After dark the 40th N.Y. came & relieved us. Now came a search after Co. & comrades. I succeeded in finding the Major & Lt. Col., the hospital & a great many killed & wounded, but the Regt. except abt a doz. men in the darkness of the woods could not be found. I was never nearer dead with cold & hunger. I however found abt a doz. men of our Regt. who had a fire & did not look further. I warmed & dried myself the best I could which was not very well as it rained in torrents, till midnight.

At that time it cleared up & a soldier who was a stranger to me made a tin cup full of coffee, the last he had, and unasked offered it to me. I took it & gave him a dollar. It completely renewed and warmed me. After that I kept warm till m'g. I did not sleep at all but passed off the night cleaning my sword & pistol & reading all my old [letters] from home.

§ MAY 6 I started at daylight to look up comrades & find who was alive, who dead. I soon found that I was generally reported among the latter. I quickly found Capt. Benson & Seward and soon after sunrise we had collected 3 Sergts. & 23 Corpls. & privates. One or two Co's. had more, but others only 8 to 10 men. The aggregate of the Regt. at that time was 190 men for duty. Two hours later the no. was increased to 300 & by 5 P.M. it was abt 450. Of the Regt. somewhere between 50 & 100 are killed or wounded. Of our Co. Corpl. Wallace is killed, Pvt. George A. Willson loses an arm & others are unaccounted for.

The enemy retreated during the night & we passed through their works at an early hour this m'g. We are now bivouaced near Williamsburgh. Victory was with us but dearly won. Michigan thank God did her whole duty.

When I went back from the front last night I found the woods & the road side strewed with dead & the moans & cries of the wounded could be heard on all sides. They were scattered around among the logs & brush so that it was almost impossible to get at them if there had been any one to do it. Those who engaged in the battle were so cold & used up that they would not attempt to care for any but themselves. Such as they ran onto they would cover up with blankets, give water to drink & leave as comfortable as possible but they would not turn out of their way to aid them unless they were acquaintances.

Many died through the night who were only slightly wounded & who might under other circumstances have been saved. This m'g several arms & legs were lying on stumps & logs by the road side where they had been amputated. Our men & the enemy were mixed together as the ground was fought over two or three times backward & forward for the space of half a mile in width & two or three times that length. The dead lay in all postures but most of them on their backs, their heads thrown back, mouth slightly open, elbows on the ground by the sides, with the hands up, folded or lying loosely across the breast or frequently one of them placed over the wound. A few had grass, sticks, dirt or their guns clutched firmly in their hands. Some hands were crossed as in prayer, some stretched up at full length. One I saw standing on his hands & knees with his head shot off. Two men were found lying opposite each other with each his bayonet through the other's body.

§ MAY 7 Weather fair. We are still encamped as before abt a mile below Williamsburgh. All our wounded are supposed to be found & cared for & our dead are by this time (3 P.M.) buried. Those of the enemy will most of them be buried to day. Their loss must exceed ours.* Thirty were in one pile, 65 in another, 150 in another this m'g which had been collected for burial & in passing over the part of the field from which they were taken I saw without search 13 bodies which were not collected. Their dead are also lying along the road & in the streets of Williamsburgh at which place are 600 of their wounded.

Our men are becoming vindictive & revengeful very fast at the sight of their dead comrades & dislike even to help bury the enemies' dead. The prisoners are driven into Williamsburgh faster than they can be taken care of. The men are very impatient at our delay & wish to join the pursuit. We shall do so as soon as provisions arrive. The eagerness of the men for battle can hardly be conceived.

The coolness & bravery of Gen. Kearney who commanded our Div. is unsurpassed by anything in the war. He repeatedly rode up to the advance in plain view where almost every man who showed

---

* In fact Federal casualties at Williamsburg came to 2,283, against 1,682 Confederate.

himself was shot in an instant. He was as cool as if it had been a review. The men had never seen him till that day. The first they saw of him was just as we came up & formed our line. The bullets were flying very thick as he came up to Col. Poe & ordered him to send 2 Co's. here & 3 Co's. there, 1 Co. to another place & keep the others here. He then turned to us & said "Men I want you to drive those blackguards to hell at once. Remember the torpedoes. Will you do it?" He was answered by a yell which reached the enemies' line above the roar of the battle & we believe & know that as to many of them the order was carried out in full.

As we passed Gen. Heintzelman, on the road coming in, he was more enthusiastic than I ever supposed he could be. He swung his hat, hurrahed for Michigan most lustily & swore as hard as ever saying "give them h--l G-d d--n them, give the steel dont wait to shoot." We would have been very glad of a chance to use bayonets but could not do it. Gen. Berry & Col. Poe are highly praised.

The conduct of Capt. Benson & Lt. Seward was most admirable. If any doubt ever existed abt Seward it is dispelled. The men look on him with pride. Benson is fairly crazy with rage & hatred toward Secesh.

One of our recruits, Chas. Allen, was found dead to day, & buried. He was a very fine boy, a student when he enlisted. He had been in the Co. but 2 weeks. The fields are strewn with guns, & accouterments, knapsacks, haversacks, coats, caps & every sort of soldiers' property. Everything indicates that they left in great haste.

§ MAY 8 I am still pretty tired & sore but owing to so many of the officers being sick or wounded I was compelled to go on guard duty to day at Williamsburgh. It is quite a place, half as large as Kalamazoo & like that the site of the State Insane Asylum & a college [the College of William and Mary]. The inhabitants are strongly Secession. Business is suspended. One can buy nothing except of Germans of whom there are but few. The inhabitants have plenty of provisions for their prisoners & wounded of whom a large number are here confined. Guard duty here is very busy work & a mixture of everything. This is a very old but pleasant place containing many things of interest if one had an opportunity to look about.

§ MAY 9 I was up nearly all night, got very little to eat. I was very tired this m'g. Abt 11 A.M. the Regt. came up on the march toward Richmond. We have traveled at a moderate rate with frequent halts till sundown. I had the most tiresome time on guard that I ever had.

We saw 2 cannon & caissons, several wagons, numerous boxes & barrels & loose cartridges which the enemy were compelled to abandon. We met several small squads of prisoners coming in under care of escorts of cavalry. One lot of 5 were trudging along alone. They said the Regt. went off & left them while they [were] eating their breakfast & they thought it would be easier to travel this way than the other & acted accordingly. One 1st Lt. of Artillery whom they brought in was very sullen but the privates seemed very jolly & entirely resigned to the fortunes of war.

§ MAY 10 We after sundown marched on 3 miles & camped near some Court House (forgotten the name) in a very large, rolling open field. I think I have never seen as fine a camping ground in Va. The plain is dry & undulating, abundance of wood & fine shade close at hand also a clear brook for washing & one of the finest springs I ever saw. The day was warm but very fine, the roads good, water abundant & of the best quality. No provisions could be had from the inhabitants. White flags were hoisted at all the houses for protection. The troops were civil & orderly. The country is beautiful & in good times must have been fruitful & pleasant.

We camped an hour before sundown [on May 10] in an oat field 17 miles from Williamsburgh. There are still some Secesh wagons strewn by the way but not so many as yesterday. We have made but 19 miles since we left our camp near Williamsburgh but as we are near the rear of the army that is doing very well. We are now from 40 to 45 miles from Richmond & our advance is probably 15 miles nearer.

Our loss (in the Regt.) on the 5th as near as can be learned is 18 killed, 39 wounded & a few missing.*

§ MAY 11 The loss of our Brigade in the late battle is now reported as killed 65, wounded 208, missing & probably killed 73.†
The 3d [Michigan] was held in reserve & lost but one man. The

---

* The 2nd Michigan's casualties at Williamsburg were officially counted as 60 — 17 dead, 38 wounded, and 5 missing.
† Officially, Berry's brigade lost 69 dead, 223 wounded, and 7 missing, a total of 299.

loss of the other 3 Regts. in killed & wounded, without the missing, is about one fifth of the whole force engaged, including the missing it is abt ¼ of the whole. One tenth is regarded as a heavy loss.

We are to remain here to day I understand. I dislike that. I cannot rest easy till we are in Richmond but the Hospt. Dept. imperatively demands rest. We must also wait for provisions & time to cook them. Several Regts. of infantry, one of Lancers & several batteries have passed during the day. The main body of the army is moving.

§ MAY 12 Eight oclock A.M. A large pontoon bridge train went along this m'g. Very stringent orders have been issued abt stragglers & marauders. They will of course have to be carried out & as agt the former should be with vigor. As to the marauders I care less. The men have seen the bodies of their wounded comrades mangled, pierced with scores of bayonets when they were lying helpless. Both at Williamsburgh & West Point officers & men who were but slightly wounded were found with throats cut from ear to ear. I have never known our men to insult or injure their dead or wounded. I do know that their dead were buried as decently & quickly as they could be & that their wounded were well cared for. I have known our men to watch with them night after night when they were themselves tired & exhausted. I was glad to see it. I would scorn to take any advantage of a prisoner or a wounded man however dishonorable may have been his conduct.

For those who are well & under arms I have no mercy. I can shoot them with as little concern as I would a wolf or a hawk. There is no unfair & dishonorable mode of warfare which they did not employ on the 5th. They displayed flags of truce & fired on our men as they approached them. They repeatedly called to us that they were our men to prevent our firing. By laying down their arms & pretending to surrender they drew our men into ambush where they were shot by others of their Regts. as well as by those who pretended to surrender. Could anyone hesitate to shoot such men?* Gen. Kearney well understood their feelings when he alluded to the torpedoes.

A good deal has been said abt brave men in the late fight. I saw

---

* Such tales, embroidered by rumor, were common in both armies after Williamsburg.

some but none like Gen. Kearney. It was not rashness. No one would call it so. It was cool, deliberate well timed bravery.

§ MAY 13 We are still in this cursed oat field. I hoped this m'g would have found us 20 miles nearer Richmond. At 9 A.M. we got orders to move at 10½. Moved abt ½ mile, halted & stacked arms. After all that is said abt toilsome marches they are not so bad as lying hour after hour on the bare ground, just plowed, in a roasting sun without tree or bush for shelter. One loses all patience & suffers both in body & mind.

We marched but 2 miles to day. Camped in the open fields near the road. Our Co. went on picket at night.

§ MAY 14 We were considerably troubled by gnats & mosquitoes. Woodticks are however our greatest annoyance. It is impossible to keep clear of them. The night was perfectly quiet & very warm. The roads are dusty. We marched soon after 11 A.M. & made 7 to 8 miles with only a halt of 10 minutes. It rained gently from 12. The road was excellent & we have never had a finer march. We have a very fine ground. Passed the place where our advance fought the enemy 4 days ago. It was only a skirmish & there was no sign of it save a few bullet marks on the trees & a few dead horses.

§ MAY 15 We were called up at 4 A.M. Marched at 6. It has rained smartly all day, begins at 6 P.M. to be cold. Did not march more than 4 or 5 miles, are now bivouacing on a large flat near Cumberland Landing on the Pamunkey River. There are here some 30 sail vessels & a large number of steamers & tugs.

We passed New Kent Court House where were 2 of the finest old oaks I ever saw. The roads are bad again. This rain will retard operations again. We are very unfortunate abt weather.

Capt. Benson saw at Williamsburgh the bodies of our wounded men whose throats had been cut from ear to ear. I saw to day a Lt. from the 4th Mich. who at West Point saw more than 100 of our men with their throats cut, others with their eyes dug out & others whose private parts were cut off & forced into their mouths. Can such men dream of success? Have we any terms but the gallows, any mercy except the point of the bayonet for them? They are unworthy a home, a country or a God.*

---

* This tale of mass atrocities at Eltham's Landing was baseless.

§ MAY 16 It rained all night but it is fair this m'g. This is a peculiar life in some respects, particularly in this that when one gets a chance to eat a meal he will if prudent, & the thing be possible put away all his stomach will contain for he never knows when or where he will get the next.

I think this abt the most important period of the war. I believe we are just at a turning point where great energy & caution must be combined. The enemy are driven near to "the last ditch." They are desperate & will fight desperately, if at all, both here & at Corinth.* Our defeat or any great delay at either place will almost certainly endanger foreign recognition & if not would certainly double the numbers, the courage & the hopes of the rebel army.

It is of the highest importance that no battle should be hazarded anywhere unless certain of success. If there be any doubt of the result at Corinth by all means let us first fight the battle of Richmond or Chickahominy. One battle virtually decides both. Our progress since the 1st of Jan. up to the latest news has been most glorious, still by a single false step our hopes of complete success might be ruined. If Halleck is beaten it will require almost super-human exertions on our part to take Richmond or perhaps to hold our own on the peninsula. I have no doubt of the result. The scales are balancing but we have the weight which will incline them most effectually.

It cannot be denied that Gen. [Joseph E.] Johnston has conducted his retreat in a masterly manner. Four hours after they left Yorktown we were in pursuit. Two hours later our cavalry attacked their rear guard. We have never allowed them to get out of sight since & they have been pushed to the utmost at every practicable point by cavalry & light artillery supported by infantry. Troops were sent with all haste to West Point to cut them off. The men were on board the transport before Yorktown was evacuated & moved without delay. Still their loss of baggage & stores has not been heavy & the number of prisoners will not exceed 5000 perhaps not more than 3000 exclusive of the wounded.

Nothing has surprised me more than the astonishing & incomprehensible stupidity or untruthfulness of newspaper reporters as

---

* The Confederates' Army of Mississippi was then taking a stand at Corinth, Mississippi, against Henry Halleck's Federal force.

shown by their accounts of the battle of Williamsburgh. I have seen several & among all hardly a single statement was true. Their unalloyed falsity surpasses what the human mind is supposed capable of, viz to tell a long story without ever accidentally relapsing into truth.

Handcock's [Winfield Scott Hancock's] brigade fought in the open field, made a brilliant charge, did excellent service & lost perhaps 300 men. Of this I have read many different accounts & it is spoken of as constituting nearly the whole battle.* As a matter of fact the greater part of the fighting was on the left where the loss was from 1600 to 1800 & the battle continued more than twice as long. This is hardly mentioned. Our brigade lost 346 & but for one acct. in the N.Y. Tribune no one would have known that it was in the battle at all. Gens. Heintzelman & McClellan say that we saved the army from defeat. Kearney is unmeasured in his praise. There is, I am told, an account of this in the Tribune which extols us more highly than we deserve. I saw in the [New York] Herald a list of 20 names purporting to be the killed & wounded of the Mich. 2d at some place not distinctly stated. Not one of these names was correctly given.

§ MAY 17 Warm & quiet. Artillery was passing all day. The regulars & Duryea's Zouaves (5th N.Y.) moved on to the front.

§ MAY 18 Very hot. We have plenty of provisions & can buy anything we wish at the landing. The Pamunkey is not more than 20 to 25 rods wide but is so deep that large vessels run up close to the shore & unload without the aid of lighters or a wharf. We are supplied here with as little trouble as if we were at Ft. Monroe.

The enemy are concentrating a large force on the Chickahominy for which reason I think we shall fight them at some other point. I hope the day will soon come. It is better to hasten matters as fast as possible.

I have now no fears abt being able to face whatever may be in store for me. The time has been when I did not know & had some misgivings of the manner in which I might be effected by the near approach of danger. There was for just a moment [at Williamsburg] a thought of home, a choking sensation & almost a tear. It was for

* At Williamsburg, on the right flank, Hancock's brigade repelled a Confederate charge and lost 100 men.

a moment only. There was a slight quiver of excitement for a moment after that & then all was cool & all the mental or moral pangs which death could have brought on that day were passed. For the next four hours I was never more calm, good natured, complacent, happy. I remember distinctly that I spoke to the men in a tone far less harsh than usual but the orders were obeyed more readily owing perhaps to the unnatural calmness. There was a pleasant eagerness, a desire to push on, to kill as many of the enemy as possible. It was as much pleasure to see them fall as to win a point in a game. It was not a vengeful, malignant joy, but was none the less intense.

I think I was never more completely master of myself. I believe that all I did was as well done as I could do it.

§ MAY 19 We pulled up at 7 A.M. & moved back one mile towards New Kent Ct. House, halted, lay on our arms four hours in a drizzling rain & then pitched tents for the night. It seems sometimes of late as if the whole object was to see how much trouble and vexation can be given us. We usually pull up at daylight, march a mile, lie on our arms in rain or hot sun till dark, then go 4 or 5 miles at double quick & halt for supper when it is too late to find either wood or water. Is it McClellan's fault or that of some one under him or is it really unavoidable?

§ MAY 20 We were called up at 2½ A.M. with orders to be ready to march in an hour. I hope we are going more than half a mile. It looks as though we might see the enemy to day.

Being ready to march & marching are quite different things. We were ready to march at 3½ as ordered but we did not start till 5. It was a fine, cool, dewey m'g & the road was good. Soon after 7 A.M. we reached Baltimore Store (5 miles) where we halted & the men pitched their tents.

I was much pleased last night at the sayings & doings of Brown and Seward, two of the laziest in the universe. The ground in our tent was wet, spongy clay into every little irregularity of which the water would in a few minutes settle. By covering it with bushes a good bed could be made. This they had neglected. They had to put all the clothes under them to keep out of the water except one blanket, which Brown declared was no better than a mosquitoe net. I was awaked at midnight by a loud altercation between them and by the aid of bright moonlight could see them both sitting upright & bitterly reproaching each other with the blame of the comfortless bed, of pains in the bones & with appropriating an undue share of the mosquitoe net. I soon laughed myself to sleep over their high flown recriminations.

There was a sharp skirmish in front yesterday & there is cannonading to day in the direction of Bottom's Bridge. We shall soon have the dangerous joy of a battle if they do not leave us again as they did at Yorktown.

§ MAY 21 A very warm day. We remain quietly in camp. Richardson's & [John] Sedgwick's Divs. with their trains moved down towards Long Bridge. Gen. R. is still anxious to know of the welfare of his old brigade. Soon after the battle of Williamsburgh it was reported to Capt. Norvell that our Regt. had behaved badly & fallen into disorder. He attempted to relate this to the Gen. The Gen. however immediately stopped him saying in a very spirited manner "Mr. Norvell that's all a d----d lie. I wont hear any more of it." Mr. Norvell disappeared but returned soon after with the true account, to which Gen. R. listened with great pleasure saying "that sounds more like it." Our men still like him better than any other officer they ever had. The whole brigade rushes out with cheers to meet him every time he comes in sight.

I had a dish of strawberries to day. They sell at one dollar per qt. Butter is 60 cts. per lb., cheese 40 cts. & other things in proportion.

§ MAY 22 An order has been issued granting whiskey rations. One gill per day. I am very glad that Col. Poe refuses to sign the requisition for our Regt. We are the only Regt. which does not draw it. I have not slept with my pants off for above 2 months to which I attribute an itching & burning of the flesh. Our contraband has become too tedious. We had to detail Lowrey from the Co. The "Shade" is so dirty, lazy & negligent that we could not live with him.

§ MAY 23 I every day wonder what will be the result of the war. In my mind there is much uncertainty. The Rebs are badly whipped but it is much easier to flog a man than to put him out of the house. What shall we do with the conquered country? with the slaves? with meddlesome foreigners? with our vast debt? with the rebels themselves?

Benson, Brown & Seward have gone after strawberries. 3 P.M. Benson, Brown, Seward & Whiting are playing Old Sledge for cigars. I am looking on. Lowrey alias "Mouth Almighty" is discoursing wonders to some boys in front of the tent. Everybody is stretched in the shade thinking of anything but marching when the bugler suddenly twangs out the assembly & we are ordered to be ready to march as quick as possible. Fifteen minutes after, our house, arms, accouterments, stores, provisions, & property of all kinds was on our backs or in the wagons. Five minutes later we were marching. We marched several miles & bivouaced at some place in the open fields. The weather is hot but the country is fine. Some say our advance is driven in; others that Richmond is evacuated. Just before we started there was heavy cannonading towards James River.

§ MAY 24 The train did not come up last night and we had no blankets. I however found some old cornstalks into which I crept & slept well. The wagons came up early in this m'g & we at once pitched our tent. It commenced raining soon after sunrise & has rained all day. We have broken camp or bivouac but once since we left Camp Mich. when it did not rain on the same day or the next. Shelter tents are the soldier's friend. By carrying a weight of two & a half pounds on his back he has always a house with him which he can with the aid of a comrade make complete & inhabitable for both in three minutes. They were considered a poor affair at first but without them we should have suffered greatly.

The Col. to day signed the whiskey requisition. The Adjutant has been with us most of the day. He swears we have more fun & jollity in our tent than in any other on the ground. In truth I have laughed more to day than in some whole weeks at home. The Adjt. was nearly sick but we gave him better quarters than he could have found elsewhere & we have nearly restored him. An Irishman of the 37th [New York] was here to day telling how fast he ran when chased by cavalry. He declared that the telegraph poles looked to him like the teeth of a fine comb.

§ MAY 25 At noon to day we have been one year in the U.S. service. Well do I remember that bright day when, on a smooth, grassy slope, declining gently down to the clear waters of the fairest river we have yet seen we swore to serve our country for three years against "all its enemies & opposers whatsoever." To most of us it was no idle oath. The heart felt what the lips uttered.

This day is as fine as that but the scenery far less beautiful. The rain ceased abt dark last night. Reveille was at 4 A.M. & we left camp at 6 A.M. Two hours later we crossed the Chickahominy, a narrow, deep, sluggish stream, at Bottom's Bridge. Soon after crossing we filed into the woods & halted for dinner.

Our march has been through quite a fine country & over much better roads than we expected. This was due to the bushes being cut away on each side so that we for the most part avoided the main road which was nearly impassable. The fences are all gone & the trains take to the fields where it is possible. We are now 12 to 14 miles from Richmond. A part of the 4th Mich. Inf. had a gallant affair with the enemy yesterday on this ground. I have seen no troops yet who equal the Wolverines in a fight.

§ MAY 26 We remain in the woods. We made a very frugal supper last night & breakfasted on coffee and crackers this m'g. It rains to night as usual. Every preparation is making for a battle. All the knapsacks & baggage of every kind have been sent across the Chickahominy & twenty rounds of cartridge extra have been issued. Everything now seems to indicate that to morrow there will be a great battle.

§ MAY 27 The weather is warm, cloudy & damp. Rain fell for 16 hours without intermission & most of the time very rapidly. When great battles are to be fought & the fate of nations is depending, such weather is almost beyond conception annoying. The Artillery sticks in the mud, Cav. & Inf. lose half their efficiency, the enthusiasm of the troops is dampened & every movement is delayed & embarrassed.

Our baggage having been sent away last night six of us slept in a shelter tent hastily put up & intended only as a sunshade. The water found its way both through & under. At daylight we were piled together after the manner of pigs, a wet, hot, steaming mass, where we lay as quiet as possible till the rain ceased. We then breakfasted on crackers & coffee & were ready for battle. I believe it is of the utmost importance that we should fight as soon as possible. I fear for the safety of our five columns in Va. There has been heavy firing to our right & to the right of Richmond I think. It is supposed to be on or near the Fredericksburgh R.R.

§ MAY 28 There was a smart shower this P.M. "Too many irons in the fire": [Gen. Nathaniel P.] Banks I hear is driven across the Potomac.* I only hope it may be no worse. If McClellan controlled

---

* Banks had been operating in the Shenandoah Valley against Stonewall Jackson.

the whole force in Va. I should have no fears but with so many departments acting without concert or under the influence of a Secretary [Secretary of War Edwin M. Stanton] whose entire good faith I doubt, there is some ground for uneasiness. Thank God there is one man at head quarters who controls all Secretaries & who always does the right thing at the right time. His confidence in McClellan is unbounded.

The action of yesterday on our right is reported a glorious affair.* There was to day some firing in that direction.

§ MAY 29 At 3 P.M. we moved abt a mile & went on picket.

§ MAY 30 The night was very warm, clear & quiet. The day was hot till 5 P.M. when there was a squall of wind & heavy rain. The thunder & lightning was unusually grand. For a dollar we purchased a rooster of a very amiable Secession lady. For a quarter additional she consented to cook it. Her husband is in the Secesh army & she is a violent rebel but the inherent good nature of herself & two sisters (young ladies) could not long be repressed. She finally acknowledged that the "Lincolnite Yankees" were not so bad as she at first supposed.

I see no prospect of being relieved. It matters not. All we have is with us & we are as much at home here as anywhere. There is considerable sickness in the Regt. We get no news or mail of any kind & we are all in the dark except as to what we see for ourselves.

§ MAY 31 There was a terrible storm of rain which lasted nearly all night accompanied by the heaviest thunder I ever heard.

We have to spend an hour every day picking off woodticks. Most of the men owing to our mode of living & the want of clean clothes are now for the first time becoming lousy. I think they got most of them from Secesh blankets picked up at Williamsburgh. Benson & Seward are both well supplied but I have thus far escaped. I heard Prentice say this m'g that he was "going to make a desperate attempt to drive the enemy from his earth works" meaning that he would try to get the lice & ticks out of his shoes & stockings.

There was yesterday considerable firing toward the right & there has been some this m'g. We returned from picket at 10 A.M. to the camp in the field whence we started. We remained there abt two hours.

Co's. D, G, and I were then ordered to report at Gen. Kearney's

---

* A Union victory at Hanover Court House.

headquarters. We had to go back a mile to reach the road which having been done we moved on at a moderate rate. We had not gone above a mile when we began to meet stragglers who reported a battle in front & that we were getting the worst of it. We went abt two miles farther & met a long train of wagons retreating in haste & in some confusion. Sick men, musicians and an abundance of cowards thronged the road. Not less than a Regt. of able bodied men passed us.

We halted in an open field to inquire for Gen. Kearney. Just then Gen. Heintzelman rode up & thinking we had come from the front inquired greatly enraged who we were & what we were doing. On being told he replied that he might have known we did not come from the front. Seeing the stragglers he ordered us to deploy, act as a guard & arrest everybody whom we found retreating. Within an hour we had arrested more than 1000 men. We were kept here till long after dark.

To be there seeing nothing but wounded men, cowardly stragglers with their doleful stories & lamentations & rascally lies, the disabled artillery & all the debris of the battlefield while the combat was going on in front & our comrades engaged was the most disagreeable & discouraging duty I ever performed. I would rather go in ten battles than suffer the anxiety of another day like this. Five Co's. of our Regt. went into battle under Col. Poe. Two Co's. under Major Dillman went in with the 37th N.Y.

§ J UNE 1, 1862 I slept but little last night. I was restless & started up at the least noise. We were relieved from guard at 8 A.M. & went to join the Regt. in the rifle pits in front. Five Co's. were out scouting but A & B remained. Just as we came up there was heavy musketry in front & beyond the field in rear of which we are stationed. It seemed to result favorably to our men & for a time is supposed the battle was over. It was however renewed toward 11 A.M. with musketry & cannonading. There is nothing certain & the most painful suspense & anxiety prevails.

Abt noon Co's. D, G, & I were sent back near where we were picketing to guard a ford. We reached the place after two hours' march & are now under Lt. Col. Williams guarding in a very careless manner what seems to me an important point. I was glad to be in motion. Anything is better than the suspense which accompanies idleness.

§ J UNE 2 The night was quiet. A light rain is followed by an intensely hot day. A working party was sent out to day which effectually blockaded this & the fords below agt Cav. & Art'y. This helps matters and will delay the enemy in case of an attack until we can obtain aid. In a short time the place might be made strong. Since dinner of the 30th I have fared sumptuously every day on hard tack & coffee. If that were not a sort of close confinement diet I should care less.

There was heavy firing all night in the direction of Richmond which was to some extent continued during the day. A great battle has been fought but we know very little of the result. Even our own loss has not yet been determined. It is only certain that Co's. A & B with their comrades of the 37th failed in a bayonet charge & retired with considerable loss. The other 5 Co's. engaged a Reb. brigade & fired at 8 rods with the regularity & precision of a drill. When the task was found hopeless they retired with the same coolness & regularity as they advanced. Col. Poe's horse was shot under him but he was unhurt. Our loss is supposed to be abt 70.

Abt 5 P.M. we started for camp where we drew rations & prepared to advance to morrow. The loss of our 7 Co's. is now known to be 57; that of the brigade 450.* Thank God every Michigan man did his duty. Troops never behaved more nobly. The 3d & 5th fought like tigers, drove the enemy a mile & only escaped being cut off by creeping back through a brushy ravine with rebel Regts. on every side. It was a mistake of Gen. [Charles D.] Jameson which sent our Regt. (5 Co's.) into battle in that position. He is a good soldier & a gentleman but acting on the statement of a damned drunken scoundrel (Col. Hayes [Alexander Hays] of the 63rd Pa.) he made a mistake. He afterwards acknowledged with great frankness & with tears in his eyes, but that did not bring the men to life.

Col. Poe had chosen the ground on which to discharge the duty assigned him. Gen. Kearney says it was the best the position afforded. Jameson ordered him to advance across an open field & it was done. Hayes called Poe a coward for not continuing the advance where it was certain to have sacrificed every man. Poe drew his revolver to shoot him & more than 20 of our men had their muskets pointed at him. His better judgment however pre-

---

* The 2nd Michigan's loss at Seven Pines was indeed 57 (10 dead, 47 wounded); the casualties in Berry's brigade came to 464.

vailed & he put up his revolver & restrained the men. Hayes was drunk but our men have sworn to shoot him at the first opportunity unless he takes back his words. He will be compelled to do so by Gen. Kearney. The expression was made too after our Regt. (5 Co's.) had recd the flying 63rd at the point of the bayonet & tried in vain to rally them.

§ JUNE 3 There was a very heavy shower of rain last night & it was very hot to day. We moved at 7 & joined the brigade a mile & a half in front. Soon after the enemy drove in our pickets directly in front. It proved to be only a reconnaissance & was not pushed beyond the exchange of a few shots. We feel quite easy here as the Mich. 7th is on picket & Gen. Richardson's command is in front of us. We have little fear of being called on to arrest stragglers. I am Acting [regimental] Adjutant. It rained at 4 P.M.

§ JUNE 4 It rained in torrents from dark last night till 9 A.M. & continued in showers all day. Horses mire to the knees on high ground in the open fields. Nothing can be done to day. Dr. Hitchcock of Kalamazoo is here aiding in the care of the sick & wounded. Although he is a comparative stranger to most of us we almost cried for joy at the sight of him. Not only our own men (Co. I) but men of other Co's. who never saw him before flocked around him as if he were a brother to them all. He says he never before realized the meaning of "onward to Richmond."

Gen. Richardson was down to see us to day & to introduce Gen. [William H.] French, one of his Brigadiers who greatly distinguished himself at Fair Oaks. He [Richardson] says that with 7500 men of his Div. he drove 50,000 Rebs, and can do it again. They fought for ¾ of an hour within 50 paces of each other. He was cheered beyond measure. There is no doubt that he is one of the best fighting Generals in the army. A large portion of the rebel dead were yesterday unburied. Heavy rain just before dark.

§ JUNE 5 It rained hard all night but the weather is now cooler & we hope the storm is past. The dead of whom many are still unburied are now nearly decomposed or consumed by maggots. Details are sent out daily to burn dead horses & bury so far as may be the human bodies. At first great holes were dug into which large numbers were thrown but the stench soon became so great that they could not be moved. A few shovels full of dirt were thrown over them & their feet, hands & often their heads were left uncovered.

§ JUNE 6 The change of weather proved to be merely from a warm rain to a cold one. Our Regt. was detailed for picket to day but owing to a change of position of other forces it became unnecessary. Gen. Kearney met a Captain yesterday & asked him where he belonged. Ans. To [Silas] Casey's Div. "Why in h--l aint you running then."

I am pleased with the posture of affairs. It looked a little cloudy for a few days but it is now all right. We have only to draw the net carefully & we are sure of the fishes.

A few of the dead still remain unburied. They are so bloated as to burst open the legs of their pants & the sleeves of their coats. Their features are entirely obliterated & the face when not consumed by maggots is but a smooth, dark shining mass of putridity, nearly as large as a half bushel.

§ JUNE 7 We were paid to day for the months of March & Apr. There was a very heavy shower of rain P.M.

§ JUNE 8 Sunday. As usual the Rebs disturbed our devotions. We were called into line early in the day by firing in front. We moved forward along the [Richmond & York River] R.R. abt a mile & after a little time moved back half that distance & camped. Our men are reported to have taken a small rifle pit with loss of 16 men.

§ JUNE 9 A busy day in the Adjutant's office. I officiated to night for the first time at Dress Parade. There was little done except reading orders.

§ JUNE 10 A very cold rain set in last night & continued nearly all day. There is a great contrast between the weather of to day & one year ago when we were roasting in Washington. The Rebs told us then that the heat would kill us all in less than 3 months. I have hit on a very labor saving arrangement. I hire Billy Mack to make the reports in the Adjutant's office. In this way I get along easily & at a small expense escape most of the labor.

Our Div. is out on a reconnaissance. Some Co's. of our Regt. are scouting still farther in advance. I of course am held with the Regt. Genls. Heintzelman, Kearney & Berry are with us. We passed over the battlefield. There are an abundance of graves & the stench is still disgusting. Col. Poe & Lt. Col. Williams are both absent sick. Major Dillman is in command. Capts. Byington & Humphrey are acting Lt. Col. & Major respectively. It does not make a remarkably efficient command.

I had yesterday a most vexatious time over the m'g report. I never made one before & there had been none made since May 26th. There were many changes & all the killed and wounded at Fair Oaks had to be accounted for. I expected to be arrested for delay before it was done.

I am often at a loss to know why it is that laxity of discipline (I can attribute it to nothing else) begets so much sickness. Under Capt. May our Co. was one of the largest in the Regt. yet had the least men for duty. Now it is the smallest in the Regt. except one & has 3 more men for duty than any other Co. There [are] 180 absent sick from the Regt. (wounded included) yet only 12 are from Co. I. Very little control is exercised as to cooking & the diet is the same in all respects as in other Co's.

§ JUNE 12 A clear warm day, on picket. Co. I captured 4 men, 3 boys, 3 horses, a mule & 3 carts all just from Richmond. One boy had a pass from the Provost Marshal & left there only 2 hours before he was taken.

Two men of Co. I (Caruthers & Tanner) were taken prisoners this m'g while scouting. They ran into their lines unaware. A Reb Sergt. & 1 man sprang up before them at 5 paces with cocked guns & notified them that they were prisoners. Our men parleyed with them a little & then making a sudden spring one of them went into the bushes & the other behind a tree. Caruthers snapped at the Sergt. but the cap did not burn. He immediately cried "forward" & the captors took to their heels. Our men did the same followed by a volley from a post nearby which they had not seen. They joined Seward who was a short distance in rear with other men & all made their way back.

§ JUNE 13 On picket. The night was very quiet. Capt. Benson's HdQrs were fired into after sunrise but no one was injured. The fire was returned with a like result. We established the line half a mile beyond where Casey's pickets were stationed & have kept it without a shot fired except the above. There was heavy cannonading toward the right this m'g — cause & effect unknown.

§ JUNE 14 A special detail was made last night for Gen. Kearney of scouts from Co. I. Corpl. Caruthers and 6 trusty men were sent & discharged their duty successfully. They lay for several hours so near the enemies' line that they could distinctly hear their conversation. We feared they would be killed or taken & were gratified in more respects than one by their safe return.

I am so glad that I discouraged Arthur from enlisting. He could not have entered service at that time & lived till now. We are compelled to be on the alert so constantly that I have ventured to sleep with pants off but once or twice since we left Ft. Monroe. It is now almost impossible to get a chance to wash your body or even to take off your shoes. Clean clothes are a rarity. This is partly owing to the water being so far from camp. I have sent my only shirt to be washed & have to wear my coat closely buttoned. Owing this we are all lousy & covered with sores & blotches. This no doubt partly owing to bad water.

Including the wounded we have 275 on the sick list. My health is remarkably good. I succeeded to day in getting a chance to wash. It refreshed me greatly. I have no fear of being sick.

Eleven scouts from the 40th N.Y. went out this m'g & 9 were captured. We are hourly expecting an attack. The weather is now hot & is beginning to be dry. The sufferings of the wounded on the field in such a day as this would be indescribable. There were not a few in the last battle who were literally eaten alive by maggots. The weather is now much hotter & there will soon be serious difficulty in obtaining water. A dead rebel soldier was to day fished out of the well where we got what was supposed to be the best water. When the weather is wet there is a great deal of surface water but it soon evaporates. There are no perennial springs. These are the hardest times we have ever seen.

Many a good soldier thinks of home, doubts if he shall ever see it again & wishes to be there. The courage & spirit of the men is however unbroken. The nearer they approach death the stronger is their hatred of Secession & the dearer is the sight of the true flag. The soldier who lives on two cups of black muddy coffee & a few squares of hard tack per day, who endures the scorching heat & the damp and chills of night, who drags his weary limbs through [mud] or dust to days of toil & nights of watching finds no fault with McClellan. He would give his life for him or for the cause he upholds.

It is only those who live well & safely at home & who are ready to seek miserable political aggrandizement on the ruins of the soldier's & patriot's reputation or of their country's cause who are constantly defaming & striving to weaken his best hopes of success. Such things do not trouble him. He is above them. But to the soldier with understanding less clear & comprehensive, who offers up home, friends, *comforts, life, all,* they seem like the painful stings of ingratitude. They hurt his feelings more than if they were applied to himself personally. The confidence of the army in McClellan is at this time unbounded.

§ J UNE 15 There was a heavy thunder shower abt 3 P.M. accompanied with very sharp lightning. It was cold afterwards. Firing on the picket line called us out very suddenly & long before the rain ceased. We stood in the rifle pit an hour. Six rebel prisoners were brought in. The 37th N.Y. became excited on picket & fired into the 4th Me. hitting several men.

§ J UNE 16 At 3 A.M. a sharp volley brought me to my feet at a bound. The line was formed but there being no more firing we returned again to quarters. I had just fallen asleep when there came a second volley. The line was formed again in less than two minutes. It was soon quiet again & we stacked arms. We went on picket at 8 A.M. I think the firing was without much occasion. The air is very still, cool & sonerous. A slight noise can be heard a great way.

§ J UNE 17 The night was cold. My blanket, usually too warm for me, was insufficient & I was glad to be up at an early hour. There was only one gun fired on our line during the night & that was by a man who tried accidentally to shoot a pig.

I saw a good article in the N.Y. Tribune concerning officers. They make the Regt. Men are willing to be made good soldiers but they will never do it themselves. It is discouraging to see how many good Regts. are spoiled for want of efficient officers.

§ J UNE 18 Our camp is a very pleasant one, beautifully shaded. Its only drawback is the want of water. There is little to be had that is drinkable & it is becoming every day more scarce. This P.M. we fell in 3 times on acct of firing on the picket line. There was a gentle shower abt sundown.

§ J UNE 19 We were in line at sunrise & marched out near the picket line to support the 20th Ind. which was attacked on their out posts. They lost 4 men but held their position. The attack was not pressed & we returned to breakfast. At 8 A.M. we went on picket. Two of Co. D were shot & severely wounded.

§ J UNE 20 The night was clear but quite dark. The wind blew in fitful gusts & not a few unfounded rumors were afloat. The conduct of some parts of the line might have been more credible. No serious alarm was raised but Co. B shot one of their own men wounding him severely in the arm. Another man of Co. D was shot this m'g while scouting. Capt. Benson's men exchanged shots with the rebs killing one. Two others were shot by our scouts & one was found who was shot yesterday by the 20th Ind. I should write many other things but for the chances of being killed or taken prisoner. I was along the lines several times last night & saw some things which although they did not much surprise me were anything but pleasant.

§ JUNE 21 The enemy threw several shot into camp this morning. A shell struck near me and threw the sand into my eyes but did not burst. I heard it very plainly & knew that it was coming near but not knowing which way to dodge I stood fast. There was quite sharp firing on the picket line abt sundown & we fell in & marched down to the rifle pits & remained till dark. This firing was on Hooker's line but abt 9 P.M. it was renewed on the left where Co. I are usually posted. We fell in again & were under arms for an hour. We were hardly in quarters before the firing was again renewed in front & we were once more in line. There seems little chance of sleep tonight.

§ JUNE 22 We marched out to the rifle pits at 2 A.M. & remained till 11. There was considerable firing on Hooker's line. That on the left proved to be a fracas among the rebels themselves.

§ JUNE 23 The day has been very quiet. We have been in line but once. There was a report this m'g that the enemy were not to be found in front. Some of our Cav. advanced carelessly & found most convincing proofs that they were still there. There seems little prospect of my being soon relieved from the Adjutant's office.

§ JUNE 24 There was I think the heaviest fall of rain last night of a few minutes duration that I ever saw. There have been several smart showers to day. We have now three good wells which supply an abundance of excellent water adding greatly to our health & comfort. I have now good quarters at the Adjutant's office. We have a plenty to eat & I am in the best of health. I keep a paper of quinine in my pocket & every m'g take a little on the point of my knife. It keeps off fevers.

There were only two Capts., 3 1st Lts. & 4 2nd Lts. in the Regt. for duty this m'g. Some are sick & some shirk. We were in line at sunrise but the day has been very quiet. I am now getting well settled down to business & like my new position.

Ten

RETREAT
FROM RICHMOND

The Peninsula campaign reached a climax with the Seven Days' Battles (June 25 to July 1, 1862), and no Yankee diarist left a better account of the confusion of that week of nonstop marching and fighting than Charles Haydon. That he even found time for his journal during this ordeal is remarkable; as he faced death it became for him a sort of last testament.

The 2nd Michigan, Berry's brigade, Kearny's division, was posted in the lines south of the Chickahominy, facing Richmond, and witnessed the first of the battles, at Oak Grove on June 25. Lee's offensive, taking shape at Mechanicsville and Gaines's Mill north of the river, was only heard by Haydon. The firing at Gaines's Mill, he wrote, was "much farther to the rear than was agreeable." His nerve failing under these attacks, McClellan retreated to the James River, and the bitterest fighting experienced by Haydon was at Glendale, on June 30. The 2nd Michigan was under fire but not engaged the next day at Malvern Hill. For six scorching weeks the Army of the Potomac lay at Harrison's Landing on the James. Finally it was ordered to give up the campaign. "Under present circumstances I am not sorry to leave the Peninsula," Haydon wrote on August 13.

* * *

§ JUNE 25, 1862 Was a clear cool day. Our Regt. & the 3d Mich. started for picket at 7 A.M. There was a pretty general movement of the troops in our Div. and in Hooker's. It is understood that certain parts of the line are to be advanced. Our left is stationary but a line of skirmishers is thrown forward extending toward the right across our picket front & Hooker's & perhaps farther. The skirmishers advance slowly a short distance when a fire is opened on Hooker's line. It gradually increased to heavy volleys & continued till about 11 A.M. when our men having gained the desired ground ceased to advance.

Everything was quiet till abt 2 P.M. when the enemy opened with field pieces & the musketry was soon after briskly renewed. The musketry soon slackened & the field pieces were reported as taken & retaken by bayonet charges. Four pieces were brought out into the edge of the woods & fired slowly till near night. The trees & bushes rendered them of little service. Abt 5 P.M. the Rebs raised a great shout & charged the battery. Our men lying concealed cut them terribly as they advanced. They gave way unable to stand the fire. For near half an hour there was a continuous & very heavy infantry fire. Several charges were made. The clear, ringing Union cheers & the sharp wild yells of the rebels were every few minutes heard with great distinctness. All we know is that the desired ground was without very great loss gained & held. The battle extended up to the right of our line but our Regt. was not engaged.*

§ JUNE 26 Was a very quiet day till abt 3 P.M. when far to the right was heard the heavy but indistinct roar of musketry. The cannon opened soon after. From that time till 8 P.M. there was the heaviest cannonade I have yet heard. It was continued with great regularity and at the rate of 25 to 40 shots per minute. At dark far along the line toward the right great cheering was heard. It passed rapidly along to our camp. News soon came to us of a great battle & victory at Mechanicsville. The camps were wild with enthusiasm. Our joy was not less lively but we could not give vent to it in the same manner. I got most awfully wet & muddy going up & down the line carrying orders & cautioning the men to unusual vigilance lest the enemy should on some other part of the line [attempt] to redeem their fortunes. Save the heavy rumble of artillery & baggage wagons along our own lines the stillness of the night was hardly disturbed by a sound.

---

* This first engagement of the Seven Days took place at Oak Grove.

§ JUNE 27 We came off picket at 10 A.M. We were called to the rifle pits at one & remained till sundown. The firing on the right was renewed at daylight. It continued till 10 A.M., a part of the time with great rapidity. Towards night there was firing far to the north & much farther to the rear than was agreeable.* Troops were seen soon after moving at double quick back along the R.R. This at once suggested that something was wrong but our men were so tired & sleepy that they paid little attention. They seemed to feel a sort of sullen, dogged determination to fight to the last where they were & not to move for anybody. A few more days & nights like the past few & they would as soon die as live. Soon after dark we were called out again & remained till after 10. The picket line is nearly broken up. The 63d Pa. ran like sheep as soon as they were fired on.

§ JUNE 28 We were called to the rifle pits at 2½ A.M. and remained till 7 when we went in for breakfast but returned immediately after. Before daylight there was fighting far to the right. We could see the explosion of the shells but could not hear the guns. For several reasons I think it best to bring this book (a pocket memorandum) to a close. I cannot send it away & I do not wish it to fall into the hands of the rebels. It is possible it may if it remains with me.

Things just now are checkered. The right wing has fallen back & we are ready for a move of some kind. I dont know what it may be. If a retreat we are the rear guard. If this should be the last news from me good bye all at home. May God bless & prosper you. Arthur will use what money I leave to complete his education. We all realize our situation but everyone is calm, cheerful & determined. We carry 150 rounds of ammunition & intend that the enemy shall have reason to remember Kearney's Div. If I fall it will be in vain for you to attempt to recover my body. Having spoken of the dark side I may say that we by no means acknowledge that we are not to be victorious. I have still great hope of success in the coming battles. I half believe that this retreat is not forced. If it be we are still powerful to hold our own in a new position.

Arthur: my boy, if I should not see you again be of good cheer

---

* Day Three saw the Battle of Gaines's Mill.

& console yourself with the thought that I died in a good cause. I would like right well to see you, Father, Eliza & all for a few minutes but it will make little difference in the end. But I have already said too much. We mean to send you news of the greatest victory of the war or at least to make like work for those who shall follow us. All the baggage has been sent away & the road is clear. The most perfect quiet prevails. The men are most of them talking in calm, subdued tones indicative of settled purpose. A few are slowly & silently walking to & fro communing with themselves. The weather is very hot. Ever since the battle of Williamsburgh I have seen some indications of what may happen.

There are many N.Y. & Penn. troops in our army. I have little confidence in them. If they were from Michigan, God bless the state, or from any of the western or New England states there would not be a shadow of doubt as to their conduct. If they run as is quite possible, we may be overwhelmed by numbers in spite of all exertions.

What tries my heart the worst is the disaster to the country if we are beaten. It is awful. Do not however despair. They will lose at least as many men as we & ours will be easier replaced. Wage the war to the last desolate acre of the accursed South. We are sure to conquer in the end. This defeat if it be one can be repaired in 30 days. If they are victorious they cannot live if we hold our ground in other places. I hope soon to see clear day through the clouds & uncertainty which now surround us. I intend to relate the events of this war beneath the shade of the glorious maples where we have passed so many happy hours.

Father: be the result what it may I thank you for having always been to me the kindest & best of parents. Eliza: placed as you were in a peculiar and difficult position as regards me you have always been more than I could have asked. Give my good wishes to all my old acquaintances.* Arthur, I advise you to make your education liberal if health will permit but by all means look to that as your help will be needed at home before the other children are old enough to assist. I wish I could see the little ones. I feel a lively

---

* With the death of his first wife (Charles's and Arthur's mother), Philotas Haydon had married a second time and fathered a second family. Charles's stepmother, Eliza, was apparently of his own generation.

interest in them although we are still unacquainted. I have written thus because we all believe that our situation is one of uncommon danger.*

§ JUNE 29 I was kept up all night by a multitude of orders. The tents were struck at 10 P.M. There was a light rain towards morning. We have destroyed everything we cannot carry. At 6 A.M. we moved off by the left flank to our left & rear halting near a sawmill. The rest of the brigade here passed us & went on further to the rear.

Everything is very quiet. There has been no firing since yesterday noon. When everything had passed we retired beyond the second line of rifle pits. We then deployed 5 Co's. across our front abt ¼ mile off & halted till one P.M. We then fell back abt ¾ of a mile. At this time Richardson's Div. was sharply engaged near the Williamsburgh road.

At 3 P.M. we retire still farther. The rest of the brigade has gone on & we are only waiting for our skirmishers. Hooker's Div. occupy the road. We have peremptory orders to join the brigade & attempt to pass them. We have to open right & left & a battery passes at full run. We continue retreating through the woods & bushes on each side & some confusion arises. The road becomes narrower & the confusion increases. Some other Regts. try to crowd through & they make matters still worse. Our Regt. & most of the others are cool & perfectly manageable. The confusion is due entirely to want of efficiency on the part of the officers. The column should at once be halted till order is restored. More artillery passes. A Regt. at double quick cuts ours in two between the 3d & 4th Co's. Three Co's. continue on & 7 Co's. are thrown off to the left on another road. We went abt ½ mile when finding that matters were becoming worse the 38th N.Y. and our 3 Co's. filed out of the road & halted till the others passed. When the road is clear we move on again. Gen. Kearney orders us to go slowly as our 3 Co's. are "the rear guard of all God's Creation." This was an encouraging prospect for us with a total of 100 men.

We reach the swamp [White Oak Swamp] at Jordan's ford, are ordered to cross, to go to the Charles City road & hold it agt all

---

* With this entry Haydon closes the volume of his journal kept since May 19.

comers. We cross the first ford, then a second one abt 60 rods wide
with water 2½ feet deep. We proceed abt a mile when a Co. of the
3d Maine encounter the enemy. We are deployed through the
woods to support them. The force of the enemy is small & soon
gives way.

Finding that they were in force nearby Gen. Kearney ordered
us to fall back across the fords. Our Co's. were left to cover the
retreat. I had hardly any expectation of escaping. The enemy
moved down rapidly but our men were soon out of the way & we
retired in line with a loss of only 3 men, on the extreme left of
the line, who were taken by a party who tried to cut us off from
the ford. Several smart volleys & a number of shells followed us
but did no harm. We crossed the fords in good time, leaving other
troops to guard them & made for another ford 3 miles lower down.

It was now dark. We marched rapidly & notwithstanding their
prayers & entreaties we were compelled to leave by the roadside
some wounded men of the 3d Maine who had been brought across
both fords. We reached the ford abt 9 P.M. & learned that Hooker's
Div. & the balance of our Regt. had crossed an hour & a half
before. We considered ourselves fortunate to have got thus far
though we were apprehensive that we should find the Rebs at the
other end of the ford. We plunged in, crossed safely & marched
till 11 P.M. The night was very dark & we did not dare to proceed
farther. Nearly choking for want of water we lay down & rested
or slept for 3 hours. We were disturbed once by a loose horse
which came galloping over us & once by picket firing.

§ JUNE 30 We were up at 2 A.M. We moved forward a mile &
found the rest of the Regt. We move on ½ mile farther & halted
in a fine open field to rest. We here made coffee, the first we had
had in 24 hours. It refreshed us very much. We have nothing but
hard crackers to eat. At noon the enemy appeared. We marched
1½ miles at double quick & then formed our line. Our brigade
was formed in columns in the woods & remained there an hour.

There is heavy cannonading on our right. We move back ½ mile
farther. Musketry opens on our left, in front & soon after on our
right. We advance to the front where a low, rude breastwork of
logs, rails, stones, turf, anything to stop bullets had been hastily
thrown up. Two batteries are in position. We are in the edge of
woods, before us is an open field 60 rods wide in the wood on the

other side of which is the enemy. The 20th Ind. were already at the work & there was no room for us. We move back abt 10 rods & lie flat down waiting for our turn.

The Rebs charge three times in heavy columns determined to break the line. The batteries double shotted with canister played on them at short range, some of the time not more than 10 rods, for an hour & a half. They were at the same time enveloped by the fire of the infantry. I never before saw such slaughter. The head of the column seemed to sink into the ground. Beyond a certain point they could not come. Four Regts. from behind the work kept up an incessant fire which was replied to by the enemy with equal rapidity.

Things remain thus till sundown when the batteries run out of ammunition. We relieve the 20th at the pits & the fire is carried on with renewed vigor. The enemy display a courage & determination known only to Americans. Darkness comes & the full moon shines forth in all its beauty but its mild, peaceful light only serves to render our aim more certain.* For an hour after dark there is a steady succession of flashes which are almost blinding. The enemy cease firing. We give tremendous cheers. They send us a terrible volley which we return. Both parties then give three cheers & the day's work is done.†

The Rebs were busy till 2 oclock carrying off their wounded. The wounded of 21 different Regts. lay on the field before us, as we learned from the Rebs themselves. Their cries & groans loaded the air, some calling for comrades, some for water, some praying to be killed & others swearing because they were not carried off the field. Our men lay close & the loss in our Regt. is light. The enemy sometimes in looking after their wounded came within a few feet of our picket line but we did not trouble them.

§ JULY 1, 1862 Gen. Richardson by hard fighting opened the road on which we are to retreat. While we held the enemy in front the army nearly all retreated. At 2 A.M. we withdraw as quietly as possible & commence our retreat. Our dead & all the wounded who could not walk had to be left. It was sad indeed the way the poor fellows begged to be taken along. It could not be done. The

---

* Haydon imagined more moonlight than there was. The moon on the night of June 30 was not yet in its first quarter.

† This engagement, Day Six of the Seven Days, was the Battle of Glendale.

most of them will die. The Rebs cannot even take care of their own wounded. Our Regt. was separated by some runaway teams & troops coming in on another road got between the parts.

At sunrise we came to a large, open, undulating field in sight of James River. It was as beautiful a country as my eyes ever beheld. The cultivated field interspersed with belts & clusters of timber & dotted with delightful residences extended several miles. The hills were quite high but the slopes gradual & free from abruptness. Wheat was in the shock, oats were ready for the harvest & corn was abt waist high. All were of most luxuriant growth. The clusters of buildings are almost like villages.

All parts of the field are favorable for Cav. & Arty. There was hard fighting on a part of it yesterday. The country was laid waste, the fences burned, the harvested grain was used by the soldiers for beds & the unharvested was trodden into the ground. The field was covered with troops. I spent two hours in ineffectual search after our lost Co's. They rejoined us soon after I returned. Here we hoped for a little rest but it was not more than an hour before we had to fall in.

We made a circuit of about 2 miles then halted & our brigade was drawn up in a column by battalions on the back side of a gently sloping hill [Malvern Hill] on the crest of which were two batteries. We had been here but a short time when the enemy appeared on the crest of another hill abt a mile off. The inclination of the ground was so slight that our brigade as well as the supports of their batteries could be seen from several points. Both parties opened with shot, shell & shrapnel. We had nothing to do but lie on the ground in the burning sun & take things just as they came.

Their shots were not wild. Almost the first shot (12 lbs. solid) struck among the N.Y. 1st as they lay on the [ground] killing two & wounding another.* One of them was thrown more than 5 ft. into the air. A shell burst in the ground not 4 ft. from Benson's head. One struck abt 10 ft. short of me in the ground & exploded nearly burying me in sand & stubble. I caught a ball from a shrapnel shell before it stopped rolling. Two others struck within reach of me. Three men of our Co. were wounded by one shot. Most of their shell burst abt 150 feet in the air & the fragments scattered

---

* The 1st New York had recently been assigned to Berry's brigade.

over a great space. The wounded were carried to the rear in considerable numbers. The loss of the brigade is 85.

The scene was exciting but I was so exhausted that despite the noise & the bullets I went to sleep. I know not how long I should have slept if the order "Fall in" had not aroused me. The 2d moved off to support another battery. I felt weak & quite used up. When I tried to lead off at double quick I reeled & came near falling. I certainly should have fallen if we had gone far. Presently the fire slackened in our locality. There is a long line of artillery on this range of hills. On a higher one in our rear are a line of heavier pieces which fire over us. From the river in rear of us the gunboats fire by signals over all with 200 lb. shells.

The firing towards night was very heavy, musketry brisk & frequent charges. Our loss is moderate, that of the enemy very severe. With another hour of daylight I believe we could utterly rout them. The cannonading was kept up till long after dark. I went onto a hill in front & saw 50 pieces of artillery playing into a piece of woods where the Rebs had taken shelter. This day's fighting has been the grandest I ever saw. It reminded me of the pictures of great battles in Europe. If our army had been fresh I should have liked all to have been risked on a battle on this field.*

§ JULY 2 We were called up at midnight & continued our retreat. Our Div. was among the first to leave. We marched 10 miles without halting to Harrison's Landing on James River. A heavy rain set in soon after daylight which lasted 20 hours. Our good roads were soon changed to mortar beds. We camped in mud & slept in mud. The enemy did not press.

§ JULY 3 A large part of the army was collected in a field in front of the landing. It commenced moving at an early hour. The enemy took a position on a hill below us & commenced throwing shot & shells among us. If they had come in force & earlier they might have done great damage. One of their shells killed 3 men & wounded 7 just to our right. A few burst near us. The fragments fell pretty thick but no one was hurt.

For all field movements the 2d, 3d & 5th Mich. are consolidated into one Regt. That one is not as large as the 2d was when we left Detroit. The 2d has 300 men & 11 officers for duty all told. Benson

---

* The Malvern Hill battle concluded the Seven Days' fighting.

was sick & went to the hospital this m'g. The fire of the enemy soon ceased & we moved down & back from the river to a large open field where we bivouaced for the night. I felt very bad in the m'g but much better in the afternoon.

§ JULY 4 Was warm, bright, glorious. All our banners were flung to wind. A national salute was fired. The music played most gloriously. Gen. McClellan came around to see us & we all cheered most heartily for country, cause & leader. The scattered Regts. are rapidly uniting. The enemy are passive so far as known.

§ JULY 9 Since last date I have been too busy in the Adjt's office to attend to anything else. The weather has been very hot & dry. We have lived quietly, resting, repairing, reorganizing, calculating losses, & regulating everything. Perfect confidence & good feeling prevail. The President was here yesterday. Kearney is bringing delinquent officers back to their Regts. Everyone has to keep his eyes wide open & attend to his business. I have had no time to think what may be our future movements beyond what are immediate & necessary. My health is good. Our Regt. has probably lost as many as 30 prisoners. Most of them were sick in Hospt. & unable to move. Corpl. Buck of our Co. I am sorry to say is among the number. Maurice Clive ran away from the Co. & was driven into the battle with stragglers & severely wounded.

§ JULY 11 The smoke & dust of our battle week having cleared away we may calculate with some certainty the results. To begin with we were in a very desperate situation, at least McClellan thought so for he himself says he resorted to the most dangerous military expedients to escape.

At Yorktown I felt the most unbounded confidence. At Williamsburgh, West Point & Fair Oaks we won undoubted victories but hardly cared for others at the same price. Since then they have followed us for a week & are still less satisfied with the result. After Fair Oaks & Stewart's raid* the thought of beating them was less prominent in my mind than that it was impossible for them to beat us. The general feeling seemed to be let *them come.*

Few expected what has followed. In one point of view our loss is great. In another we make clear gain of all that is saved. The

---

* On June 12–15 Confederate cavalry under J. E. B. Stuart had made a circuit of McClellan's army.

killed, wounded and prisoners, God knows how many, are gone, lost. The rest are better, more efficient soldiers than on the 25th of June. Before that to be outflanked or to have the enemy in rear would have produced a serious impression. Now they have been on all sides & the men care no more for them in rear than in front. We feel more certain than ever that we can whip them in a fair fight. It is true some of our Regts. did not do well. The best looking & best drilled Regt. (20th N.Y. German) that I ever saw behaved very badly. There was no time when our own Regt. was not as controllable as on Parade.

I have long been convinced that to reduce the Rebs to submission & keep them will be a very considerable, but not an impossible task. They rallied pretty quickly after Ft. Donelson. They retreated from Yorktown in better order & with less loss than I supposed they could. All this has made me anxious to see Va. reduced so that in case of necessity we could settle with the South a line of Va., Ky., Mo. & Kansas as a boundary. Then enlarge the canal from the Miss. River to Lake Mich. & from the Ohio to Lake Erie & we should be in good shape.

Though the battle of Malvern Hill was undoubtedly the grandest of the war yet in hard fighting it is not to be compared with Glendale. There we were surrounded on all sides & fired an average of 100 rounds per man.

§ JULY 15 Thermometer 103° in the shade. I have been so busy in the Adjutant's office & times have been so dull that I have done very little at journalizing of late. Intensely hot has been the weather since last date. A few drills & a Div. review by Gen. Heintzelman, Dress Parade, poor breakfasts, dinner ditto, suppers ditto have filled up the time outside the office. Inside there have been details, returns, muster rolls, reports, lists of absent officers, killed & wounded innumerable. Besides which on days when Gen. Kearney was in working mood he sent us orders faster than they could be opened & read much less obeyed. He straightens out the kinks in a manner terrible to delinquents.

Eight officers who had reported themselves sick & been sent off on the Hospital Boat without sufficient cause as he believed were at once reported absent without leave. The prospect now is that the most of them will be disgracefully dismissed from the service. Our facetious friend W. H. Seward is among the number. Next came an order saying that the large number of officers who reported themselves "present sick but who are really loafing & idling about camp was tending to demoralize the Div. & must be remedied." No officer should in future report himself sick without sending each morning, with his report, a Certificate from the Surgeon that he was *really sick*. The officers' list "present sick" at once came down from 9 to 3.

§ JULY 16 There was a fine shower last night but it now is hot as ever. Nearly all of us abt a week ago took bad colds, or rather were taken with some common malady similar to that. I have been hoarse, throat sore & a bad cough but am now much better. Everything wears a favorable look in a military view.

§ JULY 17 A smart shower at night. Everything quiet. Dr. Lyon from Kalamazoo. It is cooler to day.

§ JULY 18 We are moving our camp a short distance. We shall have better ground & more regularity but lose a good well by this means. The ground here is high but level. The ground is stiff clay & holds water perfectly. A clear puddle here will turn black & be covered with green scum within 10 hours after it falls.

Now & then a good story abt Kearney forms the chief merriment outside of what each can make for himself & comrades. They relate that once on the retreat he rode back to the rear to look after matters & was surrounded by a half dozen rebel skirmishers who presented their pieces at only a few feet off & cried out Surrender! Surrender! Kearney looked at them a moment & then cried out with the utmost contempt "You take me prisoner! Back to your Regt. you d----d hounds." At this greatly to the surprise of the rebels he put spurs to his horse & rode off at full gallop without paying any further attention to them or the bullets they sent after him.

We used to think that Heintzelman was the roughest man on the face of the earth but our opinion has changed. An officer of the Artillery who heard the conversation related to me the following scene. At Malvern Hill Gen. Heintzelman had just posted a battery. Gen. Kearney came along soon after & compelled the officer in command to move it to another place. Gen. H. soon came back & inquired who caused it to be moved. On being told he rode brim full of wrath for Gen. K. "You countermand another order of mine & I will have you arrested, Sir" said H. "Arrest my ass, G-d d--n you" said Kearney and rode off without even looking at him. Heintzelman looked after him very earnestly for near a minute. A faint smile came over his features & he himself turned around & rode slowly off leaving the battery where he found it.

§ JULY 23 The weather has been so hot & I have so many other affairs to attend to that the Journal is again neglected. I had the toothache for 3 days. Last night Dr. Lyon tried to pull it. He broke it three times & the fourth time the instruments slipped off. The tooth has not ached quite so bad since but my neck was so wrenched & twisted that it feels very curious & unpleasant. My mouth is badly cut up & troubles me about eating. On the whole I am most damndly displeased with the entire performance.

There was a review of the 3d Corps to day by Heintzelman, [John A.] Dix & others. Of all tedious things connected with the army reviews are the greatest bore. The troops looked well & marched finely. The men have been remarkably subordinate & well behaved as a general thing since we came. There is none of that lax, mutinous spirit which was so prevalent after the retreat from Manassas. Here they can get no liquor & there is no place for them to run to. A strong Provost Guard regulates affairs at the landing & they have no desire to go to any other place.

A list of names for rewards & another for promotions has been made. 'Tis said that medals of some kind are to be given & a sort of Legion of Honor formed. Nine commissioned & 4 non-comd. officers have been recommended for promotion and reward, six officers & 169 men for reward (ie, medals). Co. I has two officers & a Sergt. on the first list & 23 non-comd. officers, musicians (Underwood), & privates on the other. As in all such things there will be some unfairness & injustice. I wish I could add 6 more to the list in our Co. but it was already larger than any other in the Regt. and could not be allowed. Six more names would cover all who are in any way deserving or whom I would wish to see in any way rewarded for bravery. The list from the Regt. is not I think too large if it has been fairly chosen.

I am still officiating Adjutant & there is every prospect that I shall be for some time to come. The office has not a few advantages & is generally considered the most desirable of any below the "Field." It gives more extended acquaintance at HdQrs, a larger knowledge of business in all its branches and is in fact a very useful school of instruction in almost every branch of military affairs. It is a most desirable position for anyone who expects to be Capt. & is regarded as the legitimate road to that office. He has good quarters & no nights on guard or days on fatigue. He is expected to dress well, be neat & punctual & polite & a sort of special pleader in all the nice points of drill & etiquette. There are some of these requirements to which it would be long before I should attain.

§ JULY 26 A very warm quiet day. We had a fine Battalion Drill last night. Major Dillman surprised us all by his proficiency. He did remarkably well. The 2d is still itself. It has lost none of its Regimental pride. Pride is a great thing after all. The 2d has now the neatest & best arranged camp we have ever had. It is called the best in the Div. at least. The Inspector Genl. said this m'g that our arms were also in the best order of any in the Div. The men take hold with a willingness which they have never surpassed. I feared that the ill timed, necessary, but little understood absence of Col. & Lt. Col. might together with that of six other officers absent without leave for more than a month have produced a demoralizing effect. The 2d has however borne a high head & been unbroken in spirit amid all its misfortunes.

We need recruits. Give us 100 new men now, mix that number among the old ones & the mass will hardly feel it. The new cannot dare not do otherwise than stand. Put the same 100 into a new Regt. and they will be worth little for the next four months. We have a considerable work on hand & need to make good use of even small items.

Kearney is doing wonders for the discipline of the Div. He comes at all hours of day & night. The cry that "Kearney is coming" wakes up the men & officers quicker than if it were the enemy. It is well for them to be lively if they are not in their places for he comes like the wind. Notwithstanding all he does they will not promote him. He says it is always the same story when his name comes up. "Too rash: too d----d rash — rash in Mexico — rash everywhere — cant promote him." "The men who do the fighting never get the promotions" he says. So he told Col. Ward of the 40th N.Y., one of the bravest men & best officers in the army, been in every battle from Manassas down but never promoted.

Kearney's rashness was not a bad thing when it was acknowledged to have saved the day at Williamsburgh and Fair Oaks, nor when it saved a third of the army at Charles City Cross Roads. I speak not disparagingly of others but with more of Kearney's madness things might have been different. Many even strive to make out that he is actually crazy. The madness which has saved three of the most important battles of the war is not so bad a thing after all. I have heard more than one man say he is mad who was seeking an excuse to cover his own cowardice.

I have been having a serious time with my teeth and also with the roof of my mouth, neck & ear all caused by the mangling process applied to the tooth and surroundings. My mouth became ulcerated & was lanced to day since which it feels much better. I have had little sleep for several days and am getting nervous.

I have subscribed for the Atlantic & shall have it regularly. I cannot do without it. I have not heard from home for some time. I suppose they are busy harvesting. We saved people that trouble down here.

§ JULY 28 Phillip Kearney was around at an early hour this m'g. Last night abt 12 an order came for among many other things a Co. drill at 6 A.M. which should change to Battalion drill at 7 A.M. & continue till 8 A.M. It was so late when the order came that it was supposed that if they were on hand at 7 it would answer for the 1st m'g. We fortunately got out before he reached us but he pounced on the 3d heavily, then went for Capt. Wilson, Asst. Adjt. Genl. & put him under arrest for not issuing the order sooner.

Then he paid us a visit. First he saw a Lieut. who did not make the men under him come up to the work just right. "What are you doing there Sir? What are you good for? Your sword is given to you as a symbol of authority & if you dont use your authority I shall take it out of your hands and give it to someone who will. If you dont know your business Sir there are plenty of men in the ranks who do. I can soon find them." This done he visited Major Dillman. "Major Dillman are you a well drilled officer?" Major was stumped, did not know. "Did you make two mistakes the last time you were out?" "Yes Sir." "How did that happen?" Major started to explain. "Oh: no matter, no matter Major. It is all right," and Kearney was off before he could say anything further.

Yesterday m'g at Inspection he said publicly that we were not only a fighting Regt. but a good looking one. That we were as "Showy on Parade as gallant on the battlefield." Such things are highly gratifying to the mass of the men & none are wholly in-different to them.

Prof. Putnam of Kalamazoo is here and makes headquarters with me. There is beginning to be a great fever abt new Regts.

Everyone wants a commission in a new Regt. Almost anything to dodge hard work & bullets. It is very natural that men desire promotion. It would be a fine thing to send men from here to command in part the new Regts. but I would be very sorry to see those sent who are most anxious to go. The reputation of the 2d I fear would suffer. There will be promotions soon & in considerable numbers. I may be among the number. I hope I shall be, if I am not I shall not resign or go off without leave or apply for a place in a new Regt. just as my own is going into battle. There are men under whom I should very much dislike to serve. I can fight however under them for such men are not very troublesome on the battlefield, and that after all is the main thing.

My health is good & I can go on to the field with more zeal & confidence than ever before. I have no more fears lest my own conscience should accuse me of reluctance of spirit. One may go into battle & seem to do well when his own conscience tells him that he is most d--nably scared. I remember to have read in Caesar that at one time in his first campaign (I think) in Gaul, when matters looked unpromising, one came to him saying he must go home because of very important business, another's family was sick, a third was himself sick.

§ AUGUST 2, 1862 Hot weather. Men dying quite rapidly in some of the Regts. None in ours as yet. Health of Regt. very good. Three days ago the Rebs opened fire at midnight from the opposite shore. Scared the contrabands & sutlers, but did no great damage. The siege guns replied & soon silenced them. There is some firing almost every day. Our men yesterday crossed the river, cut down the woods & burned the buildings opposite the landing.

Col. Poe has returned. God be praised, I was afraid we should never see him again. He was greeted with most heartfelt cheers. I have not been very well to day. Took quinine toward night & feel much better. Our communication hangs on pretty slender thread but I trust it is secure.

§ AUGUST 4 This has been a hot showery day. The Div. was never under as good drill & discipline as now. Kearney is everywhere chastising the delinquents. There is no peace for the laggard under him.

§ AUGUST 5 All well.

§ AUGUST 12 Harrison's Lndg. Day before yesterday the Adjt. returned. He was immediately waited upon by the Regulators* who presented him a paper signed by all the line officers except myself. Stating that they believed he had for the last two months been unnecessarily absent, that they had lost all confidence in him as an officer, and that one & all they requested him to resign. His resignation was sent in but I suspect that Poe, to whom [Adjutant] Mahon was always a pet, took good care that it should be refused at Kearney's & hence killed at Heintzelman's. It came back last night disapproved. The Committee are not to be bluffed in this way. More anon.

On the 10th at 11 P.M. came an order to be ready to march at 2 P.M. on 11th with two days' rations in haversacks & 4 days' in wagons. All the knapsacks were sent on board of transports only in the m'g. The sick were sent away & everything made ready for the move. But where were we going? Some said cross the river & attack Petersburgh, others say to attack the enemy beyond Malvern Hill, others that we are to cross the country to Yorktown, others that we were going on board of transports, but nobody knew. Just before the time to start an order came delaying departure indefinitely.

Morning of the 12th finds us here & noon the same. I am pretty much clear of the Adjutant's office & in good time too for it has nearly upset me. I had as hard work on the march as any & in camp a great deal harder. There has been more than double the office work during my two months that there ever was before. I leave the office a perfect shadow: I have been downright sick, but not on the sick list, for more than ten days. Yesterday & now I am much better & shall soon be well as ever. The weather is most intensely hot. The flies are terribly annoying. The Band has been discharged. Right glad we were to be rid of the lazy grumbling loafers.

I think there is no doubt that we are to leave the Peninsula very soon. It will be a pretty severe blow to McClellan's reputation. We need to be if possible in a position where our presence will be an injury even when we do not fight. If we could have troubled their

---

* Haydon's allusion is to the Regulator protest movement against the North Carolina legislature in colonial times.

communication to any considerable extent Richmond must have fallen. Aside from threatening an attack we did the enemy no more harm in our late position than if we had been on the other side of the Potomac.

Charges were late in the afternoon preferred agt the Adjt. & his resignation again forwarded in connection with them. He resigned his Adjutancy at once and I am again temporarily recalled to Head Qrs.

§ AUGUST 13 I hoped that during the coming march at least I might have remained with the Co. It would have been easier for me. We have been hourly expecting to move but the order has not yet come. Nearly everything has gone & as near as I can learn the advance must have been gone full 2 days. If they will only get the wagons out of the way we can easily look out for ourselves. It is still unknown to me where we are going but Yorktown or Ft. Monroe are only too obvious. Under present circumstances I am not sorry to leave the Peninsula. The march will be a severe one in this weather.

§ AUGUST 14 Time hangs rather heavily. There seems no more prospect of moving now than 3 days ago. Some say that a large part of the troops have crossed the river & are going down the other side, others that we advance. I doubt whether we move at all.

§ AUGUST 15 At 2 A.M. comes an order to move at 5. We are up at once, got our breakfast, destroyed all the property we could not carry of which we had little save a few old tents. We moved off at 5 toward Charles City C.H., the 2d guarding the Brg. train. Though we improved every opportunity the marches were short & the halts long. It was 3 P.M. when we reached the C.H. At that point we turned to the left marching nearly north for some [time] thereby securing a clear road though a much more dangerous one. We marched 6 miles on this road at a good rate & bivouaced not far from Jones' bridge where we expect to cross the Chickahominy. We passed over a fine country & several large fields of good corn. The men used the corn in great abundance. The road was very dusty, the worst I have seen since Bull Run.

§ AUGUST 16 A cool quiet night. It is already getting far along in the forenoon & we have not heard a word abt moving. The Army of the Potomac fights pretty well but they move wonderfully slow. It seems to everyone to be of the utmost importance that this movement should be rapid yet I dare say we do not make 8 miles per day.

Col. Poe was made president of a genl. Court Martial & I judge advocate to meet at the sign post. We met accordingly & tried 3 men for stealing mules. The Brg. moved forward abt noon onto an island in the Chickahominy & bivouaced. Our train crossed & halted half a mile beyond. I rode on horseback abt 2 hours yesterday & somewhat longer to day & am beginning to be very stiff & sore.

§ AUGUST 17 I began to think to day that I was rather hasty in saying that the Army of the Potomac always moved slowly. We started at 4 A.M. & marched 24 miles at least, some say 26, before sundown. We halted 3 hours at one place to guard a road till Hooker's advance came up. We came by way of Diascund bridge from Jones' bridge where we crossed the Chickahominy & struck the Williamsburgh [road] near Roper's Church, since which time we have been on the road of our advance. It has evidently been little used. The old ruts & holes are plainly visible. The mud has in many places never dried & the road in several places for the space of more than 20 rods was still impassable. The old secession wagons still lay upset by the roadside where they were left & the shot & shells which they threw from their caissons were seemingly untouched or stuck in the mud as when we passed up. The night was cold, very cold for August. I must have rode full 35 miles to day & could scarce stand on my feet. I was never so tired.

§ AUGUST 18 I went to bed at 7, slept till 2 A.M. when I was called up for abt an hour on duty after which I slept till 5 A.M. When I first awoke I thought I should never get on my feet but a small pine being near I pulled myself up by my hands & walked off very well after a few minutes.

We reached Williamsburgh abt noon & camp just above the town. The weather has been cool during the whole march & the roads good except for the dust. There was no loss of public or private property that I saw beyond one old ambulance & 8 or 10 blankets. The enemy did not molest us at any point. I am at a loss to know why they did not. It is said that they believed our demonstrations here to be a mere ruse to cover our passage across the river & descent on the other side & that in fact they have 60,000 men on the other side to dispute the passage. Perhaps they know our real object & have sent all their available forces agt Pope* with whom we shall undoubtedly be within a week. If I ever fully recover the use of my legs again I shall be most thankful.

§ AUGUST 19 We started at 7 A.M. & made a horribly dusty march of 12 miles. The trains were slow to day & it was near noon before we were out of sight of Williamsburgh. We passed over a part of the battlefield to the right where I had ever before been. Every pine could show from 5 to 20 ball holes on either side low as a man's head to testify to the fierceness of the conflict. The idea is abroad that it was a mere skirmish. There was no such battle in the Mexican War & those who were at Williamsburgh will all tell you that they have seen nothing like it in this.

After abt 8 miles we came again to the road on which we advanced. In places where infantry could scarce wade through then we were now nearly stifled with dust. Sometimes we could not see two rods ahead. We passed Yorktown & encamped ½ mile below at dark.

§ AUGUST 20 We remained in camp till a little after noon when we marched down through Yorktown to the wharf & Gen. Kearney & staff & 2d Mich. embarked on board the steamer Empress soon after. I passed through Yorktown for the first time. It is a very old but rather pleasant town of abt 30 to 40 houses, mostly brick. The town does not cover more than ⅕ part of the ground enclosed by the work which surrounds it. Cornwallis' works are still easily seen & with some repairs might be put in a tolerable state of defence as they have already on the river side. The ground with the works is extremely rugged & uneven, impassable except by narrow crooked roads. Col. Poe says that is probably the finest earthwork in the world. The town is wholly abandoned by the inhabitants.

I took a good salt water bath before starting which cleared the dust off effectually. We did not start until some time in the evening after I had gone to bed. A man sleeping on the hurricane deck tumbled off (abt 20 ft.) into the water dragging another with him. One caught on the rudder but the other fell full a ½ mile astern before he could be reached. A moment longer & all would have been over with him.

---

* Gen. John Pope, commanding the newly formed Army of Virginia in northern Virginia.

In the execution of two utterly useless orders given by Lt. Col. Dillman I lost my haversack & contents, blanket & all my clothes, everything except canteen.

The N.Y. 1st was transferred to [David B.] Birney's Brig. to day & the 99th Pa. taken in exchange. This was done to give the command of the Brig. to Col. Poe during Gen. Berry's illness.*

§ AUGUST 21 A very quiet ride brought us without further accident abt noon opposite Aquia Creek Landing. We lay opposite the Landing abt 2 hours awaiting orders which having come we made the best possible headway for Alexandria. This seemed to please everyone though none could hardly tell why.

---

* The 1st New York's colonel, senior to Poe, otherwise would have taken the temporary command of the brigade.

Eleven

CROSS AND MAD
ALL DAY

In the four months after the evacuation of the Peninsula, the Army of the Potomac fought three major battles — Second Bull Run (a defeat), Antietam (a draw), and Fredericksburg (a defeat) — and following Fredericksburg Charles Haydon grumbled in his journal, "Cross & mad all day." Changes in the high command were frequent. After Second Bull Run John Pope lost command of the army and George McClellan regained it; after Antietam McClellan was replaced by Ambrose Burnside; after Fredericksburg Burnside would be replaced by Joe Hooker.

These were comparatively quiet times for the 2nd Michigan. It had but eleven casualties at Second Bull Run, missed the Antietam campaign entirely, and at Fredericksburg, transferred from the Third Corps to the Ninth, only came under artillery fire and lost two men. Haydon himself continued up the ladder of command — to regimental adjutant, then on September 1 to captain, leaving Company I to take command of Company E.

The period September 5 to October 26, 1862, is unrecorded here. Then or later that volume of Haydon's journal was lost. In these weeks, during which the Antietam campaign was fought, the 2nd Michigan was posted in the Washington defenses.

Haydon refused to let the discouraging events of fall 1862 discourage him for long. "There is no denying the defeat," he wrote a few days after Fredericksburg, "but I begin to be hopeful again & never felt more like fighting till the last man falls."

* * *

§ AUGUST 22, 1862 We disembarked just at dark last night, marched up & encamped opposite Ft. Lyon & west of the [Orange & Alexandria] railroad. The men recd their first full ration of soft bread since leaving this place in March. I hoped to have remained here a week or ten days. I have lived so slim for the last two or three months that my strength is perceptibly diminished. I am not out of health but merely need better food for a few days. A soldier's life is very checkered & instead of a week of rest we recd orders to march to the depot at 2 P.M. Off for Manassas, Gordonsville or some place to assist the man who always sees the enemies' backs.*

Marched to Alexandria & bivouaced in the street. Many of the men were drunk in spite of the guards. Nearly all the 1st N.Y. were tipsey. It rained at night.

§ AUGUST 23 Some of us, Col. Poe I suppose, he being the ranking officer, slept with a woman last night. At least she slept in the tent with us & he lay next to her. I believe she said she belonged to some Soldiers' Aid Society though the exact nature of the aid she did not state to me.

About 9 A.M. we went on to the cars & set out for Pope. We passed famous Manassas Junction (perhaps to be still more renowned ere another week) & reached Warrenton Junction about 2 P.M. We bivouaced for the night, got supper, detailed the picket &c when we were ordered back 1½ miles to Cedar Creek to guard the bridge. About 30 officers & all Genl. Pope's private baggage were captured by rebel cavalry at this place last night. Pope's stragglers are coming in & all sorts of rumors are afloat in regard to the battle which has been plainly heard all day. Our lady friend is still with us. There was a heavy shower at dark.

§ AUGUST 24 We marched abt 9 A.M. & halted on the R.R. abt 3 miles beyond Warrenton just before noon having forded a creek abt 3 feet deep. About 3 P.M. we moved forward ¾ of a mile.

All sorts of eatables which the country affords are suffering. Some guards of Birney's Brigade were trying to protect a field of corn. The 2d halted near & the advance was within two minutes after at the fence. Guards: Halt there, halt, cant come in here,

---

* Gen. Pope had announced in an address to his army, "I have come to you from the West, where we have always seen the backs of our enemies. . . ."

halt. By this time about 20 men were over the fence. Guards: Say, hold on there, wish you fellows would go around to the back side & not go in right here in front where we are guarding.

§ AUGUST 25 The night was clear, quiet & unusually cold. The following promotions were announced this m'g. Capt. W. L. Whipple of Co. H to be Lt. Col. 21st Mich. 1st Lt. Augustus Goebel of Co. A to be Capt. of Co. 2d Lt. C. H. Hodskin of Co. C to be 1st Lt. of A. D. L. Morrison, Commissary Sergt. to be 2nd Lt. of Co. C. Myself to be Adjutant from Augt. 10th 1st Lt. R. H. Mahon assigned to Co. I vice self promoted. This suits me very well as I am advanced one degree & can hold fast the Adjutancy or be Capt. at no distant day as I may prefer. We are abt 45 miles from Alexandria & in a fine country but provisions are short & living confounded poor.

§ AUGUST 26 We were much rejoiced to see our good Surgeon Dr. Bonine & our paroled Hosp. Steward as Asst. Surgeon. Abt 4 P.M. we marched out 4 miles on the Fredericksburgh road to relieve the 3d Michigan who were lying in wait for rebel cavalry. Living is much improved. Sheep, chickens &c are to be had on requisition properly presented.

A citizen was shot last night at his own house by a trooper. He was a notorious rebel & some justify the act while others are in favor of shooting the soldier at once. Much drunkeness & shooting both on the part of citizens & soldiers are reported at Alexandria.

§ AUGUST 27 The night was quiet with us but the enemy made a dash in our rear & destroyed the R.R. bridge at Broad Run. An Orderly came early in the m'g to tell us that our Brig. had marched an hour before he started. We marched to camp, took rations and at 10 A.M. were at Warrenton Junction & soon after at Cedar Creek bridge. Porter's [Fifth] Corps came down with us retreating from the front. We halted awhile at Cedar Creek, then crossed & marched toward Greenwich where we arrived abt 8 P.M. having marched in all about 24 miles. I left my blankets with Lowrey to go on the train supposing that we should follow the R.R. Per consequence I am without either supper or blankets.

§ AUGUST 28 At 2 A.M. I was called to convey an order to march at 3 A.M. I find myself cold & very stiff in the legs. We started at the appointed hour for the R.R. bridge across Broad Run where we arrived at 9 A.M. The Rebs had destroyed the bridge, 2 engines and a train of cars. The cars were still burning. After some delay in crossing our Brig. moved forward in column to Manassas Junction. We expected a battle at that place. The Rebs left before we arrived. They had destroyed loaded trains nearly a mile in length. A great profusion of incombustible articles were lying around but aside from a few barrels of flour we could get nothing eatable.

We halted here abt 3 hours for reports & learned that one large bridge & several small ones were burned between here & Alexandria. We then moved forward towards Centreville by way of Blackburn's Ford, crossing from the opposite direction our first battlefield. Just as we were about to leave the open field a Co. of our cavalry (several saddles empty) came back from the front on a run. We filed out to give them the road. Our Regt. might have been put in position to do something but Dillman never sees anything when he ought. The Rebs came to the edge of the woods & several of them followed 30 to 40 rods into the open field & all but one of them returned unhurt. Our Regt. opened fire on them but from their position it was ineffectual.

This little dash being over the 2d was deployed as skirmishers & advanced through the woods & fallen timber towards Centreville. Nothing occurred save the capture of two prisoners. The sun was just sinking behind the Bull Run Mts. when we planted our colors on one of the principal redoubts. The enemy had made a sharp turn to the left & the dust of their column was plainly visible abt 3 miles off. The troops which marched from Manassas Junction to the left of us opened a brisk fire of artillery on them but the day was too far gone to do much execution. It would have been fortunate if we had arrived two hours earlier but we did our best. We have marched 15 miles to day. The men had little sleep last night & hardly anything to day to eat. I have had nothing but a half ration of hard tack.

§ AUGUST 29 We moved at 5 A.M. down the road towards the old battlefield of Manassas. Cannonading opened in front abt 7 A.M. We were the advanced guard & captured abt 50 prisoners before we joined the troops which came in from the left. As soon as we came near the field Kearney seized on us & sent one Co. to hold a house, two Co's. to support a section of artillery, two Co's. as skirmishers in a piece of woods nearly in front, and 5 Co's. (with which I went) to deploy as skirmishers on the extreme right. Going out we crossed Bull Run near the Stone Bridge. We now moved forward abt a mile & a half through woods & fields recrossing the Run & finally took position in a piece of woods abt half a mile from Jackson's (Stonewall's) headquarters [at First Bull Run].

The Rebs soon got sight of us & opened with a section of artillery. They fired high & the shots splintered the trees at 8 to 10 feet from the ground most gloriously. Dillman had the "shell fever" badly & was much wilted. The firing continued with solid shot & a few shells above an hour.

I had a hearty laugh at Lt. Barden's expense. A solid 10 lb. shot struck a large black oak, abt 10 feet from the ground, under which he was lying. The splinters (the size of stove wood) knocked off his cap & battered his back smartly but without doing much damage. As he scrabbled up rubbing the dust out of his eyes & feeling wildly around for his cap his face wore a look of astonishment which would have made [me] laugh if I had have known that the next shot would be mine.

One of our batteries now opened on them from a hill behind us with most remarkable precision. The Rebs waited for abt six shots & then made off as fast as possible. A solid shot however cut down a span of horses on one gun & it was delayed long enough to get several shells which burst right among them.

We now rec'd orders to fall back across the Run. In doing this we had to cross an open field where they opened on us with shrapnel from another battery. As many as 10 pieces of the first struck within as many feet of me, & Lt. Plumb who was near had one arm badly torn. At this some of the men took the double quick but immediately came down to a walk on being ordered to do so. Their shell all exploded a little back of us & no one else was injured in crossing. We took very favorable ground on the right bank of the Run where we remained till night.

Toward the centre the battle raged hotly, with occasional intervals, from 7 A.M. till dark. We could see nothing in that direction but the contest seemed pretty equal. I think the battle will be found to far surpass in obstinacy that of last year. We saw during the afternoon another rebel battery put to flight in great haste. Some canister shot from our own guns fell among us but luckily did no harm.

§ AUGUST 30 The night was clear & quiet. We hold the same position as yesterday. I awoke destitute of rations but a soldier gave me a pancake of flour & water fried in grease & a piece of pork abt 2 inches square. This was very good but deficient in quantity so I picked up a bone which some more fortunate comrade had thrown away. This I washed & roasted & ate what little meat there was on it. I then ate 6 to 8 green peaches & pronounced my breakfast finished.

Good luck however seemed in store for me. Co. I came, Octavus being along with hard tack & coffee. I at once made a fourth addition to my breakfast. Our indefatigable Commissary (Johnston) came soon after with fresh beef & I made a fifth addition. I also procured a haversack & supplied myself for the future. My legs which before were quite limber were now fully adequate to the task of bearing my body.

There was only light skirmishing and a few shells till 1 P.M. This led to a report that the enemy had retreated. Others supposed that a great move was preparing. The fire opened pretty briskly on the centre & [left] soon after one but attracted no great attention on our part as we could not see that part of the field. It continued abt the same till after 4 P.M. when there commenced by far the most terrible fire of musketry I ever heard. The men (except those on watch) had previous to this been quietly cooking, eating, playing cards &c. They now began to lay these aside & give attention to the progress of the battle.

It was perfectly certain that the centre & left were falling back. It was however reported that a body of troops on our extreme left & heretofore liable to be cut off, having now effected a junction, the line was purposely swung back to draw the enemy from their strong, well covered position. I did not believe this report but saw its object & said nothing. The [left] continued to fall back farther & farther till abt sundown.

Our Brigade was now more than a mile in advance of the centre whereas in the original line it was somewhat retired. The order now came for the Brigade to fall back & for our Regt. to move as skirmishers by the right flank down the stream towards Centreville. The line had not moved half its length before it recd the fire of the enemies' advance. The fire being promptly returned they did not press. Subsequently the left of our line & their skirmishers became considerably mingled but the Rebs were so tired with running that they could do nothing. We moved in this way abt 1½ miles. A battery on the other side of the stream fired over us all the way at the Brigade.

Some of our men (not our Regt.) perhaps 20 were across the stream & being unable to get over were in no little trouble, but seeing the Cavalry coming they threw away everything & crossed where the water was abt 5 feet deep. Four or five short fellows who could not swim were taken. Soon after we came to a short turn in the stream where there was a ford abt knee deep. About half the line crossed at this point when we were fired on from another direction (our proper front & those who had not crossed went down the other side of the stream). The fire being returned the enemy gave back. I was with the last who crossed.

Our line was near 100 rods long & we had a half mile of open field before us. We had gone but a little way when about 2 companies of Cavalry came around the bend at full run in pursuit. Two thirds of the line by brisk running reached a corn field & formed under cover of the fence. Some 40, Benson and myself among their number were too far behind for that though we ran our very best. We shouted to them to halt & rally. They did so & we had a respectable square in short order. We were none too quick for the leader of the Cavalry a gallant fellow was within 15 rods & the rest were close behind. We gave them a volley. Two dropped at once & the leader turning his horse short around, then to the right, back to the left, fell headlong to the ground. The rest went back nearly as fast as they came but as they turned gave us a volley from their carbines which wounded 2 men. We at once took the double quick to escape the battery which now opened on us & rejoined our comrades in the corn field.

We then made for the main road where found the balance of the Regt. & Col. Poe & the Brigade. We marched in good order to Centreville. The men seemed to bear all with the utmost indifference though they swore horrible at being beaten again at Manassas. We were obliged to ford two creeks where the water was near 3 feet deep. I brought off a sword & gun extra but lost my blanket. The night was cold & sleep out of the question. As for the retreat it was orderly so far as I saw. When the Cavalry were coming down on us I could not help laughing though I had very little breath to spare, at a soldier of a N.Y. Regt. He had thrown away everything but his haversack. He was now hard pressed & cried out in his grief "Oh my God, my God, what shall I do? If I throw away my haversack I shall starve & if I dont the Rebs will catch me."

§ AUGUST 31 There was a heavy rain nearly all day. We remained at Centreville. There was some firing toward the left.

§ SEPTEMBER 1, 1862 We left Centreville abt 2 P.M. marching towards Fairfax as fast as the trains would permit. When we had gone abt 3 miles we heard cannon & soon after musketry to our front & left & at no great distance. Soon after we met a train returning with the report that the enemy held the road near Fairfax. We filed out of the road, formed line & advanced a little way when a most furious & blinding storm of wind & rain set in. The firing ceased.

Gen. Kearney rode forward alone, regardless of the storm & was killed unseen by any friend. Some say that he was killed by lightning, others by a rifle shot. A stormy end to a stormy life. Of all who have fallen in this war he is the only one for whom I have shed a tear. I have to confess that in spite of pride the news quite unmanned me. The bravest man in the Army of the Potomac has fallen. God curse the villain who shot him.*

We advanced as soon as the storm abated but it was dark & the battle over before we reached the field. Our men had driven them & left us a field covered with dead & wounded to guard. We pushed our picket line up to abt 20 rods of the enemy. One of our pickets (2d) was killed & two more taken prisoners. I had no blanket & every thread on me was as wet as it could be. The wind came up very cold from the N.W. & I never suffered more from the weather. Benson and I leaned agt a fence half dozing for an hour. When we woke he trembled so from cold that his sword dropped from his hand several times & I could hardly stand.

§ SEPTEMBER 2 At 2 A.M. we quietly left our position, all the other Regts. having gone before & favored by darkness & a high wind withdrew from the triangle which the enemy were inclosing us. We made good time & by a roundabout road reached Fairfax at sunrise. There we halted & took such breakfast as we were able to and remained till 11 A.M. The Div. then marched to Fairfax Station, thence on the road toward Pohick Church & after a march over a good road of 11 miles we camped in a most beautiful place. I had a good supper. The night was quiet but very cold.

---

* During this battle at Chantilly Kearny stumbled into Confederate skirmishers and was killed as he tried to gallop away.

§ SEPTEMBER 3 We marched at 5 A.M. passing Pohick Church, Camp Michigan & many other familiar places which we had never expected to see again. No other troops had passed over this road. Our Regt. was in advance & where we used to find mud a foot deep the ground was like rock. At noon after a march of 14 miles we camped on Hunting Creek flats between Ft. Lyon & Alexandria. There are several new Regts. here in camp. The men gaze at us in astonishment swearing that so rough & dirty a lot of fellows they never before saw.

§ SEPTEMBER 4 We are busy repairing damages, estimating losses &c and shall be ready for active service on the 6th if needed. The men are little exhausted & most of them are in excellent marching order. I feel remarkably well.

* * *

Charles Haydon's journal for the period September 5 through October 26, 1862, is missing, lost during or after the war. It was a time of inactivity for the 2nd Michigan. Heintzelman's Third Corps, battered in the Second Bull Run fighting, remained behind in the defenses of Washington during the Army of the Potomac's campaign in Maryland that was climaxed by the Battle of Antietam on September 17. The 2nd Michigan, meanwhile, was posted in its old camp southwest of Alexandria. Haydon, a newly minted captain, took command of Company E on September 13. Beginning on October 11 the regiment moved up the Potomac toward Leesburg in expectation of rejoining the army in the field. Haydon's journal resumes at a Potomac crossing due east of Leesburg.

* * *

§ OCTOBER 27 Camp near Edwards' Ferry, Md. The storm continued, both wind & rain, with great violence all night and until noon to day. Many tents were blown down & the others pursuant to orders were struck at daylight in expectation of the march. At noon however we were ordered on picket. We came down the [Chesapeake & Ohio] canal about five miles. I am now sitting on the bank of the, at this place, beautiful Potomac in the bright & cheerful evening sunshine looking southward. The river is here about 40 rods wide & from 7 to 10 feet deep. My 1st Lt. who has for a long time been detached & serving in a regular battery returned to duty with the Co. to day. He is an excellent officer &

will no doubt soon be promoted. He might have had my place if he had desired.

§ OCTOBER 28 We had a sharp frosty night but slept well two at a time. We were ordered to march for camp at daylight, arrived at 8 A.M., took breakfast & marched at 9 A.M. towards Poolesville. We filed to the left after about 2 miles & halted for dinner near Conrad's ferry. After dinner we moved forward & forded the Potomac [into Virginia] at Conrad's ford or ferry. By way of the ford the river is near half a mile broad. The water was from one to three feet deep & very cold. The bottom is covered with slippery rolling stones & sharp pointed rocks. The current is pretty swift. Several of the men fell and were well ducked but no other accidents occurred. The cold water gave considerable pain to the legs & we were very glad after a march of about two miles to halt in a field where rails were abundant. The men after their partial restraint in Maryland were particularly greedy for them. A long line of fence was lifted as if by magic & disappeared in a moment of time after the men broke ranks.

§ OCTOBER 31 About noon we pulled up and marched across to the road from Leesburgh to Winchester and bivouaced among the mountains so called, about three miles [east] of the latter place. Our camp is probably about 400 ft. higher than that of yesterday. The country is fine, the land good for farming & the grass excellent. On our road I noticed a singular kind of rock. It was a conglomerate of small stones cemented by a fine dark sand & clay. It cropped out of the ground in wave like shape, the side on which it was broken off being steep while the other has the natural dip of the strata. They were of all heights up to about 15 feet, excellent for walls or building but making in many places serious inroads on the tillable land.

There were many fine residences along the road all having a modern look, one of which I think the finest I ever saw. It is built on the side of the mountain, there being a gentle slope for some distance in front, while immediately in rear the ground rises above 100 ft. very steep but beautifully wooded with small oak, hickory & chestnut glowing in the evening sun with scarlet & gold. The house is of magnificent proportions, rich & harmonious in all its parts. The woods curve around toward the front on either side but leave a view from the house of nearly a semicircle and extending from 8 to 15 miles over a rich & romantic country. The trees are very fine on the grounds in front & are nearly all of natural growth. There is little of the artificial save the fountains four or five in number & the statuary which had been tastefully arranged to suit the character of the ground & the scenery but is now mostly removed by the owner.

§ NOVEMBER 1, 1862 Went down on the west slope of the mountains about dark on picket. No fires were allowed but the night was warm & comfortable. The eastern slope of the Blue Ridge was covered with the camp fires of our troops which had crossed the river above. Between us & them lay the Pleasant Valley 8 or 10 miles broad and fully justifying its name. As the sun went down there was a battle in the far distance southward. We could see the smoke & hear the cannon but could distinguish neither friend or foe.

§ NOVEMBER 2 Marched in & took rations preparatory to a march. The cannonading to the front is pretty brisk. We march at 3 P.M. turning to the left from the main road & proceeding by way of Mt. Gilead a short distance beyond which we bivouaced for the night without blankets. The march was very rapid as if we were to execute some flank movement.

§ NOVEMBER 3 The night was cold & we slept but little. As near as I can learn the firing of yesterday & day before was of little account being only skirmishing between cavalry & light batteries. We march from 3 P.M. until by way of Mountsville & to a place about 2 miles from Middleburgh where we bivouaced. The night was sharp, the officers' tents & blankets had not come, the cook was absent, reported arrested for a straggler & the chickens provided for supper taken from him & no wood at hand. We had a dismal prospect of lying on a pile of cornstalks all night, with hard crackers for supper.

But presently what a change — up came cook with five chickens, 4 lbs. fresh butter, 2 doz. very fine biscuits, coffee, sugar &c and by the time justice was done to these blankets came also. Thus things changed from a cold sleepless & almost supperless night to all the comforts a soldier could ask. Such a change causes an amount of jollity & good feeling little understood by those who have never tried it. Cannonading has been pretty lively to the front and right. We are well up among the mountains.

§ NOVEMBER 4 Our blankets were well coated with frost this morning and Schuetz who was pushed out of bed complained that he was "cold like hell." We remained in camp all day. Cannonading to front and right. Weather cold & raw.

§ NOVEMBER 5 Marched at 7 A.M., passed through Middleburgh which is quite a pleasant little place in which are still quite a number of rebels who were wounded in the battles of August. We crossed & recrossed the Manassas Gap R.R. at White Plains Station. We bivouaced at dark on the White Plains. There was a cold storm of rain & high wind at night. We marched to day about 14 miles.

§ NOVEMBER 6 Marched at 6½ A.M., passed through Salem, a dirty little R.R. station & thence south across a spur of the Blue Ridge by a sort of byroad making 14 to 15 miles. The road is in many places steep, rocky, narrow & full of streams so that we could only make the above distance by marching till 9 P.M. We bivouaced about 4 miles west of Warrenton. We are on the same road by which Jackson gained our rear in August last. We have been near the Blue Ridge all day. It is higher & more rugged than the Kittoctan [Catoctin] & seems but little cultivated. The weather is cold.

§ NOVEMBER 7 The night was very cold. The water in my canteen froze nearly solid. Snow fell pretty rapidly in the morning & continued nearly all day with cold high wind. Snow about 2 inches deep at night.

§ NOVEMBER 8 The weather was cold & clear. The snow had mostly disappeared at noon soon after which we moved forward about 2 miles and bivouaced again. The air was cold & there was some snow towards night.

§ NOVEMBER 9 I have not seen a newspaper since we crossed the Potomac & know only from rumor what is doing in the world. McClellan is said to be removed and great dissatisfaction exists on that account.* If it be so it indicates instability somewhere. To remove a Genl. like McClellan in the midst of movements of such importance indicates a state of wavering & uncertainty which I dread far more than the armies of Secession.

§ NOVEMBER 10 A very fine warm day. There is some firing toward the south. About 2 P.M. Lt. Young & I walked in that direction to a high hill near a place called Waterloo from which with the aid of a glass we could plainly see where the action was going

---

* On November 7 McClellan was relieved of command and replaced by Burnside.

on. It struck me at once that we were soon to move. Some 6 or 7 miles off I could see a pretty long train of wagons, some artillery & infantry all moving at a good pace to the rear. All this might mean nothing but I suggested to Lt. Young that we had better return at once to camp. We did so and just as we arrived came orders to be ready to move at a moment's notice. We also saw troops retiring on two other roads & learned from reliable sources that the enemy have again been in our rear. A little before sundown we moved forward across the Hedgeman [Rappahannock] River at Waterloo, advanced about two miles & bivouaced.

§ NOVEMBER 11 A fine bright morning. The affair of yesterday does not appear to have amounted to much. Our advanced cavalry was repulsed & the train once in motion did not stop till it crossed the Hedgeman.

§ NOVEMBER 12 We fell in early in the m'g. Soon after a train of wagons, some Regts. of Cavalry & Infantry & 3 batteries of flying artillery moved to the rear across the Hedgeman. About 1 P.M. we recrossed the river & bivouaced at the camp of the 10th.

§ NOVEMBER 13 I am vexed, annoyed & almost discouraged. As near as I can learn, the old Regts. are not to be filled up but some new & worthless Cavalry Regts. are to be formed for the reason that men think it is easier to ride than walk. Men prefer to enlist in the Cav. therefore we will have nothing but Cav. The 2d Mich. Inf. small as it is can annihilate all the Cav. Michigan has or can send into the field.

To be so much afraid of *taking* a few men when they are needed is silly in the extreme. Why dally with the d----d cowardly rascals in that way. It wont hurt them to serve their country a few months. What are men worth if they cant be used when needed. Our Regt. will I suppose die out for want of men & the officers will be mustered out of service. Half of them are now serving, myself among the number, without commissions & have been for the last two or three months.* If I take a Captain's pay I shall be liable to be punished but I have done the duty & intend to take the pay. I presume the Governor intends to hold back the commissions till the Regt. is further reduced & then refuse them altogether.

---

* The military's paperwork was in arrears, for army records show Haydon promoted to captain on September 1 and assigned command of Company E, 2nd Michigan, on September 13.

No one seems to have any heart for the war except Lincoln, some of the lower officers & the privates. We have fought well & are willing to fight till the last man falls. Still nothing is done. We are fooled, beaten, bamboozled, outflanked, hoodwinked & disgraced by half our numbers. When did the Rebels ever have occasion to boast over an encounter with the Divs. of Hooker, Richardson, Kearney? Still very little has been gained. All the devils in Hell could not stand before this army if it were led & handled as those Divs. were. Here we are late in the fall, every day of fair weather worth millions, almost in sight of the enemy & *Co. Drill* is talked of for tomorrow. Hell & furies it is enough to drive a man mad if he has one particle of regard for his country.

The railroads must be employed to transport hay from Washington which has been brought from New York by water & from God knows where to N.Y. at an expense of over $35 per ton when there are more than 200 stacks of it within 5 miles of camp which are the property of men who boast to your face of their disloyalty. Grain was obtained in the same way while our Cav. was lagging for three days in sight of more than 1000 wagonloads gathered by the wayside & drawn off as leisurely as if it were going to market. Every particle of hay, grain & fresh meat needed for the army can, in this locality, be gathered from the country. No ----- contractors must be enriched & political pimps rewarded. Do you say the inhabitants would starve. They could do as they liked about that. If they do not like this part of the country they can go somewhere else.

I would not add to the cruelties of war but having decided that there is cause for a war let us have one. I am willing to grant the enemy all the liberties I ask for ourselves. Treat the wounded kindly, prisoners decently but *prosecute* the *war*. I have seen a sick soldier refused a drink of water by a Union guard lest in getting it he or somebody else might possibly do some injury to rebel property. War is awful in the extreme but if *we* can risk *life & limb* do not hesitate over a few paltry *chattels* of the *enemy*. It is but fair that I should give to Genl. [George] Stoneman the credit for more sensible conduct. Since we crossed the Potomac his Div. has by his order made themselves comfortable. They have had hay, cornstalks, straw & when these were not handy unthrashed grain to sleep on every night. They have swept the country pretty clean of poultry, pigs, sheep & calves & the Quartermasters have taken beef cattle & a good number of horses & mules.

§ NOVEMBER 14 There was to day a fine illustration of the benefits of guarding rebel property. Three men from a N.Y. Regt. were sent beyond the lines to guard a house. They were soon after taken prisoners. Four other men of the same Regt., it being a new one very naturally straggled over to visit them & were also taken. Soon after Sergt. went over to look after his guard & was taken. Presently a Lt. went to look for his Sergt., was taken but being seen at the time by some others this rat trap was by accident broken up.

At dark we got news of an order transferring us to [William W.] Burns' Div., [Orlando B.] Willcox's [Ninth] Corps with a view it was said of consolidating our Regt. with another. Our indignation as to the consolidation knew no bounds. We held a meeting at once & resolved & swore by all the gods that we sooner than be anything save 2d Mich. Inf. would resign in a body. A committee was appointed to start for Genl. Burnside's HdQrs at daylight to protest. We were urged on by Genl. Berry through his staff officers & given to understand that it was done by Col. Poe who intended to sell us to buy a Brig. Genl'ship for himself.

As for myself I was indeed very angry & felt deeply injured by the Col's. seeming bad faith. It seemed evident that it would throw me out of the Regt. entirely or back to 1st Lt. I thought I saw very plainly why my commission was withheld. I was fully determined to resign before it came to this although to do so would have been most mortifying & unpleasant. I have now no home or business save in the army. I want to serve uninterruptedly during the war. I should feel entirely lost & desolate elsewhere so long as the war continues.

Regimental pride has always run very high with us. We have labored & fought for the glory of the 2d & to see it made anything save 2d Mich. Inf. was to make an end of all desire to excel & to destroy what we deem the best reward, next to the final success of our cause, which can be given. It would entirely break the spirit & hopes of both men & officers.

§ NOVEMBER 15 We called at an early hour on Col. Poe for a pass for 5 to Warrenton, Gen. Burnside's HdQrs, which considerably to my surprise he granted without hesitation. After he had granted the pass he asked if our business was very urgent saying that the Regt. would march before our return & he wished us present if possible. He then showed us the order transferring us to Burns' Div. The order said nothing about consolidation & I at once asked him about it. This led to a long conversation during which he said that no such thing was intended. After about half an hour the matter was mutually understood & explained to the satisfaction of all parties.

I had expected a very different scene & that we should probably all be placed in arrest. The Colonel chose his part so skillfully that I could but reproach myself for want of confidence in his good faith & such indeed was the feeling of nearly every officer in the Regt. A different course on his part would have led to the most unpleasant state of feeling. Although I could see through his move very easily, still I felt effectually blocked from doing anything further at present. Since that time he very frankly told me that I need not be surprised if the 2d & 8th [Michigan] were made one before long but it would be on terms at which I would find no fault.*

We marched at 10 A.M. & to night bivouac near Sulphur Springs. Our troops were shelled at this place this m'g & there was a battle fought here in Aug. last. Fragments of shells, solid shot & some broken guns are scattered over the ground & a number of graves are on the hill nearby. I never heard of the battle before.

§ NOVEMBER 16 We were ready to march at 5 A.M. but had to wait till near 11 for the trains to get out of the way. We then marched to the Orange & Alexandria R.R. at Bealtown [Bealeton] Station thence turned to the left & marched to our camp of Aug. 25th & 26th thence to the left again about one mile & bivouaced. A difficulty here arose between our men & the Highlanders (N.Y. 79th) about some rails which resulted in several black eyes for each party.

Our new Brigade is composed of the 46th N.Y. a German Regt., 79th N.Y. Scotch, the 2d, 8th & 17th Mich. all under command of Col. Poe.†

There is a very large & beautiful plain around Bealtown but it as well as the whole country round about is completely wasted. There is not a fence to be seen & but very few houses. We are now

---

* There would be no consolidation of the 2nd and 8th Michigan regiments.
† Poe's brigade at this time actually consisted of the 2nd, 17th, and 20th Michigan and the 79th New York.

on the road to Fredericksburgh. I rejoice at that move. I am ready to undergo & endure cheerfully all things to secure the fall of Richmond. A winter campaign is a very serious thing & I am prepared in mind for much greater hardships than I have yet known. Almost anyone can be a soldier in summer but to have served faithfully one's country in the winter of the year & of its hopes will be a lasting source of pride & gratification.

§ NOVEMBER 17 We were delayed till noon from want of rations but marched about 10 miles after dinner & bivouaced at a very fine place. By marching across the fields & on byroads a column of Infantry moved on each side & the road was left clear for baggage & Artillery. The march was in this way much more fatiguing but more troops passed over the ground. There was a light rain last night & the roads were very fine this m'g. The country of to day after the first 3 miles is barren, rocky, mostly wooded with pines. I saw to day a white slave, a girl about 18 with blue eyes, yellow hair nearly straight and a complexion lighter than a majority of Northern women. I should never have suspected her African blood if I had not seen her with other slaves.

§ NOVEMBER 18 Marched at 5 A.M. & halted at 11 A.M., having made from 10 to 11 miles. Roads good, country poor & thinly settled. I hoped that we should reach Fredericksburgh to day but we had to give way for trains.

§ NOVEMBER 19 Marched at 7 A.M. through Falmouth & arrived opposite Fredericksburgh at 2 P.M. — 9 to 10 miles. A light rain fell nearly all day. The rebels can be plainly seen in the streets of Fredericksburgh. They have 24 hours in which to remove women, children, sick soldiers &c. They are evidently running off stores & provisions very rapidly. Trains of cars came & went after our arrival. Everyone is impatient of delay. Even the rain of to day has considerably injured the roads. I hope by all means that we attempt the passage of the river to morrow.

§ NOVEMBER 20 There was some rain last night. We marched for picket at 2½ A.M. to day, the rain falling in torrents. Our batteries had nice fun with a train of cars which tried to run out of the city this m'g. The train passed through a deep cut as it came out but as soon as the engine appeared on the open ground the batteries opened & the train hastily returned under cover. The engineer tried 3 times to get out but his courage failed before he had gone more than 10 rods.

For Country, Cause & Leader

§ NOVEMBER 21 The rain fell rapidly all night & till 9 A.M. to day. Everyone was wet to the skin & there was no sleep. It was one of the most unpleasant nights we have ever experienced. We kept good fires & did not suffer much from cold. The roads begin to remind us of the Peninsula.

We miss the Regts. of the old brigade with which we served so long & especially the 37th [New York]. Why it is that our Regt. should like a wild Irish Regt. so much better than all others I could never tell, but so it is. Our men miss them very much here as they are in a fight with some of the others — generally the 79th — every day. If they were here it would be "hurrah boys be Jasus the Sicond is in a row." Many a one they & the 2d have helped each other out of.

§ NOVEMBER 22 A cold raw day. Charley Morse one of our best Sergeants was accidentally shot through the arm to day. I fear he will be unable to return to duty with the Co. again.

§ NOVEMBER 23 Still in front of Fredericksburgh. The enemy on the hills opposite. I was within pistol shot of their pickets to day. Some parts of our brigade seem to be in rather a bad condition. The guard detail of the 17th Mich. was sent back twice this m'g because they were so dirty. The Sergt. Major reported a third time with the same men saying they would have to take them as there were no clean ones in the Regt. There is an effort to get us back to the old brigade. I do not care to go.

§ NOVEMBER 25 To day ends the first half of our three years. About 600 are left out of 1080, at this rate we shall have about 300 May 25th '64. Capt. Handy's resignation was accepted last night. Underwood is discharged & both started for home to day. There are now only 6 of the original officers left. The departure of two old comrades, instructors, messmates, bedfellows, makes one feel lonely. Both were agreeable companions with whom I have spent many a pleasant hour. War makes many partings — so does peace.

§ NOVEMBER 26 To use the words of Kearney we saw the "Bull in the china shop" to day, ie we were inspected by Genl. Sumner. Kearney used to say that when he saw Sumner among his troops he could never think of him save as of a "bull in a china shop."

It rained last night & we have had a regular fall day. All one can hope for here at present is merely to preserve life, i.e., to stay along from day to day. We wander around with overcoat & gloves on or sit shivering around a smoky fire from m'g till night & then sleep cold till m'g & then repeat the same performance. We have mail about once a week & the state amusement of card playing. We often gaze at the rebel camps just across the river & wonder if they have as dull times as we & sometimes we go down to the river to talk & banter with their pickets. The country round about is destitute of provisions. Our living consists of hard tack, beef & coffee. On rare occasions a few potatoes are secured at $4.00 per bushel, a loaf of bread at 30 cts., a qt. bottle of preserves or jelly at $1.50. A more tasteless & unprofitable life I never led.

§ NOVEMBER 27 Moved camp about 1 mile to rear in order to get wood & water.

§ NOVEMBER 28 A fair cold day. Co. I was sent to Corps Hdqrs as a Provost Guard.

§ NOVEMBER 29 Marched at daylight down to the (burnt) RR bridge to support a battery which overlooks the city. The change is agreeable. We have better ground & are by ourselves. I dislike to have the Regt. mixed up with the divers commodities which constitute the brigade. The 21st Maine moved off to give us place & being a new Regt. had of course a large amount of baggage. All that they could not remove at once was immediately appropriated by our men. One worthy Capt. came back after a set of patent bullet proof breast plates which he left but finding them made into fire shovels went off without them. The Rebels are busy fortifying the hills opposite. I got the Atlantic to day & read it nearly through.

§ NOVEMBER 30 Sunday. Inspection as usual. An unfortunate quarrel arose to night between Qmr. Hill & Lt. Barden, two of our most exemplary officers. The consequence was that Lt. B. has his eyes blacked & the Qmr. came near receiving the contents of a revolver.

§ DECEMBER 1, 1862 Co. drill.

§ DECEMBER 2 We had Co. drill within 40 rods of the rebel lines. Our commands were distinctly heard by them. The weather is dry and fine.

§ DECEMBER 4 A fair, warm day. At 8 P.M. I was called on by Col. Dillman to conduct two officers & some Pvts. who had been arrested by the guard to Corps HdQrs. I marched them off between a guard with loaded guns & orders to shoot them if they attempted to escape. The officers were both drunk & suspected by Dillman with his usual stupidity of being spies. They both had horses but I would not let them ride. After much trouble I delivered them safely into the hands of Capt. Benson, Provost Marshal. I knew perfectly well that it was all nonsense to take them there but being ordered to do it I would of course comply at all hazards.

§ DECEMBER 5 Snow commenced to fall at noon & still (bedtime) continues rapidly. It looks rather dismal. The mud is already deep. The men are ragged & short of shoes & have only shelter tents which are in fact more like a dog kennel than a habitation for men. They are excellent in the field but are after all a very insufficient protection against a severe winter storm. The officers of each Co. have a thin old "A" tent. I am very deficient in clothing but hope for a supply ere long. Schuetz, Hodskin, Moore & I sat down in my tent after supper with overcoats on & played cards till we were fairly frozen out. We then went out & warmed by a smoky fire till the falling snow became more unpleasant than the cold.

§ DECEMBER 7 There have been several promotions among the line officers & a place in the non-commd. staff has been secured for Sergt. Richards of my Co. My long expected commission as Capt. came to day. I now feel as if the "two barred shoulder straps" of which the "Professor" has so much to say* are, legally at least, no imposition. Capts. Moore & I by request of the line officers called on Col. Poe this m'g to talk about the Colonelcy of our Regt. after he has laid aside the eagle & taken a star. We began right this time & the interview was pleasant though many expected it would be otherwise. Our object was to prevent the promotion of Lt. Col. Dillman who is believed by all to be a coward & otherwise incompetent. The result was entirely satisfactory.

1st Lt. John C. Schuetz Co. E left us this m'g. He has a commission in a battery & has gone to Detroit to join it. He is a good officer, one of the best feeling men I ever saw & quite a character in his way. He is a Dane, drinks his 7 gallons of lager in an evening, lifts 1500 pounds dead weight and though rather heavy built turns a summersault over a pole 5 ft. high, well educated, a fine mathematician, full of fun & jollity the whole day long. He has a pipe in his mouth ⅔ of the day, & drank at 4 years of age 31 glasses of

---

* This refers to Oliver Wendell Holmes's article "My Hunt After the Captain," about his search for his wounded son (the future Supreme Court justice), in that month's *Atlantic*.

wine in an evening at his sister's wedding. He served 3 years in the war between Schleswig Holstein & Denmark 1848–51, was wounded & very glad of a chance to get out of the country after the war was over. He is chief of the Turnverein [Society] at Detroit, an infidel of course, a faithful friend & an agreeable companion but rather full of the egotism which pervades all of his countrymen (Germans) who have served abroad. He has a pretty wife and after an absence of 1½ years is glad of a chance to see her.

Yesterday was a clear bright day but the snow thawed very little. Ice froze near 2 inches thick last night & several soldiers of this Grand Div. are reported to have frozen to death. The sun has shone all day from a cloudless sky but the snow has not softened. Our worthy 2nd Lt. J.S.M. it being Sunday m'g was seized with the idea of washing his head. When he tried about 2 minutes after to comb his hair he found it frozen stiff & sticking in all directions like porcupine quills. By getting down on all fours & holding his head to the fire he finally softened his refractory wig so as to complete the operation.

This P.M. Capt. Moore, myself & two others played "Old Sledge." I do not approve of such things on Sunday but having for the first time during the day succeeded in making fire enough to warm ourselves we felt good natured & wanted to do something & that was all that offered itself.

§ DECEMBER 8 We marched back to the brigade camp at 9 A.M. The weather is somewhat warmer.

§ DECEMBER 9 Everybody seemed seized with the idea that we were going into winter quarters & began to make preparations. We were to build a solid foundation of logs 3 to 4 feet high & put the tent on top of it. We should then have a snug commodious house 8 ft. [on a side] square whereas the available room is now owing to the slant of the tent much less. I had the logs all cut for mine when an order came to be ready to move at once. Houses were abandoned, ammunition, clothing & rations occupied exclusively our attention. As usual various rumors are afloat about the sudden change of prospects. We shall probably cross the river to morrow.

§ DECEMBER 10 We are very busy drawing clothes, rations &c. I have fitted myself comfortably out of Quartermaster's stores.

§ DECEMBER 11 We were up at 4 A.M. with orders to be ready

to march at 7. It is a still, starlight morning. The air along the surface is obscured by fog & smoke but very sonorous. The ground is frozen hard & there is everywhere a very heavy white frost.

There have been great preparations during the last two days. The rumbling of artillery, baggage wagons & bridge trains* over the frozen ground, the braying of mules & the shouting of teamsters was such that I did not sleep till after midnight. At 5 A.M. two cannon were fired just to the right of Fredericksburgh & ¾ of an hour before daylight a fire from Infantry & heavy cannonading opened in the same direction. The Infantry fire soon ceased but the artillery continued with little intermission during the day. The still air of the morning & the high semicircle of frozen hills give rise to a tremendous echo which is so prolonged that there is hardly any cessation of sound & the battle seems more furious than it really is.

One hundred & eighty pieces of artillery were unable after several hours to drive a few sharpshooters from the town so that the Engineers could lay the bridge. This work was done by about 200 of the gallant 7th Mich. in twenty minutes. Several dismounted pieces have been dragged to the rear. Large bodies of Infantry & Cavalry are massed in front & on our right. We remained in camp about a mile from the river until sundown when we moved down at double quick as if to cross, halted a few minutes & marched back to camp. A very dense black cloud of smoke concealed the town & I think a considerable portion of it is burned. Several small squads of prisoners 60 or 70 in all have been sent to the rear during the day.

§ DECEMBER 12 We were in line at daylight, marched at sunrise to the river & after a little delay, crossed just below the old R.R. bridge, at double quick & without molestation on ponton of 19 boats. The m'g was misty, smoky & very favorable for crossing. We filed to the left down the river to the lower edge of town and closed in mass on the levee under cover of a bank about 8 ft. high. Cannonading commenced about 11 A.M. near the upper bridge. About 2 P.M. the batteries in rear of us (across the river) engaged those of the enemy to our right & left. About 3 P.M. the Rebels open on us but without much effect owing to the shelter of the bank. Their

---

* It was the late arrival of these bridging pontoons that had delayed the operation.

shot either struck on the crest in front & passed thence to the opposite bank or struck in the river behind us heaving up clouds of spray. A few well directed shells scattered their fragments among us. Pvt. Eddy of Co. H was killed & a Pvt. of Co. D was wounded. Several in the other Regts. were struck, perhaps 10 in all from our brigade & some in other brigades to our right. Several pieces fell among our Co. but no one was injured. The rebels would have done well to have continued their fire of shell but they did not know the effect.

The river at this place is filled with craft which were sunk on our approach in the spring. We were first ordered to bivouac without fires on the levee. The ground was trodden into mud several inches deep & there was no choice of places. The men had already torn down several houses to get boards when, it being dark, we were marched across a small stream to the left & by going a short distance to the front reached a sheltered ravine where we had fires, good water, dry ground, plenty of hay to sleep on & hence a comfortable night though each had but a single blanket.

The town is partially burned & terribly riddled. Several dead Rebels lay in the streets as we passed along. A large amt of tobacco which had been thrown into the river was fished out by our men. It was little injured & each took as much as he wished. Although our men had little opportunity to run about they were soon well supplied with books, white shirts, petticoats, hats, bonnets, musical instruments, love letters, doll babies, pillows, bed clothing, a little money & all manner of male & female apparel & domestic furniture. The town was mostly deserted. A few women & children came up out of the cellars some crossing to our side, some to the Rebels & some remaining. The upper portion of the town was held by the enemy till near dark.

§ DECEMBER 13 Soon after sunrise we moved down the river about ½ mile & took a sheltered position near the bank. There is another bridge just below us over which large bodies of troops are passing. The m'g was very foggy & smoky till about 9 A.M. when musketry opened toward our left. It was at first scattering shots from skirmishers but soon quickened to a steady roar. Soon after the artillery opened on the plain just above & to our left. The guns made a tremendous noise in the still, frosty air of the m'g. About 11 A.M. the battle opened with great fury to the right of the town opposite Falmouth. After this there was little intermission till after dark. The sound of cannon varies only in its intensity, the musketry between a rattle & a roar & high above all came the shouts & cheers of the charges always followed by yells of defiance & the redoubled fire of the assailed. We could see little but could hear all.

Our men were crazy. At every fresh outburst they would spring from the ground & rush "en masse" to their arms which were stacked in line, stand there a few minutes waiting for an order to advance or do something. No orders coming they would gradually fall back & lie down again. This was repeated more than 20 times during the day but no order to advance came till about sundown. Eager, restless, impatient as we had been all day it was a relief to move up the hill with a prospect of sharing the fortunes of the day. We had no sooner reached the plain above than we were ordered back.

After dark I saw from the hill above a terrible contest on the right. There were two long lines of Infantry very near each other. I could not hear the guns but could see the flash & the wavering of the lines. Sometimes there was a solid sheet of flame but for the most part, twinkle, twinkle, twinkle like sparks when the fire is stirred, rapid as thought. About 20 pieces of artillery poured an enfilading fire into our ranks. The shells burst right among them. There was some reply from our side but directed mainly at the artillery. The conflict finally died away on the same ground where it opened. The greater part of our artillery has all day fired from the opposite side of the river. The town was shelled by the enemy toward dark. Large numbers of wounded & several hundred prisoners have been sent across the river. We bivouac on the ground occupied during the day.

§ DECEMBER 14 Skirmishing along the whole line & some shelling on our part. Brisk skirmish during the night. Dr. Stone of Kalamazoo came to day. We are glad enough to see him. Bivouac on the same ground.

§ DECEMBER 15 Some picket firing & the enemy shell the town. About sundown we moved up the river near to the bridge & 4 Co's. including E went on picket. Lay under shelter till dark, when E & G deployed at 5 paces, marched over the hill & took post, the men lying flat on the ground & without relief. The night was partially starlight, but the wind which blew in heavy gusts from toward the enemy drove from time to time heavy masses of black clouds across the sky. The Rebel pickets were 20 or 30 rods off &

were frequently both seen & heard. All were willing to be very watchful.

Soon after midnight came an order to move off as silently & quickly as possible by the left flank. We did so & filed around into the road. For some unaccountable reason a part of my Co. did not follow as ordered. I went back after them, came near running into the Rebel lines & was obliged to return without them. They came out soon after by another road. We moved rapidly down to the little stream which empties in just below town. The wind prevented us from hearing anything & it was only when an officer of the engineers who was at the bridge with a few men urged us to hasten over that the truth flashed on my mind.

The rest of our Regt. was over, everybody was over but us & this was the last of 5 bridges across this stream. It was torn up almost before we were off it. The town was silent as death. A few dead still lay in the streets but they had been rolled about & trampled in the mud till it was impossible to tell whether they were friend or foe. Probably very few cared & if they had it would have done no good. No living being was seen till we arrived at the bridge where a few of the engineer corps were waiting to cut it loose. We crossed at double quick & marched to our old camps.

§ DECEMBER 16 Washed & cleaned up generally. Meditated on the fortunes of war, reflections not of the most pleasing nature. Cross & mad all day. Our loss is heavy, probably 14,000 or 15,000.*

§ DECEMBER 17 Yesterday was one of unmitigated rage, hate and shame. These gradually gave way to the blues but my elastic nature has lifted the load. There is no denying the defeat but I begin to be hopeful again & never felt more like fighting till the last man falls.

§ DECEMBER 22 We have had a cold comfortless time since last date. We need a stove to warm our tent. I prefer no fire at all to a smoky mud chimney. We have blankets enough & the nights are pretty comfortable. During the day and evening when not otherwise employed we sit with overcoat & gloves on around an outdoor fire squatted a la Turk. The smoke always comes in our faces but where the heat goes is more than I can tell. If we succeed in getting warm we plunge into our hole & remain there till driven out again

---

* Federal losses at Fredericksburg were some 12,700.

by the cold. I came near freezing my ears while at breakfast a few mornings since.

We have never been more completely cut off from civilization than at present. It is impossible to buy anything here or get anything brought from abroad. One never thinks in the m'g how to enjoy himself during the day but how to get through it without positive suffering. A stove which would cost us $3.00 would make us comfortable, happy as larks. Such a one could be obtained about as easy as a drove of elephants. We have plenty of money to buy & there are plenty who want to sell to us but we cant get together.

§ DECEMBER 23 Went on picket near the town. The Rebels have thrown up a rifle pit along the river bank so that it would be very difficult for us to cross again at this point. What can be more indolent than to lie all day as we do, on the south side of a hill in the warm sun chained as it were to the spot. Our men & the Rebels seem determined to be together all the time. They never miss a chance of late. After a few words of mutual abuse & bragging comes soldiers' gossip. "Got any tobacco? Yes. Give me some. Give me some coffee & I will. What do you have to eat? What kind of houses have you got? When were you paid last? How do you like your officers? Dont you want to trade newspapers?" Then comes an exchange of jokes, bywords, drives, and an argument about the war. This m'g one of their pickets called to one of ours, "I say Yank what are you fighting about?" "I dont know." "Say Reb what are you fighting about?" "I dont know." "Lets throw our guns into the river & end the d----d war."

§ DECEMBER 24 Came in from picket at 11 A.M. Pay Rolls, Monthly Returns, Clothing Accounts &c are soon to be made hence it is absolutely necessary that there should be a fire inside the tent. At three P.M. Moore & I aided by Hoyt the cook & Benjamin the contraband with many misgivings commenced a fireplace. Three hours after, the chimney had risen to the height of 4½ feet, the work was completed. A fire is placed therein. Mirabile dictu it does not smoke. It draws stoutly, blazed cheerfully & fills the whole tent with a genial warmth.

Our house is 8 ft. [on a side] square, built 3 ft. high with pine poles on top of which is perched an "A" tent. A bed made of poles, a box, a board which answers both for table & bench constitute the furniture. At home what a state of wretchedness & poverty this would indicate. Happiness is only relative. Give me a fireplace which will not smoke & this rat hole will give me more pleasure than a king derives from his palace.

The fireplace looks like the one at home at least in this, that there is a fire in it. To be sure it is much smaller & deeper, made of mud & sticks & the jambs are of pine logs instead of neatly painted brick & there is no clean swept hearth but only the accursed soil of Virginia. There are no ornaments only swords & pistols but they gleam brightly in the firelight & have as the times go an eager & useful look. There is no conversation of friends or cheerful voices, no sounds save of bugles or drums or the soldiers without wrangling rudely over their cards.

Those who were never situated as we are will laugh if they know that with a moist eye I thus allude to home. It may be weakness but with such emotions are always mingled hate, revenge, & a determination to uphold our cause to the last & each from its contrast with the others seems more intense & positive.

If I knew the exact state of affairs around the old fireplace at home I might feel more at ease. Father has long been sick & though now reported better I half suspect that it is more from regard to my feelings than to the facts. I will hope cheerfully for the best. May Santa Claus to night fill the stockings of all the little ones as he used to mine in days of old & may "Merry Christmas" be no idle words but full of truth & meaning and good health & good cheer make glad the household.

§ DECEMBER 25 Weather warm which is fortunate for our fireplace smokes wonderfully. We made Christmas dinner on beef, hard tack & coffee. I had fortunately completed my meal when Moore made a discovery which checked him midway in his, viz that the hard tacks were full of bugs & worms. This is no uncommon thing of late but his wry face was the most laughable thing of the day.

§ DECEMBER 26 Weather warm, high wind, smoky chimney. Atlantic for January received.

§ DECEMBER 31 Weather since last date has been very pleasant. Everything here has gone well & news from home has been such that I have been entirely content. This year if I remember right began pleasantly and the end thereof is not otherwise.

Twelve

TO THE
WESTERN
THEATER

The new year brought radical change to Charles Haydon and the 2nd Michigan Infantry. Leaving the Army of the Potomac in February 1863, the Ninth Corps was sent first to the Virginia Peninsula and then two of its divisions were transferred to the western theater. Haydon and the 2nd Michigan found garrison duty in Kentucky entirely to their liking. "I board with a citizen nearby & live well," he wrote in his journal on May 15. The citizen had two pretty daughters, and when the time came to move on Haydon found the parting hard.

In April the 2nd Michigan came under command of its third (and last) colonel (after Israel Richardson and Orlando Poe), William Humphrey. Captain Haydon worked hard to bring his own command, Company E, up to the mark. During a brief but welcome furlough, word came to him that the regiment was joining in Grant's siege of Vicksburg in Mississippi. Reaching his regiment on June 19, Haydon wrote, "Next to home there is no place like the camp of the Mich. 2d."

* * *

§ JANUARY 1, 1863 This being the first of the New Year one naturally feels very much inclined to review the past & dream of the future. The last 12 months have been eventful ones with me & I may say with gratitude very fortunate ones. Many friends, comrades & acquaintances have fallen while I have remained uninjured. There are no two to whom I look back with so much regret as Genls. Kearney & Richardson.* Two braver or more loyal men never lived. The one I looked up to as the model of all that was soldierlike. The other was not so perfect in that respect but one for whom I had an affection almost as for a father. There was not a man of the 2d Michigan with whom he would not have shared his last crust of bread & hardly one who would not have marched to certain death at his bidding.

Both fell on victorious fields won in a great measure by their personal exertion & daring. If they had done as the majority do they would no doubt still have lived. Richardson complained at Antietam that he had to act as Col. for every Regt. in his Div. Kearney always insisted on doing this. Both were killed in the discharge of duties far outside of & below their rank. Kearney's spirit fought with the old Div. at Fredericksburgh. They alone gained ground & held it. Would to God we had been with them.

The red which every officer of his Div. was compelled to wear on the front of his cap when we retreated from Richmond has been decreed perpetual.† The men at their own request are allowed to wear the same on the right side of the cap. We have an appropriate badge now making at a cost of $25 each to be worn by all the officers of his Div. The red is only a square bit of flannel but is now well known throughout the army. Death it is said was to Kearney a welcome visitor but it was far otherwise to Richardson, who left a young, pretty wife & a child whom he idolized. As for myself, I shall be content if another New Year shall find me as well off as now. Thanking God for the past I commence the new year with fixed determination & unwavering hope.

§ JANUARY 7 I went on picket at 8 A.M. in command of a detail of 80 men. The air is keen, wind brisk, day quiet.

§ JANUARY 8 The night was very cold. Good fires were kept but without shelter from the wind they are of little avail. I walked to & fro the greater part of the night. All intercourse with the other side is prohibited but the pickets by whistling alternate parts

---

* Sixteen days after Kearny's death at Chantilly, Israel Richardson was mortally wounded at Antietam.

† The Kearny patch, a red diamond of flannel originated by the general to control straggling, was now (as Haydon notes) a badge of honor for the men of his old division.

of tunes which the opposite side fills up secure a sort of communication. I am now by a pleasant fire in my tent & find it far more
comfortable than a sleepless night on the banks of the Rap-
pahannock.

Stone the drummer boy of Co. I has a commission as 2nd Lt.
in the 9th Mich. Cav.

§ JANUARY 14 Lt. R. A. Beach of Co. H tendered his resignation because affairs at home required his presence. He was last
night dishonorably dismissed from the service.

§ JANUARY 15 During the last week & in fact during the last
month the weather has been warm for the season, dry & fine. We
have had innumerable drills — Battalion — Co. — Squad — Bayonet Exercise — Fencing &c. Times have passed pleasantly. I have
some few books, can study & instruct my non-commds. Jomini's
Art of War is itself a very good library for three months. The Regt.
or at least its officers are sorely vexed by the men running off to
enlist in the Regulars. When called on in Dec. we sent 30 men, 3
per Co. to fill up a Regular Battery. About a week ago they wanted
more & we refused to let them go. The men ran away at night.
We are making all the uproar about it that we can but I presume
we shall get no redress. It tends directly to the subversion of all
discipline but such in the wisdom of the Magnates at Washington
is deemed best.

The Pontoon Trains are here again & the Pioneers are ordered
to move with them carrying 6 days' rations. Where we can be going
is more than I can guess. Some say we are to cross the river above,
others that we are to use them on the road to Alexandria. I dont
see any very good place to go to just now & would therefore as
soon remain here as go on any expedition which has no especial
object. It makes little difference however for we are sworn to trudge
around the country, as a business, until mustered out by some one
either from above or below.

I have faith in Burnside but I fear that the other Genls. will not
cooperate with him. I think we shall have to proceed more cautiously in the coming campaign. Our army will not, comparatively,
be large. It must be better officered & make up in discipline. It
may be necessary to fortify some strong points for the purpose of
holding permanently the ground we gain. We can afford no rash
enterprises. Press vigorously but on well considered plans con-
quering as far as we go. It is of little use to overrun the country

if you do not succeed in destroying the armies. We cannot now pursue them to remote parts of the interior but may encroach on their borders so as to compel them to seek us.

With the Generals we now have it would be no safer to attempt the daring moves & the comprehensive strategy of Napoleon than for me to imitate Blondin at Niagara. We have many who are middling & that may ruin us. If they were all poor except one our chance would be no worse, perhaps better. McClellan having had command from the beginning, they obeyed him as it were from force of habit & he could without difficulty secure unity of action & a hearty cooperation. Each one's reputation depended on the ability with which he sustained McClellan. The glory which McClellan won was shared to some extent by all his subordinates.

Hooker, Sumner, [Franz] Sigel, [William F.] Franklin had no share in Burnside's fame. If he became conspicuous they suffered at once by the contrast. Under McClellan they were all rivals but they were obliged to pull in the same direction. As soon as he was removed their rivalry was increased, embittered & now they all pull in different directions.

Give Burnside the same control over officers & men that McClellan had & I am not sure that he would not be the better man of the two. He has it not & those who removed McClellan ought to have known perfectly well that he could not get it. If he had have won at Fredericksburgh he would have gained the confidence of the men but not that of the Generals.

§ JANUARY 16 The order to be ready to march at an early hour to morrow has been received. Where we can be going is more than I can guess. If we are to cross the river again I shall go with small hope of success. The morale of the army is not now right for such a move. If we go the little that I can do shall be done with a will but I hope it will not be tried at present. There is but little of our Regt. left & no prospect of its being recruited. Use it a little longer, turn the men over to some one else, vote the officers incompetent & send them disgraced from the service. Such is substantially the plan proposed by some of the members of the Senate.

§ JANUARY 17 We were early in readiness to move but no further orders came. The air is very keen & I am not sorry to enjoy another night by the bright blaze in our mud fireplace. I had a long talk with Capt. Young to day on the consolidation [of regiments] question. Both agreed that, although unpleasant, it is necessary & ought to be done, in an equitable manner, at once. It may throw us both out of the service on account of juniority. This we should dislike but it is something nowadays to keep off the worthless list.

[In a letter to his brother written about this time, Haydon remarks on his "long sermons in the journal . . . written for *myself*." What follows, the balance of his entry for January 17, seems to fall in that category.]

The time between the bursting of a shell in front of you & the striking of the fragments on the ground, short as it is, gives rise to the most peculiar feeling I have yet experienced. To get the full benefit you should be standing or lying perfectly idle on the ground in the direction from which the shell is to come. First the sound of the gun, instantly followed by a noise between a whiz & a yell, then say 20 rods in front & 100 feet in the air, there is the prettiest globe of dense, white smoke the size of a small haycock, eddying & unfolding in all manner of graceful shapes.

This is all you *see* but you *know* that from 10 to 200 musket balls & ragged pieces of iron will strike within the next two seconds on the acre of ground on which you stand. You hear the explosion, not so loud as the cannon, but a round compact noise, then come the fragments each one according to its shape singing a different note, varying from a sharp whiz to a low, heavy bass. The senses are so wonderfully acute that you seem to hear each one distinctly. There is no use of dodging or moving about. But where will they all strike? Will that little bullet with the shrill, piping voice pierce your body? Will that triangular chap which screams so tear out your bowels with one of his sharp points? Will that big fellow which makes that low, rushing sound be satisfied with an arm or a leg or will he take your head? Will they skip you & take someone else? Perhaps they will go too high — no — too low — no. It is soon decided — thump, rattle, bang, smash, dirt & splinters fly on every side. You are safe but looking around you see from one to a dozen poor fellows rolling headless, or writhing in agony on the ground.

One could not write in all day the thoughts which pass through his mind in those two seconds. One does not need a better opportunity to test his religion. Misdeeds are sure to find their way to the surface. These two seconds explain his spiritual condition better than all the sermons ever preached. If he is afraid to die he knows it & he knows the reason with a certainty which admits of no doubt. Those two seconds may be worth more to a man than all his previous life. If one has done his duty toward himself & others he will in that brief space of time be well repaid for it. If he has kept within the limits of his code of morals he will be very thankful. If he has not he will be more careful afterwards how he walks.

While this is passing through your brain you still see & hear all that is going on around you & have the most perfect presence of mind. Perhaps 10 seconds after you are laughing to see a comrade scratching the dust out of his eyes. What would I give if such activity of the mind & such clearness of perception could be continued & I had the power to express my thoughts in language. If you are in motion at the time or busied about anything you will feel nothing like this. It comes & goes instantly.

§ JANUARY 19 Still in camp, weather cold & clear, wood by no means plenty.

§ JANUARY 20 There was a considerable movement of troops toward the right. An order is published by Burnside saying that we are again about to meet the enemy. It seems a singular method of announcing it.

§ JANUARY 21 A terrible storm of wind & rain from the N.E. set in soon after dark last night & has continued ever since. Orders came at midnight to march at 4 A.M. in heavy order. As the rain was falling in torrents & the night was very dark & windy the prospect was anything but pleasant. Subsequently we were directed to wait further orders. At noon word came that the move was delayed by the pontoons but that we should hold ourselves in readiness to move at a moment's notice. Our tent is completely flooded, it being old & almost worthless in wet weather.

§ JANUARY 22 The rain continued with little intermission until this m'g. The air has been very damp & full of fog & mist all day. I believe our move is defeated for the present. People will have to learn that the weather & "mud" can stop military operations even when McClellan is not in command.*

§ JANUARY 23 Early in the day the troops commenced passing back from the right & most of the Infantry and Cavalry have returned to their old camps. The Artillery & bridge trains are

---

* Indeed this aborted operation would come to be known as the "Mud March."

firmly stuck in the mud. The weather was misty till near night when the sun came out for a short time.

§ JANUARY 25 On picket. Weather warm & cloudy. I have command of a detail of 97 men from the 2d. The Rebs are at work just opposite in considerable force. No communication is allowed & all the pickets can do to amuse themselves is throw stones at each other across the river.

§ JANUARY 26 Weather warm & fine. Major Genl. Ambrose E. Burnside no longer commands the Army of the Potomac. His farewell order is plain, patriotic, sensible. He never attempts to rid himself of responsibility of failure. He has always displayed a manly boldness in this respect. I must say that I have more feeling personally at his removal (that is, sympathy for the man) than I had for McClellan. He has labored hard & as I believe with the utmost patriotism & good faith; his plans have been well laid; he has done all that he could & yet has failed. The fates were against him. The laurels won on many a hard fought field are in public estimation dimmed by his late failure. Many seem more bitter on him because his last movement was stopped by the rain than they would if he had really controlled the elements himself. He undoubtedly leaves us with a heavy heart. My good wishes at least shall go with him.

A good man takes his place & the change is generally well received. "Old Joe" as the boys call him will do all that can be done by him & will keep things moving. When Hooker was asked after the battle of Fair Oaks if he could hold the position from which Casey had been driven he replied "Let Kearney support me & I will hold the gates of hell." If those two could not do it the men dont live who could.

It needs a strong arm to deal with this army just at present. Some severe remedies must be applied at once or it will be decomposed. Desertion has increased at a most alarming extent. It must *at once* be punished with *Death* speedy & certain or the army is ruined. Military discipline must be upheld with a strong hand. I hope the next move after that will be to expel that lying, thieving, contemptible class of persons known as "Reporters" from the army.

§ JANUARY 28 It was snowing when I woke this morning & it still (10 P.M.) continues without intermission. The ground is not frozen but the snow is now from 4 to 5 inches deep. There is a great deal of mud & water under it. Genl. Hooker rode the length of the picket line & in consideration of the storm sent half the men to their quarters. This is a small & a transparent act but the army is stronger in his hands by some hundreds by reason of the increased good will among the men. They had never before seen the commander of the army on the out posts in stormy weather. It was a perfectly safe act for neither party can move to do the other army great harm. Pickets are only needed to look out for spies & small marauding parties.

§ JANUARY 29 The snow was from 6 to 8 inches deep this m'g. The day has been warm & clear & the snow has thawed considerably. The pickets suffered severely. Twenty eight hours in such a storm on an exposed field with little fire & no shelter is about as much as men can endure & live. If the weather had been colder they would surely have died. My good friend Capt. Johnston was in command.

§ FEBRUARY 4, 1863 Is a very cold windy day. Genl. Hooker is making no small commotion among absentees. Two of my men whom I never saw before came back & reported for duty to day. Deserters find themselves in hot water. I have reliable information that at least four are sentenced to death.

I brought a man before the Court to day for using threatening & insulting language to the 1st Sergt. He is the first of this Co. whom I have Court Martialed. I am more & more inclined to the belief that it is better, except in aggravated cases, for a Captain to enforce discipline with his own hand than to take men before a Court. They prefer any time a smart rap over the head with the back of a sword to having their pay stopped by a Court Martial or dragging a ball & chain. The example is as good and it saves time & the reputation of the Co. It is certain & expeditious & will not require to be often repeated.

§ FEBRUARY 6 There is a very bad storm of snow, wind & rain. It has continued since daylight & seems now (9 P.M.) at its height. Last night was very cold. Moore was on picket & suffered badly.

Just after dark I was completely surprised by an order for the 9th Corps to embark at once for Ft. Monroe. We shall probably have a rough time but shall at least get 100 miles farther South. We can hardly find a less desirable place than this. Wood is so scarce where we are camped that the men have to dig the stumps deep down into the ground to get enough to cook their meals &

have a little fire in their tents. We have an immense amt of picketing. Provisions & clothing (for officers) are scarce & most unreasonably high. Hail to the old Fortress.

§ FEBRUARY 8 Benson has resigned & gone home for the purpose, he says, of entering a Cavalry Regt. I hope he will do so but I fear he intends to leave the service. I regret to say that at heart his loyalty is not of the soundest. I went on picket this m'g but was relieved in the afternoon. I think we shall leave to morrow for the land of oysters & contrabands. "Through what varieties of untried being. Through what new scenes & changes must we pass?"* The impression seems to be that we are bound for South Carolina.

§ FEBRUARY 10 Still in camp. The Corps has all gone now except two brigades. I am glad we are the last. It is much better to remain here in comfortable quarters than to go first & lie for ten days on the barren beach waiting for the others.

We had a lively time to day discussing the Kearney Badge. We refused to take the one adopted by the old Div. & have now a design of our own. It is a seven point gold Star, two inches across the extreme points, on each of which is engraved the name of one of the seven battles we fought under him. In the body of the Star is a raised gold likeness of the General with a border of enamel, the upper half red, the lower black & separated on each side by a small star. Below the likeness are two hands in the military gauntlet grasped. Under these "2nd Mich. Inf." When in uniform it is to be worn on the breast of the coat. The body of the Star can be removed & worn as a breast pin when in citizen dress.

There was much discussion as to who should be allowed to wear them. A higher degree of loyalty & heartfelt loyalty was expressed than I could even have hoped. Crego was unanimously prohibited for having expressed disloyal sentiments & for having avoided the battlefield. Four others were voted out for various reasons. Doubts were raised concerning several others. We sent a request to the 3d Mich. to join with us in procuring it. The weather is very fine.

§ FEBRUARY 12 It was thought that we would surely leave to day but night finds us still in the old camp. I am very glad as there

---

* Joseph Addison, *Cato.*

is a bad storm of wind & rain. All are gone except this brigade. I suppose there is no occasion for haste.

§ FEBRUARY 13 We marched at noon for the cars. Before leaving we burned nearly everything combustible. We came on the cars at Aquia Creek & are now (sundown) well lodged on the steamer Georgia. On the 17th of March '62 we passed this point a little earlier in the day & with quite different expectations. Things do not look bad to me now but fortune has played us so many tricks since that time that I have grown cautious & keep my hopes & fears well in reserve. We went down in full expectation of taking Richmond, five months later we came back to defend Washington; now after about six months we are once more traversing this beautiful river on some errand to us unknown. We went before with above 900 men. We go now with half that number.

§ FEBRUARY 14 The boat is not so crowded as transports usually are. Our quarters are good & the living is ditto.

Hearing that we were about to leave the Army of the Potomac the officers of the 3d Mich. sent to the officers of the 2d one keg old rye to cheer them on their way. Regrets were experienced by many at parting with such long tried & ever faithful friends which could be soothed by nothing save whiskey punch. All felt well convivial and no one went to bed till after twelve & some not till 4 A.M. At the last named hour Major Byington, 1st Lts. Plumb & Hodskin, all of the 2d, & Adjt. Genl. Reed of the 79th [New York] were so drunk as to have no very correct notion of things in general. The men as is always the case had liquor. About 3 A.M. a fight arose between some of our men & some of the 8th Mich. which caused a great noise & woke all who were asleep. Several were pretty well battered but no serious damage was done.

We were to have started at 7 last night but being fast aground at that time we did not get off till near m'g. The day was very fine, wind gentle from the east. The good feeling continued through the day but at sundown the wind freshened & we began to feel the ocean swell. The boat pitched considerably & at 9 P.M. there were only four of us left upright in the cabin. Soon after that I parted with my supper but experiencing no further inconvenience went to bed & slept well.

§ FEBRUARY 15 We arrived at the [Hampton] Roads abt 11 last night & lay at anchor till m'g. Two of the new Iron clads & abt 150 other vessels were anchored there. We then came up to Newport News passing the wrecks of the Congress & Cumberland,* landed, marched two miles up the James & have now a most delightful camp near its banks. The rank, long leafed, coarse looking pitch pine, the country level as a sheet of water, the shore redolent of sea weed & oysters are familiar to us as old acquaintances. There is a light rain but the air is soft & balmy.

§ FEBRUARY 16 A fair warm day. It was spent in laying out the camp & collecting materials. The whole Div. will have the same color line & hence will be in line of battle two or three times per day. Rain at night.

§ FEBRUARY 17 Rain & high wind all day & night.

§ FEBRUARY 18 Rain continuous since yesterday. Nothing has been or can be done toward fixing up the camp. The soil is loose sand which although not so bad without as clay, makes a much poorer floor. Everything is covered with it.

§ FEBRUARY 19 It rained till abt daylight but the balance of the day was fine.

§ FEBRUARY 21 I am tired to night. Moore & I have been at work for two days fitting up our tent. We have the best quarters since Camp Michigan. The whole camp is a very fine one. It rains to night but we have a good fire & are warm & comfortable as could be wished. We ate a good supper & drank some bottles of ale to commemorate the completion of our labors.

§ FEBRUARY 22 The rain of last evening soon changed to snow. The wind was high all night & the snow from 4 to 6 inches deep this m'g. It changed to rain & the day has been very bad. The snow is now mostly gone. The storm is one of the worst of the season.

§ MARCH 8, 1863 Since last date (when that was is more than I can recollect) we have been on the tilt each day from the time I breakfast, to wit 8 A.M. till after Dress Parade at 5½ P.M. Co. Drill, Battalion, Brigade &c with numerous inspections. Much fine work, policing &c, reviews & the like have left hardly time enough to breathe free. I have at last brought my Co. to good proficiency in drill. I have been complimented several times of late by good authority on its performances. The non-comds. recite daily in tactics.

---

* Sunk by the *Merrimack* on March 8, 1862, the day before her duel with the *Monitor*.

I reduced one Corporal to the ranks to day for appearing at inspection with a dirty gun.

Capt. Johnston & I bathed in the river to day, being the pioneers of the season. Water cold but very acceptable, rather salt to the eyes. Lt. Col. Dillman's lady & another gave me a call last night taking me quite by surprise. I had not seen a woman in my domicile for above a year. They improved the looks of it very much. I am brim full of health & strength & well content with present quarters. Desire for change is not so great here as it would be in a place less lovely.

Several schemes are at work to cause a countermarch in "Brave" Dillman's expectations as to the Colonelcy of this Regt. I have taken a large share in them. I think we shall succeed in jumping Capt. [William] Humphrey over both Lt. Col. and Major. Such is my sincere desire. If we should fail my place here would be a poor one. D. is too great a coward to demand an explanation openly (which I could give him in short order) but he would omit no chance for petty tyranny, slights & abuse. His goodness to me has of late been wonderful. If his lady had been younger & prettier I cant say how far she might have aroused my sympathy for the Col. as to the storm which is about to burst upon him. As it is I stand firm.

I quarter with my 2d Lt. The "Elder," to wit 1st Lt. James Bradley of Co. E, a man who might have made his fortune as a Methodist Preacher, stops with a friend. I have at last recovered the desk containing the Co. books & papers which I am arranging as fast as possible. I look into Charley O'Malley about once per week.

§ MARCH 18 I have been as busy since last date as one could well be. I had work enough on hand when I was called on by the officers of the line to prepare a short address on the war question for publication.* This took all my spare time for three days. I finished it last night about twelve & it was sent away this m'g.

There is a prospect of our going up to the Blackwater ere long.

---

* Haydon's address, published in the *Washington Chronicle*, took as its theme the 2nd Michigan's "desire that the war should be prosecuted till our victory is final and complete." Its target was Peace Democrats seeking the country's ruin by "harboring deserters, discouraging enlistments, by circulating false reports of the demoralization of its Army, and by urging a peace more ruinous than defeat itself."

I am well satisfied here. The men are making great improvement in military matters. Col. Williams has had a serious family quarrel in the 20th [Michigan].

An order came at 10 P.M. to move at 7 in the morning. A very considerable amt of baggage is collected & it is necessary to decide at once what must be abandoned. Of course all is haste & preparation. Where are we going? Everyone supposes to Suffolk or the Blackwater.

§ MARCH 19 Reveille was at 4 A.M. Weather cold. We marched at 9 for Newport News. Several sea going vessels lie at the wharf & we think of the South — Charleston. All doubts on this question are soon solved by going aboard our old acquaintance the Georgia. Snow commenced falling rapidly as we marched out of camp & continued with high wind all day. The Major [Byington] is in command & is a little drunker than usual, otherwise everything is after the old sort. It is now believed that we are bound for Baltimore. One year ago to day I saw Hampton Roads for the first time. On the 20th 1862 we landed. On the 20th 1863 I expect to bid them a long good bye. The weather is too rough to venture out to day. The story now goes that we are bound for the Shenandoah Valley. Several squabbles have occurred among the men. To be on a transport 12 hours without a fight would excite in my mind apprehensions of some terrible disaster.

§ MARCH 20 There was no abatement of the storm either of snow or wind during the day or night. We dare not put to sea. The boat although partly sheltered rolls heavily and there is much sickness. I am not on the list this time. Not a vessel moves from its anchorage except the little steam tugs. They have been splashing around busily all day, one moment buried in water & on the next seeming about to jump out of it entirely.

§ MARCH 21 Wind high with squalls of rain. The decks were cleared of snow & things put in order generally. There are about 200 vessels in the Roads some 25 of which are vessels of war. At 10 A.M. sealed orders were sent on board & we put out into the bay. The storm was from the N.E. & gave a very heavy swell until we reached the shelter of the E. shore. Our sealed orders, which were to be opened when we were 3 miles out, read "go to Baltimore" and that was all.

§ MARCH 22 Morning finds us at Locust Point near Baltimore. We disembarked at 10 A.M. & went on board cars on the Baltimore

& Ohio R.R. We are all pretty tired and many were sick yesterday. The weather is very fine. Major Byington is absent drunk & Ruehle is in command. I am officer of the day but have no guard. We are unable to get off before 4 P.M. at which time the men were mostly drunk or well on the way. I for want of a guard could only stand around doing what I could to preserve order which owing to the numbers & the various directions they took was but little. I tied up a few of the worst & kept as severe a face as possible till I was entirely tired out & then having asked our imbecile commander twice for a guard which he neglected to furnish I let things take their course.

As might be expected the crossed sash of the officer of the day was a central point of attraction for all apple women, Irish women who had husbands in the army, prostitutes & the inquisitive in general. Such things are always encouraged by officers & men as a sort of standing joke on the officer of the day & this Sunday at Locust Point was particularly fruitful. I stood all very complacently except in the case of one Irish woman who was particularly vexatious. She followed me like a ghost the whole day. It was "Och Captain wouldn't you eat one of my pies now? Isn't it a cigar ye'd like? Won't ye just eat one of my apples? Och Capt. dear did iver you know one Pat Mooloney who went down there to the wars?" I finally told her in no very mild language that I would throw her into the river if she did not keep out of the way. At this she clasped her hands & cried "Och Captain now you wouldn't do the like of that to a poor lone woman would ye?" I finally sent a man to upset her basket & thus got rid of her.

I lost some baggage in the m'g & the men made this a pretext for examining the inside of nearly all the houses in the vicinity swearing that they would avenge the insult to the Regt. They embraced impromptu all the women they could find but seeing the encouraging manner in which their lawlessness was received I did not trouble myself on that score.

At last we got under way but came near being thrown off the track by a rail which had been placed on the track for that purpose in open daylight. The road for several miles leads up the valley of the beautiful Patapsco. There is for several miles a succession of lovely villages hardly separated from each other. So many pretty women as came out to greet us I have not seen since the journey from Mich. in 1861. Everyone vowed to sing "My Maryland" each day of his life. We had gone about 8 miles when a drunken rascal tumbled off the cars & we had to stop to see whether he was dead or alive. He was found sitting up by the roadside swearing that he could whip any d----d rebel in Jeff's army.

While waiting for this, some girls came down to the opposite bank & we opened a conversation with them. One of them had the audacity to say that she loved the officer of the day & would give him a kiss if he would come over. She seemed very pretty at that distance & had I not been on duty I would have gone over or drowned in the attempt. As it was I could only thank her for her kindness & promise to treat with her after the war.

§ MARCH 23　We arrived at Harper's Ferry at 7 A.M., had coffee & other rations. There seemed to be little left there except the ruins of what was once a very pretty place. It is surrounded on all sides by hills very steep, almost perpendicular. The R.R. passes fairly over the town on a trestlework bridge more than 80 ft. from the ground. We reached Cumberland Md. at 5 P.M. & there took supper. The road runs along the Potomac most of the way. It is a stream of marvelous beauty flowing all the way between banks from 100 to 600 feet in height. Its usual width is about 125 yards. Water clear as crystal, current rapid.

§ MARCH 24　Reached Grafton Va. at daylight. Parkersburgh at 4 P.M. where the 2d, 17th & 79th embarked on the steamboat Majestic. It is 375 miles by rail from Baltimore to Parkersburgh. The country is mountainous all the way & the road full of sharp curves, steep grades & tunnels. We passed through 23 tunnels on the last 100 miles. Several of them were above a mile in length & the stifling coal smoke with which they were filled was by no means pleasant. Streams of water came splashing down their sides at almost every rod. On the boat an unfortunate difference occurred between some of our men & the 79th in which one of the latter was thrown overboard. He was however fished out without anything worse than the ducking. We started down the river at 9 P.M.

§ MARCH 25　On the Ohio. Our boat is new. Everything is clean & the accomodations are good. The weather is very cold & there is some snow & high wind.

§ MARCH 26　Passed Cincinnati during the night & arrived at Louisville Ky. about 10 A.M. & disembarked having traveled above 1000 miles. Although no one here expected us the ladies had a fine dinner prepared by 1 P.M. for the whole brigade. We partook in a manner which convinced them that their kindness was appreciated. We then marched out of town about a mile & encamped. There are many rebels in this place but unionism has back bone enough to make it respectable & an example to places more favored. Our introduction to the West is on the whole very pleasant. Every one is full of enthusiasm & confidence in Burnside.* We have always felt that our natural field was the West yet the idea of coming here was not much relished. We preferred the South at first but all are now well pleased. The scenery of the Ohio was not equal to my expectations. Perhaps if I had not just come from the upper Potomac it would have produced a more favorable impression.

§ MARCH 27 In camp, all quiet.

§ MARCH 28 Camp near Louisville Ky. We were paid in the forenoon. Marched to the depot soon after & about dark went on board cars on the Louisville & Nashville R.R. There was a vast amount of drunkenness among the men in spite of all efforts to the contrary.

§ MARCH 29 Some time during the night we reached Bardstown but did not leave the cars till after daylight. We marched through town & camped just outside in a very fine place. Some Rebel Cavalry are reported to have been within two miles this m'g. This is a very pleasant village of about 2000 inhabitants. Living is cheap although the country has been twice traversed by each army. The men are quiet enough now that they are sober. No plundering is allowed. The country & especially the timber remind me of Michigan. Where we are encamped are several acres of as fine whitewood, beech & maple as I ever saw. Finer water cannot be found. We have all been in fine spirits to day although we had a cold comfortless night.

§ MARCH 31 Co. E on picket. We keep a sharp lookout for guerrillas. The day is cold & squalls of snow are frequent. Very cold at night, hard frost, no fires allowed. There is a rich well cultivated country around us. There is a stream near us which is much finer than any we saw in Va. The water is clear as crystal & there are falls every few rods. The banks are of shelving rocks forming in many places apartments 100 feet in length & depth. A

---

* Gen. Burnside now commanded the Department of the Ohio.

more romantic place on a small scale I have never seen. The outlines of many scenes in Va. & Md. are far superior to anything I
have seen here but the details are by no means as fine.

§ APRIL 1, 1863 A fine warm day. There was only one thing
to break the monotony. A woman came to camp with quite a pretty
daughter about sixteen who played the violin very well. I called
her in & we listened to a few tunes. She picked up a considerable
amount of money, but the musician was much more attractive than
the music.

§ APRIL 2 Marched at 7 A.M., made ten miles & halted half an
hour for dinner. After dinner marched eight miles & bivouaced
on the fair ground at Springfield. This is the first marching of any
account since Nov. The weather was fine & the road good but the
knapsacks were heavy & the men very tired ere night. The country
is rich & well cultivated, excellent water & many fine residences.

§ APRIL 3 Up at 3 A.M. & marched at 5. Arrived at Lebanon
(ten miles) about 10 A.M. Some snow squalls during the day.

§ APRIL 4 Capt. Hodskin & I went to Louisville, bought some
clothes, went to a saloon & took supper, went to the Galt House
& put up for the night.

§ APRIL 5 We look about town a little to see what sort of a
place it is. It purports to be a city of 75,000, quite a pleasant place
in the main but not possessing many places of attraction. Business
appears to be good.

§ APRIL 6 Came back to camp & found the Regt. where we
left it, much to our satisfaction.

§ APRIL 8 I was Brig. officer of the day. Everything passed
off quietly.

§ APRIL 9 We were reviewed by Brig. Gen. [Mahlon D.] Manson. The weather was fine & the affair went off well. It is now
believed that we are sure of Humphrey for Col. No one however
can tell what may turn up. He is the best man in the Regt. who is
eligible for the place. He is not however exactly the man for Col.
He is too lax on discipline. There are no better men than the 2d
so long as they know their master. So many devils fresh from hell
would not be worse than they if not held with a strong hand.

§ APRIL 10 Col. Poe left us to day. It was a pretty serious time
& nearly all the officers & men were moist about the eyes when
they came to shake hands for the last time. I was very sorry to see
him go.

§ APRIL 11 I was appointed chairman of a committee to draft some very affecting Resolutions about Col. Poe, setting forth our deep sorrow at his departure, the gross injustice which had been done in not promoting him &c &c, his personal worth & the like.*

§ APRIL 12 I worked on the Resolutions with great zeal for I really think he deserved promotion & that by so doing the good of the service would have been furthered. I also have always regarded him as one of the best of my personal friends. The 22d Mich. had a muss with the 16th Ky. about a darkey to day & came near exchanging volleys. It was finally settled to the satisfaction of all concerned.

§ APRIL 13 I read the Resolutions to the officers & they were approved. Just as I finished an unexpected event changed the programme somewhat. A French gentleman arrived in camp & announced that he was Major of the 2d Mich. We the Captains had sent a petition to the Gov. asking that Humphrey should be Col. Poe told us that our choice decided the matter & that he had the Gov. promise in writing to that effect. If this man is Major, Dillman must be Col. and Poe must have figured the whole thing & per consequence have lied to us. I suspect such is the case. Dillman & Byington seem to understand the matter.

I at once put the Resolutions very deep down into my pocket & told Col. Dillman that if he wanted any Res. he must get someone else to write them. I hoped that he would ask me why but he did not do so. There is a firm determination on the part of the line officers to put the new Major *out* & he will have to go I think. Poe in his farewell address said there was no Regt. Regular or Vol. in the U.S. which had a better lot of officers than the 2d. Be that as it may we are very confident of being able to take care of this Regt. without any help from the outside. We are equally determined that the Gov. of Mich. shall understand that such is the case.

§ APRIL 14 The new Major went to Louisville.

§ APRIL 15 All is quiet, had brigade drill. There was a light rain.

§ APRIL 16 The new Major has not yet returned. He is accused in town of stealing shirts & diverse offences. I am on Ct. Martial

---

* After the Senate failed to confirm him as brigadier general and his volunteer's commission expired, Poe reverted to regular army status (captain) and engineering duties in the western theater.

at Genl. Manson's HdQrs. So far as I have seen the western troops they are the dirtiest lot of mortals my eyes ever beheld. This accounts I think for the great amt of sickness which has always prevailed among them. Of their drill & discipline I have had little opportunity to judge. I am glad I went into the eastern army first. Our habits are so thoroughly formed there that there is little danger of a relapse.

§ APRIL 18 Weather very warm. Nothing is heard from the new Major. I think Dillman allowed himself to be too easily fooled in that matter. The fact is both he and Byington were so delighted with the thought that they did not wish to investigate closely. Their faces are very long now & it is evident to me that they believe Humphrey will be Colonel.

I have been reading to day divers papers on the conduct of the war. Alas how many unpleasant things we have learned in the dear school of experience. I believe no other people could have stood up under such a succession of mistakes. My faith is undiminished still I no longer feel that victory is a necessity. Our Regt. & the whole army will fight well but it is with the dogged obstinacy of veteran troops having a prescribed duty to perform & not with the hilarity & confidence which used to characterize our movements. There is among our men now a sort of even, devil-may-care recklessness upon which the vicissitudes of war exert little effect. If they bear up thus under defeat what would they become after a long series of victories. Nothing could stand before them.

§ APRIL 22 Weather fine. I have been on a Court Martial for several days at Gen. Manson's Head Qrs. Col. Craddock of the 16th Ky. Inf. is President. They have a sort of off hand, cut off way of doing business without much regard to form or law. We have had very easy times in Ky. thus far still I would much rather be under Hooker. I hope to hear good news from the Army of the Potomac ere long. There is again some talk of [regimental] consolidation. I dislike to hear of it.

§ APRIL 25 Weather fine. Humphrey *is* Colonel. That is enough for one day. It is now proved I presume that the Captains of this Regt. are not so dull on some subjects as was supposed in certain quarters. Col. Poe's good faith is vindicated. That of itself is a source of great pleasure to me.

Although I bear no great love to the Lt. Col. & Major still I can but realize what my feelings would be if I were in their position.

I presume theirs are not in all respects the same as mine would be. They seem to understand the most effectual way of avenging the insult, viz to remain with us as if nothing had happened. We hoped to get rid of both of them in this way but they seem inclined to hold fast. Perhaps something can be done yet. I could say considerable more on this subject but as no one knows into whose hands it may fall in the confusion of baggage I shall refrain.

§ APRIL 26 Col. Humphrey to day issued the formal order assuming command together with a few words to the Regt. They were to the point and speak well for the new administration. The order was read at parade. The Lt. Col. was absent but the Major was present and allowed himself to be betrayed into one very foolish expression, viz "that he should not be driven in that way to resign so as to give any Captain his place." To say such a thing was very impolitic. It is true we hoped that he would do so. I had that idea in my mind some six months ago when we first laid our plans. We hoped so to speak to kill three birds with one stone, ie to put in one man whom we wanted & to put out two whom we did not want. Their tameness seems likely to disappoint us this time.

Our Chaplain preached one of his empty, sonorous sermons to day. There is no more piety about him than about the wooden horse whereon delinquent soldiers are treated to a free ride. He is cool, calculating, deceitful, all self and good authority on the practical affairs of life provided he will tell the truth. I keep on the right side of him & he has assisted me on several occasions & is willing I think to do so in some other matters. I could be Major of this Regt. if I liked but whether I will do so just now is not so certain. I think I will wait a while. I am not very urgent on the question of promotion. A Captain's place is a good one & if I were to serve in it about a year it would be no great matter.

Orders at 10 P.M. to march at 3 A.M. to morrow. Nothing known as to the direction.

§ APRIL 27 Reveille at 3 A.M. The advance started at six but the train was some what delayed & we being the rear guard did not start till 7. Marched 7 miles without halting & then stopped for dinner. Made 18 miles in all day & camped near Campbellsville. Country very fine, roads good but very dusty.

§ APRIL 28 Marched 10 miles to Green river & camped near Sublette bridge. We were rear guard again. There were many stragglers from the advance & it was only by a sound application of the flat of the sword across their shoulders that they were urged to the front. Three Regts. crossed the river by fording and went on farther. The 17th [Michigan] remained with us. The bridge at this place was burned by Morgan* in Jan. The country is rich & well watered & timbered, the landscape fine. The river is abt 50 yards wide, water clear, banks steep & rocky.

§ APRIL 29 The 17th crossed the river this m'g & marched toward Columbia. It is reported that the 20th [Michigan] have reached the Cumberland & that a skirmish has taken place. The weather is warm & showery.

§ MAY 1, 1863 Weather very fine. We still remain at Sublette bridge. I think we shall remain here to rebuild the bridge.

§ MAY 5 One year ago to day we fought at Williamsburgh. If it had been as fine a day as this we would have done much better work. The news is cheering both from East & South. If I were once more under Hooker I would be glad. I dislike to be here building log bridges away from everybody & everything while others are engaged in a soldier's legitimate duty. We are nobody at all so long as we are cooped up here. We see nobody & do nothing.

Since last date I had some difficulty with one of my men. He refused to obey orders. I took a gun & punched him pretty smartly with the bayonet a few times, then had him tied up & shall keep him at hard labor for the next month. I presume I shall have to shoot him some day. I have done nearly everything else to him that I can.

This is a dull place. Mails come by chance & there is nothing to be had save meal, eggs & whiskey. The last named article causes considerable trouble among the men. There is seldom any difficulty so long as you can keep them away from liquor & women but there always is if you do not.

§ MAY 6 There is one defect from which we suffered so much last year which does not seem as yet provided for. It is a neglect to provide proper reserves in camps of instruction to meet the wastage of the coming campaigns. If the summer's work is as vigorous as may be expected the loss to our armies from all causes cannot be less than 100,000 men. There is some talk of 20,000 men being raised in Ky. for home defense, of 20,000 in Penn. to

---

* Confederate cavalry raider John Hunt Morgan.

be used about Washington & something is said about the draft in N.Y. but no adequate provision is made to create supplies.

50,000 new men should be in camps now & be drilled in the School of the Soldier so that they could be forwarded at any time to fill the ranks of reduced Regts. in the field. Nothing produces a worse effect on the men than to let their Regts. run down in numbers so low as they have been allowed to. If the places are filled promptly they take little notice of the actual loss. If this is neglected we shall find as we did last year that we shall be on the brink of disastrous defeat for want of men just at the time when we should be gaining our greatest victories. The men for instruction should be put into secure camps, those from Mich. for instance on to some island in the lakes. Officers distinguished for rigid discipline & their qualities as instructors should be detailed from old Regts. & a few experienced soldiers placed under their command to take charge of these camps & the recruits from the first hour held strictly to their duties.

§ MAY 10 Weather is very fine. The news from the East is neither so good as we hoped nor so bad as we feared. On the whole I think we have the best of it & I believe that the offensive will be resumed again at once. Stoneman's expedition is worth everything both on account of what he did & as proof of what may be done again.*

We have a good band once more (just enlisted) which puts new life into everyone. Music is almost as necessary for soldiers as rations. Co. E goes on picket to morrow. Bradley is temporarily detailed on duty with Co. I.

There is a report to night that Richmond is taken by Keys but we are not at all disposed to believe it. Still the thing is not impossible. Our cavalry went from near Richmond direct to Keys & of course informed him that all communication with Lee was cut, that the garrison was very small, the telegraph would inform him of the high water, he could march to Richmond in 48 hours.† If previous reports are true it is possible. God grant it may be so.

---

* The Army of the Potomac, defeated at Chancellorsville on May 1–4, did not in fact resume the offensive. George Stoneman's cavalry expedition was an ineffectual part of the campaign.

† Erasmus Keyes's command, on the Virginia Peninsula, did not advance on Richmond during the Chancellorsville campaign.

§ MAY 11 We received orders at daylight to be ready to march in 25 minutes with 3 days' rations. We marched accordingly & reached Columbia about noon. The country is timbered heavily, appears to be good but is thinly settled. We passed through the town & encamped about a half mile out. From here to the Cumberland the timber is almost exclusively oak and the soil poor. The 20th [Michigan] were initiated last night near the Cumberland & paid 3 officers & 20 men killed & wounded as the price. We came out for the purpose of reinforcing but they were ordered back to this place. Co. E went on picket at night.

§ MAY 12 The 20th & Jacob's [9th Kentucky] Cavalry returned from the front this m'g.

§ MAY 13 A flag of truce came in from Morgan & we were all turned out under arms. It was sent on pretense of looking after the wounded but was really a cover for spies. It rained quite hard to day & very hard at night. We have nothing but our blankets & two pieces shelter tent for four of us & got pretty wet.

§ MAY 14 Co. E went on picket again this m'g. Our folks returned the flag of truce of yesterday & sent out two ambulances to look after the wounded.

§ MAY 15 In camp once more & a very fine one it is. I board with a citizen nearby & live well. He is the only man in this county who voted for Lincoln & is entirely sound on the main question but has some doubts about the [Emancipation] Proclamation. He has two very pretty daughters, owns no slaves, the girls & the old lady do the work, consequently everything is neat, tidy & homelike about the house. The provisions are good & well cooked, put on to the table in proper shape & the dishes succeed each other in a civilized manner, which is a thing very uncommon in the South.

The girls are pretty, intelligent & have some education and are already popular with the officers of the Regt. In point of beauty & sprightliness they are however not to be compared with the Italian sisters who were for a time the pets of the Regt. & considered as almost part of its organization. I presume however that their daily walk is much more correct & that is a great deal in these times.

I have some trouble about my Sergts. The Capt. of a Co. with Sergts. who are to be promoted stands much in the same position as a mother who has more daughters than she can easily find eligible positions in which to establish them. Promotions are very necessary to stimulate ambition & beget careful attention to duty. For a year & a half the Sergts. of this Co. were handled in the worst possible manner. It is no easy matter to bring them up to the rules of strict propriety. The senior ought to be promoted first but the thing seems impossible. I have nearly exhausted my ingenuity & have no prospect of raising him.

We are nearly as far South here as at Newport News but there is very little in the vegetation to indicate it. The maples and beech have a denser foliage surpassing in beauty anything of the kind I have seen. There are now and then along the rivers patches of tall canebrakes such as we use at home for fish poles. Aside from these one sees very little different from the timbered land at home.

§ MAY 17 Morgan is reported to have crossed the Cumberland with 3500 men & is thought to be about 18 miles from us. If such is the case we shall probably hear from him in a day or two. Nothing would please us better.

§ MAY 18 All quiet. A party of Morgan's scouts stole some horses yesterday only six miles out but there seems little probability of any movement in force.

§ MAY 22 Since last date (about the 18th) we have been in camp near Columbia. I was on picket again 3 days ago & shall continue to perform that duty once in five days till a change in the programme. The Rebs have crossed the Cumberland & are ranging the country between here & there. They carry off all the horses, all the clothing, cloth, bed clothing &c and some cattle & other provisions. They shoot or hang more or less of the citizens every day & burn some houses & other property. Their conduct is that of a horde of Arabs.

The Ky. Cav. stationed here pursue them with tolerable activity, kill some & capture a few. The citizens shoot a good many. Great numbers of horses are going north & the people themselves are fleeing for protection. We still live well at the house of our hospitable Ky. friend, entertained likewise by the bright eyes & rosy cheeks of his two pretty daughters.

1st Lt. Jos. Burger has resigned. I am sorry. He was a brave, energetic officer from the liberty inspiring hills of old Switzerland. He was possessed of a high sense of honor & propriety as well as the most unblemished integrity. A fixed rheumatism caused by exposure compelled him to leave the service.

Benson has written me for a certificate from the officers of this

Regt. as to his loyalty. I do not really believe he was at any time disloyal. An unruly tongue has however driven him out of this Regt. & estopped him from again entering service from Michigan.

§ MAY 27 We left camp at dark in light order. Marched 13 miles on the Jamestown road & bivouaced.

§ MAY 28 Marched 5 miles to Jamestown, halted & looked around the country for rebels.

§ MAY 29 A rainy day. There was some scouting and one Reb was captured by our Regt. & a few others by the Cav.

§ MAY 30 Started for home at 2½ P.M., had a race with the 8th & 79th. Marched the last 10 miles (of the 18) in two hours & in the midst of heavy rain, beat them badly.

§ MAY 31 A leave of absence came for me to day.

§ JUNE 1, 1863 We received two months' pay.

§ JUNE 2 I started for home to day. Of course there had to be an affecting separation between Kate & Mary & myself. It was not in all respects satisfactory to me. There being but little time & there being a good many people at the house I was unable to see them apart & was therefore unwilling to say many things which I desired to one while the other, who liked me much the best of the two, was present. Their small brother, a young imp, persisted in being present, and appeared perfectly crazy with delight. He immediately ran to the dining room & related to his mother in presence of the family chaplain & divers others with most astonishing correctness all he had seen & heard. This agitated the old lady considerably & caused her to make a very unnecessary visit at a time when she was not at all needed. She insisted that there had been a greater display of affection than the occasion required. In consideration however of the fact that it was not likely to be soon repeated she became serene again.

The best having been done that could be under the circumstances, I took stage for Campbellsville where I arrived at dark. I put up at a most villainous place which they called a hotel. I had several thousand dollars in money which I was bringing home for the soldiers & was not sorry when I saw a brother officer come in from Lebanon & put up for the night. Soon after we went to bed some drunken Quartermasters came & made such a row that there was no sleep to be had during the night.

§ JUNE 10 Suffice to say that I arrived safely at home, had a good time & am to start back to night. Much might be said of all I have seen & enjoyed but I have no time now. Our Corps is ordered to Vicksburgh. I have probably seen the black eyes & rosy cheeks of Mary R. for the last time. I once thought of a soldier's marriage with her.* It is undoubtedly better for both that the ceremony was not performed. The sharing of my pay would not in the end have been a compensation for the chances of permanent settlement which she would have lost. Furthermore I suspect she would have pleaded more strongly for the continuance of the contract than would have been pleasant. Even in a legal point of view things might turn up which would make it difficult.

I left home, went to Decatur. I put up at a hotel & had a good sleep before (2 A.M.) car time. I consider myself on the road to Vicksburgh. It was harder parting with the folks at home than I expected. After all there is no place quite like home even to a soldier. The ever changing scenes and companions which render transient the attachments to other places seem to strengthen it as to this. I suppose everyone's happiness & good nature has its own level. If it is forced above the level one day by outward circumstances it falls as far below on the next by way of reaction. The ebb is equal to the flood.

§ JUNE 11 I took the cars at 2 A.M. & reached Michigan City about 5 A.M. I fell in with Major Huston & Lt. Rexford of the 4th [Michigan] Cavalry. We strolled around town till 9.50 A.M. & then left for Indianapolis where we arrived abt sundown. I here fell in with a Mich. man belonging to the Commissary Dept. of our Div. Left the place abt dark.

§ JUNE 12 Reached Louisville about 2 A.M. Stopped at the Louisville Hotel. I find that the rear of our Div. is about 24 hours ahead of us. I fall in with my 1st Lt. who is Asst. Qmr. of the Corps & who says he has a boat which will start for Cairo in a few hours. At 5 P.M. he assures me that his boat will leave. I make all haste to reach that place, wait till 7 P.M. & learn that his boat will not leave under 24 hours & that it will probably be 4 days going to Cairo. I make for the cars at top speed & reach them just in time.

I swore for a few minutes abt Qmrs. in general & my Lt. in particular, then relapsed into a sleep which was unbroken till we

---

* Presumably "Mary R." was Haydon's Michigan acquaintance, not his Kentucky one.

changed cars at Mitchell. I slept well after that, with one exception, till we reached Centralia at sunrise. Some one at the opposite end of the car, without any previous arrangement, tried to get into bed with somebody else & there was considerable noise & the conductor was called &c.

§ JUNE 13 We take breakfast at Odin & leave for Cairo about 9 A.M. where we arrive abt 5 P.M. I lost no time in going on board the steamer Atlantic bound for Memphis. The weather is very hot & I have felt more fears of sickness to day than at any time since I joined the army. At sundown we find ourselves afloat on the Father of Waters, the river of Iniquity & Disasters.

§ JUNE 14 I was up at sunrise. The m'g is fine & cool & I am feeling remarkably well. The boat is tied to the shore & some 15–20 men are engaged in a very unyankeelike manner backing wood on board. We are soon sweeping down the long curves at a good rate. The shores are low but not at this season wet. There is [no] kind of traveling like steamboating. If one could take his own house with him he would not be more comfortable.

The Miss. River is a curious place for speculations on theology but I nevertheless indulged quite extensively to day and considered matters in a most serious light. I am slightly inclined to the belief that Mr. Pope's (not the Genl.) saying "What ever is — is right" announces the true doctrine.* A man has only to follow the prompting of his own nature. This however destroys free will & fixes everyone's fate even to the smallest act beyond his control. This leads to very curious results & conclusions. It is a plausible, easy going theory & would be a good one for me if I only believed it. It *seems* to be very correct, still I have little faith in it.

The opposite theory looks well in some respects but I cant see its foundations. In the one you get good conclusions from seemingly bad premises, in the other you get seemingly bad conclusions from good premises. I try to think honestly on such matters. I do not care enough about it either way to be bigoted or prejudiced.

We reached Memphis about 10 P.M.

§ JUNE 15 We are still at Memphis on board the Atlantic. The rear of our Div. left here yesterday. I am anxious to be off. Night finds us still at Memphis. The day has been hot. I strolled around

---

* Alexander Pope, *An Essay on Man.*

town awhile in the m'g. It is not a bad looking place. There is a large amt of cotton here, probably 30,000 bales. During the balance of the day I remained on board playing spectator. Contrabands were busy with drays hauling cotton. The boat hands labored hard in piling hard tack, pork, bales of hay &c on our decks. I would be almost anything sooner than a deck hand on a Miss. steamboat. The soldiers hauled in a great many big bellied, lubberly catfish weighing from 20 to 40 lbs. each and for further amusement rolled the female contrabands about all ends uppermost. The passengers read novels, smoked cigars, drank cherry cobblers, mint juleps &c.

§ JUNE 16 We were to have been off at an early hour without fail but a dispute arose between the Captain of the boat & the post Qmr. in consequence of which we were delayed till noon. There was a fine shower about 3 P.M. There was never a journey on which it is more absolutely necessary to take things cool than on this. It is however no easy matter. We get no news from Vicksburgh but most of the boats from that way have more or less shot holes in them. We reach Helena, Ark. (70 miles) in six hours. This is encouraging. Here is a considerable body of troops. We start after ½ hour convoyed by Gunboat No. 4.

§ JUNE 17 When I awoke I found the boat tied up at Napoleon, Ark. which is said to have been one of the wickedest little towns in the South West. It is now nearly deserted. Learning that there is a body of Rebs up in the country about a mile the boat is pulled out into the river & anchored. Someone, whether from the gun boat or town I know not, fired the buildings nearest us & about a dozen were burned. The boat had to be moved to keep clear of the fire. The gun boat has reached the end of its beat & we have been waiting all day for a convoy. Time hangs heavily. There was a fine shower this afternoon.

We have as passengers about a dozen officers whose Regts. are below, a few citizens, my friend Buckingham of the Commissary Dept. A reporter for the [New York] Herald who but for the business he is in would appear to be a very fine man. A reporter for some other paper, a regular jackass of a chap, has the generosity to make a great deal of sport for others at his own expense.

§ JUNE 18 The convoy came up last night with 3 boats and we pulled out abt sunrise. There were six boats beside the convoy & several barges in tow loaded with hay and coal. It was slow business until abt 2 P.M. when our boat & 2 others ranged ahead & took a

15 mile gait. The country along the river looks better to day. Many of the houses have been burned but those which remain have a more decent look. The low sand flats are not numerous or so extensive & the plantations are not all of them covered with old girdlings. The country is more thickly settled. The weather is quite comfortable.

§ JUNE 19 We found ourselves this m'g at Young's Point, La. opposite the mouth of the Yazoo. I went ashore and looked about but could get no definite news of the Regt. Soon after we started up the Yazoo, came about 12 miles to Snyder's Bluff. We found the Regt. about 2 miles back from the river & about 15 miles from Vicksburgh. It is a very rough, broken country & I think pretty healthy for this latitude. I am in good health & spirits and find the Regt. ditto. Next to home there is no place like the camp of the Mich. 2d.

Thirteen

NO DOUBT
THAT I WAS HIT

Rather than taking part directly in the siege of Vicksburg, the 2nd Mich-
igan was part of the force posted to the north along the Yazoo River to
guard against any attempt by Joseph E. Johnston's Confederate forces to
relieve the besieged city. Following Vicksburg's surrender on July 4, 1863,
Grant turned troops eastward against Johnston at Jackson, Mississippi's
capital. It was there, on July 11, at the head of his company storming a
Rebel position, that Charles Haydon was seriously wounded.

His journal for the next few months is sketchy as his recuperation went
slowly, hampered by setbacks. "I have felt little like journalizing for some
time," he wrote on September 18. At a military hospital in Cincinnati he
suffered from deep depression, which only eased after he obtained a medical
leave to complete his convalescence at home in Michigan.

In mid-December 1863 Haydon set out to rejoin his regiment, now at
Knoxville, Tennessee, leading a wagon train (he had been promoted to
lieutenant colonel) through a harrowing 160-mile journey from central
Kentucky. He reached the camp of the 2nd Michigan on the last day of
the year "& was very cordially received even by those from whom I least
expected it."

* * *

§ JUNE 20, 1863 We are really down South — Latitude 32° 20′,
a degree south of Charleston, on a line with the great desert of

Africa. Everything looks new and at this point not very pleasing. The hills are not high but the ground is in all conceivable shapes & so full of ravines as to be almost impassable. The water is brackish & bad, very bad. The woods are oak, basswood, sycamore, cottonwood, magnolia, palmetto &c. They are so full of underbrush, briars, nettles, poisonous weeds and such like that it is very unpleasant & difficult to get through them. The trees are loaded with the long grey Southern moss which hangs from the limbs in clusters & sheets from 2 to 10 feet in length (perpendicular) and swings loose in the wind. This gives to everything a sort of dull sombre appearance. It looks old, very old, as though everything was on the decline.

Canebrakes such as we buy at home for fish poles are very abundant & are used by the men for almost everything. There are some *alligators,* a good many snakes, lizards everywhere, plenty of mosquitoes, flies, bugs, tarantulas, horned frogs & other infernal machines too numerous to mention. I have not been far into the woods. I went up to the edge once to day & very cautiously looked in a little way then walked off. I am not much afraid of snakes but I do not wish to provoke any unnecessary collision. They say that in the woods snakes & lizards tumble down on your head every few steps but could not swear to that. There are blackberries & wild plums in abundance, ripe & inviting.

There was terrific firing at Vicksburgh this m'g commencing before daylight. How I wish we could go down to the front where there is something doing. I saw Lt. Col. [Dwight] May and several other acquaintances from Michigan.

Our Regt. got very drunk on the way here. Moore and Montague had their hands full with Co. E. I have had experience enough in loading drunken soldiers onto boats & cars. They act like devils. If they should act so when sober it would not take long to adjust matters but in this case you have to tolerate some things which you would not at any other time. The men know perfectly well that as a rule the officers want to get drunk as bad as they do & that if it were not for the responsibility & their presence they would.

Still I do not believe that many of them would drink much after they had been out of the army a few days. A soldier never knows one day where he may be the next & his hold on the future being so uncertain he crowds the present to the utmost. "Eat drink & be merry for to morrow you die."* I know by experience how powerfully those words appeal to the desires & if I do not indulge in wine as others do I presume it is only because other things please me more.

After some months of hard fare you arrive in a city. There is no one there who knows you except comrades who never tell tales. You have money & opportunity. Everything within you says there is no law or restraint here. Do as you please. "Let joy be unconfined."† It may be your last chance. Everyone seems to think you are doing exactly right & to be anxious to help you in all your undertakings. Be careful & you will meet your Chaplain or hear his voice in the next room. But enough of this. Those who have tried it know all about it & those who have not can never learn from mere description.

There must be an increase of sickness if we remain here long. I am not much afraid of disease but can see the possibility of hard times ahead. The darkies are jubilant. "God bless Massa Lincum" say they all. They do nothing now but gather blackberries & plums to sell together with their master's property to soldiers. I saw a planter try to stop one who threw down his hoe & was walking off. He called out to him "where are you going?" "Oh I'se gwine to 'list — yah, yah, yah" was the reply & off he went & three others after him.

Their employment as soldiers is looked upon here with much more favor than in the Army of the Potomac. They are pretty well posted & are nearly all anxious to fight. It is thought here that they will make good soldiers. I find that my late journey amounts to about 2000 miles & that of the Regt. to about 1200 miles. There is no further need of troops in this vicinity.

§ JUNE 21 I went out with Capt. Moore & Lt. Bradley and picked blackberries. The supply is unlimited. The day has been cool & quiet.

§ JUNE 23 The day as usual was warm & the dust is the worst I have ever seen. There is a light rain to night. It is much needed. Many of the Regts. have to go more than a mile for water. The firing at Vicksburgh is regular but not rapid. We have some pros-

---

* A coinage from Luke 12:19 ("take thine ease, eat, drink, and be merry") and Isaiah 22:13 ("let us eat and drink; for tomorrow we shall die").
†Byron, *Childe Harold's Pilgrimage.*

pect of a brush here. [Joseph E.] Johnston is reported to have crossed the Big Black. We got a paper of the 16th to day from which we learn that Lee is in Penn. How damnable slow the conscription is. With 50,000 new troops Lee's army could never reach Va. [again]. As it is I fear a mere repulse & a successful retreat.

Our people are just commencing what ought to have been completed two months ago. We are fortifying at this point. It is of the utmost importance that Vicksburgh should be off our hands very soon so that the troops can be used elsewhere. On discipline & conscription the Govt. is fearfully weak. Why dally and take months over taking a few men. What are they good for if not to use when needed. Put them into the field & make it safer for them to stay there than to try to get away.

§ J UNE 24 We were called out at 4 A.M. for fatigue & worked on rifle pits till sundown. The day was hot but a large amt of work was accomplished. I never saw men take hold better. We shall be ready for Johnston shortly. There are all manner of rumors of doings in the outside world but we pay little heed to them. The firing at Vicksburgh has been very heavy all day.

§ J UNE 25 A very warm day. There has been very heavy firing at Vicksburgh especially toward night. The report of the capture of Port Hudson is confirmed.* Report also says that our mail boat is sunk in the river above; that some of our batteries were blown up at Vicksburgh &c but we get no news from reliable sources.

§ J UNE 27 Yesterday was much like to day which has been hot with some prospect of rain. When you keep quiet you do not appreciate the heat but as soon as you exercise it becomes evident enough. It is so constant, regular & all pervading as scarcely to be perceptible till you try to work. You are bathed in perspiration almost as soon as you conceive the idea of doing anything. A good amt of labor can however be performed without very much danger.

The country is not so bad after all as I was at first led to believe. There are not so many snakes or other infernal machines as was represented. The alligators eat some soldiers but if the soldiers would keep out of the river they would not be eaten. We have very good water now & are living pretty well. It is a paradise compared

---

* Port Hudson, Louisiana, also under Federal siege, would not surrender until July 8.

with Harrison's Ldg. Vicksburgh is not yet taken but the news is favorable. We get very little news from abroad.

§ JUNE 28 Sunday. There was a fatigue party out to day but there was no inspection except at the option of Co. Comdrs. There are so many Penn. officers in this Corps that one can hardly breathe free. We shall do little I fear till we get clear of some of them.

I learned to day considerably to my surprise that two young ladies of my acquaintance at Kalamazoo both of the highest circle had found "babies for their cradles before they had husbands for their beds." The soldiers will have to go home to reform the morals of the people or to make morals for them for I conclude there can be little left to reform. News from Vicksburgh is cheering but not very important. We get no mail from home.

§ JUNE 29 At 8 A.M. we recd orders to march in an hour. We marched to Flower Hill Church abt 7 miles south east. The dust is full 4 inches deep, fine & light as flour. The weather is exceedingly warm. The heat reflected from the sand seems to scorch like a blaze of fire. Water is very scarce. The woods along the road are very fine. The trees are many of them very large, 6 to 10 ft. in diameter, with leaves more than double the size of the same kinds in Michigan. The magnolias were in full bloom the white flowers contrasting beautifully with the incomparable green of the leaves. Peaches seem to grow wild. Fig trees are common & are loaded with green fruit.

The soldiers could not forget even amid their toils that there was a time (so says tradition) when a single fig leaf was all that concealed the charms of woman. As for association's sake they caressed the leaves some discussion arose as to the fitness of Eve's choice for her first & at that time her only garment. It being the first article used to conceal her loveliness some were inclined to look upon it with disfavor. It was however soon suggested that the concealment was so slight that her charms half concealed, half disclosed were more exciting than if seen in their full glory. I suppose Eve did not think that her simple efforts at dress making & modesty would be discussed by her boys after so many years. I have no doubt she was a fine lady & very beautiful but altogether too fond of apples.

§ JUNE 30 I was not well to day but I would not go on the sick list. I had a bad diarhoae, was sick at the stomach, vomiting &c and limber as to the legs. I ate too many blackberries last night. I think I saw 100 bushels of them on 4 acres. The weather is terrible hot & I have felt very much wilted all day. I finally made up my mind to feel bad to day unless something unusual happened. I peeled a quantity of sweet gum bark & chewed it to regulate my bowels. I ate nothing & resolved to be well to morrow. There are a plenty of green corn, cucumbers, squashes &c but I am a little afraid of them although I saw the Surgeon eating of them.

§ JULY 1, 1863 I am in fine health & spirits. The weather is more moderate. About noon Montague is driving a stake with an axe. The axe slips off the helve & gives me a cut & a bruise on the leg just below the knee. It is quite unpleasant but I think I shall not be compelled to lie off.

2nd Lt. Fred. Wilkinson's resignation granted to day. 2nd Lt. D. C. Morrison cashiered for drunkenness by a Ct. Martial order recd to day.

Nothing can exceed the beauty of the evenings in this latitude. There is one great drawback. The infernal jiggers alias sand fleas eat the very flesh off one's bones. These are not the proper jiggers but a sort of red flea.

§ JULY 2 I am quite lame to day but otherwise in good condition. They are talking about a fight near here but I can see few indications of it. I distrust the capability of the general officers of the [Ninth] Corps & fear that a battle would not add much to our reputation. Our Regt. about a year ago was used to fighting without much aid from field officers & now that it has a Colonel it may go through decently on its own hook. The Regt. was called out for fatigue at 3 A.M.

§ JULY 4 Early in the morning there were rumors of the surrender of Vicksburgh all of which were happily confirmed in the afternoon. At 4 P.M. an order was recd to march at once. We marched about 7 miles towards the [Big] Black River.

§ JULY 5 We lay in camp till abt noon & then marched two miles toward Black River. Camped in a very fine place, beautiful oak woods, cool & open. Water scarce. Killed a very large rattlesnake in camp.

§ JULY 6 There was much talk abt moving suddenly & we fell in several times but remained all day in camp. There was a light rain at night.

§ JULY 7 We marched at noon across the Black & through abt 2 miles of cypress swamp. Weather very hot, many men drop down from its effects. After we got out of the swamp it was cooler and we marched very leisurely till dark.

Soon after sundown there were signs of rain and abt 9 P.M. commenced one of the worst storms I ever saw. The wind blew very hard, the rain fell in perfect torrents drenching one to the skin in a moment's time. The thunder & lightning I never saw surpassed. The road which was very dusty before now became so slippery that we could hardly stand & it was impossible except during the flashes to see a person two feet in front. We marched four abreast with arms locked to keep from slipping & felt our way before us like blind men. We bivouaced abt 11 P.M. The rain had ceased & we were chilly enough. Fortunately there were plenty of rails near. A good fire & a cup of coffee soon fitted us for a sound sleep in wet blankets.

§ JULY 10 By very ill arranged & toilsome marches (not because of their length) we arrived last night within abt 6 miles of Jackson. We were up early & advanced very slowly & stopped for dinner abt 3 miles from the city. Just as we had finished there were a few shots in front & word came that the enemy were about to attack. The 79th N.Y. were hastily deployed as skirmishers & supported by the 2d, advanced through a large corn field to see what could be found in front. The whole force followed close after & by dark we crossed the [Vicksburg & Jackson] railroad & passed the Insane Asylum with only a few stray shots from the enemies' scouts. The day was very hot. Five men of my Co. were sunstruck. We bivouaced in line. Since crossing the Black the country has been almost one continuous corn field. A very large proportion of the land is cultivated & the country is much the finest which I have seen in the Confederacy.

§ JULY 11 We were up at 3 A.M. I had very little supper & no breakfast. Our clothes are constantly wet with sweat & having no water to wash we are suffering terribly from sores, eruptions & a breaking out of the skin which makes one almost raw & feels as though he were in the fire.

A little before sunrise the 2d was deployed as skirmishers covering the front of our brigade and connecting with others on the right & we all slowly advanced. The skirmishers had orders to advance till they drew the fire of the rebel batteries if possible. We had gone but a little way when some Regts. to the right of us which seemed to be resting carelessly received a brisk fire which appeared to be pretty effective. They moved to the rear in very quick time, sent out skirmishers & advanced again. A few shots fell near but no one was struck. We moved forward across a very difficult ravine & gained good cover under a fence with an open field beyond.

Here we encountered a moderate but well directed fire from skirmishers at long range. The whistling of the balls animated the men greatly. Chas. Smith of my Co. recd a severe shot in the leg & some others of the Regt. were struck. We lay here abt an hour when an order came to advance at double quick. We had before us abt 100 rods of open field, then a narrow steep ravine through which runs a brook, then a hill, thick bushes, further on a corn field fence with rifle pits at a short distance. Between us & the fence there were as we have since learned three Regts. of Infantry.

We crossed the open at a run & without much loss, the men full of fire, yelling like devils, Kearney's name being uppermost in their cry. I never felt more eager. Their skirmishers flew before us. We sprang down into the ravine & up the other bank. I tumbled back once & did not get up as quick as most of the others. When I did I found a narrow terrace & another steep bank. The Co. had all halted at the bank & seemed waiting to see who should go up first. I swore a most substantial oath (being indignant at them for stopping) & then we all made a dash at the hill.

It was so steep that only three or four got up at first. The Rebs were about three rods off. I made abt half the distance to them when I was whirled around & laid on my back suddenly, very suddenly & in a manner which left no doubt in my mind that I was hit. All who came up with me shared the same fate.

When I first became conscious, which was very soon, I lay on my back wondering what was to come next. I tried to get up but could not stir so much as a finger, nor could I speak although I could see & hear all that was doing, the trees above & the bullets around. Our men had halted at the brink of the hill so that I lay between the fires. I tried two or three times to rise but finding I could not move I began to reflect on other matters. I now observed that my hands were laid across my breast & in fact that my whole position was that of the greater part of those killed in battle. I then began to question myself as to whether I were not really dead.

I soon discarded this idea but still felt certain that I must die very soon. My whole feeling became one of wonder & curiosity as to the change which I believed I was about to experience. I was in

no pain bodily & no mental anxiety. After abt 2 minutes I heard
Sergt. Keyser of my Co. cry out to the men "G-d d--n your souls
are you going to leave the Capt. lying there?" A second after
he with eminent danger to himself sprang forward & caught
me by the arm. The instant he touched me I sprang to my feet.
Just then the Regt. went past on a charge driving the enemy before them. I tried to give my Co. a word of encouragement but
my throat was so full of blood that I strangled when I attempted
to speak.

With the aid of the Sergt. I walked back to the brook & lay down
partly in it. He gave me water to drink & poured it over me in
large quantities. I soon got up again & with his aid walked back
50 to 60 rods & lay down again. I could speak pretty well now but
still threw up large quantities of blood from the lungs. I was soon
able to walk again & started but met some men with a stretcher
who carried me to the field hospital. But for the aid of the Sergt.
I should have fallen into the hands of the enemy as the Regt. being
wholly unsupported was very soon compelled to fall back.

My Co. numbered for the fight 18 men & 2 officers. One man
was killed & four wounded. Both officers were wounded, Lt. Montague receiving a severe flesh wound below the knee. The Regt.
lost 58 killed & wounded.* I never saw better fighting done but
the want of support rendered it of little avail beyond the mere
number of the enemy killed which was however very considerable.

On arriving at the Hospt. my wound was dressed, my chances
of recovery discussed, some encouragement was given by the Sur-
geons & I resolved to get well. I was laid on a blanket under a tree
& soon after ate a good dinner to make up for the want of breakfast. No very severe pain to day. The ball struck me in the right
shoulder abt an inch below the collar bone & passed out just at
the lower edge of the shoulder blade.

§ JULY 12 I had very little sleep last night but feel quite comfortable this m'g. We were moved back towards night abt a mile
to get out of range of the cannon. About 4 days after this I was
taken with a fever which lasted two days & left me so low that I
could hardly speak. It was about the 18th I think when our corps
started back to Snyder's Bluff. At first they intended to leave me

---

* The 2nd Michigan's losses were officially listed as 9 killed, 40 wounded, and 10
  missing, a total of 59.

& a few others for the rebels thinking that we would die if they attempted to move us. Finally however we were taken. I was carried 10 miles on a stretcher & rode the rest of the way in an ambulance. We were 2½ days on the way & I reached Snyder's Bluff with very little life in me. With good care I revived rapidly. On the 28th I was able to make the following notes.*

§ JULY 28 Heavy shower of rain, high wind, tent nearly blown down. In default of wine we drink milk punch 3 times a day. Our living is passable. I can write or read very little — too weak. I am beginning to walk again. I am very tired of lying abed. Wound doing well.

§ JULY 29 Weather cool & pleasant. I have walked 30 or 40 rods to day & have felt well except a toothache. A great many men of the Div. are dying but none of our Regt.

§ JULY 30 They gave us some assurance that we would start north to morrow. It delights us beyond measure. Lt. Col. Dillman resigned.

§ JULY 31 We were disappointed about starting to day. I am doing well but the weather is hot & the bed very tiresome. I long for good northern air. I live as well as I can but that is none of the best.

§ AUGUST 1–27, 1863 We went on board Augt. 1st & on the 12th arrived at Cincinnati where I was at once sent to the Marine Hospt. Soon after embarking I was taken with the most terrible pain I ever suffered. It continued for several days. I believe that morphine was all that kept me from jumping overboard. I declined gradually during the whole journey. At Hospt. I had excellent care & again slowly revived.

§ AUGUST 28 Marine Hospital, Cincinnati, Ohio. Journal resumed. This cool comfortable day finds me feeling pretty, ie nearly, free from pain & at 10 A.M. sitting at the table pencil in hand. I arrived here Augt. 12th weak & exhausted by the journey of 1200 miles up the rivers. For several days I suffered much & improved very little. The pain finally subsided & I am gaining strength quite rapidly. The wound is healing slowly but well. I am anxious to be at home but shall not be able to leave here for some weeks.

---

* This entry and part of the preceding one were written retrospectively, no earlier than July 28 and perhaps later.

§ August 29 The weather is cool, almost cold. Breakfast was a little poorer than usual. There was no change as to kind but a diminution of quality. Recd a letter from Capt. Young. The nurse who has taken care of me (a very faithful man) was sent away & a new & extremely awkward chap substituted.

§ August 30 Sunday. Weather cool & that is about all.

§ September 2, 1863 All the officers have been moved upstairs into one large room. I dont like the arrangement at all. Dr. Davis the Surgeon in charge has returned from temporary absence. He is a very pleasant man but has a professional fondness for probes &c as I learned on his first visit. They all keep feeling around after pieces of bone in the wound as if all the bones in my body were broken & the pieces crammed into this bullet hole. I am doing very well but might do better. I am lonesome, gloomy, impatient. I wish I were at home or with my Regt.

§ September 4 There came near being a row here last night. Some rowdies tried to make a lame soldier who was outside the yard hurrah for Vallandigham.* He balanced himself on one crutch and laid the other over their heads with a will, calling lustily for his comrades. They as many as were able were not slow in coming to the rescue. As soon as they could get him away they all ran to a stone pile & let drive with might & main at the crowd which had now collected, at the same time calling to their comrades inside to hand on guns & pistols. Fortunately the police interfered. Three persons in the crowd were badly hurt & some stones were thrown into the Hospt. Soldiers know how to deal with traitors.

Four of the officers start for home on "leave" to night.

§ September 5 I went outside the yard to day for the first time. The jar of walking on pavement hurt me a little but I walked about 40 rods & back. It did me good mentally more than physically. My body is better now than my mind. I see nothing but sick men, brick walls, dust & coal smoke. I really doubt sometimes whether I am quite myself. It does not seem as if I knew more than half as much as I used to. I try to play checkers but I am all of a tremble before the first game is through. An hour of pleasant conversation would raise me more than a week of this dullness. A

---

* Clement Vallandigham, exiled from the Northern states, was running in absentia for the governorship of Ohio on an antiwar platform.

good many people come here but I dont fancy them & wont talk with them. Things looked better outside than I expected & I feel much encouraged thereby.

§ SEPTEMBER 18 I have felt little like journalizing for some time back. I am greatly improved in health. I could stand quite a march so far as my legs are concerned but the shoulder is not yet healed & the arm needs time before it will be servicable. As I am now Lt. Col. I do not need leg service so much as I used to.*

Yesterday I went out to dinner. Mrs. Caldwell our worthy matron got me into a rather unpleasant position but I came out pleasantly after all. She took me to the house of a friend to dine. I supposed she would remain of course but she went away & left me to my own resources. I found myself at a very elegant establishment with three very agreeable ladies, entire strangers. I would rather have been differently situated but seeing that there was no escape I resolved to make the best of it & accordingly spent two or three hours very agreeably. Had a fine dinner & found my host a very jolly man but too busy to stay longer than to eat his dinner. I went to the theater (Wood's) at night. "The Castle Spectre" was played.

§ SEPTEMBER 19 Went to the theater (Pike's Opera) this P.M., play "Wake Not the Dead." I can walk abt the city now as much as I like.

§ SEPTEMBER 21 I started for home.

§ SEPTEMBER 22 I did not leave Detroit till after dark.

§ SEPTEMBER 23 I arrived at Decatur at 3 A.M. pretty tired, slept a few hours & reached home at 9 A.M.

§ OCTOBER 24, 1863 Since the above I have been getting well as fast as I could. My wound is not yet entirely healed. There was snow yesterday. I do considerable duck shooting, have good success.

§ OCTOBER 29 I spent 4 days in Kalamazoo, came home to day. I had a fine time visiting my old friends.

§ DECEMBER 6, 1863 Sunday night at home. I am sitting by the cheerful old fire place in the dining room. I am nearly well & shall to morrow start for the land of cotton, treason & desolation. The journey for a part of the way bids fair to be anything but

---

* Haydon was promoted to lieutenant colonel on September 11, to rank from July 3.

pleasant. I doubt however that the reality will be as bad as the picture of imagination. If it is true that distance lends enchantment to things beautiful it is doubly true that it lends terror to those which are doubtful.

My leave of absence does not expire till the 10th & I shall journey slowly back to the Marine Hospt. I can tell all about going away from home so much better to morrow that I shall leave it till then. "Sufficient for the day is the evil thereof."*

§ DECEMBER 7 I went to Kalamazoo. Everybody who has been to the wars once knows what it is to leave home for a second campaign.

§ DECEMBER 8 I went to Detroit. Stopped at the Exchange.

§ DECEMBER 9 I went out early & looked about the city. I found my visit a failure. The person I desired to see was elsewhere. I learn that the old 2d is nearly used up. There is hardly enough left to be called a Regt. I met several old acquaintances about town.

§ DECEMBER 10 I started at 10 last night & reached Cincinnati at 11 A.M. to day. It is a dark cloudy day and on the whole rather lonesome. I reported at the Hospt. after dinner. I shall not be discharged till I find some means of going to the Regt. I stop at the Gibson House. I saw Lt. Col. Richardson of the 27th Mich. I was glad enough to see anyone from the Corps. I wish I was with the Regt. again instead of lying here idle. I took a sip from a bottle of wine I brought from home to raise my spirits. I went to Wood's Theater at night and saw Miss Matilda Heron in a poor play made up from [the novel] East Lynn or the Earl's Daughter.

§ DECEMBER 11 Rainy. My wound broke open last night & bled considerably. I went to the hospital & had it dressed. I do not apprehend any trouble from it. What is duller than to be lying here without business or acquaintances. It is worse than solitary confinement. I shall be off as soon as possible. I went to Wood's. Saw Miss Heron play Oliver Twist.

§ DECEMBER 12 By being too inquisitive to day I got into more business than I desired. Having heard that Col. Leasure† had an office in the city for the forwarding of men to the Corps I gave him a call just to inquire about matters & things. Consequence I

---

*Matthew 6:34: "Sufficient unto the day is the evil thereof."
† Col. David Leasure then commanded the brigade to which the 2nd Michigan was assigned.

was seized upon at once & ordered to proceed to Crab Orchard [Kentucky] & take command of a detachment of 280 men which is going to the front as an escort to a large train. We have to carry 20 days' rations. A jolly prospect. I went to Pike's Opera. Saw Miss Lucille Western as Nancy Sykes in Oliver Twist.

§ DECEMBER 13 The weather is very warm & there has been a drizzling rain for 3 days. The roads will be as bad as they can be made. I am all ready for a start.

§ DECEMBER 14 I was up at 4 A.M., took the cars at Covington at 6 A.M. & ran off the track before we got out of the city. Reached Nicholasville at noon & took the stage for Crab Orchard. The weather is cold & raw but not stormy.

In the stage was a lady who had been everywhere, seen everybody and told all about everything she had seen, how polite everyone was to her, how good she felt at one time, how bad at another. In short she talked for six hours without the slightest intermission. She had with her a small boy who contrived with great dexterity to put his feet on everybody in the coach at intervals of about five minutes. There was a newly married couple on the back seat & the bride's sister was with them. The bride was radiant with smiles at all she had enjoyed & the sister with what she hoped to enjoy. The young man sat between them & they overlaid him in a manner quite exciting to beholders. Being a tall man he managed to keep his head above the sea of ribbons & laces which overflowed the balance of his person. A short man would have been smothered. I have not been free from toothache since I left Detroit.

§ DECEMBER 15 I reached Crab Orchard abt midnight & stopped at the dirtiest hotel I ever saw without exception. The detachment is not ready but I hope it soon will be. There is as usual much confusion & delay. The weather is warm & fine. At 8 P.M. there came an order from Gen. [Jeremiah T.] Boyle which was understood to take away my men to another place. If it were not for my trunk I would be very glad to see them go. Without that I could get through in six days. I have been busy with red tape all day but have accomplished little.

§ DECEMBER 16 After much labor, swearing & red tape I left town at 1 P.M. with 155 men, 4 officers & 7 wagons. I have found nothing of the train I was to convoy. The men are a mixed lot of convalescents, stragglers &c from the Corps. With hard labor we made about 2 miles. The wagons stuck fast in the mud every few rods. I went back to town and made arrangements to lighten our load about 2000 lbs. We have a tent & stove. We can live passably. The weather is cold & threatens snow. Thus we passed the first half day & the first 2 miles of the journey (160 miles) to Knoxville. I lost all patience & vowed I would start if we did not get a mile. We have six mules per wagon & I have a miserable rosinante horse from the Govt. stable for myself.

§ DECEMBER 17 We started at 8 A.M. but the mules balked at the outset & delayed us half an hour. There were divers other delays & on the whole we were glad to halt just after passing through Mt. Vernon, having made ten miles. We met Gen. Burnside this morning & I had the honor of shaking hands with him & a moment's conversation. I saw Capt. Poe our former Col. at Mt. Vernon & had a long talk with him. I first learned from him of the death of Major Byington from wounds recd in the great sortie of the 2d at the siege of Knoxville [on November 24].

One wagon rolled over & over to day. The men are a promiscuous lot & brought together for the first time. The officers are strangers to each other & to the men. There is no organization but they did rather better to day than yesterday. There was a heavy shower last night & there have been squalls of rain & snow all day. It requires much patience & perseverance to get along. Our Surgeon Dr. Willets of the 8th Mich. was rolled together with his horse headlong down a bank but fortunately escaped unhurt.

§ DECEMBER 18 It froze very hard last night & there were heavy squalls of snow this morning. The roads bore the wagons for the most part but breaking where the mud was deepest the going was rather worse than yesterday. We however made passable headway till noon whence we came to so bad a hill that with having to pass another train we did not get over till 4 P.M. We camped soon after having made only 5 or 6 miles all day. Our wagonmaster is a very tall man & rides a very small mule. The mule aforesaid lay down with him to day in the middle of a stream and ducked him completely under. This, considering the weather, was not very comfortable.

§ DECEMBER 19 The night was very cold & between that & toothache I got very little sleep. I dozed just long enough to dream of home. The ground froze very hard but the deepest holes will not yet bear. One of the men slipped & dislocated his shoulder this morning. We started at 8 A.M. but the wagons having to ford a stream twice it was noon when we reached Rockcastle river, three miles.

The men mostly avoided the fords. One big, fat, lazy dutchman putting his feet on the axle & hanging to the end board with his hands tried to cross with less trouble. The water was about 3 feet deep & as might be expected the mules stopped just in the middle. The dutchman clung stoutly but his posterior sank "gradually low" into the cold water & then with characteristic intelligence he let go with his hands instead of his feet & went under head foremost.

One man crossed the ford in a wagon & then when I ordered him to assist at the second by riding a lead mule he tried to excuse himself by saying that he could not ride. I told him he must do it or cross on foot & have his rations stopped. He finally got on but the mule threw him, greatly to my delight, all under in the middle of the stream. He ran bellowing to shore & the mules came near drowning.

It snowed a little in the morning but it was clear & very cold during the day. We were two hours ferrying across Rockcastle river. We began the ascent of Wild Cat mountain but made only one mile. Camped on a very steep narrow place by the roadside & killed a beef which we picked up on the way.

§ DECEMBER 20 We took turns last night in sitting up to keep the fire & in this way we slept a part of the time very well. The roads were hard as rock & as rough as could be. We spent four hours getting up a steep slippery hill but having passable roads the rest of the way made 7 miles. The wagonmaster came near breaking his arm. The day was bright but so cold that the ground did not soften in the least. There are great sheets of ice along the cliffs and mountain sides. The country is very rugged & hardly cultivated at all. Inhabitants are few in number & very poor.

§ DECEMBER 21 The night was not as cold as to prevent sleep. We started early on a good road & reached Camp Pitman at 10 A.M. We were delayed till 1 P.M. drawing forage. We made abt 5 miles farther and camped. At a house nearby I saw a fair young woman tending a baby. Of course I said it was a very fine one & asked if it was hers. "Yes." "Where is your husband, Madame?" "I have none." "Oh: widow." "No Sir." "Never married?" "No." "Must have been unfortunate then?" "Yes Sir I was very, but the young man gave me $50 to settle & I said no more about it." Cheap enough thought I to myself.

§ DECEMBER 22 Weather fine, roads much better. We made 12 miles to day. The men's feet have been nearly frozen, are very sore & give much trouble. We have for two days been meeting the stragglers from a train captured near Tazewell [Tennessee]. The road is full of refugees from Georgia & Tennessee. They are very poor, ignorant & dirty but their loyalty atones for a good deal.

§ DECEMBER 23 Weather cold with raw wind & flurries of snow. Roads fair. We passed Barboursville & encamped a mile beyond. Sundry complaints came to me this morning from citizens that the men had been plundering. This did not surprise but it somewhat annoyed me. To one woman who seemed very poor I gave two dollars. I told the others I was very sorry & would do them the best service in my power by marching off as quick as possible. Our forage is all gone & we have to halt here to gather more if possible from the country. I regret the delay very much.

§ DECEMBER 24 The night was very cold but the day beautiful. I sent out a foraging party which procured* 30 bushels of corn & half a ton of hay. We had an Inspection. I corrected the rolls & examined the state of the rations. "Tis the night before Christmas" — not exactly the Christmas of civilization yet I have seen many worse days & nights than this. This delay has been very irksome to me. I begrudge every minute till I am with the Regt. Inasmuch as I shall have no time to morrow I drank to night the last of a bottle of wine I brought from home & wished Merry Christmas to everyone who deserves it.

§ DECEMBER 25 We made full 12 miles. Several men are sick and were delayed somewhat by them. Our road has been along the Cumberland river. It is a very pretty stream. The hills to the height of 300 ft. or more on either side. We are now two miles from Cumberland Ford & 15 miles from the Gap. We camped in a snug little ravine running back from the river. Wood & water are plenty. We picked up another stray ox to day & killed him for supper.

§ DECEMBER 26 Opened with a cold drizzling rain. The roads were very heavy for both men & teams. I was compelled to halt after making 8 miles. We crossed the Cumberland Ford. The hills

---

* In his original notes for this date, Haydon used the verb *seized*.

are several hundred ft. high on either side & their tops were shrouded in clouds & mist.

§ DECEMBER 27 The morning was damp & there was heavy rain from 1 P.M. till after dark. We made 11 miles, passed Cumberland Gap at noon & camped 5 miles beyond at Powell river. We have scant forage for morning & there are no posts from which we can draw. We must push on as fast as possible & pick up what we can by the way. We have been in three states to day. Our view of the mountains was much obscured by clouds & mist. It cleared up for a few minutes & afforded a hasty view. The scenery about the Gap is very grand & the place might be rendered one of immense strength. The highest peak rises at an angle of about 75° & the summit is near 1000 feet above where most of the troops are quartered. On this are 8 pieces of artillery.

I had little chance to look about. It requires all my time & attention to keep things going. I have however succeeded as well as I could expect. There is some degree of organization & efficiency among the men notwithstanding the unfavorable circumstances under which we started. I rather enjoy the journey. The country is much better since we crossed the mountains.

§ DECEMBER 28 It rained till near daylight but the day has been cold & clear. We started at the usual hour. We passed through Tazewell at noon & camped a little beyond. Being entirely out of forage I sent out three teams which returned at night with as much wheat in the bundle as they could bring. To morrow & next day will come the danger if any from the rebels. We are pretty well prepared for them & if we are not stopped we shall reach the Corps in 3 days. I had some trouble with one of the men this morning & I feared that I should be obliged to strike him before I could enforce obedience but did not. We drank a little hot whiskey & water before going to bed to night.

§ DECEMBER 29 We started at 7½ A.M. and except an hour for dinner were on the road till 5 P.M. We forded Clinch river & we are now camped about a mile from it. The roads were very heavy & deep in the forenoon. The country is mountainous but fertile in the valleys. We overtook a supply train of 115 wagons 19 days from Crab Orchard. The guard had deserted it & we are taking it upon ourselves to see it through. Weather cold and fair. We see rebels to morrow if at all.

§ DECEMBER 30 The train started 7½ A.M. & we acted as rear

guard to it till we reached the vicinity of Maynardville & beyond the reach of danger. We then took a road to the left leading to Blaine's Cross Roads. The road nearly all day has been along the beds of shallow streams. We made abt 12 miles. The country is mountainous but the valleys are fertile & generally cultivated. These mountains are full of coal. In many places the road is cut through solid beds of it. It is not mined for want of transportation. I presume that minerals abound.

§ DECEMBER 31 There was a heavy shower of rain & high wind last night. We started at the usual hour, roads very bad, reached Corps headquarters at noon, turned over men, rations, teams &c. I joined the Regt. & was very cordially received even by those from whom I least expected it.

I called on Col. Humphrey comd'g the brigade & arranged about promotions in the Regt. I went to arrange about being mustered* & about mess affairs. I have plenty of work on hand. Times are hard & things look gloomy. I think there can be improvement. I have had a good experience in coming over the mountains. Hard fare is not new to me. I dined with the staff at Corps HdQrs. & supped with Col. Humphrey at Brigade HdQrs.

---

* That is, to be officially sworn in as lieutenant colonel of the 2nd Michigan.

Fourteen

A VALLEY FORGE
WINTER

While Charles Haydon was recuperating from his wounding, the 2nd Michigan had endured the Confederate siege of Knoxville (November 17 to December 5, 1863), losing 93 men killed and wounded there. As Haydon discovered on his return, the lifting of the siege did not end the suffering of the Michigan men, and he termed it their Valley Forge experience. They had to cope with harsh winter conditions on half rations or less. "The small quantity on hand & the prospect of its becoming daily less adds anxiety to actual suffering," he wrote.

The three-year enlistment of the 2nd Michigan would be up on May 25, 1864, and as second-ranking officer that winter Haydon campaigned strenuously for re-enlistment. If three-quarters of the men signed on again, regimental integrity would be honored, status as "veteran volunteers" assured, and, most important, a thirty-day furlough granted. With a certain amount of sleight of hand Haydon succeeded in his campaign. In his journal he also indulged himself in his continuing discussion of military leadership, in which he found the Ninth Corps singularly lacking.

At last, on February 10, 1864, came the long-awaited order to start for Michigan and the regiment's re-enlistment furlough. February 21 found Charles Haydon in Cincinnati, more than halfway home. "I passed the day quietly, it being Sunday," he wrote. It was the final entry in his journal.

* * *

§ JANUARY 1, 1864 This is a very cold & perhaps I might say a very cheerless day. There was a heavy storm of wind & rain last night. It cleared off cold with some snow & high wind. We have much smoke and very little fire, none at all inside the tents. I tried to be mustered again to day but did not succeed — too much red tape. I dined with Capt. Moore. The coffee froze in our saucers but we made way with the greater part of a roast goose. The men are almost naked & barefooted, rations & tents very scant. We get rations of flour from grown & sick wheat. The bread made from it is of a dirty buckwheat color & frequently causes sickness at the stomach. Everything is worn out & tattered. I have been trying to do a little work but for the most part I sit shivering over the fire. Very little can be done in the way of office work.

§ JANUARY 2 I was very cold last night & slept but little. I was determined ere another night to have a tent with a fire in it. Accordingly I have one. It is a very rude arrangement as yet but I can keep warm to night & to morrow I will arrange things better. I have done little else to day but one night will repay my trouble. Our men have for 3 days at a time been compelled to live on parched corn. Corn in the ear was the only ration issued and there was no opportunity to grind it. I was delighted to night by a letter from home.

§ JANUARY 3 My chimney is finished & a bed & table are built. I wrote several letters & other documents. I went again to the circumlocution office & came very near being mustered; so near in fact that I expect to succeed in a day or two. I made a short speech to the men to try to induce them to reenlist. Co. E and some others have done so amounting in all to about 70. The weather is milder. We keep up good spirits & many more are willing to reenlist than I should suppose under the circumstances. I wonder at the fidelity & patriotism of the men.

§ JANUARY 4 There was an Inspection this morning. Hardly a man in the Regt. had any stockings. I saw several whose bare feet came in contact with the frozen ground at every step. The balance of their clothing is little better. All the hardships which time & reality have attributed to Valley Forge are equalled. I have been very busy with office business. I spoke to the men again about reenlisting. No exertion has heretofore been made but it seems likely at present that the required number ¾ can be obtained. In that case we can soon go home. I froze my feet slightly coming over the mountains & they are so sore I can hardly walk.

§ JANUARY 5 I was engaged a part of the day on a Board of Survey. I spent some time in looking after enlistments. We have now enough men enlisted to carry us home.

§ JANUARY 6 This morning when the men were called on to swear in [re-enlist], several of them backed out & we are left in the lurch again. I & several others went to work & have nearly regained the number & have them sworn in. Some of the officers do nothing & I suspect they are secretly dissuading the men. The late inspection shows that of 1100 men in our brigade 400 are without shoes. Of those who had covering for the feet more than half had supplied themselves with boots at the expense of a month's wages per pair. Only 3 men in our Regt. had stockings.

§ JANUARY 7 The 2d is enrolled among the Veteran Volunteer Regts. & will soon be off for home. In spite of all our exertions up to 11 A.M. to day the matter was in doubt. At that time I was obliged to report to Gen. [Edward] Ferrero whether the requisite three fourths was obtained. It was not, but rather than lose the chance I ran the risk & reported that it was. I then notified the men that the matter was decided. A considerable number thinking they were likely to be left in the lurch came forward & were sworn. Our list was soon raised far above the required number.

It is already talked that it would be a fine thing to fill up the Regt., make Col. Humphrey Brigadier & give me his place. I think they are hasty, still it is a thing to be looked after. I never was greedy about promotions, still when one place is filled it is well to be looking toward the next, remembering always that the best way of getting a higher position is to attend carefully to the duties of the one you already hold.

§ JANUARY 8 The Veterans have increased to 167 most of whom have been mustered. Snow fell about two inches deep last night. The weather is very sharp. We made requisition for raw hides to day & each man is to make shoes after his own style. Heretofore my bedding had been limited to one blanket & my overcoat. I was to day fortunate enough to obtain another blanket. I have seen but two newspapers since Dec. 17th, the latest was Dec. 24th.

§ JANUARY 9 I have as usual been very busy with enlistment papers. The weather is clear & very frosty.

§ JANUARY 10 I have as usual been very busy with office work. Last night is thought to have been the coldest of the season. I awoke about 4 A.M. & got up to build a fire. I was so cold that I could not tell whether my feet were on the ground or off. I purchased another blanket to day. Snow is about two inches deep.

§ JANUARY 11 To night an order came changing the brigades. It returns Col. Humphrey to the Regt. & relieves me of course from command. I am very glad indeed to be rid of it just at this time. It will lighten my labors at least one half.

§ JANUARY 12 It is not quite so cold. Provisions are very short. I have thus far had enough meat, bread (mostly corn), coffee & sugar. It is a long time since the men have had more than half rations (from the Govt.) of those articles. The small quantity on hand & the prospect of its becoming daily less adds anxiety to actual suffering. The army has rarely full rations for one day in store & no certain source of supply. There is a mess of four line officers near me. I heard one of them this morning call to their cook "Joe is there anything for breakfast?" "Nothing but coffee Sir." At noon the question is repeated. "Joe is there anything for dinner?" Joe answers briskly "O yes, Sir. I got a pound & a half of meal from the Commissary." This constituted the dinner of four officers & their cook, all of whom had breakfasted on coffee.

My health is excellent & my appetite quite surprising. When I was coming over the mountains I used to eat ¾ of a pound of hard tack for dinner every day. A pound is a full day's ration. Here they never issue more than 6 to 8 ounces per day & that very seldom. My box of hard tack is all gone. The flour we get makes me sick. We have fine air & water & the general health is good.

We expect to start for home soon but I fear there will be delay. Fifty times a day you can hear the men saying "I wish Burnside would come back." They think no one else cares for the 9th Corps. If he was here I know we should fare better.

§ JANUARY 13 Col. Humphrey is detailed on Court Martial so I still remain in command. The weather is mild. The Adjutant came to me to night with the complaint that he had had nothing but one ear of corn all day to eat. This is more due to his inactivity than absolute necessity. He is one of those Germans who like to sit in the corner & smoke all day. He is a very good office Adjutant but deficient in energy.

A very singular case came before me this morning. Few who do not know the South in war time would believe it. I was writing in my tent when the orderly came in & said a boy wanted to see me. I told him to send him. A lad of 17 years appeared. The short of his story was this. His aunt, a young woman of 25, had granted indulgence to a man of our Regt. on the promise of five cents. The man went off without paying. The boy came to make complaint. I dismissed the case.* Capt. Poe told me he could seduce every woman in Tenn. with one haversack full of coffee.

One more case & I close the picture of life in Tenn. A friend of mine stayed over night at a house where there was a young woman of fair features & engaging manners. Her kindness to him reached the utmost bounds of female generosity. He was very short of money but on leaving felt compelled to share with her his purse, light as it was. He handed her ten cents intending to apologize for the smallness of the sum. Before he had time however she looked up to him & very innocently exclaimed "bless me Sir I haven't a cent in change."

§ JANUARY 14 Monotonous.

§ JANUARY 15 The papers of the Veteran 2d are so nearly completed that I am going to take things a little easier to night. I have never been busier than since I returned to the Regt. The Adjt. is new. The Regt. had been for 2 months in charge of its most incompetent Captain. Everything was in arrears. The new organization had to be effected & I had besides a considerable amount of private business. From early in the morning until late at night I have worked. We have to march to Strawberry Plains to morrow. We got half a bushel of dried apples last night & I have lived mainly on apple sauce to day.

§ JANUARY 16 We marched to Strawberry Plains & across the Holston river. The roads were very bad. The men are in rather poor spirits because they were lengthening the road home. I never saw richer land than along the valley of the Holston. In an old cornfield the ears were as high as my head when on horseback. Wheat stubble was knee high & very thick.

§ JANUARY 17 We unexpectedly find ourselves in good quarters. At noon to day I was ordered to take the Regt. (Col. Humphrey

---

* In his original notes Haydon wrote, "As he could not identify the man I dismissed the case."

is at Knoxville) into a large building near the railroad bridge which was formerly used as a Seminary. The 23d Mich. had just moved out leaving as dirty a place as I ever saw. There is a room for each Co. & there are four rooms for the officers. There is a good fire place in each. I fear we shall not enjoy it long for if we do not go home we expect to be ordered to the front. We have had nothing to eat to day but meat & apple sauce. Gen. Wilcox [Orlando B. Willcox] has assumed command of our Corps. I was introduced to him to day. I am glad to see him back. I have more confidence in him than in [Robert B.] Potter.

§ JANUARY 18 Has been a rainy bad day. Col. Humphrey returned from Knoxville to day. He could not buy one particle of anything eatable. There has been a general falling back of trains & troops from the front to day. The roads were heavy & the men straggled badly. It is said these troops moved to the front four days since to get provisions. To day they came back destitute. I do not believe the Govt. has two days' rations in East Tennessee for the troops stationed there.

§ JANUARY 19 There was a cold rain & high wind during the night & snow fell about two inches deep toward morning. The troops which came in from the front had a hard night. The forces are still falling back on Knoxville. Our baggage was sent over the river during the night. There are rumors that our retrograde is forced & hurried but I see little indication of it at the front. A Quartermaster was arrested for circulating such a report which seems to indicate its truth. The railroad bridge which was completed only a week ago is to be burned & some of the baggage will be destroyed. As for rations there can be no great loss. Men & officers have to live mainly at their own expense. The beef cattle & the hogs die by dozens of starvation. When they get too weak to drive they are killed for our use. There is danger that all the Govt. animals will die for want of forage. Our own breakfast consisted of one biscuit for five of us & some fried pork — dinner, meat — supper the same. About 10 P.M. we got four ounces of flour per man.

§ JANUARY 20 We got some more flour this morning & there being an abundance of cattle too poor to drive we had plenty of provisions. Just before supper when we were all talking about going home & what we would do when we got there, an order came to fall in instanter. We complied, stacked arms, loaded our baggage, waited half an hour & then went back to supper. A dash was made on our picket line.

§ JANUARY 21 Just after midnight we were ordered to cross the river at once. We moved about two miles down the railroad, turned off into the woods & bivouaced. We had no blankets but wood was plenty. I leaned against a tree & slept well from 3 till 7 A.M. Every expedient is resorted to for food. Raw corn & wheat are roasted, boiled, fried, pounded, ground in coffee mills &c. We have a very fine camp among the cedars. The bridge was destroyed during the night. There were scattering musket shots from 10 A.M. & artillery opened & continued slowly till dark. One man of Co. K was wounded. The teams have gone to the rear with our baggage & blankets. In spite of short rations the utmost cheerfulness & good feeling prevails. The band played a few good tunes to night. I pity the poor inhabitants whom we leave in our rear. We discovered a cave which we explored to night. It extended about 100 feet & there flowed a fine stream of water through the lower apartment.

§ JANUARY 22 At one A.M. we marched across the railroad to the wagon road & along that toward Knoxville. We had to drag two pieces of artillery by hand or abandon them, the horses having all died of starvation. At 9 A.M. we had made only seven miles. We halted & ate some beef. Horses came from Knoxville & relieved us of the cannon. We came on two miles farther & halted to make coffee. When it was nearly ready the rebel cavalry fell upon our rear & we had to form line. They captured the Surgeon of the 17th Mich. & some stragglers. They came very [near] getting our Chaplain who had stopped to get a Methodist dinner out of the inhabitants. The Surgeon was delayed by the charms of a fair one whom he saw by the wayside.

Finding they did not press we moved back half a mile farther, formed again & drank our coffee. We then moved slowly back to within three miles of Knoxville, exchanging scattering shots with them as we went. Their force was all cavalry & ours all infantry. Neither party seemed anxious to make any great demonstrations. A Lieut. of the 46th N.Y. was killed. Gen. Wilcox & a Lieut. of the 27th [Michigan] were slightly wounded. We had a fine view of the Smoky Mts. in N.C. as we came along. This is the first time I ever saw that state. We had meat for supper.

§ JANUARY 23 We passed a third night without blankets. The

roads freeze hard enough to bear artillery. So long as we have plenty of wood there is however but little trouble in sleeping. We bivouaced in line about three miles from Knoxville. We got some flour. If our men had not stolen about three days' rations from the 23rd Mich. & some from other sources I hardly know how we should have lived. The day is very fine & warm. I am Brigade Field Officer of the Day.

§ JANUARY 24 We marched at 8 A.M. through Knoxville & down the railroad to Erin Station five miles below. I saw a scaffold in Knoxville where the Rebels hung several union men & where our folks hung several Rebels & are going to hang some more to day. I saw Parson Brownlow standing at the door of his house.* The town is very dirty & smallpox prevails to a great extent. The bands played as we passed through town & all were in high spirits.

The men have been on short rations so long that they do not march as they used to. They start off well enough but their strength soon gives out. The air is as soft & balmy as an evening in June. The country is fine.

§ JANUARY 25 We could hardly imagine finer weather. We have been fixing up camp. I bathed to day, water pretty cold. The flour we get is so black & bad that we use parched corn instead of bread.

§ JANUARY 26 The weather is uncomfortably warm. Three of our men were taken in the late retreat. When we look the whole thing over it appears one of the most bungling & disgraceful affairs on record. We lost from 50 to 100 prisoners & probably $150,000 worth of property. We went night & day with most indecent speed back to Knoxville followed by a Regt. or two of Cav. which could have been scattered to the winds by our Regt. alone. The 9th & 23d Corps driven like a flock of sheep before a squad of Cav. No fault can be imputed to anyone below the star for all were willing & eager to chastise their teasers.

If there ever was a Corps cursed with Genls. it is the 9th. First comes Major Gen. Park [John G. Parke], a mild, polite worthless sort of man. Next Brig. Gen. Wilcox [Willcox], a pleasant, gentlemanly man devoid of fighting qualities who earned his promotion by being taken prisoner at the first Bull Run. He has however the

---

* William G. Brownlow, a onetime Methodist preacher, was a strongly Unionist Knoxville newspaperman who had been imprisoned by the Confederate authorities earlier in the war.

rare merit of not being a drunkard. Next Brig. Gen. Potter, a puffy, bloated, red faced N.Y. city politician. Next Brig. Gen. Ferrero, who before the war had a good reputation as a dancing master & who has written a very readable book on that art. I have some respect for him for he has the merit of personal courage in a high degree & is always willing to fight if the others will let him. To command our brigade we have Col. Pierce (formerly Gen. Pierce) [Ebenezer W. Peirce], the hero of Big Bethel. Though I have no respect whatever for his ability I have a good deal for his perseverance. When he found he was not fit to be a Genl. he resigned, went home, enlisted as a Private, lost an arm at 2d Bull Run & has risen to the position of Colonel.

Forage is more abundant here & rations a little fuller. Our Regt. has not however seen a full ration since the day they left Crab Orchard, Ky. early in Sept. So far as the country is concerned we have seen none which pleased us more than East Tennessee.

§ JANUARY 27 Weather as fine as yesterday. Recd a letter from home dated Jan. 4th.

§ JANUARY 28 Weather superb. I am officer of the day. Half rations are now issued which being a considerable increase causes general good feeling. The sick of the Corps do not exceed two per cent. There is some prospect of going home.

§ JANUARY 29 The weather is like the Indian Summer of the north except that there is no smoke. No fires are needed. We are ordered to start for home Feb. 1st. The joy of the men knows no bounds.

§ JANUARY 30 There was a light shower last night but the weather is fine to day.

§ JANUARY 31 Four P.M. we are ready to start at daylight to morrow for the north when the order is suspended & another follows warning us to be ready to move at a moment's notice. A squad of Reb. Cavalry has appeared somewhere. That is enough to scare old Foster* out of his wits & render the presence of our 200 men necessary for the salvation of East Tenn. I wish there was some way to make Major Generals keep their word. I presume we shall have to leave here between two days & burn half our rations

---

* John G. Foster commanded the Department of the Ohio.

& baggage as at Strawberry Plains. All our men who have not reenlisted have been assigned to the 17th Mich.

I bought a good five year old colt to day of Kentucky racing stock for $50. Weather fine.

§ FEBRUARY 1, 1864 There was a heavy shower last night but the day is warm & fine. We lay in camp till about 4 P.M. & then marched toward Knoxville. We passed through the town, crossed the river & bivouaced without blankets about a mile beyond. The number of times Foster was, in the minds of officers & men, consigned to the lower regions could not be enumerated on this page.

§ FEBRUARY 2 At 8 A.M. we were ordered back to camp at Erin Station. Weather delightful. I am officer of the day. There was a squall of wind & rain abt dark.

§ FEBRUARY 3 Weather colder. Nothing doing.

§ FEBRUARY 4 Weather fine.

§ FEBRUARY 5 We were notified that there would be an Inspection by Gen. Foster. We made ready & waited till about sundown when the Gen. passed along the road with four women in an ambulance. Thus ended his first visit to the 9th Army Corps. As for provisions we have meat & meal & that is all. The men get half rations from the Govt. & we get what we can.

It is reported that placards are posted in Knoxville to the effect that the Rebs have offered to lay down their arms provided the officers are received on the same terms which are offered to the men. No credit is given to the rumor. Although I sincerely desire the war to be ended yet such a rumor always causes an involuntary feeling of regret at first. In spite of my better judgment there is a feeling that I am about to be turned out of employment, that my "occupation is gone." I cannot see why it is that this rude half savage & seemingly comfortless life has such attractions.

There is also a rumor that the President has called for 500,000 more men. If this be true something may yet be done for officers of the old Regts. As it is they have been dealt with very unfairly. Owing to their reduced numbers promotions have almost ceased in the old Regts. & officers who entered service two years later are above us simply because their Regts. are full enough to come within the rules for promotion.

Times are dull, there is little to read, little to do & very little to eat.

§ FEBRUARY 6 There were light squalls of rain & a few flakes of snow, the first we have seen in near a month.

§ FEBRUARY 7 I am officer of the day. A long expected order has arrived & we have to send all our horses to Kingston (35 miles) to forage. I disliked very much to send mine off in that way but there is no help for it. Every particle of grain in the country is required for the men. They only receive from 8 to 11 ozs. of meal per day whereas they should have 22 ozs. At headquarters we live almost totally on meal and parched corn. The meat we get is so poor & stringy that it is hardly eatable. Weather fair but quite cool.

§ FEBRUARY 8 Very dull. Weather clear, wind cold & raw.

§ FEBRUARY 10 Gen. [John M.] Schofield has come. Gen. Foster has gone. We are ordered to proceed to Loudon & take boat for Chattanooga. We are going home via Nashville & Louisville R.R. if we are not stopped again.

§ FEBRUARY 11 We got out to the R.R. at 11 A.M., all the leave taking, cheering &c having been previously accomplished. We marched 14 miles along the R.R. The 17th, 20th & 27th [Michigan] marched ½ mile out to take leave of us. Took supper with a violent old Reb. Supper very good & the man one of the blandest imaginable.

§ FEBRUARY 12 Marched to Loudon 12 miles. Arrived at 10 A.M., crossed the river & waited all day for cars. I bear witness that the Tennessee is one of the finest rivers I ever saw, water clear as crystal. Saw Gens. [T. T.] Garrard & Schofield for the first time.

§ FEBRUARY 13 Slept last night on the warehouse steps. Left Loudon at 1 P.M. We were very fortunate in starting when we did for if we had remained in camp at Erin Station 2 hours longer our order would have been countermanded. Many Regts. have had more difficulty than we. We arrived at Chattanooga abt 9 P.M. The country from Kingston to 50 miles west is very fine. We yesterday reached the land of full rations once more. We brought along abt 100 Rebel deserters.

§ FEBRUARY 14 We remained on the cars at Chattanooga till 5 A.M. We could not see much of the battlefield in the darkness. I was up most of the night looking after affairs. When we went to our car we found it filled with female contrabands & their squalling progeny who had taken possession in our absence. This was too much for my philanthropy & I turned them out in a hurry. When I woke up this m'g we were among the mts. of Georgia or Alabama.

As is often the case that which is least useful is most interesting. We saw some fine rocks during the day. The amt of force required to guard the road is very large.

§ FEBRUARY 15 We reached Nashville at 1 A.M. Rain had been falling for 12 hours & the cars were leaky. We stopped in the depot warehouse. Interesting scenes among East Tennessee immigrants. We went into the barracks at 10 A.M. Went on board cars at 5 P.M. & left Nashville at 8, ran till noon.

§ FEBRUARY 16 We had a fine night's rest. Weather very cold in the m'g. Reached Louisville at 4 P.M., stopped at the soldiers' home. Had very poor quarters. Most outrageous cold.

§ FEBRUARY 17 Remained at Louisville. Weather cold & I have taken a very severe cold & am almost sick. I went to the Theater. Play by D. & W. with Mrs. Farrel. House thin & cold, play dull.

§ FEBRUARY 18 I recd orders at 11 from Col. Humphrey to march at once across the river to the cars bound for Cincinnati. While I was hastening to comply a second order came to go by boat. We accordingly find ourselves on board the U.S. Mail Boat Gen. B. bound for Cincinnati. Dinner on board an Ohio River steamboat is different from [the railroad] & the change is not unpleasant.

§ FEBRUARY 19 I passed the night in a very satisfactory manner. There was a great amt of floating ice & in some places the river was frozen two inches deep clear across. This delayed us considerably. Sometimes it almost stopped our progress. We reached Cincinnati at 7 A.M., landed, quartered the troops in the 5th St. Barracks & myself at the Gibson House. Went to Pike's Opera at night, heard M'lle Vestrali as Gamea in the Jewish Mother. House very full, performance fine. Everybody well pleased.

§ FEBRUARY 20 Life in Cincinnati passes very well. If Uncle Sam desires our services in this place we can remain provided only that he come down by times with funds. I went to night to Wood's Theater, saw Mr. J.W.B. as Richard 3d. I was well pleased with the performance. M.H. was as comic as usual & Mrs. K. of course delighted everybody. There were however some drawbacks. Everybody had a bad cold & coughed. The audience was very large but evidently not well read in Shakespeare. They needed someone to tell them where to cheer & when to laugh. For want of that they sometimes put in at the wrong place & came near turning the sublime into the ridiculous.

We tried to get the Col. to go but he declined out of deference to the conference. He however came out with a most ferocious black mustache, changed by barber's magic & on the whole looked so rakish that a knight of industry tried to persuade him into the company of the fair sex. I only wonder that he did not succeed.

§ FEBRUARY 21 I passed the day quietly, it being Sunday. I was most of the time in my room engaged in private affairs.

*　*　*

This final entry in Charles Haydon's journal gives not a hint of his condition. However, the "very severe cold" he mentioned in his February 17 entry must have rapidly worsened, for he soon reported himself to the Marine Hospital in Cincinnati, where he had recuperated from his wounding. Very probably his normally sturdy constitution had been weakened by his wounding and then his early return to strenuous duty, for on March 14, 1864, in the Cincinnati military hospital, he died. The cause of death is listed on the army's medical records as "cerebro-spinal congestion," a form of pneumonia. Haydon's body was returned home to Michigan for interment. What survived him is the journal of a good soldier.

Index